RIVERSIDE TEXTBOOKS
IN EDUCATION

MEASURING INTELLIGENCE

A GUIDE TO THE ADMINISTRATION OF THE NEW
REVISED STANFORD-BINET TESTS OF INTELLIGENCE

BY

LEWIS M. TERMAN

Professor of Psychology
Stanford University

AND

MAUD A. MERRILL

Professor of Psychology
Stanford University

HOUGHTON MIFFLIN COMPANY

BOSTON · NEW YORK · CHICAGO · DALLAS
ATLANTA · SAN FRANCISCO

The Riverside Press Cambridge

COPYRIGHT, 1937

BY LEWIS M. TERMAN AND MAUD A. MERRILL

The Riverside Press

CAMBRIDGE · MASSACHUSETTS

PRINTED IN THE U.S.A.

EDITOR'S INTRODUCTION

TWENTY-ONE years ago Terman's *The Measurement of Intelligence* was issued as the tenth volume in the Riverside Textbooks in Education Series, and in introducing it to the public the editor of the Series made, in part, the following statement, all of which seems pertinent to the present edition:

> The present volume appeals to the editor of this series as one of the most significant books, viewed from the standpoint of the future of our educational theory and practice, that has been issued in years. Not only does the volume set forth ... the large importance for public education of a careful measurement of the intelligence of children, but it also describes the tests which are to be given and the entire procedure of giving them. In a clear and easy style the author sets forth scientific facts of far-reaching importance, facts which it has cost him, his students, and many other scientific workers, years of patient labor to accumulate....
>
> The educational significance of the results to be obtained from careful measurements of the intelligence of children can hardly be overestimated. Questions relating to the choice of studies, vocational guidance, schoolroom procedure, the grading of pupils, promotional schemes, the study of the retardation of children in the schools, juvenile delinquency, and the proper handling of sub-normals on the one hand and of gifted children on the other — all alike acquire new meaning and significance when viewed in the light of the measurement of intelligence as outlined in this volume. As a guide to the interpretation of the results of other forms of investigation relating to the work, progress, and needs of children, intelligence tests form a very valuable aid. More than all other forms of data combined, such tests give the necessary information from which a pupil's possibilities of future mental

growth can be foretold, and upon which his further education can be most profitably directed.

The publication of this revision and extension of the original Binet-Simon scale for measuring intelligence, with the closer adaptation of it to American conditions and needs, should mark a distinct step in advance in our educational procedure. It means the perfection of another and a very important measuring-stick for evaluating educational practices, and in particular for diagnosing individual possibilities and needs. Just now the method is new, and its use somewhat limited, but it is the confident prediction of many students of the subject that, before long, intelligence tests will become as much a matter of necessary routine in schoolroom procedure as a blood-count now is in physical diagnosis. That our schoolroom methods will in turn become much more intelligent, and that all classes of children, but especially the gifted and the slow, will profit by such intellectual diagnosis, there can be but little question. . . .

The original volume and its scales have now been before the public for twenty-one years, and the sales, not only in the United States, but in England and other countries comprising the British Commonwealth of Nations, have been exceedingly gratifying to both author and publishers.

Inspired by a desire not only to perfect and extend the scales, but to make them still more useful by preparing a second scale that should be equivalent in range, difficulty, reliability, and validity, Dr. Terman began, ten years ago, a complete revision and extension of the original Stanford-Binet scales, basing the revision and standardization upon larger and more representative groups. In this undertaking Dr. Merrill joined as collaborator. The work proved of greater magnitude and more laborious than had at first been expected, but now, after ten years of painstaking research, two new and equivalent scales, each more extensive than the original both in range and in number of tests, and each providing for greater objectivity in scoring, are at last ready for public use and are here so offered. While the original Stanford-Binet scale remains as valid as before, the new scales, with their wider range and with the advantages each offers for retesting by the other and as a safeguard against coaching, and with their far more accurate standardization, present so much larger possibilities for usefulness that the old scale probably will soon be entirely superseded by the new.

An examination of the manuscript of the present volume leads the editor again to state that the work in its new form, as in the old, represents a distinct contribution to educational procedures, and to predict for the revision a usefulness even greater than that enjoyed by the original edition.

ELLWOOD P. CUBBERLEY

PREFACE

THE Stanford revision of the Binet-Simon intelligence scale has
had a wider field of usefulness than anyone could have foreseen
at the time of its publication in 1916. It has become the
standard clinical method for the evaluation of intellectual
status and is used, not only in clinical practice, but also as a
tool of research with a wide variety of subjects, including de-
fectives, delinquents, the retarded, the gifted, the normal, and
the psychopathic.

In view of the numerous and important services which such
a system of tests is called upon to perform, it has seemed to us
desirable to make the new revision as thoroughgoing as possible. We have accordingly provided two scales instead of one,
have extended them so as to afford a more adequate sampling
of abilities at the upper and lower levels, have defined still
more meticulously the procedures for administration and scoring, and have based the standardization upon larger and more
representative populations. Besides these major improve-
ments, many others of less crucial importance have been in-
corporated.

Although the task of revision has required ten years for its
completion, and has been carried through with constant aware-
ness of the sources of error involved in test construction, nothing approximating perfection can be claimed for the results.
The tools of psychology, particularly those dealing with the
more complex mental processes, belong to an entirely different
order of precision from those employed by the physical scien-
tist. So far as one can now see, they always will. Apart from
possible criticisms of the general plan on which the scales have
been constructed, there are doubtless minor imperfections
which only extended use will disclose. Even so, it is hoped

that this revision of the Binet method will long provide a common standard by which to gauge the intellectual level of human subjects from early childhood to the end of life's span.

In the course of so extensive an undertaking the authors have naturally incurred a heavy load of indebtedness to many persons: to the Social Science Research Council of Stanford University for its generous support of the project; to our highly competent and devoted assistants, Helen Campbell, Helen Green, Lois Kulmann, Barbara Mayer, Margaret Murray, Melita Oden, and Wilhelmina Warkentin, who assisted in gathering the standardization data; and to the school administrators and teachers throughout the country whose unanimous and whole-hearted co-operation greatly facilitated the testing program which provided the fundamental data. Miss Mayer and Mrs. Oden, in addition to their work as field examiners, have carried through the arduous task of scoring all the tests and getting out the major part of the statistical data. Grateful acknowledgment is made of the expert assistance rendered by Dr. Paul Buttenwieser and Dr. Quinn McNemar in the statistical treatment of results, and of the help given by Mrs. Alice McAnulty Horn in formulating the plans for Hollerith coding.

LEWIS M. TERMAN
MAUD A. MERRILL

CONTENTS

PART I — THE NEW REVISION

PART II — INSTRUCTIONS FOR ADMINISTERING FORM L

xi

CONTENTS

LIST OF FIGURES

LIST OF TABLES

PART I

THE NEW REVISION

CHAPTER I

ESSENTIAL FEATURES OF THE REVISION

THE major faults of the original Stanford-Binet scale have long been recognized. Although affording a satisfactorily valid and reliable measure over a fairly wide intermediate range, it was especially defective at both extremes. Abilities below the mental level of four years or above that of the average adult were very inadequately sampled. In the range from five to ten years the standardization was surprisingly correct, considering the rather small number of subjects on which it was based, but above ten it yielded scores that were progressively too low. A number of tests in the scale were unsatisfactory because of low validity, difficulty of scoring, susceptibility to coaching, etc. The instructions both for administration and scoring in numerous instances lacked the precision which is necessary to insure objectivity and comparability of results. Finally, one of the severest limitations to the usefulness of the scale was the fact that no alternative form was available for use in retesting or as a safeguard against coaching.

In the revision here offered we have provided two scales which differ almost completely in content, but are mutually equivalent with respect to difficulty, range, reliability, and validity. The scales are designated as Form L and Form M. In content Form L bears greater resemblance to the original Stanford-Binet, but neither form can be recommended above the other. Both, we believe, are relatively free from the grosser faults of the old scale. They cover a far wider range, they are more accurately standardized throughout, the tests provide a richer sampling of abilities, and the procedures have been more rigidly defined. On the whole they are somewhat less verbal than the old scale, especially in the lower years.

The revision utilizes the assumptions, methods, and principles of the age scale as conceived by Binet. There are of course other systems of tests which are meritorious, but for the all-round clinical appraisal of a subject's intellectual level the Binet type of scale has no serious rival. It is not merely an intelligence test; it is a method of standardized interview which is highly interesting to the subject and calls forth his natural responses to an extraordinary variety of situations. The arrangement of the tests in year groups makes the examination more interesting to the examiner by enabling him to grasp the evidence as it comes in. There is a fascination in the use of an age scale that does not fade out with experience. Each examination is a new adventure in which every step is interesting and meaningful. The variety provided by the ever-changing tasks insures the zestful cooperation of subjects and is at the same time based upon what we believe to be sound psychological theory. It is a method which, to paraphrase an oft-quoted statement by Galton,[1] attempts to obtain a general knowledge of the capacities of a subject by the sinking of shafts at critical points. In our revision we have greatly increased the number of shafts and have sunk them at points which wider experience with tests has shown to be critical.

The scale devised by Binet contained 54 tests, and the first Stanford revision increased the number to 90. Each form of the new revision contains 129 tests. Below the five-year level tests are now located at half-year intervals, the gaps which existed at years eleven and thirteen have been filled, and the scale has been given more top by the addition of two supplementary superior adult levels. In the selection of tests we

[1] In a footnote to an article by James McKeen Cattell, "Mental Tests and Measurement," *Mind*, 1890, *15*, 373.

have tried to correct such inadequacies of the old scale as its too verbal character at the lower levels and its too great dependence upon rote memory at the upper. For the younger subjects the scale has been made incomparably more interesting and also more valid by the liberal use of diminutive objects, brightly colored cubes, wooden beads, and other attractive materials. In general, however, the content of the new scales resembles that of the old and includes such well-known tests as comprehension, absurdities, word-naming, drawing designs, memory for digits, giving differences and similarities, defining abstract terms, etc.

Our efforts to increase the number of non-verbal tests were successful chiefly at the lower levels. Like other investigators we have found that it is extremely difficult to devise non-verbal tests for the upper levels which satisfy the requirements of validity, reliability, and time economy. At these levels the major intellectual differences between subjects reduce largely to differences in the ability to do conceptual thinking, and facility in dealing with concepts is most readily sampled by the use of verbal tests. Language, essentially, is the shorthand of the higher thought processes, and the level at which this shorthand functions is one of the most important determinants of the level of the processes themselves.

One of the important aims of the revision was to secure greater objectivity of scoring. Where judgment is involved in evaluating responses to an item, definite principles and classified illustrations have been given to guide the examiner. Ease and objectivity of scoring have in fact often played a crucial rôle in the selection and rejection of test items. The part played by subjective judgment cannot be wholly eliminated from a test of the Binet type, but we have tried to bring it as near as possible to the irreducible minimum.

Hardly less important than the selection of suitable tests has been the selection of subjects for use in the standardization of the scales. We have devoted more than ordinary effort to secure a representative sampling of the white child population in the United States between the ages of two and eighteen years. Besides increasing the number of subjects tested to 100 at each half-year level below six, to 200 at each age between six and fourteen, and to 100 at each age from fifteen to eighteen, we have made a stubborn attempt to avoid sampling errors inherent in age, grade location, nationality, and geographical distribution. We do not flatter ourselves that we have been entirely successful, but our data represent a much closer approximation to an unbiased sampling than has heretofore been attained in the standardization of any scale for individual examining. The fact that the same subjects were used in the standardization of Form L and Form M has made it possible to guarantee almost perfect equivalence of the scores yielded by the two scales.

For reasons elsewhere set forth (page 24 ff.) we have retained both M.A. and I.Q. scores. We have provided, however, a table whereby the latter (and, indirectly, the former) may be readily converted into standard scores.

CHAPTER II

DEVELOPMENT AND STANDARDIZATION OF THE SCALES

PRELIMINARY SELECTION OF TESTS

WORK on the revision was begun with a survey of the literature on the old Stanford-Binet and a study of every kind of intelligence test item that had been used or suggested. The search for suitable material yielded thousands of test items, some of them of unknown value and most of them of unknown difficulty. The first principle of sifting was to give preference, other things equal, to types of test items that experience had shown to yield high correlations with acceptable criteria of intelligence. Such items were assembled in as great variety as possible and with special attention to promising types of non-verbal tests. Practical considerations which had to be taken into account included ease of scoring, appeal to the subject, time requirement, and convenience of administration. For one or another of these reasons a large number of otherwise excellent tests had to be rejected. Prominent among tests which have universally proved their worth are analogies, opposites, comprehension, vocabulary, similarities and differences, verbal and pictorial completion, absurdities, drawing designs from copy and from memory, memory for meaningful material and for digits, etc.

General preliminary researches on particular types of tests and special problems of method were undertaken by qualified graduate students under our direction in the laboratory. Two of these [1] which dealt with scoring methods for the vocabulary test will be described in connection with a discussion of that

[1] Cf. Part II, p. 303.

7

test. Bailey's [1] study of the ability of children to make comparisons from memory and Rulon's [2] study of the verbal absurdities test yielded information that was of value concerning two important types of tests. Deal's [3] experiments on weight discrimination to determine the effect of differences in instructions and of different series of weights demonstrated that, at the age levels where the test was applicable, geometrically equal increments in the weight series did not produce equal sense distances nor make the series equally difficult at every point. On the basis of this study we selected the optimal weight series and directions only to discard the test finally because of its poor showing in the statistical analysis of the standardization data.

After the mass of test items had been assembled and critically examined, the material which seemed to be the most promising was selected for experimental trial. This tryout was preliminary rather than final and was intended to effect the elimination of the least satisfactory tests and to give the approximate age location of those retained for further trial. It utilized about a thousand subjects in the vicinity of Stanford University for whom mental ages had been determined by the original Stanford-Binet scale. The new items were too numerous to permit the administration of all to this entire group of subjects; instead, each test was given to at least twenty subjects of each mental age in the range in which it was applicable. Curves of percents passing at successive mental ages were plotted and the steepness of these curves afforded a graphic indication of the validity of the tests. A majority of the curves covered the entire range from the men-

[1] Bailey, Babette Frances. *An Experimental Study of the Ability of Children to Make Comparisons from Memory.* Unpublished M.A. Thesis, Stanford University, 1930.

[2] Rulon, Philip J. *An Experimental Study of the Verbal Absurdities Test.* M.A. Thesis, Stanford University, 1928.

[3] Deal, Bonnye. *Weight Discrimination as a Test of Intelligence at the Lower Mental Levels.* M.A. Thesis, Stanford University, 1929.

tal age group yielding 100 per cent of passes to that yielding 100 per cent of failures. In preparation for the final tryout each test was given a provisional age location at the level where the proportion of passes was approximately 50 per cent.

It will be understood, of course, that the final selection of tests and their standardization were based upon unselected populations and not upon mental age groups as determined by any other scale. The use of such groups in the first experimental trial of test items was largely a measure of economy; in preliminary sifting the method is much more effective per unit of time than is the use of chronological age groups.

Mental age groups were not available for the preliminary tryout of items in the pre-school range, and chronological age groups had to be used. As not many of the test items could be given to any one child at this level, it was necessary to utilize about 500 pre-school subjects. Lists were made up for the required ages by consulting birth registrations, after which the cooperation of parents was enlisted by mail or telephone communication. Most of these subjects were secured in one community of about 65,000 population.

This preliminary tryout provided the necessary data for the selection of tests for the provisional scales. As we have already stated, the retention or rejection of items was based upon several criteria. In order of importance these were: (1) validity, (2) ease and objectivity of scoring, and (3) various practical considerations such as time economy, interest to the subject, the need for variety, etc.

Validity in turn was judged by two criteria: (1) increase in the percents passing from one age (or mental age) to the next, and (2) a weight based on the ratio of the difference to the standard error of the difference between the mean age (or mental age) of subjects passing the test and of subjects failing it. The use of such a weighting scheme was prompted by the obvious advantage of being able to utilize the data for all of the subjects who were tested with a given item. Since this weight is based upon the total number of successes and failures for the item in question, and because it is a unitary index, it affords a better basis for judging the relative validity of items than a series of percents passing.

Increase in percents passing at successive chronological ages is indirect but not conclusive evidence of validity. Height, for example, increases with age, but is known to be practically uncorrelated with brightness. Increase in percents passing by mental age is better, but exclusive reliance upon this technique predetermines that the scale based upon this criterion will measure approximately the same functions as that used in selecting the mental age groups. In the present case this was not objectionable, since the purpose of the revision was to provide scales closely comparable to the old with respect to the mental abilities tested.

FORMATION AND USE OF THE PROVISIONAL SCALES

When the sifting process described above had been completed, a sufficient number of promising tests remained to make up two provisional scales for final tryout. In order to insure having the requisite number of surviving tests to make two complete scales, it was necessary to provide a margin of safety in the provisional batteries by the inclusion of more tests than would be ultimately needed. This margin of safety had to extend throughout the entire range. Provisional Form L contained 209 tests and provisional Form M 199. As we have stated in Chapter I, the number of tests in the completed scale is 129 in each form, only a small number of which are identical in the two forms. The margin of safety allowed (about 30 per cent) was none too large.[1]

---

[1] A report on rejected tests and reasons for their unsatisfactoriness will be presented in a later volume.

In the application of the provisional scales to the more than 3000 subjects upon whom the standardization was based, the testing in all cases covered a very comprehensive age range. The examination of each subject was extended downward through an age level in which there were no failures and upward through an age level in which there were no successes, according to the provisional standards of scoring. All subjects included in the standardization data were given both forms of the test, half of them taking Form L first, half of them Form M first. The average time required for administering the two forms to a subject was approximately three hours. The two forms were given not less than a day and not more than a week apart. It was often not possible to complete the examination on one form at a single sitting. The number of sittings required for a subject depended upon several factors: the amount of scattering of successes and failures, the fatigability of the subject, school schedules, the convenience of teachers and parents, etc.

All of the testing was done by seven thoroughly trained examiners working as full-time research assistants. All were of graduate status and well grounded in the theory and practice of mental testing. In special preparation for the present undertaking they were given two months of intensive instruction and practice in the administration of the provisional scales. In this connection much attention was given to uniformities of examining procedure, minimum range of testing, the recording of responses, the tentative standards for scoring, etc. Every effort was made to insure that each test would be given, recorded, and scored as nearly as possible in the same way by all the examiners. Recording of responses was to be so complete as to permit later rescoring on more lenient or less lenient standards. In order that unforeseen contingencies might be dealt with uniformly, the examiners were instructed to report all questions and uncertainties to the central office so that uniform rulings could be made for all the examiners to follow. An important feature of the preliminary training concerned the procedures laid down to insure representative samplings of the child populations in communities where the testing was to be done.

THE SELECTION OF SUBJECTS

In order to secure a representative group of school children, we chose them from different sections of the country, trying to avoid selective factors due to social and economic status. We chose average schools, and, as far as possible, recruited the pre-school group from the siblings of school cases. All subjects are American-born and belong to the white race. There has been no elimination of any particular nationality groups.

Geographical distribution. Seventeen different communities in eleven states were sampled to secure the 3184 subjects upon whom our final standardization was based. During the first year devoted to testing, three of the examiners worked in different communities in California, one in Nevada, one in New York, one in Colorado, and one in Kansas. During the second year testing was done in two communities in California, two in Virginia, one in Vermont, one in Texas, two in Minnesota, and a number of communities (chiefly rural) in Indiana and Kentucky. The same examiners were employed. The selection of localities for the second year's testing was based upon certain considerations in regard to the sampling which had resulted from a study of the socio-economic levels of the first 1500 subjects.

Socio-economic status. Four estimates of the socio-economic status of the subjects tested during the first year were made in an effort to appraise the group and to guide in the selection of next year's subjects.

The Sims Questionnaire [1] was given to two grade groups, between the fifth and the eighth, in each school that supplied subjects for the revision standardization. Our data indicate no such reliability for the questionnaire as Sims reports (a correlation of .94 between paired siblings), and, as the published norms are inadequate to serve as a criterion for our sampling, we have been able to make but little use of this estimate of social and economic level.

Classifications of the occupations of fathers of the first 1500 cases were made according to the Barr rating scale,[2] the Taussig five-grade grouping, and a grouping arranged by Goodenough [3] based on the census classification and affording a basis for comparison with the occupational distribution of employed males in the United States in 1930.

The mean Barr rating on occupational status of fathers was 9.34 for a population of 1572 cases. Terman [4] found a mean Barr rating of 8.88 for employed adult males of the general population of the United States based on figures reported in the 1920 census. The mean of 8.88 for the general population corresponds to the Barr rating of gardener; the mean of 9.34 for fathers of our group to a Barr rating of carpenter (9.37).

The Taussig classification gave:

I.	Professional	8.79%
II(a).	Semi-professional and higher business	15.21
II(b).	Business and clerical	18.49
III.	Skilled labor	42.08
IV.	Semi-skilled labor	6.7
V.	Unskilled labor	8.72

[1] Sims, Verner M. *The Measurement of Socio-Economic Status*. Bloomington, Public Schools Publishing Company, 1928.

[2] Cf. Terman, Lewis M. *Genetic Studies of Genius*, vol. 1. *Mental and Physical Traits of a Thousand Gifted Children*. Stanford University Press, 1925, pp. 66–72.

[3] Goodenough, F. L., and Anderson, J. E. *Experimental Child Psychology*. New York: Century, 1931. Appendix A.

[4] Terman, Lewis M., *op. cit.*, p. 71.

The Goodenough classification, which afforded a basis for comparison with the 1930 census figures, was as follows:

TABLE I[1]

Occupational Group	Percentages of Employed Males in U.S.	Percentage Distribution of Known Occupations of Living Fathers of Revision Cases		
		1st Sample	2d Sample	Total
I..........	3.1	7.5	1.2	4.5
II..........	5.2	11.1	4.2	7.8
III..........	15.0	28.3	22.4	25.5
IV..........	15.3	6.3	24.2	14.9
V..........	30.6	31.8	31.0	31.4
VI..........	11.3	8.8	9.9	9.4
VII..........	19.5	6.2	7.1	6.6
Total N......	38,077,804	1438	1319	2757

Group I is professional; Group II, semi-professional and managerial; Group III, clerical, skilled trades, and retail business; Group IV, farmers; Group V, semi-skilled occupations, minor clerical positions, and minor businesses; Group VI, slightly skilled trades and other occupations requiring little training or ability; and Group VII, day laborers (urban and rural).

All of the figures indicate that the first year's sampling is least adequate in the case of the rural group. Accordingly we took care to include several additional rural communities in the selections for the following year. Two of the examiners spent the entire year testing in rural districts, one in country schools in southern Indiana and Kentucky, the other in a country village in Vermont. A third spent three months testing in a rural community in Minnesota and another about the same amount of time testing the child population of a backwoods village of Virginia.

Our rural sampling is still inadequate. Following the census

[1] By permission of D. Appleton-Century Company.

classification, according to which areas having a population density of less than a thousand per square mile are listed as rural, about thirty per cent of our cases are drawn from rural communities as against fifty per cent of the population of the United States under nineteen years of age. The figures in Table 1 for the total 2757 cases (cf. column five) indicate that class VII (urban and rural day laborers) includes a disproportionately small number of cases.

It is also apparent from the table that the distribution is slightly skewed in the direction of superiority of occupational status. This deviation from the census figures probably represents a trend in the right direction inasmuch as the census figures for employed males over ten years of age include Negroes, who, of course, represent on the whole a lower occupational group. Though the lower occupational groups tend to have larger families than those of higher occupational status, this differential birthrate factor tends to be offset by the inclusion in the lower occupational groups of more of the *young* men unskilled by reason of lack of experience and training, who have not yet established families.

Selection of school cases. Schools of average social status were selected in each community. Then in each school our examiners tested all of the children between the ages of six and fourteen who were within one month of a birthday in whatever grade enrolled. Our data include 200 such cases, 100 boys and 100 girls, at each age level from six to fourteen.

The advanced group, aged fifteen to eighteen, presented the greatest difficulties of selection. Dozens of studies have shown that the regular academic high school is highly selected, how highly depending on the nature of the community and on various other factors. In some localities the presence of factories tends to withdraw children from school as early as the law permits. The laws in the various states differ with respect to the compulsory school age and there are differences in the degree of rigor of enforcement of the existing laws. Certain communities have continuation or part-time schools and technical high schools which are usually attended by less highly selected groups. The indications are that the industrial depression in these years, 1930–32, operated to keep the older children in school since there were fewer jobs available to withdraw them.

Only a hundred cases were to be tested at each of these upper age levels, according to our schedule, fifty boys and fifty girls. There were many different kinds of secondary schools to choose from and there was more selective elimination. Instructions to the examiners were intended to insure that the advanced group would be as nearly as possible continuous with the intermediate, with no break between fourteen and fifteen years. The compulsory school age was taken into account, the general character of the population, and the type of secondary education that was offered. In each community the school census was consulted to determine the amount of elimination after age fourteen. We made certain that some of the twelve-, thirteen-, and fourteen-year-olds who had gone on to high school were included, also some of the slow fifteen- and sixteen-year-olds who were still in the intermediate school.[1] A few cases who had graduated from high school were included and a few who had dropped out of school without completing high school. These out-of-school groups were sampled by choosing siblings of school children in numbers proportional

---

[1] The following illustration will show how a given number of fifteen-year-old children were selected from a school system. Suppose eight fifteen-year-old boys are to be selected from a certain school. In the school in question the distribution of fifteen-year-old boys is as follows:

Grade	6	7	8	9	10	11
Number of fifteen-year-olds	1	0	6	20	10	1
Per cent of fifteen-year-olds	3	0	16	52	26	3
Number to be chosen	0	0	1	4	2	1

Possibly a retarded sixteen-year-old boy will be found in the seventh grade and none in the eighth grade, so that in the selection of the next age group a rough balance may be worked out.

TABLE 2. AGE-GRADE DISTRIBUTION OF SUBJECTS IN SCHOOL

Grade	Age															
	4½	5	5½	6	7	8	9	10	11	12	13	14	15	16	17	18
Post Grad. H.S.																1
Out: H.S. completed															1	6
Out: did not complete H.S.														4	12	11
Part-time school														4	5	6
12														4	24	39
11													5	25	36	29
10												5	28	34	22	7
9											9	40	40	19	7	2
8										5	59	104	25	10	1	
7									3	64	90	37	6	1		
6								2	72	88	34	12	3			
5							2	72	95	31	8	2				
4							82	98	27	12	3					
3						1	96	25	6	2						
2					90	118	22	5	1							
1				130	99	64	2									
Kdgn.	10	60	78	53	11	20										
Spec. class		1		1	1					1	1					
Total N	10	61	78	184	202	203	204	201	204	204	204	202	107	102	108	101

to the amount of elimination at ages above fourteen. However, the number of out-of-school cases tested falls somewhat short of the actual proportions chosen by reason of limitation of time and the difficulty of locating the desired cases.

Table 2 (page 17) shows a distribution by age and grade of our school cases.

Selection of the pre-school subjects. In order to make sure that our pre-school group, too, was a continuation of the same distribution, we chose as far as possible younger sibs of the school groups. The chief sources through which these younger children were secured were: (1) birth records; (2) school census; (3) school siblings; (4) kindergartens; (5) well-baby clinics of city or county health centers; (6) day nurseries; (7) nursery schools conducted by settlement houses; and (8) personal report. When the field work was first begun, the pre-school children of one community were secured largely through the agency of the local parent-teacher association, ladies' aid society groups, and personal report. But the cases chosen in this way made up such a highly selected sample that we found it necessary to eliminate the whole group.[1] Needless to say, this error was not repeated.

The extent to which various sources were utilized in selecting our cases differed widely from one community to another, depending upon the local conditions. In some of the rural counties in Indiana and Kentucky, birth records were almost unknown and a school census non-existent, while in other communities birth records and school census reports yielded practically complete lists of the pre-school children of the community to which the other sources added but little. Great care was exercised in the large population centers to include representative groups; if a school in a suburban district which had been chosen as average on the advice of superintendent and counselors seemed to include too large per-

[1] The mean I.Q. of the group so selected was 112.7.

centage of higher occupational groups it was offset by a tenement district center.

All of the examiners secured lists of siblings from the school children in all schools where testing was done. Names not secured in this way were added from school census reports and birth records, where these were available, and were further supplemented by personal reports from children, teachers, and neighbors. In one city about a hundred cases were secured through the well-baby clinics of city health centers which made up a group similar to the school group in the same localities. Twenty-five additional cases [1] were secured from a day nursery, from nursery schools conducted by two settlement houses, and from a nursery school which enrolled children representing an occupational cross-section of one of the cities.

In the smaller communities, from seventy-five to eighty per cent of the pre-school child population of the appropriate ages was examined. The first contact with the mother was made by letter explaining in untechnical terms the purpose of the study and asking her cooperation. This was followed up by a telephone call or personal visit. About three per cent of the mothers refused to allow their children to be tested because they were "not interested" or did not "believe in it." Other reasons given for refusing were illness, inconvenience, "too busy," etc. The majority of the children aged four and over were examined in an unused room at the neighborhood school building where they were brought either by the mother or by the examiner who called for and returned children whom the mother was unable to bring. The majority of the children under four were tested in their own homes.

Since a number of our pre-school subjects were attending kindergarten, we made a comparison between this group of 132 children aged four and a half to five and a half and a group

---

[1] The mean I.Q. of this group computed separately to determine whether the group was significantly different from the whole was 98.8.

of 115 children of the same age who were not in kindergarten, in order to determine the effect of selection in the kindergarten group. The average I.Q. of 132 kindergarten children was found to be 102, while that of the same age group not in kindergarten was 103.

The problems of testing in rural communities are many and varied. At some seasons of the year the roads in some of the rural sections were all but impassable; the schools, most of them two- or three-room establishments, had few children at exact ages and the next school district was many rough miles away; homes where the pre-school children were tested were often inaccessible and miles apart. Nevertheless, few of the children under fourteen were missed, and the willingness of the teachers and parents to cooperate with the "testing teacher" was very heartening. Indeed, we found everywhere in both rural and urban communities a most cordial response and willing cooperation.

Nationality of descent. The subjects of our group were all American-born white children. In the case of the pre-school group the parents also were American-born, but we made no effort to control the selection in regard to nationality of descent. In fifty per cent of the cases both parents were born in the United States.

Table 3 summarizes the data concerning the birthplace of parents of children on whom the tests were standardized. The forty-two different countries represented have been classified into eight groups as follows: Group I, United States; II, England, Ireland, Scotland, Canada, Australia, and New Zealand; III, Norway, Sweden, and Denmark; IV, Austria, Hungary, Germany, and Holland; V, Belgium, France, Spain, and Portugal; VI, Italy; VII, Russia, Finland, Poland, Latvia, Esthonia, and Lithuania; and VIII, a miscellaneous group of twenty other nationality groups.

TABLE 3. BIRTHPLACE OF PARENTS

Group	I	II	III	IV	V	VI	VII	VIII
Birthplace of both parents	1588	55	49	25	7	64	21	31
Birthplace of one parent only	289	105	59	49	6	28	22	37
Birthplace of father	1715	112	79	52	8	85	35	51
Birthplace of mother	1752	103	78	47	12	67	28	46

DERIVATION OF THE FINAL SCALES FROM THE STANDARDIZATION DATA

The primary tasks in arranging the final scales were two: (1) elimination of the less satisfactory tests, and (2) the achievement of an age arrangement of the retained tests which would make the mean mental age of each age group of subjects identical with mean chronological age, giving a mean I.Q. as close as possible to 100. However, before either of these tasks could be undertaken, it was necessary to check and rescore all of the blanks. Although the seven examiners had scored the responses provisionally as the tests were given, it was inevitable that individual variations should occur in the application of the rules which had been laid down. In testing so many subjects, unexpected situations occur and types of responses are encountered which cannot be foreseen. The rescoring was all done at Stanford University by Miss Mayer and Mrs. Oden under the direction of the authors. As the rescoring was done, lists of satisfactory and unsatisfactory responses were made up for each test item. The better part of a year was required to go through the more than six thousand blanks in this way.

In order to save time and to insure accuracy in the statistical data on which the final selection and rearrangement of the tests would be based, Hollerith techniques were used. For each subject all of the successes and failures on both Form L and Form M were punched on Hollerith cards, together with such supplementary data as serial number of the subject, age, sex, school grade, nationality of descent, occupational status of father, geographical location, and the total number of tests passed in the two forms. Approximately 30,000 cards were required for this purpose, or an average of about ten for each subject. The data on age, sex, school grade, geographical location, examiner, and form of test first given were punched separately on each card of a given subject, in order that they might be correlated with successes and failures on any test in either scale. By means of the Hollerith sorter it was then possible to plot for each test the curve showing per cent of subjects passing in successive ages throughout the range, also the curve of per cent passing by successive intervals of composite total score on the two forms. This was done for the sexes separately as a basis for eliminating tests which were relatively less "fair" to one sex than the other. It was possible, also, to compare the scores on the form given first with those on the form given second, to study the effect of practice, and to allow for it in the computation of the composite I.Q.'s. The correlation of each test with composite total score (equivalent to correlation with mental age) was computed separately for each test, thus providing a basis for the elimination of the least valid tests. One important use of the Hollerith data was in connection with the balancing of the two scales; it was important that at each level the two scales should be as nearly alike as possible with respect to the relative difficulty of the tests located at that level and with respect to their correlation with total score.

The "correct" standardization of an age scale depends, of course, upon the age location of the separate tests and upon the amount of credit (months of mental age) allowed for passing them. Other factors, such as the intercorrelation of the tests and the shapes of the curves of percents passing, are also involved. It is at present not possible to lay down, in advance, rules which if followed will cause the scale to yield a mean I.Q. of 100 at each level. In the present revision, as in the original Stanford-Binet, it has been necessary to work empirically by revising and re-revising until an arrangement of the tests was formed which achieved the desired goal. In the case of Form L, six successive revisions were necessary to accomplish the result, but once this had been done for Form L, it was possible to achieve at once an equally good result with Form M by arranging its tests so as to match those of Form L at each age level with respect to difficulty, validity, and shape of curves of percents passing by age. The standardization procedure involved not only the shifting about of tests in a given form, but also shifting them from one form to the other, modifying the standard of scoring to make a given test easier or harder so as to make it fit a given age level, etc. In making such shifts and modifications several other considerations had to be kept in mind, such as the necessity of variety among the tests of each form, correlation with total score, sex differences, ease of scoring, appeal to subject, time requirements, etc.

Detailed report of the data regarding the individual tests of the two scales, including validity, sex differences, age improvement, and influence of schooling will have to be deferred to a later volume. The effective outcome of the study can be judged from the material presented in the following chapter, which shows that the two scales measure essentially the same thing throughout their course, that they are closely equivalent in difficulty, that their standardization is approximately correct at all levels, and that they are equally fair to the sexes. The fact that the mean I.Q.'s for our standardization group tend to run slightly above 100 is the result of intentional adjustment to allow for the somewhat inadequate sampling of subjects in the lower occupational classes.

UNITS OF MEASUREMENT

Indices of developmental level. Three indices of developmental level have been used by psychologists: mental age, point (or raw) score made up of admittedly unequal units, and a statisticised point score composed of units allegedly equal. In practice the first two reduce to one, for raw point scores are commonly converted at once into age norms and thus become in effect mental age scores. The choice is accordingly between a mental age score and an "altitude" score composed of supposedly equal linear units ranging upward from an established zero point in the manner of a yardstick. Only one intelligence scale of the latter type has been fully worked out, that for Thorndike's CAVD test.[1] The advantage of a scale which starts at zero and increases by equal units is that it permits one to add, subtract, multiply, and divide scores. As measured by such a scale, a subject who scores 20 is presumed to be twice as intelligent as one who scores 10, and half as intelligent as one who scores 40.

However, the CAVD technique is open to criticism from a number of points of view. One may first of all raise the question whether such expressions as "A is twice as intelligent as B," or "half as intelligent as C," have any real psychological meaning. Thorndike has tried to give them meaning by positing a theory of intelligence which explains intellectual differences as solely a function of the *number* of established neural bonds, but for reasons we cannot here enter into, we are unable to accept his proof that area and altitude of intelligence are perfectly correlated. His view seems to us an oversimplification of the complex and in direct opposition to most of the recent trends of psychological theory.

Secondly, the only available statistical procedure for making an equal-unit scale rests on the assumption that in an un-

[1] Thorndike, E. L. *The Measurement of Intelligence.* New York, 1926. 616 pp.

selected population the distribution of intelligence follows strictly the normal curve. This may or may not be true. There are biological characters for which it is not true, and intelligence may conceivably be one of them. The question could be answered for intelligence if we had an equal-unit scale to begin with, but we are in the unfortunate position of having to assume the answer in advance in order to derive the equal-unit scale. It is the old problem of lifting oneself over the fence by one's bootstraps.

The expression of a test result in terms of age norms is simple and unambiguous, resting upon no statistical assumptions. A test so scaled does not pretend to measure intelligence as linear distance is measured by the equal units of a foot-rule, but tells us merely that the ability of a given subject corresponds to the average ability of children of such and such an age. This was all that Binet claimed to accomplish, and one can well doubt whether the voluminous output of psychometric literature since his day has enabled us to accomplish more. We have accordingly chosen to retain this least pretentious of units for the estimation of mental level.

There are, however, certain characteristics of age scores with which the reader should be familiar. For one thing, it is necessary to bear in mind that the true mental age as we have used it refers to mental age on a particular intelligence test. A subject's mental age in this sense may not coincide with the age score he would make in tests of musical ability, mechanical ability, social adjustment, etc. A subject has, strictly speaking, a number of mental ages; we are here concerned only with that which depends upon the abilities tested by the new Stanford-Binet scales.

Another characteristic of the mental age unit is that we do not need to assume for it uniformity of magnitude from year to year. Indeed the unit appears definitely to decrease with age, if we can judge by the ease or difficulty with which adjacent mental ages can be discriminated.   For example, the difference between one-year and two-year intelligence is so great that any one can sense it, while even a psychologist might have difficulty in discriminating between the mental levels of twelve years and thirteen years on the basis of ordinary observation.   Certainly the magnitude of the mental age unit shrinks rapidly as mental maturity is approached, just as annual increments in height decrease as the child approaches physical maturity.   The difference in intellectual ability between the average child of fifteen and the average child of sixteen is so small that it can barely be detected by the most elaborate mental tests.   Probably not one twelve-months-old child in a million has reached the mental level which is normal to the average child of two years, but almost half of the fifteen-year-olds have reached the level which is average for sixteen years.   Increments beyond this point have not been clearly demonstrated for unselected subjects.

Finally, the reader should understand that mental ages at the upper end of the Stanford-Binet scales are not true "mental ages," but instead are more or less arbitrary scores designed to permit the computation of I.Q.'s of superior older subjects.   The magnitude of these units in score points has been adjusted in such a way as to give approximately the same distribution of I.Q.'s for adult subjects as is found for children. The adjustment assumes that in terms of an absolute scale (if we had one), the distribution of brightness scores of adult subjects would follow the same curve as the distribution for unselected children of a given age.

The index of brightness.   We want to know not only the intellectual level (mental age) of a subject, but also his brightness or dullness in comparison with others of his age.   As already stated, we have continued to use the I.Q. for this purpose.   Alternative units which might be considered in this connection are percentile scores and standard scores.

Percentile scores are the least desirable of all because they are the most misleading to anyone who is not versed in statistics. It is very difficult to make the average person understand that a given percentile difference near the median is much less than the same percentile difference near the extremes; for example, that the difference between the 50th and 55th percentiles is trifling compared to the difference between the 90th and 95th percentiles. Percentile scores have the additional disadvantage that they do not lend themselves to correlational and many other forms of statistical treatment.

The standard score (sometimes called "sigma" score, "Z" score, or "T" scores) is commonly preferred by research workers. It gives a subject's rating in terms of his deviation from the mean of the group with which he is compared. For example, if a thousand unselected ten-year-old children have a mean raw score of 120 points on a given test, and the standard deviation of the raw-score distribution for the group is 20, a subject's raw score of 140 becomes a standard score of +1; a raw score of 160 becomes standard score +2, etc. In order to avoid negative scores for subjects who test below the mean, one may assign some arbitrary positive value (say 50) to a standard score of zero, and some other arbitrary value (say 10) to the S.D. of the distribution. Then a subject who tests 1 S.D. below the mean is scored 40; 2 S.D. below the mean, 30; 2.5 S.D. above the mean, 75, etc. These so-called "T" scores have, of course, all the properties of standard (or sigma) scores, since they are but another expression of the same thing.

The merit of standard scores lies in the fact that a deviation of 2 S.S. is presumably twice as great as a deviation of 1 S.S. In the illustration above, a "T" score of 70 is just twice as far from the mean 50 as a "T" score of 60. From the statistical point of view, every advantage is in favor of the standard score. Why, then, have we not discarded the I.Q. index of brightness in favor of some kind of standard score index?

One reason is that the majority of teachers, school administrators, social workers, physicians, and others who utilize mental test results have not learned to think in statistical terms. To such a person a rating expressed as "+2 sigma" is just so much Greek. They have, however, gradually accumulated considerable information in regard to the educational and behavioral correlates of various grades of I.Q. They know, for example, that an I.Q. of 80 signifies a particular grade of dullness, one of 50 a particular grade of mental deficiency, etc. If necessary they could in the course of time acquire an equal amount of information about the concrete significance of standard scores. It has taken twenty years for the groups of workers in question to reach their present stage of skill in the interpretation of I.Q.'s; it would probably take another twenty years to reach the same stage in the interpretation of standard scores.

For the convenience of research workers we have provided a conversion table (Table 8) from which it is possible to read off the standard scores corresponding to any particular I.Q., so that those who wish to use standard scores exclusively may do so.

As it has turned out, the I.Q.'s yielded by the new Stanford-Binet scales are themselves standard scores within a reasonably small margin of error. This comes from the fact that the S.D.'s of the I.Q. distributions of the different age groups show a marked tendency to cluster in the neighborhood of 16 I.Q. points, from which it follows that an I.Q. of 116 corresponds fairly closely to a standard score of +1; an I.Q. of 132 to a standard score of +2, etc. One can therefore say that, so far as practical uses of the scales are concerned, the I.Q.'s which they yield are about as free from objectionable features as true standard scores.

Whatever index of brightness is used, some will claim too much from it and others too little. The uninformed will read meaning into it which it does not connote and the overenthusiastic will, in too exclusive dependence upon it, ignore other lines of information which should be taken into account. The hypercritical, on the other hand, will continue to oppose its use on grounds which are largely irrelevant: because it is often misunderstood or misused; because it is influenced by environment as well as by endowment; because it does not measure social adaptability; because it does not always predict accurately success in school or success in life, etc.

There are psychologists who so dread the misunderstanding and misuse of their concepts that they would prefer to keep them strictly esoteric, as theologians once did and as physicians still sometimes try to do, but one can hardly take seriously the suggestion that the results of mental age tests should be reported exclusively in terms intelligible only to the psychometrician. The sensible alternative is to employ the simplest indices available and as rapidly as possible acquaint teachers, school counselors, social workers, and physicians with their significance and their limitation.

ADULT MENTAL AGE

It will be recalled that in the original Stanford-Binet, adult mental age was tentatively placed at sixteen years, and that chronological age above this point was disregarded in computing the I.Q.'s of older subjects. The correct placement must take account of the age at which unselected subjects cease to improve in mean score. Unfortunately, the precise determination of this terminal age is complicated by the fact that it is extremely difficult to secure truly unselected test-populations above the age of fourteen or fifteen. Since the less intelligent pupils tend to drop out of school earlier than the more gifted, the age gain in test-score commonly found with high-school populations is largely spurious. As elsewhere noted, no effort was spared in the present investigation to secure as representative populations as possible to the age of eighteen. The task was facilitated by the extremely unfavorable employment situation at the time the tests were made, which operated to reduce considerably the school elimination normally occurring after fourteen; and we believe that we have succeeded in minimizing, if not wholly escaping, the usual effects of selection at the upper ages.

For our data the yearly gain begins to decrease after the age of thirteen and by the age of sixteen it has become approximately zero. Chronological age beyond sixteen has therefore been entirely disregarded in computing the I.Q. In view of the fact that age improvement ceases gradually rather than abruptly, we begin at thirteen years to disregard increasing fractions of successive chronological age increments. From thirteen to sixteen we cumulatively drop one out of every three additional months of chronological age and all of it after sixteen. The appropriate chronological age divisors to be applied in computing I.Q.'s of subjects over thirteen years are shown in Table 4. However, the actual use of this table for finding an I.Q. is obviated by the fact that the appropriate allowances have already been made in the complete I.Q. tables on pages 417 to 450. It was found empirically by the use of the trial and error method that this adjustment, in conjunction with the credit allowances finally adopted for tests passed in the three Superior Adult levels, makes the distributions of I.Q.'s of the older subjects resemble closely those of the younger, as presumably should be the case on an ideal scale.

In this connection it should be noted that mental ages above thirteen years cease to have the same significance as at lower levels, since they are no longer equivalent to the median performances of unselected populations of the corresponding chronological ages. A mental age of fifteen years represents the norm for all subjects who are sixteen years of age or older.

Beyond fifteen the mental ages are entirely artificial and are to be thought of as simply numerical scores. As such they are useful in marking off the higher intellectual altitudes measured by the scale and in providing a basis for computing a subject's I.Q. score.

TABLE 4. CORRECTION TABLE FOR HIGHER CHRONOLOGICAL AGES

Actual C.A.	Corrected C.A. Divisor	Actual C.A.	Corrected C.A. Divisor	Actual C.A.	Corrected C.A. Divisor
13–0	13–0	14–0	13–8	15–0	14–4
13–1	13–1	14–1	13–9	15–1	14–5
13–2	13–1	14–2	13–9	15–2	14–5
13–3	13–2	14–3	13–10	15–3	14–6
13–4	13–3	14–4	13–11	15–4	14–7
13–5	13–3	14–5	13–11	15–5	14–7
13–6	13–4	14–6	14–0	15–6	14–8
13–7	13–5	14–7	14–1	15–7	14–9
13–8	13–5	14–8	14–1	15–8	14–9
13–9	13–6	14–9	14–2	15–9	14–10
13–10	13–7	14–10	14–3	15–10	14–11
13–11	13–7	14–11	14–3	15–11	14–11
				16–0 and above	15–0

THE ABBREVIATED SCALES

When limitations of time make it necessary, the starred tests of either form may be used as an abbreviated scale. The time requirement is thus reduced by one-third and the measure yielded is still reliable enough for most purposes. The probable error of an I.Q. based on an abbreviated test is about 20 per cent higher than for the complete scale. (Table 11.) The starred tests have been selected so as to be as representative of the entire scale as possible with respect to variety, difficulty, interest to subject, sex differences, and validity as measured by correlation with total score. The result is a high correlation between I.Q. scores for the entire scale and those for the abbreviated scale of the same form. Nevertheless, there are individual cases in which the I.Q. yielded by the abbreviated scale is as much as 8 or 10 points too high or too low, and it is therefore strongly recommended that the entire scale be administered unless limitations of time absolutely forbid.

CHAPTER III

STATISTICAL ANALYSIS OF SCORES[1]

THIS chapter will be limited to a summary presentation of the most essential facts bearing upon the accuracy with which the scales have been standardized, I.Q. variability in relation to age, reliability of scores, practice effects, relation of scores to the socio-economic status of parents, and the equivalence of scores on the new scales to those yielded by the original Stanford-Binet. A more detailed statistical treatment of the data is reserved for separate publication. Among the topics so reserved are successes and failures on the separate tests by age, validity of the separate tests, sex differences, effects of schooling, sibling resemblances, and the results of a factorial analysis of the intellective functions which the scales measure.

ACCURACY OF STANDARDIZATION

The primary criterion to be satisfied in the standardization of an intelligence scale of the Binet type is that the mean mental age score for unselected subjects of any chronological age shall agree closely with the mean chronological age, or, stated in other words, that unselected subjects of any age shall earn a mean I.Q. of approximately 100. In the accomplishment of this result two main difficulties are encountered: (1) the selection of representative populations at each age, and (2) the proper allocation of tests to the various age levels. The methods employed in meeting these difficulties have been described in the preceding chapter. The accuracy with which

[1] For assistance in the preparation of this chapter the authors are greatly indebted to Dr. Paul Buttenwieser and Dr. Quinn McNemar.

the standardization fits the selection of subjects on which it has been based is indicated by the I.Q. means in Tables 5 and 6.

The means given are for the sexes combined, inasmuch as the sex differences were of relatively small magnitude. A few tests in the trial batteries which yielded largest sex differences were early eliminated as probably unfair. A considerable number of those retained show statistically significant differences in the percentages of success for boys and girls, but as the scales are constructed these differences largely cancel out. For our samples the means below 6 years tend to run about 2 points higher for girls, from 6 to 13 years about 2 points higher for boys, and above 13 years about 4 points higher for boys. It is possible that a part of the sex difference found is due to biased sampling.[1]

The number of subjects from 1½ to 18 years of age for whom complete tests were made by both Form L and Form M was 3184. It was found necessary, however, to omit 181 subjects from the standardization group because of evidence indicating clearly that they represented a too favorable selection from the general population. The omitted subjects included the entire group of preschool subjects tested in Colorado.[2] This omission accounts for the fact that the N's for ages 2 to 5 in Tables 5 and 6 are smaller than those in Table 7. Subjects to the number of 93 were also tested at the age level of 1½ years for the purpose of establishing the difficulty of individual test items. I.Q.'s for this group were not computed for the reason that only a minority of the subjects at this age are adequately measured by the scales.

Table 5 gives for each scale the raw I.Q. means for the age groups from 2 to 18, and also the smoothed values from 2½ to 17. Because of the probable errors of the means (averag-

---

[1] As we have already stated, the data on sex differences will be presented in a later publication.

[2] Factors responsible for the biased sampling are given on page 18.

ing about 1.3 for the smaller groups and 0.8 for the larger groups) the smoothed values give a somewhat truer indication of the correctness of standardization for the groups in question.

TABLE 5. I.Q. MEANS BY AGE FOR THE STANDARDIZATION GROUP

Age	N	Form L		Form M	
		Raw	Smoothed	Raw	Smoothed
2	76	107.5±1.3		104.0±1.2	
2½	74	109.9±1.6	107.4	108.3±1.6	105.7
3	81	104.8±1.4	107.8	104.8±1.4	107.1
3½	77	108.0±1.3	105.1	108.2±1.3	105.5
4	83	102.5±1.3	104.7	103.5±1.2	104.8
4½	79	103.7±1.2	103.5	102.7±1.2	103.4
5	90	104.3±1.0	103.1	104.0±1.0	103.0
5½	110	101.4±0.9	102.2	102.2±0.9	102.8
6	203	101.0±0.6	101.4	102.1±0.6	102.6
7	202	101.8±0.8	101.7	103.5±0.7	103.0
8	203	102.4±0.7	102.8	103.3±0.7	104.1
9	204	104.3±0.8	103.7	105.4±0.8	104.6
10	201	104.5±0.8	104.4	105.0±0.8	105.0
11	204	104.3±0.9	104.1	104.7±0.8	104.2
12	202	103.6±0.9	104.0	102.9±0.9	103.8
13	204	104.0±0.8	102.8	103.7±0.8	102.6
14	202	100.9±0.8	102.6	101.2±0.8	102.5
15	107	102.8±1.2	101.7	102.6±1.3	101.9
16	102	101.3±1.1	103.0	101.9±1.2	103.3
17	109	104.8±0.9	104.4	105.4±0.9	104.9
18	101	107.3±1.2		107.3±1.1	

Reference to the occupational classification of fathers in Table 1 (page 14) shows the sample on which the scales were standardized to have been somewhat overweighted with subjects from the higher socio-economic levels. Although for reasons already stated we believe that some departure from the census classification in this direction is defensible, we present in Table 6 the age means for the composite scores of the L and M scales adjusted to show the values that would have been obtained for a representative sampling of the native-born white population as classified by parental occupation in the 1930 census. To accomplish this correction the subjects were divided according to father's occupation into the seven classifications of the Goodenough occupational scale,[1] and at each age level the mean I.Q. (composite of L and M) was computed separately for each of these seven groups. These means were then weighted, at each age level, according to the 1930 census frequencies for the respective groups (see Table 1), and combined into a weighted composite mean for each age level from 2 to 18 years. Table 6 gives both the raw and smoothed values for the composite L–M means based upon this adjustment.

TABLE 6. COMPOSITE L–M I.Q. MEANS ADJUSTED FOR 1930 CENSUS FREQUENCIES OF OCCUPATIONAL GROUPINGS

Age	N	Raw	Smoothed
2	76	102.1	
2½	74	104.7	103.3
3	81	103.2	104.1
3½	77	104.3	102.2
4	83	99.2	101.6
4½	79	101.2	100.8
5	90	101.9	100.4
5½	110	98.2	100.0
6	203	100.0	99.8
7	202	101.2	100.8
8	203	101.1	102.0
9	204	103.6	102.7
10	201	103.5	103.0
11	204	101.9	102.2
12	202	101.2	101.6
13	204	101.8	101.0
14	202	100.0	101.3
15	107	102.0	101.3
16	102	101.8	103.3
17	109	103.2	103.8
18	101	106.3	

[1] This scale is now known as the Minnesota Scale for Occupational Classification

Figure 1 gives the distribution of the composite of the adjusted L–M I.Q.'s for the standardization group in terms of the per cent of cases at each of the ten-point I.Q. intervals. In view of the effort made to secure a representative standardization group, and in view of the accuracy with which the scales have been adjusted for difficulty throughout the age range, the curve shown in Figure 1 probably gives the clearest picture available of the intellectual differences which obtain among American born white children of the ages in question.

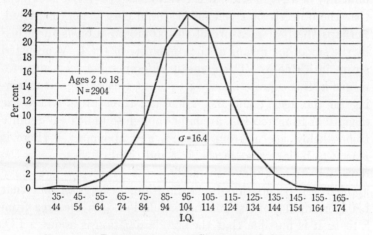

FIGURE 1. DISTRIBUTIONS OF COMPOSITE L–M I.Q.'S OF STANDARDIZATION GROUP

There are two questions of prime importance in connection with the accuracy of standardization. These concern (1) the equivalence of scores on the two scales and (2) the relative difficulty of a given scale at the various age levels.

Table 5 shows that the two scales agree very closely in mean I.Q. at almost every age level. The only difference greater than 1.7 I.Q. points (between raw means) is at age 2, where it is 3.5. The average difference is 0.8 points. If we omit age

2 the average difference is 0.67 points. Of the twenty-one age groups, seven show higher age means for Form L (average discrepancy 1.1 points), twelve show higher values for Form M (average discrepancy 0.77), and two show perfect agreement. The smoothed means in Table 5 show even closer agreement, the largest difference amounting to only 1.7 points and the average difference 0.56 points. We may conclude, therefore, that the scales are almost perfectly equated for difficulty at all levels.

Regarding the second of the above questions, the relative difficulty of a given scale at the various age levels, it is evident that the objective striven for has been closely approximated. Perhaps the best measure of this approximation is furnished by the smoothed means of the composite of the L–M adjusted scores in Table 6. The greatest difference between any two means in this column is only 4.3 points, this difference obtaining for the ages 3 and 6. There are three areas where the deviations from 100 I.Q. are large enough to indicate a definite trend: below age 4, from 8 to 12, and above 15. There is reason to believe that in the first and third of these areas the deviation trends, notwithstanding the correction we have applied for occupational classification, reflect a somewhat biased sampling of the general population. In the area from 8 to 12 it is possible that the standardization is about 2 I.Q. points in error in the direction of too great leniency. We may conclude that the major inequalities of difficulty known to exist in the old scale have been eliminated and that the scales now available are more accurate tools than have hitherto been available for the measurement of mental growth by repeated testing over a period of years.

I.Q. VARIABILITY IN RELATION TO AGE

The use of I.Q. scores rests on the assumption that variability in terms of I.Q. remains approximately constant from age to age, or, stating it in another way, that variability in terms of mental age is directly proportional to chronological age. Only to the extent that this assumption is true does the I.Q. score have consistent meaning, as otherwise a given I.Q. at one age might be equivalent to a much higher or lower I.Q. at another age. Numerous investigations have shown that scales of the Binet type when carefully standardized do show a marked tendency to yield constant I.Q. variability, at least from fairly early childhood to the adolescent period. Thus, for example, the proportion of four-year-olds with a mental age of five years (I.Q. 125) agrees closely with the proportion of eight-year-olds who test at ten or of twelve-year-olds who test at fifteen. Similarly, the proportion of five-year-olds who test at four (I.Q. 80) agrees closely with the proportion of ten-year-olds who test at eight.

An empirical demonstration of the facts on this point offers considerable difficulty. Apart from fluctuations of the obtained values from the true values because of limited size of samplings, there is the risk of greater selective curtailment of the sampling at certain ages than at others. One could be sure, for example, that a sampling of six-year-olds (age 6–0) obtained entirely from the school enrollment would be seriously curtailed at the lower extreme, since the mentally less advanced are less likely than the mentally bright to have entered school by this age. Such would especially be the case if no kindergarten were available. One can safely assume that a strictly school sampling above the age of thirteen or fourteen years will also be curtailed at the lower extreme, because of the greater tendency of dull children to leave school. Notwithstanding our strenuous effort to correct for these and other errors of sampling, complete success is hardly to be expected, and a considerable degree of irregular fluctuation in the found magnitudes of I.Q. variability from age to age could reasonably be attributed to these sources of error.

Table 7, which presents the data with respect to I.Q. variability and age, shows that the standard deviations of I.Q.'s fluctuate around a median value slightly in excess of 16 points, and that at each age the values agree closely for the two scales.[1] Since inspection of the values reveals no marked relationship between I.Q. variability and C.A. over the age range as a whole, we may accept 16 points as approximately the representative value of the standard deviation of I.Q.'s for an unselected population. Attention, however, should be drawn to ages six and twelve, where the relatively low and high values respectively are deviations too extreme to be explained as purely chance fluctuations. The high variability

TABLE 7. I.Q. VARIABILITY IN RELATION TO AGE

C.A.	N	σ L I.Q.	σ M I.Q.
2	102	16.7	15.5
2½	102	20.6	20.7
3	99	19.0	18.7
3½	103	17.3	16.3
4	105	16.9	15.6
4½	101	16.2	15.3
5	109	14.2	14.1
5½	110	14.3	14.0
6	203	12.5	13.2
7	202	16.2	15.6
8	203	15.8	15.5
9	204	16.4	16.7
10	201	16.5	15.9
11	204	18.0	17.3
12	202	20.0	19.5
13	204	17.9	17.8
14	202	16.1	16.7
15	107	19.0	19.3
16	102	16.5	17.4
17	109	14.5	14.3
18	101	17.2	16.6

[1] The variabilities given are for the sexes combined, as the sex differences in this respect were too small to be reliable.

at age twelve might conceivably be ascribed to the differential age of the onset of pubescence, although it has yet to be demonstrated that pubescence is significantly related to the rate of mental growth. Whether the atypical I.Q. variability at age six resides in the character of the sampling at that age, or whether it is perhaps an artifact of the nature of the scale at that level cannot be determined from the available data. In the lack of positive proof to the contrary, we are probably justified in assuming that the true variability is approximately constant from age to age. Repeated tests of the same subjects from early childhood to maturity will be necessary to determine whether this assumption is in accord with the facts.

Figure 2 shows the distributions of the adjusted composite L–M I.Q.'s for three age levels: 2 to 5½, 6 to 12, and 13 to 18. It is evident from inspection of these curves that I.Q. variability as measured by the new scales is approximately the same for the three levels.

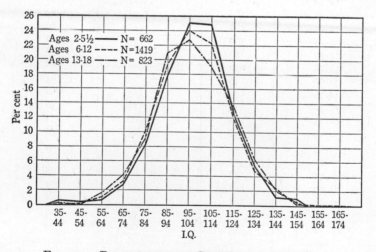

FIGURE 2. DISTRIBUTIONS OF COMPOSITE L–M I.Q.'S AT THREE AGE LEVELS

STANDARD SCORES

Since many workers, for purposes of research, prefer to express intelligence test ratings in terms of standard scores, we are providing a table whereby I.Q.'s may be transmuted into these measures (Table 8). For the reasons enumerated above, we recommend that a given I.Q. be treated as signifying the same standard score at any age. We consider this a defensible procedure, since any errors that it may entail are probably less serious than those which would result from deriving standard scores on the basis of the unsmoothed values of the standard deviation of I.Q. at the different age levels.

TABLE 8. I.Q. EQUIVALENTS OF STANDARD SCORES

Standard Score	I.Q.	Standard Score	I.Q.
+5.00	180	− .25	96
+4.75	176	− .50	92
+4.50	172	− .75	88
+4.25	168	−1.00	84
+4.00	164	−1.25	80
+3.75	160	−1.50	76
+3.50	156	−1.75	72
+3.25	152	−2.00	68
+3.00	148	−2.25	64
+2.75	144	−2.50	60
+2.50	140	−2.75	56
+2.25	136	−3.00	52
+2.00	132	−3.25	48
+1.75	128	−3.50	44
+1.50	124	−3.75	40
+1.25	120	−4.00	36
+1.00	116	−4.25	32
+ .75	112	−4.50	28
+ .50	108	−4.75	24
+ .25	104	−5.00	20
.00	100		

PRACTICE EFFECTS

Inasmuch as both scales were administered to all the subjects with an interval of from one to a few days between testings, it has been possible to determine the practice effect with considerable accuracy. The mean increase in I.Q. on the second test is the same from L to M as from M to L. The amount of increase shows no noticeable trend in relation to size of I.Q., but varies according to the age of the subjects. Table 9 summarizes the data on practice effect.

TABLE 9. PRACTICE EFFECTS IN RELATION TO AGE

Age Group	Mean increase in I.Q. on second test
2 and 2½ years.............	2.6
3 and 3½ years.............	4.4
4 and 4½ years.............	2.5
5 and 5½ years.............	2.0
6 and 7 years.............	2.1
8 and 9 years.............	2.1
10 and 11 years.............	2.2
12 and 13 years.............	2.4
14, 15, and 16.............	2.1
17 and 18 years.............	4.0

As we have already stated, in the statistical treatment of results the practice effect was subtracted from the I.Q. of the second test. First, however, the observed values of practice effect at the different age levels were smoothed, and integer deductions were substituted for fractional ones. The subtractions actually applied were as follows:

Ages 2 to 4½	3 I.Q. points
Ages 5 to 16	2 I.Q. points
Ages 17 to 18	3 I.Q. points

One cannot, of course, infer from the above data the amount of practice effect when the tests are separated by a longer time interval. Extensive data from retests with the old Stanford-Binet indicate that when the *same scale* is repeated a small effect

43

may persist for several months, and that in the case of subjects who have been given the test several times, the practice effect may become a more or less serious matter. If the two scales now available are used alternately, a subject may be retested at relatively brief intervals without risking any appreciable vitiation of the results by reason of practice effects.

RELIABILITY OF THE SCALES AND PROBABLE ERROR OF SCORES

The reader should not lose sight of the fact that a test with even a high reliability yields scores which have an appreciable probable error. The probable error in terms of months of mental age is of course larger with older than with young children because of the increasing spread of mental age scores as we go from younger to older groups. For this reason it has been customary to express the P.E. of a Binet score in terms of I.Q., since the spread of Binet I.Q.'s is fairly constant from age to age. However, when our correlation arrays were plotted for the separate age groups they were all discovered to be distinctly fan-shaped. Figure 3 is typical of the arrays at every age level.

From Figure 3 it becomes clear that the probable error of an I.Q. score is not a constant amount, but a variable which increases as I.Q. increases. It has frequently been noted in the literature that gifted subjects show greater I.Q. fluctuation than do clinical cases with low I.Q.'s — a phenomenon which has usually been ascribed to scale defects, faulty standardization at the upper levels, or the alleged instability of gifted children. However, we now see that this trend is inherent in the I.Q. technique itself, and might have been predicted on logical grounds. It is reasonable to expect that a subject's fluctuation in mental age score will be proportional, not to the variability of his chronological age group, but

44

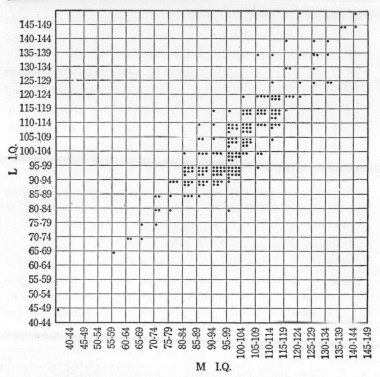

M I.Q.

FIGURE 3. SCATTER PLOT OF CORRELATION BETWEEN L
AND M I.Q.'S AT C.A. 7

to the variability of his mental age group. Thus, the probable
error of a test-score of an eight-year-old boy with a mental age
of twelve should resemble the typical probable error of that
group characterized by a mental age of twelve — viz., the
twelve-year group.[1]

It follows that the P.E.$_{I.Q.}$ must be expressed as a function
of the I.Q., a procedure which is empirically verified by the
observations summarized in Table 10. It follows equally
that the reliability coefficient is inadequate for I.Q. data unless

[1] So far as the authors know, the above facts were first pointed out by Dr. Quinn
McNemar.

45

reliabilities are derived separately for various I.Q. levels. From the average differences listed in Table 10, we may derive the standard error of a test score for the corresponding I.Q. levels,[1] and from these values we can deduce the appropriate reliability by solving the equation $\sigma_{\text{I.Q.}} = \sigma_{\text{dist.}} \sqrt{1 - r_{11}}$ for r_{11}, assuming the standard deviation of the I.Q. distribution as 16.4, the most typical value. (See Table 7.)

TABLE 10. AVERAGE DIFFERENCE BETWEEN L AND M I.Q.'S
(as empirically observed)

Ages 3–18 combined

I.Q. Level	N	Av. Diff.
130 and over	154	5.92
110–129	872	5.55
90–109	1291	5.09
70–89	477	4.35
Below 70	57	2.49

TABLE 11. ERRORS OF MEASUREMENT AND DERIVED RELIABILITIES FOR VARIOUS I.Q. LEVELS

I.Q. Level	$\sigma_{\text{I.Q.}}$ (derived from av. diff. between L and M I.Q.'s)	P.E._I.Q.	Equivalent to reliability of
130 and over	5.24	3.54	.898
110–129	4.87	3.29	.912
90–109	4.51	3.04	.924
70–89	3.85	2.60	.945
Below 70	2.21	1.49	.982

It will be seen from Table 11 that in general P.E._I.Q. is approximately .03 times the I.Q. The chances are even that a score which falls in the I.Q. range 90 to 109 does not differ from the true score on such a scale by more than 3 points, and the chances are five to one that it does not differ from the true score by more than 6 points, or twenty-two to one that it is not in error by more than 9 points. The probable error of a score above 130 I.Q. is approximately 3.5 points, and for a score below 70 I.Q. it is only about 1.5 points. The chances

[1] See McNemar, Quinn. The expected average difference between individuals paired at random. *Jour. of Genet. Psych.*, 1933, **43**, 438–439.

are twenty-two to one that a score below 70 on one of these scales is not in error by more than 4.5 points. The extreme accuracy of the scales at the lower I.Q. levels will be gratifying to those who make frequent use of the test for clinical purposes and who are rightly concerned with the dependability of their findings. The probable errors just given represent the situation for the scale as a whole. When different age levels are treated separately it is found that the situation for the age range above 6 is appreciably more favorable than this, and for the range 2 to 6 appreciably less favorable. The probable errors for the abbreviated scales composed of the starred tests are about 20 per cent greater than those for the unabbreviated.

The last column of Table 11 gives the reliabilities which correspond to the average differences between L and M I.Q.'s as given in Table 10. It will be seen that these reliability values range from .98 for subjects below 70 I.Q. to approximately .90 for subjects above 130 I.Q. For subjects near 100 I.Q. the reliability is .925.

The above reliabilities are unquestionably more meaningful than the reliabilities that would be found by correlating Form L against Form M. However, the latter were computed, separately for the twenty-one age groups, and were found to range from .85 to .95, with a median of .91. The median for ages 2 to 6 was .88 and for the ages above 6 it was .93.[1]

---

[1] It should be mentioned, in this connection, that the foregoing coefficients cannot be directly compared with the reliabilities customarily reported for intelligence tests. Since the subjects were all within four weeks of a birthday or half-birthday, the spread of ability at each level is restricted to the variability of a single-age group. If reliabilities had been computed by correlating mental age score on L against mental age score on M for several age groups combined, as is often done in establishing mental-test reliability, the coefficients so obtained could have been sharply (but spuriously) increased. Doubling the standard deviation of mental age score in this fashion would raise an r_{11} of .909 to .977. Even basing the reliabilities on a twelve months' age range, instead of the range of two months which was employed, would have raised the median figure from .91 to approximately .915. Basing them on school grade groups (grade 1, grade 2, etc.), as is customary in computing reliabilities of achievement tests, would have raised the value still higher. Therefore, our median reliability of .91 is probably as good as, or better than, a majority of coefficients of .92 to .95 which one finds reported in the literature of psychometrics.

SCORES IN RELATION TO SOCIO-ECONOMIC STATUS OF PARENTS

Reference has already been made to the correlation between intelligence and socio-economic status. In the army data the mean test-scores of recruits, classed according to civilian occupation, regularly decreased from the higher to the lower occupational levels. Numerous subsequent studies have shown that a similar relationship exists between the intelligence of children and parental occupation. Our data are in agreement with previous findings. The results are summarized in Table 12, which gives the mean I.Q., by ages, for subjects grouped according to father's occupation.

TABLE 12. MEAN I.Q.'S (L–M COMPOSITE) ACCORDING TO FATHER'S OCCUPATION

Father's Occupational Classification	Chronological Ages			
	2–5½	6–9	10–14	15–18
I. Professional	116.2	114.9	117.5	116.4
II. Semi-professional and managerial	112.4	107.3	112.2	116.7
III. Clerical, skilled trades, and retail business	108.0	104.9	107.4	109.6
IV. Rural owners	99.1	94.6	92.4	94.3
V. Semi-skilled, minor clerical, minor business	104.3	104.6	103.4	106.7
VI. Slightly-skilled	95.1	100.0	100.6	96.2
VII. Day laborers, urban and rural	93.6	96.0	97.2	97.6

It is hardly necessary to stress the fact that these figures refer to *mean* values only, and that in view of the variability of the I.Q. within each group the respective distributions greatly overlap one another. Nor should it be necessary to point out that such data do not, in themselves, offer any conclusive evidence of the relative contributions of genetic and environmental factors in determining the mean differences observed.

It may be of interest to note that Group IV, composed of rural children, drops in mean I.Q. after the preschool age, whereas Groups VI (semi-skilled) and VII (unskilled) improve in mean I.Q. with the beginning of the schooling period. These trends are too small to be very reliable and should be regarded merely as suggestive. Even if the trend were reliable it would require an extensive research, carefully planned for the purpose, to determine whether the lowered I.Q. of rural children can be ascribed to the relatively poorer educational facilities in rural communities, and whether the gain for children from the lower economic strata can be attributed to an assumed enrichment of intellectual environment that school attendance bestows.

Our subjects have been classified into two groups which we have designated as rural and urban. The urban group is here defined to include all subjects from areas having a population density of 1000 or more per square mile, and the rural group all others. Figure 4 shows the I.Q. distributions for the two

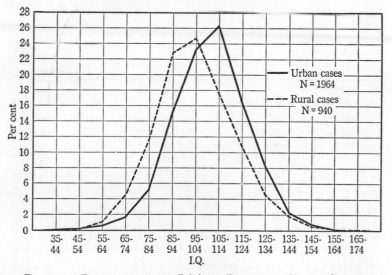

FIGURE 4. DISTRIBUTIONS OF I.Q.'S OF RURAL AND URBAN GROUPS

groups. The respective means are 105.7 and 99.2. The distributions in Figure 4 are of I.Q.'s which have not been adjusted for occupational sampling. Our data agree in general with earlier investigations of intellectual differences between urban and rural children.

EQUIVALENCE OF OLD STANFORD-BINET SCORES TO NEW SCALES

In order to determine the extent to which scores on the old Stanford-Binet may be considered equivalent to results yielded by the new scales, we have given the former test to 178 subjects of the revision group. These subjects, ranging in age from five to eighteen years, were retested with a mean interval of five months between examinations. For the age group five to twelve, (N = 123) the Stanford-Binet I.Q. correlates .864 with L I.Q., .852 with M I.Q., and .877 with the L–M com-

TABLE 13

C.A.	N	Mean I.Q.	
		Stanford-Binet	L.M. Composite
5 and 6	40 *	100.3	97.4
7	19	103.9	101.2
8	19	101.2	98.0
9	16	101.8	104.0
10	17	96.7	96.5
11	21	101.1	100.3
12	15	104.9	108.5
13	13	99.6	102.2
14	13	89.3 (91.5) **	96.2
15 and 16	16	91.1 (96.2) **	97.3
17 and 18	13	96.5 (103.0) **	103.2

* Of the 40 cases in this group, 24 were given only Form L. These are not included in the total of 178.

** Stanford-Binet I.Q.'s were computed on the basis of an adult mental age of 16. The starred values in parentheses are the I.Q.'s that would have been obtained by adopting the present chronological age adjustment above 13.

posite I.Q.; for the group aged thirteen to eighteen, ($N = 55$) the corresponding correlations are .884, .906, and .896. These correlations are vitiated somewhat by the fact that the old Stanford-Binet, as judged by standardization of the new revision, yields mental ages slightly too high at the younger ages and somewhat too low at the older levels. This trend is apparent from examination of Table 13, which shows, age by age, the correspondence for this limited sample between Stanford-Binet I.Q.'s and L–M composite I.Q.'s.

Data are also available on 120 additional cases who had previously been tested with the Stanford-Binet and who were given the L Scale by student testers. The intervals between testings ranged from one to six years. The ages ranged from 5–0 at the time of testing with the Stanford-Binet to 18–0 at the time of testing with the L scale. Correlation between original Stanford-Binet I.Q. and L I.Q. = .925 ($\sigma_{L\,I.Q.} = 24.8$; $\sigma_{S-B\,I.Q.} = 20.9$). This correlation is about as high as the respective reliabilities of the scales would permit, and we may therefore conclude that the new scales are measuring almost exactly the same functions as are measured by the original Stanford-Binet.

RESULTS OF RETESTS OF FIFTEEN HUNDRED SEVENTEEN
SCHOOL CHILDREN **

CA* at first examination	N	Mean IQ old scale	Mean IQ revised scale	σ_{S-B} IQ	σ_L IQ	D/σ_D of means	r S–B vs. L IQ	Mean interval in years between tests	σ interval in years
5	149	104.00	97.25	14.20	15.60	3.90	.64	5.16	1.94
6	806	98.00	94.60	13.25	15.95	4.66	.70	5.42	1.88
7	154	89.10	86.15	13.05	15.00	1.84	.76	5.04	1.86
8	122	89.20	88.70	11.95	15.60	0.28	.75	4.59	1.77
9	114	87.04	86.34	13.27	18.68	0.33	.80	4.03	1.62
10	93	84.25	83.90	10.50	14.30	0.19	.75	3.66	1.53
11	79	91.55	85.15	10.40	15.40	3.06	.77	3.01	1.12
Av.	...	91.88	88.87	12.37	15.79	....	.74	4.42	

* CA 5 = 4–6 to 5–5

** The above table, from an article by Maud A. Merrill on *The Significance of I.Q.'s on the Revised Stanford-Binet Scales*, published in the *Journal of Educational Psychology* (1938), *29*, 641–651, shows the results of retests of 1517 school children originally tested with the 1916 Scale.

CHAPTER IV

GENERAL INSTRUCTIONS

ESSENTIAL REQUIREMENTS OF A VALID TEST

IN ORDER to secure a valid result in the use of the Stanford-Binet scales, three requirements must be satisfied: (1) the standard procedures must be followed; (2) the child's best efforts must be enlisted by the establishment and maintenance of adequate rapport; and (3) the responses must be correctly scored. It can hardly be said that any one of the three is more important than the others, for all are absolutely essential. Unless the tests are given in strict accordance with the procedures by which they were standardized, the examiner can never be sure what his results mean. If he has failed to enlist the subject's best efforts, the only thing certain is that the resulting score will be too low in some unknown degree. Unless he has learned to score the responses according to the rules which have been laid down, his data will not be comparable to the norms.

ADHERENCE TO STANDARD PROCEDURE

Control of conditions. The purpose of a standard procedure is to make possible the observation of the subject's behavior under controlled conditions. The test method, to the extent that it does control the conditions under which the behavior is called forth, is an experimental method, and as such it yields results which are valid for the specific conditions in question. The procedure for giving these tests has been carefully standardized for each test situation and should be followed without deviation. With a view to securing greater uniformity of results, we have simplified the procedure and have made the instructions as definite as possible. The burden on the examiner's memory has been somewhat lightened by adherence to certain principles of uniformity. Special rules, such as permitting the examiner to give the subject an illustration in one test but not in another of the same general type, have been avoided.

It cannot be too strongly emphasized that unless a standard procedure is followed, the tests lose their significance. The chief danger is in unintentionally and unconsciously introducing variations which will affect the subject's response. One who has not had thorough training in psychometrics is unable to appreciate how seriously the omission, alteration, or addition of a single phrase may influence the response.

For the examiner to follow a standard procedure does not at all imply that his manner need be stilted or formal; on the contrary, the procedure has been so planned as to provide the basis for an easy and natural approach to each of the problem situations presented. The directions have been made as simple and natural as possible in order that they may serve as an apparently spontaneous and informal presentation of the tasks. They are not to be thought of as armchair pronouncements which often break down in the concrete test situation. They have been developed "on the job" and with painstaking attention to practical considerations. Many of them have evolved into their present form only after several revisions.

Avoidance of giving help. One serious danger in even minor departures from the standard formula arises from the examiner's conscientious desire to see the child perform to the limit of his ability. The desire is wholly commendable, provided it does not lead the examiner to give help in ways that are not permissible, a thing which one can easily do without being aware of it. What we want to know is not whether the subject could do the assigned task with an undefined amount of help, or under special conditions which may appeal to the examiner as reasonable, but whether he does accomplish it under the precise conditions specified in the manual of directions.

If the subject does not understand the question, or asks what is meant, it is permissible to explain only by repeating the pertinent part of the formula, unless an alternative form of the question is given in the manual to take care of such an emergency. The examiner may even repeat the question more than once if the child remains silent, but except in the case of young children repetition is not often called for and in general is to be avoided. It will, of course, be understood that under no circumstances may the items of any of the memory tests be repeated, such as digits, sentences, words, stories, etc. It is never permissible to repeat the question after an unsatisfactory response has been given, however sure the examiner may be that the subject is capable of answering correctly. School children are accustomed to regard the teacher's repetition of a question which has been incorrectly answered as an invitation to try again, but in giving Binet tests, second trials are against the rule. The rule has, however, one exception: if the subject's response indicates that a part of the formula has been misunderstood because of the examiner's faulty enunciation or the subject's imperfect hearing, the entire formula is repeated. When in the vocabulary test, for example, a subject sometimes defines the word *tap* as "something you wear on your head," it is obvious that he has understood the examiner to say *cap*.

Another difficulty arises when the subject gives a response which cannot be scored because of ambiguity or lack of clearness as to the meaning it was intended to convey. This situation is especially likely to arise in giving the vocabulary test. In order to bring out a scorable response in such cases the examiner should say, "Tell me what you mean," or "Explain what you mean." The only other permissible follow-up questions are noted in the directions. The scoring manual indicates the general types of responses that should be further questioned, but it is of course impossible to anticipate in the instructions all the special cases that will be encountered. In pressing for an explanation there is always danger that the subject will think the examiner is dissatisfied with his response and change it; on the other hand, the subject may be done an injustice if the examiner fails to determine whether the meaning which the response was intended to convey would satisfy the requirements for passing the test. The word *connection* may be defined by the statement, "Connection means to connect," or one of the verbal absurdities may be responded to by the mere repetition of the critical phrase. In either case the subject's meaning will usually be made clear by the request, "Explain what you mean."

Order of presenting the tests. The tests of each year group should be given in the order in which they appear in the manual and record booklet. The order is one which gives a minimum of monotony and also takes account of the effect of one test upon another. The order in which the separate items appear within a given test is based upon relative difficulty of the items and the value of a particular item as a starter, and it is advisable not to alter the order of presentation. For example, the level of difficulty of the second and third items of the "ingenuity" test hinges upon the use that the subject is able to make of the experience he has gained in the solution of the first and simpler problem. Serial testing — that is, giving all the tests of one type consecutively (digits, sentences, etc.) — is not permissible if the test score is to be interpreted in terms of the established norms. It has been urged in defense of this practice that time is saved by the busy clinician, since he does not have to repeat the instructions for each recurring test as the series becomes more difficult, and that there is an advantage in establishing a "mental set" for repeating digits, giving similarities, or the like. The method in question is indefensible if for no other reason than that it changes the difficulty of the test items by an unknown amount. Perhaps a mental set for repeating digits makes this test easier, but a special experiment would be necessary to determine whether and to what extent this is true. It is conceivable that boredom from being kept too long at a monotonous task would more than offset the advantage of mental set, and decrease the score.

In order to secure the child's best effort, however, it is sometimes necessary to change the test sequence. For example, if the child shows resistance toward a certain type of test, such as repeating digits, drawing, etc., it is better to shift temporarily to a more agreeable task. When the subject is at his ease again, it is usually possible to return to the troublesome tests with better success. Such difficulties are particularly likely to be encountered in the testing of pre-school children. This group presents so many special problems that we have felt it necessary to give a separate discussion of the techniques of pre-school testing.

THE IMPORTANCE OF RAPPORT

The examiner's first task is to win the confidence of the child and to overcome any timidity he may feel in the presence of a stranger. Unless rapport has first been established, the results of the first tests are likely to be misleading. The time and effort necessary for accomplishing this are variable factors, depending upon the personality of both the examiner and the subject. It is impossible to give specific rules for the guidance of the examiner in establishing rapport. The address which flatters and pleases one child may excite disgust in another. The examiner must himself be genuinely interested and friendly or no amount of skilled technique will enable him to establish a sympathetic, understanding relationship with children. There are people who lack personal adaptability to an extent that makes success in this field for them impossible. Such a person has no place in a psychological clinic.

Nothing contributes more to satisfactory rapport than keeping the child encouraged. This can be done in many subtle, friendly ways; by an understanding smile, a spontaneous exclamation of pleasure, an appreciative comment, or just the air of quiet understanding between equals that carries assurance and appreciation. Any stereotyped comment following each test becomes perfunctory and serves no purpose other than to punctuate the tests. In general it is wise to praise frequently and generously, but if this is done in too lavish and stilted a fashion it is likely to defeat its purpose. The examiner should remember that he is giving approval primarily for effort rather than for success on a particular response. To praise only the successful responses may influence effort in the succeeding tests. Praise should never be given between the items of a particular test, but should be reserved until the end of that test. Under no circumstances should the examiner permit himself to show dissatisfaction with a response, however absurd it may be. With younger children, especially, praise should not be limited to tests on which the child has done well. Young children are characteristically uncritical and are often enormously pleased with very inferior responses. In praising poor performances of older subjects, the examiner should remember that the purpose of commendation is to insure confidence and not to reconcile the subject to an inferior level of response. In the case of a failure that is embarrassingly evident to the child himself, the examiner will do well to make some excuse for it. Expressions of commendation should be varied and should fit naturally into the conversation.

Although the examiner should always encourage the child

to believe that he can answer correctly if he will only try, he must avoid the common practice of dragging out responses by too much urging and cross-questioning. To do so often robs the response of significance and is likely to interfere with the maintenance of rapport. While the examiner must be on his guard against mistaking exceptional timidity for inability to respond, he must also be able to recognize the silence of incapacity or the genuineness of an "I don't know."

The competent examiner must possess in a high degree judgment, intelligence, sensitivity to the reactions of others, and penetration, as well as knowledge of and regard for scientific methods and experience in the use of psychometric techniques. No degree of mechanical perfection of the tests themselves can ever take the place of good judgment and psychological insight of the examiner.

THE APPRAISAL OF RESPONSES

Mastery of the scoring rules. Detailed instructions for scoring the tests of both Form L and Form M are given in Part II. It is, of course, very necessary for the examiner to acquaint himself thoroughly with the scoring rules there laid down. It is as important to know what constitutes a satisfactory response as it is to use the correct procedure in presenting the problem to the subject. We have aimed to secure objectivity of scoring by indicating as clearly as possible the guiding principles involved, and by giving numerous examples of satisfactory and unsatisfactory responses.

The examples given are verbatim responses copied from our case records, and they accordingly resemble closely the types of responses any examiner may expect to secure. They are not, however, a random sampling of such responses. In general we have given only a few examples of responses which were so obviously either satisfactory or unsatisfactory that no one would fail to score them correctly. A majority of the illustrations have been selected from responses which are nearer the borderline. The difficult task of the examiner is to learn to distinguish the barely plus responses from those which are barely minus. Among the samples are also illustrations of ambiguous responses which call for further questioning.

It will be found that the responses have been scored from a common-sense point of view, making the differentiation between plus and minus as free from arbitrary, artificial, and academic distinctions as possible. In the same spirit the examiner must free himself from purist prejudices regarding ungrammatical speech and be as willing to credit a correct response awkwardly expressed as one that is given in the best literary form. It is necessary to be very alert in order to judge whether the poorly formulated answer really carries the correct meaning.

Avoidance of the "halo" effect. Scoring must be kept free from the "halo" effect. Each response must be judged on its own merits without regard to other successes or failures. The examiner must guard against allowing his scoring to be influenced by the general impression he has formed of the subject's ability. There is a natural tendency to overestimate the ability of the sprightly, self-confident, talkative child, and the examiner has to be very careful to avoid scoring the responses of such a subject too leniently. He must not temper his scoring by any conviction that the subject could have answered correctly if he had really tried; his task is to score the response which has actually been given. The halo effect will be reduced by making a full record of the responses.

Scoring not purely mechanical. Although it would be impossible to overemphasize the importance of mastering thoroughly the scoring rules which have been laid down, the fact remains that the scoring of Binet tests can never be made as objective as the stencil scoring of some of the pencil-and-paper tests. Even the veteran examiner now and then encounters a novel type of response which he finds difficult to classify as plus or minus. A good many of the tests occasionally bring a response so near the borderline that the most competent examiners would not agree unanimously in scoring it. The task of those who would use the Stanford-Binet scales is to learn to score each test as nearly as possible the way it was scored in the process of standardizing it. Only in the degree to which they accomplish this task will their results be comparable with the established norms. Considerable practice as well as careful study of the instructions is necessary in order to acquire a ready skill. At best, however, the instructions are far short of being "fool-proof." Formulas are not adequate substitutes for scientific judgment or for common sense.

While one could wish that the Binet scale were entirely free from subjectivity of scoring, this limitation is the price that is paid for its great flexibility and richness as compared with tests which are stencil-scored. The price is not excessive in view of the greater psychological insight that the Binet type of test affords. Improved forms of this test will doubtless continue to appear, but the method itself is not likely to be superseded.

ADMINISTERING THE TESTS

The surroundings. The most desirable testing-room is one to which the child is accustomed and where he feels at ease, but which is free from distracting stimuli. An unused schoolroom is particularly good even with such attention-compelling elements in the total situation as the clumping of small feet through the adjacent halls, slamming doors, and distant voices. These things are all familiar aspects of the usual working situation. They are reassuring to a child who is inclined to be a bit timid and are to be preferred to the bare clinic room without even the comforting presence of ordinary furnishings. It is our experience that excellent testing may be done under very inadequate physical conditions. If children are easily distracted, it must be remembered that the undivided attention of the examiner and the ever-varied test situations are powerful counter-attractions. Each new task is short and interesting.

The clever examiner avoids hampering too much the freedom of the wriggly youngster between tasks. It is easier to command undivided attention for the few moments of a given task if the atmosphere is easy and informal and there is not too great insistence on sitting still. The importance of making the child comfortable, physically as well as mentally, is obvious. He should have a comfortable position and proper light for working. Light directly in the child's face is especially to be avoided.

The presence of others. Of all the distracting influences the presence of another person is one of the most objectionable, especially if that person is the child's mother or teacher. Contrary to what one might expect, the presence of a stranger is a much less disturbing influence. It is easier to test the child in a classroom full of student observers than in the most ideal clinic room with the mother present. If the child is alone with the examiner, he is more at ease from the mere fact that he does not feel that he has a reputation to sustain. Parents and teachers have for so long been centers of reference and authority in the child's world that in their presence he cannot free himself from the psychological "field forces" which they exert upon him. Even if they betray no sign of approval or disapproval of the responses given, their presence tends to inhibit spontaneity and to act as a distracting influence that interferes with the establishment of rapport between the child and the examiner. In the case of a shy child it is often advisable to have the mother come into the examining room with the subject and then withdraw as soon as he has become adapted to the situation. With very young children it is often necessary to have the mother present during the entire test.[1]

Manipulating the testing material. The examiner must have his material arranged in such a manner that he loses no time fumbling around to find the needed card, watch, or pencil. Such delays both jeopardize rapport and needlessly prolong the test. It is particularly important that the material be systematically arranged when much object material is to be used, as in the testing of young children. The various cards which are used in the administration of the scale should be clipped into a binder. We have found it convenient to keep the object material for each test in a small compartment of the testing-box and where possible to mount the objects on a card for ready presentation. Miniature dogs, cats, scissors, and thimbles are much too tempting for tiny hands to resist, and they require tactful management to avoid grief. At any rate, there is no difficulty in securing the child's avid interest in such things!

Duration of the examination. About the only danger of fatigue lies in making the examination too long. The fact that the required tasks are novel and interesting to a high degree insures that under ordinary conditions fatigue is not likely to interfere to any appreciable extent. An hour is ordinarily not too long for a test except in the case of the younger children. Testing time may even extend to an hour and a half without noticeable loss of interest or signs of weariness. Children vary so markedly in their test reactions that it is impossible to predict the time requirements for a given test. It is sometimes desirable to introduce a few minutes' intermission; in exceptional cases a test requires so much time that it is necessary to break it up into two sittings. The examination of a young child can usually be completed in half

[1] See discussion of testing pre-school children, pages 68 ff.

an hour to forty minutes, that of an older child in about an hour. The experienced examiner requires considerably less time than the novice.

Desirable range of testing. The examination should be begun ɛt the point where the child is likely to succeed, but not without some effort. If the starting point is too difficult, the child may become discouraged and refuse to try; if it is much too easy, he is not sufficiently challenged and becomes over-confident. In determining where to begin one must take into account the chronological age, the grade placement, general behavior, and any other pertinent information that may be available. In the case of children who are presumably somewhere near average in ability, it is usually good practice to begin with the group of tests just below the child's chronological age. However, if the examiner has overestimated the subject's intelligence and there is a failure in the tests of that group, it is necessary to go back and give all of the tests of the previous age group, and so on until a level has been reached where all of the tests are passed. This point is the basal age level. In like manner, the examination should be carried up the scale until an age level has been found in which all of the tests are failed. Thus, in effect the subject is given the entire scale, although actually he is given only that portion of the scale which marks off the upper and lower limits of his ability. It sometimes happens that a subject passes all of the tests at a higher age level than the one in which the first failure occurs. Again he may pass tests beyond the age group at which he has failed all the tests. In testing normal children little error will result if we go back no farther than the first year in which no failures occurred, and if we stop with the first year in which there was no success. In computing mental age, all successes and failures are taken account of, including any failures that may have occurred below the basal age level, and successes beyond the first year at which all tests have been failed.

63

The abbreviated scales. If a briefer survey test is desired in a given case where pressure for time is a factor, it is possible to score on the basis of the starred tests only, by distributing the allotment of credit for the year level to the tests of the abbreviated scale. Thus, four tests at year VIII would receive 3 months each, instead of the 2 months' credit allowed for each when all six tests are given; at Average Adult level four tests given instead of the usual eight would increase the credit for each test from 2 months to 4 months. That is, the total amount of credit for the tests of a given year group remains the same.

It sometimes happens that the examiner starts out to give the entire scale and after giving all the tests of two or three year groups finds that it is impossible to finish the examination in the time available. If we assume that an additional sitting would not be feasible, the examiner has but two choices: (1) he may continue to give all the tests as far as possible, in which case no tests at all would be given in the higher levels at which some successes would have been possible; or (2) he may change in mid-stream to the abbreviated scale with the prospect of being able to carry the examination through the highest levels at which successes are likely to occur.

The latter choice is, of course, the correct one. If the examination is broken off abruptly at a point where most of the tests are being passed, no reliable estimate can be made of the score that would have resulted had the examination been completed. The other choice permits the computation of a score which is only a little less reliable than if the entire scale had been given. The correct procedure for computing the score in such cases is to assign the regular amount of credit for each test passed at the levels where all the tests are given, and the proportionately larger amounts at the levels where only the starred tests have been used.

Scattering of successes. It may be a matter of concern to

examiners familiar with the old scale that successes and failures should be scattered over a wider range on the revised scale than on the old one. The reason for this is that the magnitude of the intervals between successive age levels has been decreased both in the lower and the upper parts of the scale: at the lower in order to secure a more adequate sampling of abilities in the period which is characterized by a rapidity of mental growth unequaled at any later stage of development; at the upper in order to permit the inclusion of additional age levels designed to give the scale more top. The result has been a richer sampling of abilities and a greater range of successes and failures.

Whatever the nature of intelligence may be, its manifestations in the individual are uneven. One individual will do better with one kind of material than he does with another. Thus, A may succeed well on tasks involving immediate recall, whereas in drawing designs he may function at a lower level. Abilities are always manifested and measured in relation to experiences and training, and the behavioral composite which we call intelligence is of necessity modified and moulded by these factors. No cross-section view of the performances characteristic of children *en masse* at particular age levels will ever be found to be perfectly characteristic of a given individual.

Finding mental age. The tests at each level cover the preceding period of mental development. For example, if a child is to be credited with a basal mental age of three years he must score plus on all six of the tests listed under the heading year III. Thus, the tests listed under each age heading relate to the age period immediately preceding the heading in question. The six tests under the heading year V cover the period from IV-6 to V; the six tests under the heading year VI cover the period from year V to year VI. Since the age periods are divided into six months, intervals from years two to five, we count one month toward mental age for each of the six tests at a given level in this part of the scale. From year six to fourteen each year group represents an interval of twelve months and we therefore count two months toward mental age for each of the six tests at these levels. Above year XIV, in order to make I.Q.'s for the upper age levels comparable with I.Q.'s at the lower levels, the number of age levels has been increased and the tests at these levels have been given heavier weighting. Accordingly, the number of tests at the Average Adult level is eight and each test is given 2 months' credit, making a total of 16 months' credit for this level. At Superior Adult level I, each of the six tests receives 4 months' credit, Superior Adult level II has six tests at 5 months each, and Superior Adult level III six tests at 6 months each. It is possible for an adult to earn an I.Q. of 152 on this scale.

To find the mental age, the subject is first credited with all the tests (and the corresponding years and months) below the point where the examination begins, which, of course, is at a year group in which all the tests are passed. To this assumed credit is added 1 month for each test passed up to and including year V, 2 months for each passed in years VI to Average Adult inclusive, 4 months for each success in Superior Adult I, 5 months for each success in Superior Adult II, and 6 months for each success in Superior Adult III.

The question arises how mental age is computed when a test has been spoiled in the giving, as occasionally happens. At the pre-school level an alternative test may be substituted in such cases. At the middle and upper levels there are no alternative tests and the total credit for a given level must be apportioned among the remaining tests. For example, if one of the tests at year X has been spoiled and has to be discarded, the 12 months' credit allowed for this year group is equally divided among the remaining five tests, giving each a value of

2.4 months. If three of these five have been passed, the total credit earned at this level is 7.2 months. The same rule applies in case a test has been omitted by oversight or for lack of time to give it. *Under no circumstances, however, may an alternative test be substituted for a test which has been failed.*

The following illustrations of mental age computation will make the process clear:

Suppose a child, aged four years and two months (written 4–2), passes all of the tests at year III, five at year III–6, three at year IV, two at year IV–6, two at year V, and one at year VI. The total credit earned is as follows:

	Years	Months
Year III, all plus. Basal year level.............	3	.....
Year III–6, 5 tests passed, credit 1 month each....	.....	5
Year IV, 3 tests passed, credit 1 month each......	.....	3
Year IV–6, 2 tests passed, credit 1 month each....	.....	2
Year V, 2 tests passed, credit 1 month each.......	.....	2
Year VI, 1 test passed, credit 2 months each......	.....	2
	3	14 or

Mental Age score, 4–2

Suppose in the case of an older subject the distribution of successes and failures has been as follows: six tests at year XIII were passed, four at year XIV, four at A.A., three at S.A. I, two at S.A. II, and two at S.A. III.

	Years	Months
Year XIII, all plus. Basal year level............	13	.....
Year XIV, 4 tests passed, credit 2 months each....	.....	8
Year A.A., 4 tests passed, credit 2 months each....	.....	8
Year S.A. I, 3 tests passed, credit 4 months each	.....	12
Year S.A. II, 2 tests passed, credit 5 months each....	.....	10
Year S.A. III, 2 tests passed, credit 6 months each...	.....	12
	13	50 or

Mental Age score, 17–2

An adult subject who has passed all the tests at the A.A. level, five at S.A. I, all at S.A. II, and three at S.A. III is scored as follows:

67

	Years	Months
Credit presupposed, years II to XIV	14	. . . . .
Year A.A., 8 tests passed, credit 2 months each. . . .	. . . . .	16
Year S.A. I, 5 tests passed, credit 4 months each. . .	. . . . .	20
Year S.A. II, 6 tests passed, credit 5 months each. .	. . . . .	30
Year S.A. III, 3 tests passed, credit 6 months each.	. . . . .	18
	14	84 or

Mental Age score, 21–0

The importance of checking all calculations of mental age scores cannot be overemphasized. All operations must be performed at least twice to reduce the chances of clerical errors.

The computation of I.Q. The I.Q. is the quotient of mental age (M.A.) divided by chronological age (C.A.). Although the computation is a very simple process, it is found in practice to give rise to many errors. These occur both in converting years and months into months and in the division which follows such conversion. In order to reduce the number of errors from this source, and also to save the examiner's time, we have provided "I.Q. tables" (pages 415–450). From these tables M.A. and C.A. being given, it is possible to read off the I.Q. directly without computation of any kind.

The only place where confusion is likely to arise is in the case of subjects who are between the ages of 13 and 16. As has already been explained (pages 29 ff.), we no longer cease counting C.A. abruptly at a given age, but by degrees. Up to 13–0 the entire C.A. is counted; beyond 16–0, none of it. The C.A. of a subject who is between the ages of 13–0 and 16–0 is counted as 13–0 plus ⅔ of the additional months he has lived. This means that a true C.A. of 14 is counted as 13–8; a true C.A. of 15 as 14–4; a true C.A. of 16 as 15–0, which is the highest divisor used in the computation of an I.Q. A table has been provided (page 31) for the ready conversion of any true C.A. between 13–0 and 16–0 into the "adjusted C.A."

68

THE TESTING OF PRE-SCHOOL CHILDREN

Because of the special problems involved in dealing with young children in a test situation, pre-school testing requires its own technique. Young children do not easily become absorbed in an externally imposed task; their attention is easily distracted and they are quickly fatigued. Their responses are likely to be influenced by hunger, restlessness, desire to please the examiner, timidity, and a hundred other motives and circumstances. They are much less motivated than older children by competition or the desire to measure up to a standard. Such personality traits as shyness, dependence, and negativism are apt to determine the behavior patterns to a more marked extent than is the case with older children whose social experience has accustomed them to conform to a more stereotyped pattern.

Particular care should be taken to see that a young child is physically comfortable. He should never be tested when he is hungry, or tired, or in need of a nap. If he begins to show fatigue, the test should be discontinued. Where possible, a low table and child's chair should be used.

In general it will be found desirable to exclude observers, particularly parents, teachers, or siblings. In the case of a very young child, or even an older one who is timid or dependent, it may be desirable to have one parent present, but never both, and never another child. In such cases the parent should be instructed to keep in the background, allowing the examiner to manage the situation and the child in his own way. The parent must be warned never to reword a question or to say anything which would suggest the answer.

The initial approach to the child is of the greatest importance in securing the best test results. How to meet this situation is something the examiner will have to determine in each case for himself. The same technique is not suitable for all subjects. It is generally wise to allow the child time to accustom himself to the new situation before beginning the examination. With a shy or timid child it is advantageous to direct his attention away from himself either by ignoring him or by interesting him in other things.

The examiner will find it an aid to equip himself with some toys for use in getting acquainted with the child. A box of small toys is easy to carry, and interesting to a child. Needless to say, these should never be the same as any of the test material, nor should the child ever be entertained with any of the object material from the tests. Apart from the risk of invalidating a test which has not yet been given, the material is likely to be damaged. The examiner should at all times be in control of the situation and not allow the child to dominate the proceedings.

Great care must be exercised to keep the child motivated. His desire for approval and his natural curiosity are among the most potent aids the examiner has. Thus it becomes the examiner's task to keep the child encouraged and confident by liberal praise and by taking advantage of every bit of curiosity shown. When attention lags, it is often possible to stimulate curiosity by the promise of interesting material to come. When the usual methods to secure motivation are ineffective it is sometimes helpful to promise a reward, such as the privilege of playing with specified toys, returning to his home, etc.

In the drawing tests, the examiner will find the use of a crayon or thick pencil desirable for young children, both because it evokes greater interest, and also because it is easier for them to manipulate than the ordinary pencil.

The tests have been made as interesting and varied as possible, but certain of those which have proved to be the best measures of intelligence are not among the most interesting to the child. It often requires great ingenuity and resourcefulness on the part of the examiner to keep the child's attention on the task long enough for him to become interested in it. On the other hand, some of the testing material is so interesting that it may divert the child's attention from the task of the test. Of course, the examiner must never give the directions for the use of any of the object material while the child is handling it, since it may then be impossible to know whether the response is purposeful or just a random activity. Also, the items of a test should never be presented until the examiner is sure he has the child's attention. Without first securing attention there is considerable danger of wasting a test because of the rule against repeating it once a response, however perfunctory, has been given; there is also danger of failing to get a response for a test in which an item cannot be repeated under any circumstances, such as Memory for Digits.

In pre-school testing it is the examiner, even more than the child, who must constantly be adapting himself to new situations and meeting emergencies. It is impossible to give hard and fast rules for the conduct of the examination, but it cannot be emphasized too strongly that it must be a standardized, controlled experiment with the procedure as rigidly adhered to as possible. It is not always possible with young children to preserve the order of giving tests. The examiner must be skilled in stopping short of the point at which urging will tend to arouse or intensify negativism; in sensing when it is desirable to go on to a more pleasing test with the idea of returning to the troublesome one at a more favorable moment. He may find a time when the child is less negativistic, or he may be able later to present the material in a more attractive way. He should make it his goal to leave no test which the child has not attempted. On the other hand, the examiner must not be deceived by the child who is eager to proceed to something more to his liking and gives an offhand answer rather than one which is representative of his best effort.

PART II

INSTRUCTIONS FOR ADMINISTERING FORM L

YEAR II

1. *Three-Hole Form Board [1] (Must precede Three-Hole Form Board: Rotated, Year II-6)

Material: Form board 5"×8" with three insets for circle, square, and triangle.

Procedure: Present the board with the blocks in place. Place the board so that the base of the triangle will be towards the subject. Say, "*Watch what I do.*" Remove the blocks, placing each before its appropriate recess on the side toward S.[2] Then say, "*Now put them back into their holes.*" Allow two trials. Return the blocks to the board for a second trial and repeat the procedure.

Count it a trial when the child has arranged the pieces to his satisfaction as indicated by pushing back the board or looking up at the examiner.

Score: 1 plus.[3] All three blocks must be placed correctly.

2. Identifying Objects by Name

Material: Card with toy cat, button, thimble, cup, engine, and spoon attached.

Procedure: Show the card with the six small objects attached and say, "*See all these things? Show me the kitty.*" "*Put your finger on the kitty.*" "*Where is the kitty?*"

[1] This test occurs also in Form M at Year II, Test 4.

[2] S. refers to the subject and E. will be used to designate the examiner.

[3] That is, one success in the two trials passes the subject. This form of abbreviation is used throughout.

NOTE. — The tests marked with a * constitute an abbreviated scale, for use in case there is not time to give a complete test. See page 64.

In order ask for: (a) kitty, (b) button, (c) thimble, (d) cup, (e) engine (train, choo-choo), (f) spoon. It is not permissible to ask for the objects by any special names other than those specified in the instructions.

Score: 4 plus. The child must designate the object by pointing to it.

3. *Identifying Parts of the Body (Same as II–6, 2)

Material: Large paper doll.

Procedure: Show the paper doll and say, *"Show me the dolly's hair."* Same for mouth, ear, and hands.

(a) Hair, (b) mouth, (c) ear, (d) hands.

Score: 3 plus. The child must clearly indicate the parts on the paper doll.

4. Block Building: Tower

Material: Twelve 1-inch cubes.

Procedure: Place the blocks in confusion before the child and then build a four-block tower out of his reach, saying, *"See what I'm making!"*

Then, pushing the blocks toward the child, say, " *You make one like this.*" *"Make yours* (pointing) *right here.*" E.'s tower is left standing while the child is attempting to build another. If E.'s tower is knocked over it should be rebuilt. Illustrate several times if necessary.

Score: The child must build a tower of four or more blocks in imitation of E.'s tower and in response to E.'s request, not spontaneously either before or later, as it is purposive behavior in which we are interested rather than the spontaneous play activities involving manipulation of material. The tower must stand by itself at the four-block stage.

5. *Picture Vocabulary** (Same as II–6, 4; III, 2; III–6, 2; IV, 1)

Material: Eighteen 2″× 4″ cards with pictures of common objects.

Procedure: Show the cards one at a time. Say, *"What's this?"* *"What do you call it?"*

Score: 2 plus.   See scoring standards, pages 195 ff.

6. *Word Combinations* [1] (Same as M, II, 6)

Procedure: Note the child's spontaneous word combinations at any time during the interview.

Score: See scoring standards, page 197.

Alternate

Obeying Simple Commands (Same as III–6, 1)

Material: Block, spoon, cat, cup, thimble.

Procedure: With the objects on the table in a row as follows, block, spoon, cat, cup, thimble, say:

(a) *"Give me the kitty."*

(b) *" Put the spoon in the cup."*

(c) *" Put the thimble on the block."*

Replace the objects in the same order after each trial. It is sometimes necessary to repeat each command several times if the child has made no move toward carrying out your request.

Score: 2 plus.

[1] This test occurs also in Form M at Year II, Test 6.

YEAR II-6

NOTE: If the Three-Hole Form Board (II, 1) has not already been given, it should be given before Test 1 of this group.

1. *Identifying Objects by Use (Same as III–6, 5)

Material: Card with cup, shoe, penny, knife, automobile, and iron attached.

Procedure: Show the card with the six small objects attached and say, "*Show me what* ...." or "*Which one* ......" or "*Show me the one that* ......"

(a) "...... *we drink out of.*"
(b) "...... *goes on our feet.*"
(c) "...... *we can buy candy with.*"
(d) "...... *we can cut with.*"
(e) "...... *we ride in.*"
(f) "...... *we use to iron clothes.*"

Score: 3 plus. The child must designate the object by pointing. If he points incorrectly, the response is scored minus even though he may have given the correct name.

2. Identifying Parts of the Body (Same as II, 3)

Material: Large paper doll.

Procedure: Show the paper doll and say, "*Show me the dolly's hair.*" Same for mouth, ear, and hands.

(a) Hair, (b) mouth, (c) ear, (d) hands.

Score: 4 plus. The child must clearly indicate the parts on the paper doll.

3. *Naming Objects

Material: Chair, automobile, box, key, fork.

Procedure: Present the objects one at a time. Have the child name each. Say, *"What is this?"* *"What do you call it?"* Present in the order:

(a) Chair, (b) automobile, (c) box, (d) key, (e) fork.

Score: 4-plus. See scoring standards, page 199.

4. *Picture Vocabulary (Same as II, 5; III, 2; III–6, 2; IV, 1)

Material: Eighteen 2″ × 4″ cards with pictures of common objects.

Procedure: Show the cards one at a time. Say, *"What's this?"* *"What do you call it?"*

Score: 9 plus. See scoring standards, pages 195 ff.

5. *Repeating 2 Digits

Procedure: Say, *"Listen; say 2."* *"Now, say 4–7,"* etc.

(a) 4–7, (b) 6–3, (c) 5–8.

Pronounce the digits distinctly and with perfectly uniform emphasis at the rate of one per second.

Score: 1 plus. The series must be repeated in correct order without error.

6. Three-Hole Form Board: Rotated (II, 1 must precede)

Material: Form board used in II, 1.

Procedure: With the board in position 1 (the base of the triangle toward the child), remove the blocks from the board while the child watches. Place each block before its proper recess on the side toward the child. Then rotate the board, while the child watches, to position 2 (with the apex of the triangle toward the child), and say, *"Put them*

all back where they belong."   No time limit.   Give two
trials, repeating the same procedure for the second trial.
   Score: 1 plus.   All three blocks must be placed correctly.

Alternate

Identifying Objects by Name (Same as II, 2)

Material: Card with cat, button, thimble, cup, engine,
and spoon attached.

Procedure: Show the card with the six small objects attached and say, "*See all these things?   Show me the kitty.*"
"*Put your finger on the kitty.*"   "*Where is the kitty?*"

In order ask for: (a) kitty,   (b) button,   (c) thimble,
(d) cup,   (e) engine (train, choo-choo),   (f) spoon.

Score: 5 plus.   The child must point to the object.

YEAR III

1. Stringing Beads

Material: Box of 48 kindergarten beads all of the same
color, 16 round, 16 square, 16 cylindrical, and a pair of
18-inch shoestrings.

Procedure: String one bead of each shape, saying, "*Now
let's play this game.   Watch.*"   Then, giving S. another
string, say, "*Let's see how many we can put on.*"   Continue
stringing beads while the child works on his chain, urging
as often as necessary.   If S. seems to be selecting a particular shape, tell him any bead will do.   Time limit, 2 minutes.

Score: 4 beads.   Count each bead that has been pulled
on the string beyond the metal tip, even though in manipulation it may have slipped off again.

2. *Picture Vocabulary (Same as II, 5; II–6, 4; III–6, 2; IV, 1)

Material: Eighteen 2″ × 4″ cards with pictures of common objects.

Procedure: Show the cards one at a time. Say, "*What's this?*" "*What do you call it?*"

Score: 12 plus. See scoring standards, pages 195 ff.

3. *Block Building: Bridge [1]

Material: Twelve 1-inch cubes.

Procedure: Place the blocks in confusion before the child and then proceed to build a bridge of three blocks beyond the child's reach, saying, "*See if you can make one like this.*" "*Make yours* (pointing) *right here.*" E.'s bridge is left standing. Illustrate several times if necessary.

Score: The structure may be unsteady, but is counted satisfactory if it stands. The base blocks must not be touching. They must be bridged by a third which rests on both. The response is still scored plus if the child continues to build by adding towers to his bridge.

The bridge must be built in response to E.'s request and not spontaneously at some other time during the test.

4. *Picture Memories

Material: Four cards with animal pictures.

Procedure: Show card (a) and ask, "*What is this?*" " *Yes, it's a cow* (or *moo-cow*)." If the child does not name it correctly, tell him the name. Take the card away and say, before showing card (A), " *Now we are going to find it!*" Then show card (A) and ask, "*Where is it?*" If necessary, say, "*Show me,*" or " *Put your finger on it.*"

[1] This test occurs also in Form M at Year III, Test 1.

Show card (b) and, pointing to each object, ask, *"What is this?"* If the child does not name it correctly, tell him. Take the card away as before and say, before showing card (B), *" Now we are going to find them!"* Then show card (B) and ask, *"Where are they?"* Be careful to avoid naming the objects when you are asking the child to locate them from memory.

Score: 1 plus. S. must clearly indicate the correct objects. Additional enumeration makes the response minus.

5. Copying a Circle

Material: Circle printed in record booklet.

Procedure: Give the child a pencil and, pointing to the circle in the booklet, say, *"Make one just like this." "Make it right here."* Give three trials, repeating the directions for each trial. Do not allow S. to trace the model.

Score: 1 plus. See scoring standards, pages 201 f.

6. *Repeating 3 Digits

Procedure: Say, *" Listen; say 4–2." " Now, say 6–4–1,"* etc.

(a) 6–4–1, (b) 3–5–2, (c) 8–3–7.

Pronounce the digits distinctly and with perfectly uniform emphasis at the rate of one per second.

Score: 1 plus. The series must be repeated in correct order without error after a single reading.

Alternate

Three-Hole Form Board: Rotated [1] (Same as II–6, 6)

Material: Form board used in II, 1.

Procedure: With the board in position 1 (the base of the triangle toward the child), remove the blocks from the

[1] This test occurs also as an alternate in Form M at Year III.

board while the child watches.   Place each block before its proper recess on the side of the triangle toward the child. Then rotate the board, while the child watches, to position 2 (with apex of the triangle toward the child), and say, *"Put them all back where they belong."*   No time limit.   Give two trials.   Repeat the same procedure for the second trial.

Score: 2 plus.   All three blocks must be placed correctly.

YEAR III–6

1. *Obeying Simple Commands (Same as II, Alt.)

Material: Block, spoon, cat, cup, thimble.

Procedure: With the objects on the table in a row as follows, block, spoon, cat, cup, thimble, say:

(a) *"Give me the kitty."*

(b) *"Put the spoon in the cup."*

(c) *"Put the thimble on the block."*

Replace the objects in the same order after each trial. It is sometimes necessary to repeat each command several times if the child has made no move toward carrying out your request.

Score: 3 plus.

2. *Picture Vocabulary (Same as II, 5; II–6, 4; III, 2; IV, 1)

Material: Eighteen 2″ × 4″ cards with pictures of common objects.

Procedure: Show the cards one at a time.   Say to the child, *"What's this?"*   *"What do you call it?"*

Score: 15 plus.   See scoring standards, pages 195 ff.

3. Comparison of Sticks

Material: Match sticks, cut to 2-inch and 2½-inch lengths.

Procedure: Place the two sticks on the table before the child in the positions indicated below and about an inch apart. Say, *"Which stick is longer?"* *"Put your finger on the long one."* Give three trials, alternating the relative positions of the long and the short sticks. In case one of the first three trials is failed, give three additional trials, continuing to alternate the positions of the sticks.

(a) _____   (b) _____   (c) _____

_____   _____   _____

Score: 3 of 3 or 5 of 6.

4. Response to Pictures I

Material: Three pictures, Dutch Home, River Scene, Post Office.

Procedure: Present the pictures in the following order: Dutch Home, River Scene, Post Office. Say, *"Look at this picture and tell me all about it."* If there is no response, repeat the request: *"Tell me all about it."* If the child names one or two things in a picture and then stops, urge him on by saying, *"Tell me more about it."* Only one question of this type, however, is permissible. Do not remove the picture until it is clear that no further response is forthcoming.

Score: 2 plus. See scoring standards, pages 204 ff.

5. *Identifying Objects by Use (Same as II–6, 1)

Material: Card with cup, shoe, penny, knife, automobile, and iron attached.

Procedure: Show S. the card with the six small objects

attached and say, *"Show me what ......"* or *"Which one ......"* or *"Show me the one that ......"*

  (a) *"...... we drink out of."*
  (b) *"...... goes on our feet."*
  (c) *"...... we buy candy with."*
  (d) *"...... we can cut with."*
  (e) *"...... we ride in."*
  (f) *"...... we use to iron clothes."*

Score: 5 plus.   S. must designate the object by pointing. If he points incorrectly, the response is scored minus even though he may have given the correct name.

6. *Comprehension I

  Procedure: Ask,
  (a) *"What must you do when you are thirsty?"*
  (b) *"Why do we have stoves?"*

If there is no response, repeat the question, asking, *"What must you do when you are thirsty?"*

Score: 1 plus.   See scoring standards, pages 206 f.

Alternate

Drawing Designs: Cross

  Procedure: Give the child a pencil and, as you draw a cross making the diagonal lines about two inches in length (×), say to him, *" You make one just like this."* Illustrate once only.   Give one trial.

  Score: See scoring standards, pages 207 f.

YEAR IV

1. *Picture Vocabulary (Same as II, 5; II–6, 4; III, 2; III–6, 2)

    Material: Eighteen $2'' \times 4''$ cards with pictures of common objects.

    Procedure: Show the cards one at a time. Say, *"What's this?"* *"What do you call it?"*

    Score: 16 plus. See scoring standards, pages 195 ff.

2. *Naming Objects from Memory

    Material: Automobile, dog, shoe, cat, spoon, engine, doll, scissors, thimble, box.

    Procedure: Place the automobile, dog, and shoe in a row before the child in the order indicated from his left to his right. Call his attention to each object, asking him to name it. Accept whatever name he gives. If he hesitates, name it for him. Then say, *" Now shut your eyes tight so that you can't see them."* Screen the test objects from his sight and cover the *dog* with the small box cover. Remove the screen and say, *" Look! Which one did I hide?"* If the child points without naming the hidden object, say, *" Yes, what is it?"* Repeat the procedure for (b) and (c), hiding in turn the engine and then the doll.

    (a) Automobile, *dog*, shoe.

    (b) Cat, spoon, *engine*.

    (c) *Doll*, scissors, thimble.

    Score: 2 plus. The child must designate the object either by its correct name or by the name he used when it was first shown to him.

86

3. Picture Completion: Man (Same as V, 1)

Material: Incomplete drawing of a man.

Procedure: Point to the incomplete drawing in the record booklet and say, *"What is this?"* Whether the child recognizes it or not, say, *"It is a man, isn't it? (or Yes, it's a man). See, he has only one leg. You finish him. Make all the rest of him."* If S. stops after making the missing leg only, believing he has completed the task, say, *"Make all the rest of him."* If, however, S. begins with an arm or some part other than the leg and then stops, accept the response as complete without further urging. If S.'s addition is unrecognizable, ask, *"What is this?"*

Score: 1 point. See scoring standards, pages 209 ff.

4. *Pictorial Identification

Material: Card with pictures of objects.

Procedure: Show the card and say, *"Show me what ......"* or *"Which one ......"* or *"Show me the one that ......"*

(a) *"...... we cook on."*

(b) *"...... we carry when it is raining."*

(c) *"...... gives us milk."*

(d) *"...... has the longest ears."*

(e) *"...... shines in the sky at night."*

(f) *"...... catches mice."*

If S. names the object without pointing to it, ask him to point.

Score: 3 plus. Naming the object is not sufficient. The child must point to it on the card.

5. *Discrimination of Forms

Material: Two cards with 10 forms, one to be cut up so that the forms may be placed one at a time on the other card at "X."

Procedure: Show the uncut card with the forms and say, *"See all of these things?"* Place the circle of the duplicate set at "X" and say, *"Find me another one just like this,"* at the same time passing your finger around the circumference of the circle. If there is no response, say, *"Do you see all of these things?"* Indicate the other forms. *"And do you see this one?"* pointing to the circle at "X" again. *"Now find me another one just like this."* Correct an error on the circle by saying, *"No, find one just like this,"* again passing the finger around the outline of the figure. If S. still fails to find the circle, show him. S. is not given credit for finding the circle after correction. Give no further help. Present the square next, then the triangle, and then the other forms in any random order that differs from the order of their arrangement on the large card.

Score: 8 plus.

6. Comprehension II

Procedure: Ask,

(a) *"Why do we have houses?"*

(b) *"Why do we have books?"*

Score: 2 plus. See scoring standards, page 212.

Alternate

Memory for Sentences I

Procedure: Say, *"I want you to say something for me. Say, 'big boy' (or 'big girl')."* *"Now say, 'I am a big boy' (or 'girl')."* *"Now say ......"*

(a) *"We are going to buy some candy for mother."*
(b) *"Jack likes to feed the little puppies in the barn."*
If S. hesitates, urge him to try by asking him to *"Say it."*
It is, of course, never permissible to repeat the sentence.
Score: 1 plus.   No error.   Errors include omissions, substitutions, additions, changes in words or in the order of words, but *not* contractions, e.g., "we're" for "we are."

YEAR IV–6

1. Aesthetic Comparison

Material: Three cards with pairs of pictures for comparison.

Procedure: Show each card in turn and ask, *"Which one is prettier?"*

Score: 3 plus.

2. *Repeating 4 Digits

Procedure: Say: *"I am going to say some numbers and when I am through I want you to say them just the way I do. Listen carefully, and get them just right."*   Before each series repeat, *"Listen carefully, and get them just right."*   Pronounce the digits distinctly and with perfectly uniform emphasis at the rate of one per second.

(a) 4–7–2–9,   (b) 3–8–5–2,   (c) 7–2–6–1.

Score: 1 plus.   The series must be repeated in correct order without error after a single reading.

3. *Pictorial Likenesses and Differences (Same as VI, 5)

Material: Six cards with pictures.

Procedure: Present card (a) and say: *"See these crosses that are just alike?   Here's one* (pointing) *that is* not *like the others. Put your finger on the one that is* not *the same as the others."* Make sure that S. points out the one that is different. No further illustration. Repeat for each of the following cards, *"Put your finger on the one that is* not *the same as the others."* Card (a) is used for illustration only.

Score: 3 plus. Card (a) is not included in the score.

4. Materials

Procedure: Say, *"What is a chair made of?"* Same for *dress* and *shoe.*

(a) Chair, (b) dress, (c) shoe.

Score: 2 plus. See scoring standards, pages 214 f.

5. *Three Commissions

Procedure: After getting up from the chair and moving with the child to the center of the room, say: *" Now I want you to do something for me. Here's a pencil. I want you to put it on that chair over there; then I want you to shut (open) the door; and then bring me the box which you see over there* (pointing in turn to the objects designated). *Do you understand? Be sure to get it right. First you put the pencil on the chair, then shut (open) the door, then bring me the box. Go ahead."* If S. asks what to do next say merely, *"Go ahead."*

Do not repeat the instructions again or give any further aid whatever, even by the direction of the gaze. If the child stops or hesitates it is never permissible to ask what comes next.

Score: All three commissions must be executed and in the proper order. See scoring standards, pages 215 f.

6. *Opposite Analogies I (Same as VII, 5)

> *Procedure:* Say,
> (a) *"Brother is a boy; sister is a ......"*
> (b) *"A table is made of wood; a window of ......"*
> (c) *"A bird flies; a fish ......"*
> (d) *"The point of a cane is blunt; the point of a knife is ....."*
> (e) *"An inch is short; a mile is ......"*
> *Score:* 2 plus.   See scoring standards, pages 216 f.

Alternate

Pictorial Identification (Same as IV, 4)

> *Material:* Card with pictures of objects.
> *Procedure:* Show the card and say, *"Show me what ....."*
> or *"Which one ......"* or *"Show me the one that ......"*
> (a) *"...... we cook on."*
> (b) *"...... we carry when it is raining."*
> (c) *"...... gives us milk."*
> (d) *"...... has the longest ears."*
> (e) *"...... shines in the sky at night."*
> (f) *"...... catches mice."*

If S. names the object without pointing to it, ask him to point.

Score: 4 plus.   Naming of object is not sufficient.   S. must designate it on the card.

YEAR V

1. *Picture Completion: Man (Same as IV, 3)

> *Material:* Incomplete drawing of a man.
> *Procedure:* Point to the incomplete drawing in the record booklet and say, *"What is this?"*   Whether the child recog-

nizes it or not, say, "*It is a man, isn't it?* (or *Yes, it's a man*). *See, he has only one leg. You finish him. Make all the rest of him.*" If S. stops after making the missing leg only, believing he has completed the task, say, "*Make all the rest of him.*" If, however, S. begins with an arm or some part other than the leg and then stops, accept the response as complete without further urging. If S.'s addition is unrecognizable, ask, "*What is this?*"

Score: 2 points. See scoring standards, pages 209 ff.

2. Paper Folding: Triangle

Material: Six-inch squares of paper.

Procedure: Say, "*Watch what I do.*" Make sure that the child is watching while you fold one of the $6'' \times 6''$ sheets once along the diagonal making a triangle; then fold this triangle once through the middle to make a triangle half as large.

Give the child another square of paper and say, "*Now you do it. Make one just like this.*" Leave the folded paper exposed, but pressed flat against the table.

Score: See scoring standards, pages 217 f.

3. *Definitions

Procedure: Say, "*What is a ball?*" If necessary, urge by saying, "*You know what a ball is. Tell me what a ball is.*" Use the same formula for *hat* and *stove*.

(a) Ball, (b) hat, (c) stove.

Score: 2 plus. See scoring standards, pages 218 f.

4. Copying a Square

Material: Square printed in the record booklet.

Procedure: Give the child a pencil and say, pointing to the square in the booklet, "*Make one just like this. Make it right here."* Give three trials, repeating the directions for each trial. Do not allow S. to use the side of one square as part of another, or to trace the model.

Score: 1 plus. See scoring standards, pages 219 ff.

5. *Memory for Sentences II

Procedure: Say, *"I want you to say something for me. Say, 'big boy'* (or *'big girl'),"* depending on the sex of the subject. *" Now say, 'I am a big boy'* (or *'girl')." " Now say ......"*

(a) *"Jane wants to build a big castle in her playhouse."*

(b) *"Tom has lots of fun playing ball with his sister."*

If S. hesitates, urge him to try by asking him to *"Say it."*

Score: 1 plus. No error. Errors include omissions, substitutions, additions, changes in words or in order of words.

6. *Counting Four Objects

Material: Four blocks, 4 square beads, and 4 pennies.

Procedure: Present the objects in a row, one series at a time, first the 4 blocks, then the 4 beads, and then the 4 pennies. Remove each preceding series before presenting the next in order. Ask for each series, *" How many? "* S. is not asked to count or to point, but it is permissible for him to do both.

Score: 2 plus. If S says *"four,"* but on counting gets some other number, or if he counts any series several times, obtaining a different result each time, the response is scored minus.

Alternate

Knot [1]

Material: Pair of 18-inch shoestrings. Pencil.

Procedure: Say, *"Watch what I do. I'm tying a knot*

[1] This test occurs also as an alternate in Form M at Year V.

around this pencil." Tie a single knot (not a bow), then present the other shoelace and say to the child, "*You take this other piece of string and tie the same kind of knot around my finger. Make one just like this one*" (pointing to the examiner's knot).

Score: Any sort of knot which does not come undone is acceptable.

YEAR VI

1. *Vocabulary

Material: Vocabulary card.

Procedure: Say, "*I want to find out how many words you know. Listen, and when I say a word, you tell me what it means. What is an orange?*" Vary the form of the question to avoid a stilted manner of presentation, e.g., "*What does ...... mean?*" "*Tell me what a ...... is,*" or give just the word without further question. If S. hesitates, urge him to try by saying, "*Just tell me in your own words; say it any way you please. All I want to know is whether you know what a ...... is.*" If the child can read, give him the vocabulary card and let him look at each word as you read it.

If the child's meaning is not clear, that is, if his response can't be scored either plus or minus without further explanation, say, "*Tell me what you mean,*" or "*Tell me more about it.*"

Since the words have been arranged in the order of their difficulty for approximately 3000 subjects, we have found that there is very little likelihood of success beyond the point where six consecutive words have been failed.

Score: 5 plus. See scoring standards, pages 302 ff.

2. *Copying a Bead Chain from Memory I

Material: Box of 48 kindergarten beads all of the same color, 16 round, 16 square, and 16 cylindrical.

Procedure: Place the box of beads on the table before the child and say, *"Watch what I do."* While S. watches, make a chain of 7 beads using alternately square and round beads and say, *"When I'm through, I'm going to take this one away and see if you can make one just like it."* When complete, let S. look at it for 5 seconds. Remove the chain and, giving him a shoestring, tell the child to make one just like it. Allow not more than 2 minutes.

Score: No error in pattern. See scoring standards, page 222.

3. Mutilated Pictures

Material: Card with mutilated pictures.

Procedure: Show S. the card with the mutilated pictures and, pointing to each in turn, ask, *"What is gone in this picture?"* or *"What part is gone?"* If the child hesitates, further urging is sometimes necessary to elicit a response. Vary the question by asking, *"What isn't there?"* Avoid pointing to the missing part in designating the object.

(a) Wagon, (b) shoe, (c) teapot, (d) rabbit, (e) glove.

Score: 4 plus. See scoring standards, pages 223 f.

4. *Number Concepts

Material: Twelve 1-inch cubes.

Procedure: Place the blocks in a pile on the table before S. In order that the examiner may be sure just how many blocks the child means to indicate, we use a sheet of white paper for him to put his blocks on. Say, *"Give me ......* *blocks. Put them here,"* pointing to the sheet of paper.

After each choice replace the blocks in the pile. Ask, in turn, for *three* blocks, *nine, five,* and *seven*. Sometimes the child thinks that in order to designate the correct number of blocks he has to pick them all up in his hand at once. In such a case say, " *You don't have to take them all in your hand at once.*" It is important for the examiner to avoid suggesting the correct response; for example, do not wait expectantly when S. stops after having placed too few blocks on the paper, nor should you hasten to remove the blocks, after he has given you the correct number, without making sure that he has really finished.

(a) 3,   (b) 9,   (c) 5,   (d) 7.

Score: 3 plus.

5. * Pictorial Likenesses and Differences (Same as IV–6, 3)

Material: Six cards with pictures.

Procedure: Present card (a) and say: "*See these crosses that are just alike?   Here's one* (pointing) *that is* not *like the others.   Put your finger on the one that is* not *the same as the others.*"   Make sure that S. points out the one that is different.   No further illustration.   Repeat for each of the following cards, " *Put your finger on the one that is* not *the same as the others.*"   Card (a) is used for illustration only.

Score: 5 plus.   Card (a) is not included in the score.

6. Maze Tracing

Material: Maze paths with three positions marked (see record booklet).

Procedure: Show S. the first maze and say, pointing to the little figure on the path, "*This little boy lives here, and here* (pointing) *is the schoolhouse.   The little boy wants to go to school the shortest way without getting off the sidewalk.   Here is the sidewalk. Show me the shortest way. Mark it with your pencil, but don't go off the sidewalk. Start here and take the little boy to school the shortest way.*"

Then show the second maze and say, "*This other little boy lives here* (position 2). *Show me the shortest way for* him *to go to school. Don't go off the sidewalk.*"

Likewise, for the third maze say, "*And this boy lives here* (position 3). *Show me the shortest way for* him *to go to school. Don't go off the sidewalk.*"

In case the child starts tracing without marking the path with the pencil, say, "*Make it so I can see it.*"

Score: 2 plus. See scoring standards, page 225.

YEAR VII

1. Picture Absurdities I

Material: Four pictures: (a) Man with umbrella, (b) man with saw, (c) dog and rabbit, (d) man and woman sitting in the rain.

Procedure: Show the pictures in the order indicated and ask for each in turn, "*What's funny (foolish) about that picture?*" If the child's response is ambiguous without further explanation, ask, "*Why is it (that) funny (foolish)?*"

Score: 3 plus. See scoring standards, pages 226 f.

2. *Similarities: Two things

Procedure: Say, "*In what way are ...... and ...... alike?*"

(a) *Wood and coal.*
(b) *Apple and peach.*
(c) *Ship and automobile.*
(d) *Iron and silver.*

97

It is often necessary to insist a little if S. is silent or says he doesn't know. It is permissible to repeat the original question or to add, "*How are they the same?*" or "*In what way are they alike?*" When a difference is given for (a) say, "*No, I want you to tell me how they are* alike. *In what way are wood and coal the same?*" If the child persists in giving differences, make no further comment after the other pairs.

Score: 2 plus. See scoring standards, pages 228 ff.

3. * Copying a Diamond

Material: Diamond printed in the record booklet.

Procedure: Point to the model in the booklet and, giving S. a pencil, say, "*Make one just like this. Make it right here.*" Give 3 trials. For the second and third trials say, "*Now, make another one just like this. Make it here.*"

Score: 2 plus. See scoring standards, pages 230 ff.

4. Comprehension III

Procedure: Say,

(a) "*What's the thing for you to do when you have broken something which belongs to someone else?*"

(b) "*What's the thing for you to do when you are on your way to school and see that you are in danger of being late?*"

(c) "*What's the thing for you to do if another boy* (or *girl*, depending on the sex of the subject; or *another person*, for adults) *hits you without meaning to do it?*"

Score: 2 plus. See scoring standards, pages 232 f.

5. * Opposite Analogies I (Same as IV–6, 6)

Procedure: Say,

(a) "*Brother is a boy; sister is a* . . . . . ."

(b) "*A table is made of wood; a window of* . . . . . ."

(c) *"A bird flies; a fish ......"*
(d) *"The point of a cane is blunt; the point of a knife is ......"*
(e) *"An inch is short; a mile is ......"*
Score: 5 plus.   See scoring standards, pages 216 f.

6. *Repeating 5 Digits

Procedure: Say: *"I am going to say some numbers and when I am through I want you to say them just the way I do. Listen carefully, and get them just right."* Before each series repeat, *"Listen carefully, and get them just right."* Pronounce the digits distinctly and with perfectly uniform emphasis at the rate of one per second.

(a) 3–1–8–5–9,   (b) 4–8–3–7–2,   (c) 9–6–1–8–3.

Score: 1 plus.   The series must be repeated in correct order without error after a single reading.

YEAR VIII

1. *Vocabulary

Material: Vocabulary card.
Procedure: Say: *"I want to find out how many words you know.   Listen, and when I say a word, you tell me what it means.   What is an orange?"*.   Vary the form of the question to avoid a stilted manner of presentation, e.g., *"What does ...... mean?"* *"Tell me what a ...... is,"* or give just the word without further question.   If S. hesitates, urge him to try by saying: *"Just tell me in your own words; say it any way you please.   All I want to know is whether you know what a ...... is."*   If the child can read, give him a printed copy of the word list and let him look at each word as you read it.

If the child's meaning is not clear, that is, if his response can't be scored either plus or minus without further explanation, say, "*Tell me what you mean,*" or "*Tell me more about it.*" Continue until six consecutive words have been failed.

Score: 8 plus. See scoring standards, pages 302 ff.

2. Memory for Stories: The Wet Fall

Material: Card with printed selection on it.

Procedure: Say: "*Here is a story about 'The Wet Fall.' Listen carefully while I read it because I shall ask you questions about it.*" Give the child a copy of the selection and let him follow it as you read it aloud.

The Wet Fall

"Once there was a little girl named Betty. She lived on a farm with her brother Dick. One day their father gave them a Shetland pony. They had lots of fun with it. One day, when Dick was riding on it, the pony became frightened and ran away. Poor Dick fell into a ditch. How Betty laughed when she saw him! He was covered with mud from head to foot."

Remove the child's copy of the selection and proceed to ask him the following questions:

(a) "*What is the name of this story?*"
(b) "*What was Betty's brother's name?*"
(c) "*Where did they live?*"
(d) "*Who gave the pony to them?*"
(e) "*What did the pony do?*"
(f) "*What happened?*"

Score: 5 of 6. See scoring standards, pages 233 ff.

3. *Verbal Absurdities I

Procedure: Read each statement and, after each one, ask, *"What is foolish about that?"* If the response is ambiguous without further explanation, ask, *"Why is it (that) foolish?"*

(a) "They found a young man locked in his room with his hands tied behind him and his feet bound together. They think he locked himself in."

(b) "A wheel came off Frank's automobile. As he could not get the wheel back on by himself, he drove his automobile to the shop for repairs." (If S. calls the wheel a tire in his response, repeat the item, saying, *"It was a* wheel *that came off Frank's automobile. As he could not get the wheel back on ..."* etc.)

(c) "I read in the paper that the police fired two shots at a man. The first shot killed him, but the second did not hurt him much."

(d) "An engineer said that the more cars he had on his train the faster he could go."

Score: 3 plus. See scoring standards, pages 235 ff.

4. *Similarities and Differences

Procedure: Say, *"I'm going to name two things and I want you to tell me how they are* alike *and how they are* different. *In what way are ...... and ...... alike, and how are they different?"* If in (a) or (b) S. omits either of the comparisons, ask, *"And how are they the same (or different)?"* Make no comment concerning omissions in (c) and (d)

(a) *Baseball and orange.*   (c) *Ocean and river.*

(b) *Aeroplane and kite.*   (d) *Penny and quarter.*

If his response indicates that S. has recalled *baseball* as *football*, *orange* as *lemon*, or *river* as *lake*, repeat the original question.

Score: 3 plus. See scoring standards, pages 239 ff.

5. *Comprehension IV

Procedure: Ask,

(a) *"What makes a sailboat move?"*

(b) *"What should you say when you are in a strange city and someone asks you how to find a certain address?"*

(c) *"What should you do if you found on the streets of a city a three-year-old baby that was lost from its parents?"*

Score: 2 plus. See scoring standards, pages 241 f.

6. Memory for Sentences III

Procedure: Say, *"Listen, and be sure to say exactly what I say."*

(a) *"Fred asked his father to take him to see the clowns in the circus."*

(b) *"Billy has made a beautiful boat out of wood with his sharp knife."*

Score: 1 plus. No error. Errors include omissions, substitutions, additions, changes in words or in order of words.

YEAR IX

1. Paper Cutting I (Same as XIII, 3)

Material: Six-inch squares of paper.

Procedure: Taking one of the sheets, say,

(a) *"Watch carefully what I do. See, I fold the paper this way* (folding it over once through the middle, making a rectangle). *Now I will cut out a piece right here"* (indicating). At the center of the creased edge cut an opening that is about half an inch square. Leave the folded paper exposed, but pressed flat against the table. The fragments cut from the paper should be kept out of sight. Indicating the $3'' \times 3''$ square in the booklet, say, *"Make a drawing*

here to show how this paper would look if it were unfolded
(opened). *Draw lines to show where the paper would be
creased and show how and where it would be
cut.*" If S. omits either the creases or the
cuts, repeat, "*Draw lines to show where
the paper would be creased and show how
and where it would be cut,*" emphasizing the pertinent
words.

(b) For the second sheet say, "*Now watch what I do.
See, I fold the paper this way* (folding the sheet over in the
middle). *Then I fold it this way* (folding it again in the middle, but at right angles to the first fold). *And now I will
cut out a piece right here.*" Cut off the corner formed by
the intersection of the folds. The cut should
be made about three quarters of an inch from the
corner. Then say, as before, "*Make a drawing
here to show how this paper would look if it were*
unfolded (opened). *Draw lines to show where the paper
would be creased and show how and where it would be cut.*"

Score: 1 plus. See scoring standards, pages 242 ff.

2. Verbal Absurdities II (Same as XII, 2)

Procedure: Read each statement and, after each one,
ask, "*What is foolish about that?*" If the response is ambiguous, say, "*Why is it (that) foolish?*"

(a) "Bill Jones's feet are so big that he has to pull his
trousers on over his head."

(b) "A man called one day at the post office and asked if
there was a letter waiting for him. 'What is your name?'
asked the postmaster. 'Why,' said the man, 'you will find
my name on the envelope.'"

(c) "The fireman hurried to the burning house, got his
fire hose ready, and after smoking a cigar, put out the fire."

(d) "In an old graveyard in Spain they have discovered a small skull which they believe to be that of Christopher Columbus when he was about ten years old."

(e) "One day we saw several icebergs that had been entirely melted by the warmth of the Gulf Stream."

Score: 3 plus. See scoring standards, pages 244 ff.

3. *Memory for Designs (Same as XI, 1)

Material: Card with two designs.

Procedure: Before showing the card say, "*This card has two drawings on it. I am going to show them to you for ten seconds, then I will take the card away and let you draw from memory what you have seen. Be sure to look at both drawings carefully.*" Then show the card for 10 seconds, holding it

at right angles to the child's line of vision and with the designs in the position given in the plate. At the end of approximately 4 seconds say, quietly, "*Look at both.*" Have S. reproduce the designs immediately, and note which is the top of his drawing.

Score: 1 plus or 2 with half credit each. See scoring standards, pages 248 ff.

4. *Rhymes: New form

Procedure: Say, "*You know what a rhyme is, of course. A rhyme is a word that sounds like another word. Two words rhyme if they end in the same sound, like 'hat' and 'sat.' Now I want you to:*

(a) "*Tell me the name of a color that rhymes with* head."

(b) "*Tell me a number that rhymes with* tree."

(c) "*Tell me the name of an animal that rhymes with* fair."

(d) "*Tell me the name of a flower that rhymes with* nose."

Score: 3 plus. See scoring standards, page 240.

5. *Making Change

> *Procedure:* Ask, *"If I were to buy four cents' worth of candy and should give the storekeeper ten cents, how much money would I get back?"* Same for 12–15; 4–25 cents.[1]
> *Score:* 2 plus.

6. *Repeating 4 Digits Reversed

> *Procedure:* Say, *"I am going to say some numbers, and I want you to say them backwards. For example, if I should say 5–1–4, you would say 4–1–5. Ready now; listen carefully, and be sure to say the numbers backwards."* Before each series repeat, *"Ready now; listen carefully, and be sure to say the numbers backwards."* Rate one per second.
> (a) 8–5–2–6, (b) 4–9–3–7, (c) 3–6–2–9.
> *Score:* 1 plus. The series must be repeated backwards in correct order without error after a single reading.

YEAR X

1. *Vocabulary

> *Material:* Vocabulary card.
> *Procedure:* Say, *"I want to find out how many words you know. Listen, and when I say a word, you tell me what it means. What is an orange?"* Vary the form of the question to avoid a stilted manner of presentation, e.g., *"What does ...... mean?" "Tell me what a ...... is,"* or give just the word without further question. If S. hesitates, urge him to try by saying, *"Just tell me in your own words; say it any way you please. All I want to know is whether you know what a ...... is."* Give S. a printed copy of the word list and let him look at each word as you read it.

[1] No time limit.

If the child's meaning is not clear, that is, if his response can't be scored either plus or minus without further explanation, say, *"Tell me what you mean,"* or *"Tell me more about it."* Continue until six consecutive words have been failed.

Score: 11 plus. See scoring standards, pages 302 ff.

2. Picture Absurdities II

Material: Picture, Frontier Days.

Procedure: Present the picture and ask, *"What's foolish about that picture?"* If the response is ambiguous, ask, *"Why is it (that) foolish (funny)?"*

Score: See scoring standards, pages 254 f.

3. *Reading and Report

Material: Card with selection printed on it.

Procedure: Hand the selection to S. and say, *"I want you to read this out loud as well as you can."* Pronounce for S. any word he is unable to make out, allowing not more than 5 seconds' hesitation. Each word which the examiner has to pronounce for the child counts as an error. Record the time in seconds and the number of errors made in reading the selection. When S. has finished say, *"That's very good. Now, tell me what you read. Begin at the beginning and tell me everything you can remember."* When S. stops ask, *"And what else?"*

Score: 10 memories; not more than 2 errors in reading; time 35 seconds or less. See scoring standards, pages 255 f.

4. *Finding Reasons I

Procedure: Say:

(a) *"Give two reasons why children should not be too noisy in school."*

(b) *"Give two reasons why most people would rather have an automobile than a bicycle."*

If S. gives only one reason and stops, do not try to elicit the second by further questioning, but, before giving the next item, hesitate long enough to give S. an opportunity to remember himself that he is expected to give two reasons. If in either case S. asks how many reasons he has given, read his response to him so that he may decide for himself.

Score: 2 plus. See scoring standards, pages 256 ff.

5. *Word Naming

Procedure: Say: *" Now I want to see how many different words you can name in one minute. Just any words will do, like 'clouds,' 'dog,' 'chair,' 'happy.' When I say, 'Ready,' you begin and say the words as fast as you can and I will count them. Ready; go ahead."* Do no urging unless the child hesitates for 10 seconds, in which case say, *"Go ahead as fast as you can. Any words will do."* If S. gives sentences or counts, stop him, saying, *"Counting* (or *sentences) not allowed. You must name separate words. Go ahead as fast as you can."*

Score: 28 words. See scoring standards, pages 258 f.

6. Repeating 6 Digits

Procedure: Say, *"I am going to say some numbers and when I am through I want you to say them just the way I do. Listen carefully, and get them just right."* Before each series repeat, *"Listen carefully, and get them just right."* Pronounce the digits distinctly and with perfectly uniform emphasis at the rate of one per second.

(a) 4–7–3–8–5–9,   (b) 5–2–9–7–4–6,   (c) 7–2–8–3–9–4.

Score: 1 plus. The series must be repeated in correct order without error after a single reading.

YEAR XI

1. *Memory for Designs (Same as IX, 3)

Material: Card with two designs.

Procedure: Before showing the card say, *"This card has two drawings on it. I am going to show them to you for ten seconds, then I will take the card away and let you draw from memory what you have seen. Be sure to look at both drawings carefully."* Then show the card for 10 seconds, holding it at right angles to the child's line of vision and with the designs in the position given in the plate. At the end of approximately 4 seconds say, quietly, *"Look at both."* Have S. reproduce the designs immediately, and note which is the top of his drawing.

Score: 1½ plus. See scoring standards, pages 248 ff., 259.

2. *Verbal Absurdities III

Procedure: Read each statement and, after each one, ask, *"What is foolish about that?"* If the response is ambiguous, say, *"Why is it (that) foolish?"*

(a) "The judge said to the prisoner, 'You are to be hanged, and I hope it will be a warning to you.'"

(b) "A well-known railroad had its last accident five years ago and since that time it has killed only one person in a collision."

(c) "When there is a collision the last car of the train is usually damaged most. So they have decided that it will be best if the last car is always taken off before the train starts."

Score: 2 plus. See scoring standards, pages 259 ff.

3. *Abstract Words I

   Procedure: Say, "*What is* ......*?*" or "*What do we mean by* ......*?*"

   (a) Connection, (b) compare, (c) conquer, (d) obedience, (e) revenge.

   Score: 3 plus. See scoring standards, pages 261 ff.

4. Memory for Sentences IV

   Procedure: Say, "*Now listen, and be sure to say exactly what I say.*"

   (a) "*At the summer camp the children get up early in the morning to go swimming.*"

   (b) "*Yesterday we went for a ride in our car along the road that crosses the bridge.*"

   Score: 1 plus. No error. Errors include omissions, substitutions, additions, changes in words or in the order of words.

5. Problem Situation

   Procedure: Say, "*Listen, and see if you can understand what I read.*"

   "Donald went walking in the woods. He saw a pretty little animal that he tried to take home for a pet. It got away from him, but when he got home, his family immediately burned all his clothes. *Why?*"

   Score: See scoring standards, pages 264 f.

6. *Similarities: Three things

   Procedure: Say, "*In what way are* ......, ..., *and* ...... *alike?*"

   (a) *Snake, cow, sparrow.*

109

(b) *Rose, potato, tree.*

(c) *Wool, cotton, leather.*

(d) *Knife-blade, penny, piece of wire.*

(e) *Book, teacher, newspaper.*

A little urging is sometimes necessary to secure a response. If S. hesitates or says he doesn't know, urge him to try by repeating the question or asking, "*How are they alike?*"

Score: 3 plus. See scoring standards, pages 265 ff.

YEAR XII

1. *Vocabulary

Material: Vocabulary card.

Procedure: Say: "*I want to find out how many words you know. Listen, and when I say a word, you tell me what it means. What is an orange?*" Vary the form of the question to avoid a stilted manner of presentation, e.g., "*What does ...... mean?*" "*Tell me what a ...... is,*" or give just the word without any further question. If S. hesitates, urge him to try by saying, "*Just tell me in your own words; say it any way you please. All I want to know is whether you know what a ...... is.*" Give S. a printed copy of the word list and let him look at each word as you read it.

If the subject's meaning is not clear, that is, if his response can't be scored plus or minus without further explanation, say, "*Tell me what you mean,*" or "*Tell me more about it.*" Continue until six consecutive words have been failed.

Score: 14 plus. See scoring standards, pages 302 ff.

2. *Verbal Absurdities II (Same as IX, 2)

Procedure: Read each statement and, after each one, ask, *"What is foolish about that?"* If the response is ambiguous, say, *"Why is it (that) foolish?"*

(a) "Bill Jones's feet are so big that he has to pull his trousers on over his head."

(b) "A man called one day at the post office and asked if there was a letter waiting for him. 'What is your name?' asked the postmaster. 'Why,' said the man, 'you will find my name on the envelope.'"

(c) "The fireman hurried to the burning house, got his fire hose ready, and after smoking a cigar, put out the fire."

(d) "In an old graveyard in Spain they have discovered a small skull which they believe to be that of Christopher Columbus when he was about ten years old."

(e) "One day we saw several icebergs that had been entirely melted by the warmth of the Gulf Stream."

Score: 4 plus. See scoring standards, pages 244 ff., 267.

3. Response to Pictures II

Material: Picture, Messenger Boy.

Procedure: Say, *"Look at this picture and tell me all about it."*

Score: See scoring standards, pages 267 f.

4. Repeating 5 Digits Reversed

Procedure: Say: *"I am going to say some numbers, and I want you to say them backwards. For example, if I should say 5–1–4, you would say 4–1–5. Ready now; listen carefully, and be sure to say the numbers backwards."* Before each series repeat, *"Ready now; listen carefully, and be sure to say the numbers backwards."* Rate one per second.

(a) 8–1–3–7–9,   (b) 6–9–5–8–2,   (c) 5–2–9–4–1.

Score: 1 plus. The series must be repeated backwards in correct order without error after a single reading.

5. ***Abstract Words II** (Same as XIV, 6)

Procedure: Say, "*What do we mean by* ......*?*" or "*What is* ......*?*"

(a) Constant,   (b) courage,   (c) charity,   (d) defend.

Score: 2 plus. See scoring standards, pages 269 f.

6. ***Minkus Completion** ¹ (Same as S.A. I, 3)

Material: Selection printed on last page of record booklet.

Procedure: Have S. fill in the missing word for each blank in the selection printed in the record booklet. Say, "*Write the missing word in each blank. Put just one word in each.*"

(a) One cannot always be a hero, ... one can always be a man.

(b) The streams are dry ...... there has been little rain.

(c) ...... either of us could speak, we were at the bottom of the stairs.

(d) He is ...... well grounded in Geography ...... his brother, ... he is not so quick in Arithmetic.

If S. cannot read, it is permissible to read the words for him, indicating each. If necessary, write in the missing word that S. dictates.

Time limit, 5 minutes.

Score: 2 sentences plus. See scoring standards, page 271.

---

¹ This test occurs also in Form M at Year XII, Test 2.

YEAR XIII

1. Plan of Search

Material: Circle with a small gap in the side next the child (see record booklet).

Procedure: Give S. a pencil and, showing him the circle in the record booklet, say: "*Let's suppose that your purse with a lot of money in it has been lost in this big field. Take this pencil and start here* (pointing) *at the gate, and show me where you would go to hunt for the purse so as to be sure not to miss it.*" If S. fails to understand that he is to mark the path, add, "*Mark it with the pencil to show me where you would go to hunt for the purse.*"

If S. stops before there is evidence whether or not any plan governs his procedure, say, "*But suppose you hadn't found it yet, show me everywhere you would go to look for it.*" No further questioning or urging.

Score: See scoring standards, pages 272 f.

2. Memory for Words

Procedure: Say, "*Now listen, and be sure to say exactly what I say.*"

(a) "*Cow, sand, glass, chair, bell.*"

(b) "*Grace, truth, worth, peace, doubt.*"

Score: 1 plus. No error. Errors include omissions, substitutions, additions, changes in words or in order of words.

3. *Paper Cutting I (Same as IX, 1)

Material: Six-inch squares of paper.

Procedure: Taking one of the sheets, say,

(a) "*Watch carefully what I do. See, I fold the paper this way* (folding it over once through the middle, making a rectangle). *Now I will cut out a piece right here"* (indicating). At the center of the creased edge cut an opening that is about half an inch square. Leave the folded paper exposed, but pressed flat against the table. The fragments cut from the paper should be kept out of sight. Indicating the $3'' \times 3''$ square in the record booklet, say: *"Make a drawing here to show how this paper would look if it were* unfolded (opened). *Draw lines to show where the paper would be creased and show how and where it would be cut."* If S. omits either the creases or cuts, repeat, *"Draw lines to show where the paper would be creased and show how and where it would be cut,"* emphasizing the pertinent words.

(b) Fold the second sheet once in the middle, and then fold it again in the middle but at right angles to the first fold. Then cut off the corner formed by the intersection of the folds. The cut should be made about three quarters of an inch from the corner. Repeat the instructions as before.

Score: 2 plus. See scoring standards, pages 242 ff., 274.

4. *Problems of Fact [1]

Procedure: Say, *"Listen:*

(a) *"A man who was walking in the woods near a city stopped suddenly, very much frightened, and then ran to the nearest policeman, saying that he had just seen hanging from the limb of a tree a ...... a what?"* (If the reply is *"man,"* say, *"Tell me what you mean; explain it."*)

(b) *"My neighbor has been having queer visitors. First a doctor came to his house, then a lawyer, then a minister (preacher, priest,* or *rabbi). What do you think happened there?"* (If the response is *"a death,"* etc., check by asking what the lawyer came for.)

---

[1] This test occurs also in Form M at Year XIII, Test 5.

(c) "*An Indian who had come to town for the first time in his life saw a white boy riding along the street. As the white boy rode by the Indian said, ' The white boy is lazy; he walks sitting down.' What was the white boy riding on that caused the Indian to say, ' He walks sitting down'?*"

Score: 2 plus.   See scoring standards, pages 274 ff.

5. *Dissected Sentences [1]

Material: Cards on which disarranged words are printed in capitals.

Procedure: Show the sentences one at a time in the order indicated.   Before giving S. the first sentence, say, with the card in your hand but held so that S. can't see the words until you have completed your instructions: "*Here is a sentence that has the words all mixed up so that they don't make any sense. If the words were changed around in the right order they would make a good sentence. Look carefully, and tell me how the sentence ought to read.*"   Pronounce for S. any word he does not know, but give no further help.[2]   For (b) and (c) say, "*Now tell me how this one ought to read.*"   Time, 1 minute each.

(a) FOR THE STARTED AN WE COUNTRY EARLY AT HOUR.

(b) TO ASKED PAPER MY TEACHER CORRECT I MY.

(c) A DEFENDS DOG GOOD HIS BRAVELY MASTER.

Score: 2 plus, or equivalent in half credits.   See scoring standards, pages 276 f.

---

[1] This test occurs also in Form M at Year XIII, Test 3.

[2] In the 1916 revision the examiner was permitted to read the first sentence correctly if the subject was unable to succeed with it.   In the present test no illustration is given.

6. * **Copying a Bead Chain from Memory II**

Material: Box of 48 kindergarten beads all of the same color, 16 round, 16 square, and 16 cylindrical.

Procedure: Make a 9-bead chain, holding the string so that S. can see, and say, *"Watch carefully what I am making because I am going to take this one away and see if you can make one just like it."* Use, in order, 2 round, 1 square, 1 round, 1 cylindrical, 1 round, 1 square, and 2 round beads, making a chain like the sample.

$$\bigcirc\ \bigcirc\ \square\ \bigcirc\ \square\ \bigcirc\ \square\ \bigcirc\ \bigcirc$$

When complete, let S. look at it for 5 seconds. Remove the chain and tell him to make one just like it. Time limit, 2 minutes.

Score: No error.

YEAR XIV

1. * **Vocabulary**

Material: Vocabulary card.

Procedure: Say, *"I want to find out how many words you know. Listen, and when I say a word, you tell me what it means. What is an orange?"* Vary the form of the question to avoid a stilted manner of presentation, e.g., *"What does ...... mean?"* *"Tell me what a ...... is,"* or give just the word without further question. If S. hesitates, urge him to try by saying, *"Just tell me in your own words; say it any way you please. All I want to know is whether you know what a ...... is."* Give S. the vocabulary card. containing the word list and let him look at each word as you read it.

If the subject's meaning is not clear, that is, if his response can't be scored plus or minus without further explanation, say, "*Tell me what you mean,*" or "*Tell me more about it.*" Continue until six consecutive words have been failed.

Score: 16 plus.   See scoring standards, pages 302 ff.

2. *Induction

Material: Six sheets of tissue paper 8½″× 11″.

Procedure: Take the first sheet, and saying, "*Watch what I do,*" fold it through the middle and then, in the center of the folded edge, cut out a small notch.   Then say, "*How many holes will there be when the paper is unfolded?*" Unfold the sheet and spread it out so S. can count the holes, thus calling his attention to the correct number.

Take a second sheet of paper and fold it as before, saying, "*When I folded it this way and cut out a piece, you remember it made one hole in the paper.   This time we will give the paper another fold and see how many holes there will be.*" Then proceed to fold the paper again, this time at right angles to the first fold, cut out a notch from the folded edge, and ask, "*How many holes will there be this time when the paper is unfolded?*" Let S. see the result as before and place this sheet on the other, proceeding to the third sheet.

Continue in the same manner with sheets 3, 4, 5, and 6, adding one fold each time at right angles to the preceding one.   In folding each sheet recapitulate the results, saying thus, with the sixth sheet, "*When we folded it this way there was* one *hole; when we folded it again there were* two; *when we folded it again there were* four; *when we folded it again there were* eight; *when we folded it again there were* sixteen; *now tell me how many holes there will be if we fold it once more?*" Be careful to avoid saying, "When we folded it once, twice, three times ......" Do not unfold the last sheet, but this time express approval regardless of the correctness of the response, and if S. gives the correct response for the sixth sheet, say, *"Give me a rule so that I can know each time how many holes there are going to be."*

If the rule is given spontaneously before the sixth folding it is not necessary to continue. It is not permissible to ask for the rule until all six parts have been given. Nothing must be said which could remotely suggest the operation of the rule.

Score: Plus if the rule is grasped by the time the sixth sheet is reached; that is, S. may pass after five incorrect responses, provided the sixth is correct and the governing rule can then be given. See scoring standards, pages 277 f.

3. Picture Absurdities III [1]

Material: Picture, The Shadow.

Procedure: Showing the picture, ask, *"What's foolish about that picture?"* If the response is ambiguous, say, *"Why is it (that) foolish?"*

Score: See scoring standards, pages 278 f.

4. *Ingenuity (Same as A.A., 6)

Procedure: The problem is given orally and may be repeated if necessary. (a) *"A mother sent her boy to the river to bring back exactly 3 pints of water. She gave him a 7-pint can and a 4-pint can. Show me how the boy can measure out exactly 3 pints of water using nothing but these two cans and not guessing at the amount. You should begin by filling the 7-pint can first. Remember, you have a 7-pint can and a 4-pint can and you must bring back exactly 3 pints of water."* [2]

---

[1] This test occurs also in Form M at Year XIV, Test 2.

[2] If the subject fails, we do not explain the solution. The procedure differs in that respect from the 1916 revision.

Use the same formula for (b) and (c).

(b) 8-pint can and 5-pint can to get 11 pints. Begin by filling the 8-pint can.

(c) 4-pint can and 9-pint can to get 3 pints. Begin by filling the 4-pint can.

The subject is not allowed to use pencil and paper. If he resorts to a method that involves guessing, tell him that he must *measure* out the water without guessing. Explain, also, if necessary, that it is a fair problem, not a catch. Encourage him to keep on trying during the 3-minute period allowed for each problem, but if he has failed on the first problem it is not necessary to go on to (b) and (c).

Score: 1 plus. See scoring standards, page 279.

5. Orientation: Direction I

Procedure: Read the following directions distinctly, emphasizing the critical words:

(a) *"Which direction would you have to face so that your* left *hand would be toward the* east?"

(If S. points or says, " *That way,*" say, "*What is the* name *of the direction you would have to face?"* etc.)

(b) *"Suppose you are going* west, *then turn to your* right; *what direction are you going now?"*

(c) *"Suppose you are going* north, *then turn to your* left, *then turn* right; *what direction are you going now?"*

(d) *"Suppose you are going* south, *then turn* left, *then turn* right, *then turn* left *again; what direction are you going now?"*

(e) *"Suppose you are going* north, *then turn* left, *then* left *again, then* right, *and then* right *again; what direction are you going now?"*

It is permissible to repeat the directions if S. becomes confused or cannot remember the problem.

Score: 3 plus.

6. *Abstract Words II (Same as XII, 5)

   Procedure: Say, *"What do you mean by ......?"* or
   "What is ......?"
   (a) Constant,   (b) courage,   (c) charity,   (d) defend.
   Score: 3 plus.   See scoring standards, pages 269 f., 280.

AVERAGE ADULT

1. *Vocabulary

   Material: Vocabulary card.
   Procedure: Say: *"I want to find out how many words you
   know.   Listen, and when I say a word, you tell me what it
   means.   What is an orange?"* Vary the form of the question to avoid a stilted manner of presentation, e.g., *"What
   does ...... mean?"* *"Tell me what a ...... is,"* or give
   just the word without any further question.   If S. hesitates,
   urge him to try by saying, *"Just tell me in your own words;
   say it any way you please.   All I want to know is whether
   you know what a ...... is."* Give S. the vocabulary card
   containing the word list and let him look at each word as
   you read it.
   If the subject's meaning is not clear, that is, if his
   response can't be scored plus or minus without further explanation, say, *"Tell me what you mean,"* or *"Tell me more
   about it."* Continue until six consecutive words have been
   failed.
   Score: 20 plus.   See scoring standards, pages 302 ff.

2. *Codes

   Material: Message and code printed in capitals in the
   record booklet.
   Procedure: Show S. the code given in the record booklet

and say: " *Here is a message that has been written two ways.
This is what we want to say, 'Come to London'* (pointing)
and here it is in code (pointing and reading the letters).
*Each letter here in the code stands for a letter up here in the
message.*" Indicate each letter, or letters, in the code and
the corresponding letter in the message. " *You figure out
how it goes, what the system is, and then write H U R R Y in
code.*"

If the first code is solved correctly, say, when presenting
the second, " *Now figure this one out and then write H U R R Y
in this code.*" If there is more than one error on the first
code, it is unnecessary to give the second. If necessary,
explain to S. that a code is a way of sending secret messages.
It is permissible for S. to write out the alphabet as an aid if
he wishes, but E. must in no way suggest his doing so or
assist him with the alphabet. Time limit, 3 minutes each.

(a) C O M E   T O   L O N D O N
     D P N F   U P   M P O E P O

(b) C   O   M   E   T   O   L   O   N   D   O   N
     BD   NP   LN   DF   SU   NP   KM   NP   MO   CE   NP   MO

Score: 1½ plus.   See scoring standards, pages 280 f.

3. *Differences Between Abstract Words

Procedure: Say, "*What is the difference between:*
(a) "*Laziness and idleness?*"
(b) "*Poverty and misery?*"
(c) "*Character and reputation?*"
Score: 2 plus.   See scoring standards, pages 281 ff.

4. Arithmetical Reasoning

Material: Three cards on which are printed arithmetical
problems.

Procedure: Present each card and say, "*Read this out

loud and give me the answer." With the printed problem still before him, have S. find the answer without the use of pencil or paper. It is not permissible, if the subject gives an incorrect answer, to ask him to solve the problem again. The following exception, however, is made to this rule: If the answer given to the third problem indicates that *yard* has been read as *feet*, S. is asked to re-read the problem carefully (aloud) and to tell how he solved it. No extension of the time limit is allowed for this correction, however. No further help may be given.

(a) If a man's salary is $20 a week and he spends $14 a week, how long will it take him to save $300?

(b) If 2 pencils cost 5 cents, how many pencils can you buy for 50 cents?

(c) At 15 cents a yard, how much will 7 feet of cloth cost? Time limit, 1 minute each.

Score: 2 plus.

5. Proverbs I

Procedure: Say, *"Here is a proverb, and you're supposed to tell what it means. For example, this proverb, 'Large oaks from little acorns grow,' means that great things may have small beginnings. What does this one mean?"*

(a) *"A burnt child dreads the fire."*

(b) *"He who would eat the kernel must crack the nut."*

(c) *"A drowning man will catch at a straw."*

Score: 2 plus. See scoring standards, pages 283 ff.

6. *Ingenuity (Same as XIV, 4)

Procedure: The problem is given orally and may be repeated if necessary.

(a) *"A mother sent her boy to the river to bring back exactly 3 pints of water. She gave him a 7-pint can and a 4-pint can.*

Show me how the boy can measure out exactly 3 pints of water using nothing but those two cans and not guessing at the amount. You should begin by filling the 7-pint can first. Remember, you have a 7-pint can and a 4-pint can and you must bring back exactly 3 pints of water." [1]

(b) 8-pint can and 5-pint can to get 11 pints. Begin by filling the 8-pint can.

(c) 4-pint can and 9-pint can to get 3 pints. Begin by filling the 4-pint can.

Time limit, 3 minutes each.

The subject is not allowed to use pencil and paper. If he resorts to a method that involves guessing, tell him that he must *measure* out the water without guessing. Explain, also, if necessary, that it is a fair problem, not a catch. Encourage him to keep on trying during the 3-minute period allowed for each problem, but if he has failed on the first problem it is not necessary to go on to (b) and (c).

Score: 2 plus. See scoring standards, pages 279, 286.

7. Memory for Sentences V

Procedure: Say, *"Now listen, and be sure to say exactly what I say."*

(a) *"The red-headed woodpeckers made a terrible fuss as they tried to drive the young away from the nest."*

(b) *"The early settlers had little idea of the great changes that were to take place in this country."*

Score: 1 plus. No error. Errors include omissions, substitutions, additions, changes in words or in order of words.

[1] If the subject fails, do not explain the solution.

8. Reconciliation of Opposites (Same as S.A. II, 5)

Procedure: Say, *"In what way are* ...... *and* ......
alike?"

(a) Heavy and light.   (d) More and less.
(b) Tall and short.   (e) Outside and inside.
(c) Sick and well.   (f) Asleep and awake.

Even though S. is failing the items, all six must be given.
If, as sometimes happens, S. fails to grasp the idea until
several items have been given, a correction of the preceding items is accepted if offered spontaneously. If S. says
they are opposite, repeat the question with emphasis on
alike.

Score: 3 plus. See scoring standards, pages 286 ff.

SUPERIOR ADULT I

1. *Vocabulary

Material: Vocabulary card.

Procedure: Say: *"I want to find out how many words you
know. Listen, and when I say a word, you tell me what it
means. What is an orange?"* Vary the form of the question to avoid a stilted manner of presentation, e.g., *"What
does* ...... *mean?" "Tell me what a* ...... *is,"* or give
just the word without any further question. If S. hesitates, urge him to try by saying, *"Just tell me in your own
words; say it any way you please. All I want to know is
whether you know what a* ...... *is."* Give S. the vocabulary card containing the word list and let him look at each
word as you read it.

If the subject's meaning is not clear, that is, if his
response can't be scored plus or minus without further
explanation, say, *"Tell me what you mean,"* or *"Tell me*

more about it." Continue until six consecutive words have been failed.

Score: 23 plus.   See scoring standards, pages 302 ff.

2. Enclosed Box Problem

Material: Any small cardboard box.

Procedure: Show S. a box and say:

(a) *"Listen carefully.   Let's suppose that this box has 2 smaller boxes inside it, and each one of the smaller boxes contains a little tiny box.   How many boxes are there altogether, counting the big one?"*

(b) *"Now let's suppose that this box has 2 smaller boxes inside it and that each of the smaller boxes contains 2 tiny boxes.   How many altogether?"*

(c) *"Now suppose that this box has 3 smaller boxes inside it and that each of the smaller boxes contains 3 tiny boxes. How many boxes are there altogether?"*

(d) *"Now suppose that this box has 4 smaller boxes inside it and that each of the smaller boxes contains 4 tiny boxes. How many are there altogether?"*

Score: 3 plus.

3. *Minkus Completion (Same as XII, 6)

Material: Selection printed in the record booklet.

Procedure: Have S. fill in the missing word for each blank in the selection printed in the record booklet.   Say: *"Write the missing word in each blank.   Put just one word in each."*

(a) One cannot always be a hero, ... one can always be a man.

(b) The streams are dry . . . . . . there has been little rain.

(c) . . . . . . either of us could speak, we were at the bottom of the stairs.

(d) He is ...... well grounded in Geography ...... his brother, ... he is not so quick in Arithmetic.

Time limit, 5 minutes.

Score: 3 sentences plus. See scoring standards, pages 271, 289.

4. *Repeating 6 Digits Reversed [1]

Procedure: Say: "*I am going to say some numbers, and I want you to say them backwards. For example, if I should say 5–1–4, you would say 4–1–5. Ready now; listen carefully, and be sure to say the numbers backwards.*" Before each series repeat, "*Ready now; listen carefully, and be sure to say the numbers backwards.*" Rate, one per second.

(a) 4–7–1–9–5–2, (b) 5–8–3–6–9–4, (c) 7–5–2–6–1–8.

Score: 1 plus. The series must be repeated backwards in correct order without error after a single reading.

5. *Sentence Building

Procedure: Say, "*Now make up a sentence that has in it the three words:*

(a) "*Benefactor, institution, contribution.*"

(b) "*Civility, requirement, employee.*"

(c) "*Attainment, fortune, misery.*"

Score: 2 plus. See scoring standards, pages 289 ff.

6. Essential Similarities [2]

Procedure: Say, "*What is the principal way in which ...... and ...... are alike?*"

(a) Farming and manufacturing.

(b) Melting and burning.

(c) An egg and a seed.

Score: 2 plus. See scoring standards, pages 291 f.

[1] This test occurs also in Form M at Superior Adult Level I, Test 4.

[2] This test occurs also in Form M at Superior Adult Level I, Test 3.

SUPERIOR ADULT II

1. *Vocabulary

Material: Vocabulary card.

Procedure: Say: "*I want to find out how many words you know.   Listen, and when I say a word, you tell me what it means.   What is an orange?*"   Vary the form of the question to avoid a stilted manner of presentation, e.g., "*What does ...... mean?*"   "*Tell me what a ...... is,*" or give just the word without any further question.   If S. hesitates, urge him to try by saying, "*Tell me in your own words; say it any way you please.   All I want to know is whether you know what a ...... is.*"   Give S. the vocabulary card containing the word list and let him look at each word as you read it.

If the subject's meaning is not clear, that is, if his response can't be scored either plus or minus without further explanation, say, "*Tell me what you mean,*" or "*Tell me more about it.*"   Continue until six consecutive words have been failed.

Score: 26 plus.   See scoring standards, pages 302 ff.

2. *Finding Reasons II

Procedure: Say:

(a) "*Give three reasons why some people use typewriters which cost so much when they could get pen and ink for a few cents.*"

(b) "*Give three reasons why a man who commits a serious crime should be punished.*"

If S. stops after giving one or two reasons, do not try to elicit more reasons by further questioning, but, before proceeding to the next item, hesitate long enough to give S. an opportunity to continue. If for either (a) or (b) S. asks how many reasons he has given, read his responses to him so that he may decide for himself.

It occasionally happens that the subject says he does not believe a man who commits a serious crime should be punished. In such a case, ask him to give the commonly accepted reasons.

Score: 2 plus. See scoring standards, pages 293 ff.

3. *Repeating 8 Digits

Procedure: Say: *"I'm going to say some numbers and when I am through I want you to say them just the way I do Listen carefully, and get them just right."* Before each series repeat, *"Listen carefully, and get them just right."* Rate, one per second.

(a) 7–2–5–9–4–8–3–6
(b) 4–7–1–5–3–9–6–2
(c) 4–1–9–3–5–8–2–6

Score: 1 plus. The series must be repeated in correct order without error after a single reading.

4. *Proverbs II

Procedure: Say: *"Here is a proverb, and you are supposed to tell what it means. For example, this proverb, 'Large oaks from little acorns grow,' means that great things may have small beginnings. What does this one mean?"* If the illustration has already been given at the Average Adult level in the preceding proverb test, it may be omitted here. Say instead, *"Here is another proverb. What does this one mean?"*

(a) *"A bird in the hand is worth two in the bush."*
(b) *"You can't make a silk purse out of a sow's ear."*

Score: 2 plus. See scoring standards, pages 295 f.

5. Reconciliation of Opposites (Same as A.A., 8)

Procedure: Say, *"In what way are ...... and ......*
alike?"

(a) Heavy and light.   (d) More and less.
(b) Tall and short.   (e) Outside and inside.
(c) Sick and well.   (f) Asleep and awake.

Even though S. is failing the items, all six must be given.
If, as sometimes happens, S. fails to grasp the idea until
several items have been given, a correction of the preceding
items is accepted if offered spontaneously. If S. says they
are opposite, repeat the question with emphasis on *alike*.

Score: 5 plus. See scoring standards, pages 286 ff., 296.

6. Repeating Thought of Passage: Value of Life [1]

Procedure: Say, *"I am going to read a short paragraph.*
When I am through you are to repeat as much of it as you can.
You don't need to remember the exact words, but listen care-
fully so that you can tell me everything it says." Then read
the following selection:

"Many opinions have been given on the value of life.
Some call it good, others call it bad. It would be nearer
correct to say that it is mediocre, for on the one hand our
happiness is never as great as we should like, and on the
other hand our misfortunes are never as great as our
enemies would wish for us. It is this mediocrity of life
which prevents it from being radically unjust."

Score: See scoring standards, pages 297 f.

[1] This test occurs also in Form M at Superior Adult Level II, Test 6.

SUPERIOR ADULT III

1. *Vocabulary

Material: Vocabulary card.

Procedure: Say, "*I want to find out how many words you know. Listen, and when I say a word, you tell me what it means. What is an orange?*" Vary the form of the question to avoid a stilted manner of presentation, e.g., "*What does ..... mean?*" "*Tell me what a ...... is,*" or give just the word without any further question. If S. hesitates, urge him to try by saying, "*Just tell me in your own words; say it any way you please. All I want to know is whether you know what a ...... is.*" Give S. the vocabulary card containing the word list and let him look at each word as you read it.

If the subject's meaning is not clear, that is, if his response can't be scored either plus or minus without further explanation, say, "*Tell me what you mean,*" or "*Tell me more about it.*" Continue until six consecutive words have been failed.

Score: 30 plus. See scoring standards, pages 302 ff.

2. *Orientation: Direction II

Material: Card on which the problem is stated.

Procedure: Let S. look at the card while you read the problem aloud and while he is solving it. Do not allow S. to use pencil and paper.

(a) "*I drove west for two miles; then I turned to my right and drove north for half a mile; then I turned to my right again and drove two miles further. What direction was I going then?*" Pause for S. to respond, and then ask,

(b) *"How far was I from my starting point when I stopped?"*

Score: 2 plus.   See scoring standards, page 299.

3. *Opposite Analogies II

Procedure: Say:

(a) *"A rabbit is timid; a lion is ......"*

(b) *"The pine tree is evergreen; the poplar is ......"*

(c) *"A debt is a liability; an income is ......"*

Score: 2 plus.   See scoring standards, page 299.

4. Paper Cutting II

Material: Six-inch squares of paper.

Procedure: Taking one of the sheets, say, *"Watch carefully what I do.   See, I fold the paper this way* (folding it over once through the middle), *then I fold it this way* (folding it again so that the second fold is parallel to the first), *and then this way* (folding it again in the middle, but this time at right angles to the first two folds).   *Now I will cut out a piece right here."*   Cut out a small triangular piece from the side which presents only two edges.   Leave the folded paper exposed, but pressed flat against the table. The fragments cut from the paper should be kept out of sight.   Indicating the 3" × 3" square in the booklet, say, *"Make a drawing here to show how this paper would look if it were* unfolded (opened).   *Draw lines to show where the paper would be creased and show how and where it would be cut."*   If S. omits either the creases or the cuts, repeat, *"Draw lines to show where the paper would be creased and show how and where it would be cut."*

Score: See scoring standards, pages 300 f.

5. *Reasoning

Material: Card on which problem is stated.

Procedure: Let S. look at the card while you read the problem aloud and while he is solving it.

"*I planted a tree that was 8 inches tall. At the end of the first year it was 12 inches tall; at the end of the second year it was 18 inches tall; and at the end of the third year it was 27 inches tall. How tall was it at the end of the fourth year?*"

Do not allow S. to use pencil and paper. If the answer is 40 inches, ask S. to explain how he got it. Time limit, 5 minutes.

Score: See scoring standards, page 300.

3. Repeating 9 Digits

Procedure: Say: "*I am going to say some numbers and when I am through I want you to say them just the way I do. Listen carefully, and get them just right.*" Before each series repeat, "*Listen carefully, and get them just right.*" Rate, one per second.

    (a) 5–9–6–1–3–8–2–7–4
    (b) 9–2–5–8–4–1–7–3–6
    (c) 4–7–2–9–1–6–8–5–3

Score: 1 plus. The series must be repeated in correct order without error after a single reading.

PART III

INSTRUCTIONS FOR ADMINISTERING
FORM M

YEAR II

1. * Delayed Response

Material: Three small pasteboard boxes and a small toy cat.

Procedure: Place the boxes in a row about two inches apart. Say, *"Look, I'm going to hide the kitty and then see if you can find it again."* Make sure that the child is watching and then hide the cat first (a) under the *middle box*, then (b) under the box at E.'s *right*, and then (c) under the box at E.'s *left*. Screen the boxes each time and count aloud from 1 to 10 at the rate of 1 per second. Remove the screen, and say, *" Now find the kitty!"* The child's *first* choice in each trial must be the correct one.

Score: 2 plus. If in any trial E. has been unable to prevent two boxes from being turned over simultaneously, that trial is scored minus.

2. Identifying Objects by Name

Material: Card with dog, ball, engine, bed, doll, and scissors attached.

Procedure: Show the card with the six small objects attached and say, *"See all these things? Show me the dog."* *" Put your finger on the dog."* *"Where is the dog?"*

In order ask for: (a) dog, (b) ball, (c) engine (train, choo-choo), (d) bed, (e) doll, (f) scissors (shears). It is not permissible to ask for the objects by any special names other than those specified in the instructions.

Score: 4 plus. The child must point to the objects.

NOTE. — The tests marked with a * constitute an abbreviated scale, for use in case there is not time to give a complete test. See page 64.

3. Identifying Parts of the Body

Material: Large paper doll.

Procedure: Show the paper doll and say, *"Show me the dolly's hair."* Same for eyes, feet, and nose.

(a) Hair, (b) eyes, (c) feet, (d) nose.

Score: 3 plus. The child must clearly indicate the parts on the paper doll.

4. * Three-Hole Form Board [1]

Material: Form board $5'' \times 8''$ with 3 insets for circle, square, and triangle.

Procedure: Show the board with the blocks in place. Place the board so that the base of the triangle will be toward the subject. Say, *"Watch what I do."* Remove the blocks, placing each before the appropriate recess on the side toward the child. Then say, *"Now put them back into their holes."* Allow two trials. Return the blocks to the board for the second trial and repeat the procedure.

Count it a trial when the child has arranged the pieces to his satisfaction as indicated by pushing back the board or looking up at the examiner.

Score: 1 plus. All three blocks must be placed correctly.

5. * Picture Vocabulary (Same as II–6, 4; III, 2; IV, 1; V, 1)

Material: Seventeen $2'' \times 4''$ cards with pictures of common objects.

Procedure: Show the cards one at a time. Say, *"What is this?"* *"What do you call it?"*

Score: 2 plus. See scoring standards, pages 328 ff.

[1] This test occurs also in Form L at Year II, Test 1.

6. *** Word Combinations** [1]

Procedure: Note the child's spontaneous word combinations at any time during the interview.

Score: See scoring standards, pages 197 f., 330.

Alternate

Naming Objects (Same as II–6, 3; III, 5)

Material: Shoe, watch, telephone, flag, jack-knife, stove.

Procedure: Present the objects one at a time. Have the child name each. Say, *"What is this?"* *"What do you call it?"*

Present in the order: (a) Shoe, (b) watch, (c) telephone, (d) flag, (e) jack-knife, (f) stove.

Score: 3 plus. See scoring standards, pages 330, 331.

YEAR II–6

1. *** Identifying Objects by Use** (Same as III, 3)

Material: Card with stove, bed, pipe, chair, dustpan, and scissors attached.

Procedure: Show the child the card with the six small objects attached and say, *"Show me what......"* or *"Which one......"* or *"Show me the one that......"*

(a) *"...... we cook on."*

(b) *"...... we sleep in."*

(c) *"...... a man smokes."*

(d) *"...... we sit on."*

(e) *"...... we sweep the dust into."*

(f) *"...... we cut with."*

Score: 4 plus. The child must point to the object. If he points incorrectly, the response is scored minus even though he may have given the correct name.

[1] This test occurs also in Form L at Year II, Test 6.

2. **Motor Coordination**

> *Material:* Toy egg-beater.
> *Procedure:* Demonstrate several revolutions, saying, *"See this? You make it go the way I do."* Present the egg-beater in position for the child's preferred hand. Give three trials, demonstrating before each trial.
> *Score:* One complete turn of the handle in any trial is plus.

3. * **Naming Objects** (Same as III, 5)

> *Material:* Shoe, watch, telephone, flag, jack-knife, stove.
> *Procedure:* Present the objects one at a time. Have the child name each. Say, *"What is this?"* *"What do you call it?"*
> Present in the order: (a) Shoe, (b) watch, (c) telephone, (d) flag, (e) jack-knife, (f) stove.
> *Score:* 4 plus. See scoring standards, page 331.

4. * **Picture Vocabulary** (Same as II, 5; III, 2; IV, 1; V, 1)

> *Material:* Seventeen $2'' \times 4''$ cards with pictures of common objects.
> *Procedure:* Show the cards one at a time. Say, *"What is this?"* *"What do you call it?"*
> *Score:* 7 plus. See scoring standards, pages 328 ff.

5. * **Repeating 2 Digits**

> *Procedure:* Say, *"Listen; say 2."* *"Now say 5–8,"* etc.
> (a) 5–8, (b) 7–2, (c) 3–9.
> Pronounce the digits distinctly and with perfectly uniform emphasis at the rate of one per second.
> *Score:* 1 plus. The series must be repeated in correct order without error.

6. Obeying Simple Commands

Material: Block, button, dog, box, scissors.

Procedure: With the objects on the table in a row as follows, block, button, dog, box, scissors, say,

(a) *"Give me the dog."*

(b) *"Put the button in the box."*

(c) *"Put the scissors (shears) beside the block."*

Replace the objects in the same order after each trial. It is sometimes necessary to repeat each command several times if the child has made no move toward carrying out the request.

Score: 2 plus.

Alternate

Stringing Beads (Same as IV, 2)

Material: Box of 48 kindergarten beads all of the same color, 16 round, 16 square, 16 cylindrical, and a pair of 18-inch shoestrings.

Procedure: String one bead of each shape, saying, *"Now let's play this game. Watch."* Then, giving S. another string, say, *"Let's see how many we can put on."* Continue stringing while the child works on his chain, urging as often as necessary. If S. seems to be selecting a particular shape, tell him any bead will do. Time limit, 2 minutes.

Score: 2 beads. Count each bead that has been pulled on the string beyond the metal tip, even though in manipulation it may have slipped off again.

YEAR III

1. *Block Building: Bridge [1]

Material: Twelve 1-inch cubes.

Procedure: Place the blocks in confusion before the child and then proceed to build a bridge of three blocks beyond the child's reach, saying, " *You make one like this.*" "*Make yours* (pointing) *right here.*" E.'s bridge is left standing. Illustrate several times if necessary.

Score: The structure may be unsteady, but is scored satisfactory if it stands. The base blocks must not be touching. They must be bridged by a third which rests on both. The response is still scored plus if the child continues to build by adding towers to his bridge.

The bridge must be built in response to E.'s request and not spontaneously some other time during the test.

2. *Picture Vocabulary (Same as II, 5; II–6, 4; IV, 1; V, 1)

Material: Seventeen $2'' \times 4''$ cards with pictures of common objects.

Procedure: Show the cards one at a time. Say, "*What is this?*" "*What do you call it?*"

Score: 10 plus. See scoring standards, pages 328 ff.

3. *Identifying Objects by Use (Same as II–6, 1)

Material: Card with stove, bed, pipe, chair, dustpan, and scissors attached.

Procedure: Show the child the card with the six small objects attached and say, "*Show me what......*" or "*Which one......*" or "*Show me the one that......*"

[1] This test occurs also in Form L at Year III, Test 3.

(a) " . . . . . . *we cook on.*"
(b) " . . . . . . *we sleep in.*"
(c) " . . . . . . *a man smokes.*"
(d) " . . . . . . *we sit on.*"
(e) " . . . . . . *we sweep the dust into.*"
(f) " . . . . . . *we cut with.*"

Score: 5 plus. The child must point to the object. If he points incorrectly, the response is scored minus even though he may have given the correct name.

4. Drawing a Vertical Line

Procedure: Give the child a pencil and, drawing a vertical line, say to him, " *You make one like this.*" "*Make it here.*" Illustrate once only. Give one trial.

Score: See scoring standards, pages 332 ff.

5. * Naming Objects (Same as II–6, 3)

Material: Shoe, watch, telephone, flag, jack-knife, stove.

Procedure: Present the objects one at a time. Have the child name each. Say, "*What is this?*" "*What do you call it?*"

Present in the following order: (a) Shoe, (b) watch, (c) telephone, (d) flag, (e) jack-knife, (f) stove.

Score: 5 plus. See scoring standards, pages 331, 334.

6. Repeating 3 Digits

Procedure: Say, "*Listen; say 4–2.*" "*Now say 7–4–9,*" etc.

(a) 7–4–9, (b) 9–6–1, (c) 2–5–3.

Pronounce the digits distinctly and with perfectly uniform emphasis at the rate of one per second.

Score: 1 plus. The series must be repeated in the correct order without error after a single reading.

Alternate

Three-Hole Form Board: Rotated [1] (II, 4 must precede)

Material: Form board used in II, 4.

Procedure: With the board in position 1 (the base of the triangle toward the child), remove the blocks from the board while the child watches. Place each block before its proper recess on the side of the triangle toward the child. Then rotate the board, while the child watches, to position 2 (with the apex of the triangle toward the child), and say, *"Put them all back where they belong."* No time limit. Give 2 trials. Repeat the same procedure for the second trial.

Score: 2 plus. All 3 blocks must be placed in the correct holes.

YEAR III-6

1. * Comparison of Balls

Material: Card with large and small sphere.

Procedure: Show the card and ask, *"Which ball is bigger?"* *"Put your finger on the big one."* Give 3 trials alternating the relative positions of the large and small balls. In case one of the first three trials is failed, give 3 additional trials, continuing to alternate the positions of the balls.

Score: 3 of 3 or 5 of 6.

2. Patience: Pictures

Material: Two cards with pictures cut in two vertically.

Procedure: Place the two halves of the card before the

---

[1] This test occurs also as an alternate in Form L at Year III.

child so that the cut edges are toward the outside, as indicated in the figure.

(a) Say, "*Put these two pieces together
and make a ball.*"

(b) Place the two halves of the other
card before him and say, "*Put these two pieces together and
make a pig.*"

Score: 1 plus.   See scoring standards, pages 334 f.

3. *Discrimination of Animal Pictures** (Same as IV–6, 1)

Material: Two cards with pictures of animals.

Procedure: Place card number 2 under the first card so
that the rabbit in the lower left corner is framed by the
rectangular slit in card 1.   Say, "*See all of these animals?
Find me another one just like this up here,*" pointing to the
rabbit in the frame.

Correct an error on the rabbit by saying, " *No, find me
one just like* this," again pointing to the rabbit.   If S.
still fails, show him the rabbit.   S. is *not* given credit for
finding the rabbit after correction.   Proceed from left to
right in order.   R to L for the middle row, and L to R for
the top row.   Say, "*Find me another one just like* this *one,*"
for each animal.   Since the items of this test have not been
arranged in the order of their difficulty, it is not safe to
assume that failure on the first few items indicates inability
to pass the test.

Score: 4 plus.

4. *Response to Pictures I** (Same as VI, 4)

Material: Three pictures, Grandmother's Story, Birthday Party, Wash Day.

Procedure: Present the pictures in the following order:
Grandmother's Story, Birthday Party, Wash Day.   Say,

"Look at this picture and tell me all about it." If there is no response, repeat the request, *"Tell me all about it."* If the child names one or two things in a picture and then stops, urge him on by saying, *"Tell me more about it."* Only one question of this type, however, is permissible. Do not remove the picture until it is clear that no further response is forthcoming.

Score: 2 plus. Level I. See scoring standards, pages 335 ff.

5. Sorting Buttons

Material: Twenty half-inch buttons, 10 black and 10 white. Small box.

Procedure: Empty the button box onto the table in front of the child and place the box cover beside the box ready for sorting the buttons. Take a button of each color from the mixed pile in front of the boxes, saying, as you illustrate: *"See, the black buttons go in this box, and the white buttons go in that box. Now you put all the black buttons in that box and all the white buttons in this box."* Time limit, 2 minutes.

Score: No error. Errors made in the process of sorting, if corrected spontaneously, are disregarded in scoring.

6. * Comprehension I

Procedure: Ask,

(a) *"What must you do when you are hungry?"*

(b) *"What must you do when you are sleepy?"*

If there is no response, repeat the question, asking, *"What must you do when you are ......?"*

Score: 1 plus. See scoring standards, page 339.

Alternate

Matching Objects

Material: Twelve 1-inch cubes.

Procedure: Use 2 sheets of white paper, putting them on the table in front of the child and then placing the blocks in a pile beside the papers:

(a) Take 1 block from the pile and put it on one of the sheets of paper, saying, "*See what I have put on my paper. You take one and put it on your paper.*" Replace both blocks on the pile after the trial.

(b) Then take 4 blocks, placing them in a row on your paper about an inch apart and say, "*Now see what I have. You take this many and put them on your paper.*" Replace the blocks on the pile, as before, and proceed in the same way for (c) and (d).

(c) Take 2 blocks and say, "*Now this many.*"

(d) Take 3 blocks and say, "*Now this many.*"

It is important for the examiner to avoid suggesting the correct response; for example, do not wait expectantly when S. stops after having placed too few blocks on his paper, nor should you hasten to remove the blocks after he has given you the correct number without making sure that he has really finished.

Score: 3 plus.

YEAR IV

1. *Picture Vocabulary (Same as II, 5; II–6, 4; III, 2; V, 1)

Material: Seventeen 2″ × 4″ cards with pictures of common objects.

Procedure: Show the cards one at a time. Say, "*What is this?*" "*What do you call it?*"

Score: 12 plus. See scoring standards, pages 328 ff.

2. Stringing Beads

Material: Box of 48 kindergarten beads all of the same color, 16 round, 16 square, 16 cylindrical, and a pair of 18-inch shoestrings.

Procedure: String one bead of each shape, saying, "*Now let's play this game. Watch.*" Then, giving the child another string, say, "*Let's see how many we can put on.*" Continue stringing the beads while the child works on his chain, urging as often as necessary. If S. seems to be selecting a particular shape, tell him any bead will do. Time limit, 2 minutes.

Score: 7 beads. Count each bead that has been pulled on the string beyond the metal tip, even though in manipulation it may have slipped off again.

3. * Opposite Analogies I (Same as VI, 6)

Procedure: Say:
(a) "*Brother is a boy; sister is a . . . . . .*"
(b) "*In daytime it is light; at night it is . . . . . .*"
(c) "*Father is a man; mother is a . . . . . .*"
(d) "*The snail is slow; the rabbit is . . . . . .*"
(e) "*The sun shines during the day; the moon at . . . . . .*"
Score: 2 plus. See scoring standards, pages 340 f.

4. * Pictorial Identification

Material: Card with pictures of objects.

Procedure: Show the card and say, "*Show me what . . . . . .*" or "*Which one . . . . . .*" or "*Show me the one that . . . . . .*"

(a) " . . . . . . *can fly.*"

(b) " . . . . . . *swims in the water.*'

(c) " . . . . . . *do we read.*"

(d) " . . . . . . *tells us the time.*"

(e) " . . . . . . *does the hen lay.*"

(f) " . . . . . *grows on a tree.*"

If S. names the object without pointing to it, ask him to point.

Score: 3 plus.   Naming the object is not sufficient.   The child must point to it on the card.

5. Number Concept of Two

Material: Blocks and beads.

Procedure:

(a) Take 2 blocks and put them in front of S.   Ask, "*How many?*"

(b) Remove the blocks and present 2 square beads. Ask, as before, "*How many?*"

(c) Remove the beads and place 4 square beads before S.   Say, "*Give me 2 beads and you take 2.*"

Score: 2 plus.   Counting aloud is permissible.   (c) is scored plus if the blocks are separated two and two even though the child makes no effort to *take* his two.

6. * Memory for Sentences I

Procedure: Say, "*I want you to say something for me. Say, 'big boy'* (or *'big girl').*"   "*Now say, 'I am a big boy'* (or *'girl').*"   "*Now say.... .*"

(a) "*I like to eat ice-cream cones.*"

(b) "*My watch has two hands.*"

(c) "*Give me just one of them.*"

If S. hesitates, urge him to try by asking him to "*Say it.*"   It is, of course, never permissible to repeat the sentence.

Score: 2 plus.   No error.   Errors include omissions, substitutions, additions, changes in words or in order of words.

Alternate

Discrimination of Animal Pictures (Same as III–6, 3; IV–6, 1)

Material: Two cards with pictures of animals.

Procedure: Place card number 2 under the first card so that the rabbit in the lower left corner is framed by the rectangular slit in card 1.   Say, *"See all of these animals? Find me another one just like this up here,"* pointing to the rabbit in the frame.

Correct an error on the rabbit by saying, *"No, find me one just like* this," again pointing to the rabbit.   If S. still fails, show him the rabbit.   S. is *not* given credit for finding the rabbit after correction.   Proceed from left to right in order. R to L for the middle row, and L to R for the top row.   Say, *"Find me another one just like* this *one,"* for each animal. Since the items of this test have not been arranged in order of their difficulty, it is not safe to assume that failure on the first few items indicates inability to pass the test.

Score: 6 plus.

YEAR IV-6

1. * **Discrimination of Animal Pictures** (Same as III–6, 3)

   Material: Two cards with pictures of animals.

   Procedure: Place card number 2 under the first card so that the rabbit in the lower left corner is framed by the rectangular slit in card 1.   Say, *"See all of these animals? Find me another one just like this up here,"* pointing to the rabbit in the frame.

Correct an error on the rabbit by saying, " *No, find me one just like* this," again pointing to the rabbit.   If S. still fails, show him the rabbit.   S. is *not* given credit for finding the rabbit after correction.   Proceed from left to right in order.   R to L for the middle row, and L to R for the top row.   Say, *"Find me another one just like* this *one,"* for each animal.   Since the items of this test have not been arranged in order of their difficulty, it is not safe to assume that failure on the first few items indicates inability to pass the test.

Score: 7 plus

2. * Definitions

Procedure: Say, *"What is a key?"*   If necessary, urge by saying, *"You know what a key is.   Tell me what a key is."* Use the same formula for *dress* and *bed.*

(a) Key,   (b) dress,   (c) bed.

Score: 2 plus.   See scoring standards, page 342.

3. Repeating 4 Digits

Procedure: Say, *"Listen, I am going to say some numbers and when I am through I want you to say them just the way I do.   Listen carefully, and get them just right."*   Before each series repeat, *"Listen carefully, and get them just right."* Pronounce the digits distinctly and with perfectly uniform emphasis at the rate of one per second.

(a) 4–7–3–1,   (b) 5–2–8–3,   (c) 9–4–1–7.

Score: 1 plus.   The series must be repeated in correct order without error after a single reading.

4. * Picture Completion: Bird

Material: Incomplete drawing of a bird (in record booklet).

Procedure: Point to the incomplete drawing in the record booklet and say, "*What is this?*" Whether, the child recognizes it or not, say, "*That's a bird*" (or "*Yes, it's a bird*" or "*Yes, it's a duck*"). "*You make the rest of the bird.*" If S.'s addition is unrecognizable, ask, "*What is this?*"

Score: 1 point. See scoring standards, pages 343, 344.

5. Materials

Procedure: Say, "*What is a house made of?*" Same for *window* and *book.*

(a) House,   (b) window,   (c) book.

Score: 2 plus. See scoring standards, pages 343, 345.

6. *Comprehension II (Same as V, 5)

Procedure: Ask,

(a) "*What do we do with our eyes?*"

(b) "*What do we do with our ears?*"

Score: 1 plus. See scoring standards, page 345.

Alternate

Patience: Pictures (Same as III–6, 2)

Material: Two cards with pictures cut in two vertically.

Procedure: Place the two halves of the card before the child so that the cut edges are toward the outside, as indicated in the figure.

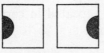

(a) Say, "*Put these two pieces together and make a ball.*"

(b) Place the two halves of the other card before him and say, "*Put these two pieces together and make a pig.*"

Score: 2 plus. See scoring standards, pages 334 f., 345.

YEAR V

1. *Picture Vocabulary (Same as II, 5; II–6, 4; III, 2; IV, 1)

Material: Seventeen $2'' \times 4''$ cards with pictures of common objects.

Procedure: Show the cards one at a time. Say, *"What is this?"* *"What do you call it?"*

Score: 14 plus. See scoring standards, pages 328 ff.

2. *Number Concept of Three

Material: Blocks and beads.

Procedure: Place the blocks before S. and say,

(a) *"Give me 3 blocks."* Then place the box of beads before him and say,

(b) *"Give me 3 beads."*

(c) *"Give me 2 blocks and 1 bead."*

Score: 2 plus. For (c) the order of presentation is disregarded.

3. Pictorial Similarities and Differences

Material: Twelve $2'' \times 4''$ cards.

Procedure: Present card (a) and say, *"See these two trees? They are just alike, aren't they? Just the same."* Then show card (b), *"But these two aren't alike* (pointing), *one is round and one is square."* Cards (a) and (b) are used for illustration only. No further illustration. Show card (1) and say, *"Now look at these two. Are they alike? Are they the same?"* For each successive pair, exposing one card at a time, say, *"And these. Are they alike? Are they the same?"*

Score: 9 plus.

4. * Patience: Rectangles

Material: Two rectangular cards, each 2 × 3 inches, one divided diagonally into two triangles.

Procedure: Place the uncut card on the table with one of its longer sides toward the child. Beside it lay the two halves of the divided rectangle with their hypotenuses turned from each other, as shown in the figure. Then say, *"One of my cards has been cut in two; you put these two pieces* (touching the two triangles) *together to make a whole one just like this"* (pointing to the uncut card). If the first attempt is a failure, record minus and replace the pieces, saying, *" No, I want you to put these two pieces together to make a whole one just like this."* After a successful trial, say, *"Do it again."* If a piece is turned over, turn it back and do not count that trial. A trial is counted when the child leaves the pieces in some position. Give 3 trials. No time limit.

Score: 2 plus.

5. * Comprehension II (Same as IV–6, 6)

Procedure: Ask,

(a) *"What do we do with our eyes?"*

(b) *"What do we do with our ears?"*

Score: 2 plus. See scoring standards, pages 345, 346.

6. Mutilated Pictures

Material: Card with mutilated pictures.

Procedure: Show S. the card with the mutilated pictures and, pointing to each in turn, ask, *"What is gone in this picture?"* or *"What part is gone?"* If the child hesitates, further urging is sometimes necessary to elicit a response.

Vary the question by asking, *"What isn't there?"* Avoid pointing to the missing part in designating the picture. For (d) ask, *"What is gone in the boy's face?"*

(a) Table, (b) coat, (c) cat, (d) head, (e) bird.

Score: 3 plus. See scoring standards, page 347.

Alternate

Knot [1]

Material: Pair of 18-inch shoestrings. Pencil.

Procedure: Say, *"Watch what I do. I'm tying a knot around this pencil."* Tie a single knot (not a bow), then present the other shoelace and say to the child, *" You take this other piece of string and tie the same kind of knot around my finger. Make one just like this one"* (pointing to the examiner's knot).

Score: Any sort of knot which does not come undone is acceptable.

YEAR VI

1. Number Concepts

Material: Twelve 1-inch cubes.

Procedure: Place the blocks in a pile on the table before S. In order that the examiner may be sure just how many blocks the child means to indicate, we use a sheet of white paper for him to put his blocks on. Say, *"Give me ...... blocks. Put them here,"* pointing to the sheet of paper. After each choice replace the blocks in the pile. Ask, in turn, for 2, 10, 3, and 6 blocks. Sometimes the child thinks that in order to designate the correct number of blocks he has to pick them all up in his hand at once. In such a case

[1] This test occurs also as an alternate in Form L at Year V.

say, "*You don't have to take them all in your hand at once.*"
It is important for the examiner to avoid suggesting the
correct response; for example, do not wait expectantly
when S. stops after having placed too few blocks on the
paper, nor should you hasten to remove the blocks, after
he has given you the correct number, without making sure
that he has really finished.

(a) 2,   (b) 10,   (c) 3,   (d) 6.

Score: 3 plus.

2. * Copying a Bead Chain

Material: Box of 48 kindergarten beads all of the same
color, 16 round, 16 square, 16 cylindrical.

Procedure: Place the box of beads on the table before
the child and say, "*Watch what I do.*" While S. watches,
make a chain of 8 beads using 2 round, 1 cylindrical, 2
round, 1 cylindrical, and 2 round beads, making a chain

like the sample.   Leaving this chain exposed, say, " *You
make one just like this. Be sure to make it just like this.*"
At the child's first error, say, "*Make it just like* this *one*,"
pointing to the model.   Time limit, 2 minutes.

Score: No error in pattern.   See scoring standards,
page 348.

3. * Differences

Procedure: Say, "*What is the difference between .....*"
(a) " *A bird and a dog?*"
(b) "*A slipper and a boot?*"
(c) "*Wood and glass?*"

If S. does not seem to understand, say, "*You've seen a bird and you've seen dogs. Now, tell me the* difference *between a bird and a dog.*"
Score: 2 plus. See scoring standards, pages 348 ff.

4. * **Response to Pictures I** (Same as III–6, 4)
Material: Three pictures, Grandmother's Story, Birthday Party, and Wash Day.
Procedure: Present the pictures in the following order: Grandmother's Story, Birthday Party, Wash Day. Say, "*Look at this picture and tell me all about it.*"
Score: Level II, 2 plus. See scoring standards, pages 335 ff., 350.

5. **Counting 13 Pennies**
Material: Thirteen pennies.
Procedure: Place thirteen pennies in a horizontal row before the child. Say, "*See these pennies. Count them out loud and tell me how many there are. Count them with your finger, this way* (pointing to the first one on E.'s right). *One. Now, go ahead.*" Do not count further for S. If S. gives a number without pointing, say, "*No, count them with your finger, this way,*" starting him as before. Give 2 trials.
Score: 1 plus. Counting must tally with pointing.

6. * **Opposite Analogies I** (Same as IV, 3)
Procedure: Say:
(a) "*Brother is a boy; sister is a ......*"
(b) "*In daytime it is light; at night it is ......*"
(c) "*Father is a man; mother is a ......*"
(d) "*The snail is slow; the rabbit is ......*"
(e) "*The sun shines during the day; the moon at ......*"
Score: 4 plus. See scoring standards, pages 340 f., 351.

YEAR VII

1. Giving the Number of Fingers

Procedure: Ask: *" How many fingers have I on one hand?" " How many on the other hand?" " How many on both hands together?"* If the child begins to count in response to any of the questions, say, *" No, don't count. Tell me without counting,"* and repeat the question.

Score: All three questions must be answered correctly and promptly (approximately 3 seconds) without the necessity of counting. Some subjects do not understand the question to include the thumbs. We disregard this if the number of fingers exclusive of thumbs is given correctly.

2. Memory for Sentences II

Procedure: Say, *" Listen; be sure to say exactly what I say."*
(a) *" Betty has made a pretty dress for her doll out of blue ribbon."*
(b) *" My baby brother wants Santa Claus to bring him a great big drum."*
Score: 1 plus. No error. Errors include omissions, substitutions, additions, changes in words or in order of words, but not contractions, such as "Betty's" for "Betty has."

3. * Picture Absurdities I

Material: Three pictures: (a) Man on limb, (b) man on scales, (c) cat and mice.
Procedure: Show the pictures in the order indicated and ask for each in turn, *"What's funny (foolish) about that picture?"* If the child's response is ambiguous without further explanation, ask, *"Why is it (that) funny (foolish)?"*
Score: 2 plus. See scoring standards, pages 351 ff.

4. *Repeating 3 Digits Reversed

Procedure: Say, "*I am going to say some numbers, and I want you to say them backwards. For example, if I should say 5–1–4, you would say 4–1–5. Ready now; listen carefully, and be sure to say the numbers backwards.*" Before each series repeat, "*Ready now; listen carefully, and be sure to say the numbers backwards.*" Pronounce the digits distinctly and with perfectly uniform emphasis at the rate of one per second.

(a) 2–9–5,   (b) 8–1–6,   (c) 4–7–3.

Score: 1 plus.   The series must be repeated backwards in correct order without error after a single reading.

5. *Sentence Building I

Procedure: Say, "*I'm going to tell you something about 'dog–cat' — 'The dog runs after the cat.'   Now* you *make a sentence about*

(a) 'Horse, bigger, dog.'
(b) 'Boy, fell, leg.'
(c) 'Child, flowers, meadow.' "

If the child hesitates, urge him on by saying, "*I told you something about 'dog–cat.'   Now you tell me something about ......*"

Score: 2 plus.   See scoring standards, pages 353 ff.

6. *Counting Taps

Procedure: Say, "*Listen; I am going to tap on the table, and I want you to tell me how many times I tap. Listen carefully.*" Illustrate first with two taps, correcting the child's response if he gives the wrong number, and if necessary repeating the illustration. Do not screen the hand while tapping. To produce uniform sounds we use a fountain pen cap for tapping. Rate about one per second.

Before each series say, "*Listen again.*" Then ask, "*How many this time?*"

Tap successively   (a) 7,   (b) 5,   (c) 8.

Score: 3 plus.

YEAR VIII

1. *Comprehension III

Procedure: Ask,

(a) "*What should a man do if he comes home and finds that a burglar has robbed his house?*"

(b) "*Why is a train harder to stop than an automobile?*"

(c) "*What should a man do if he finds that he is earning less money than it takes to live on?*"

Score: 2 plus.   See scoring standards, pages 355 ff.

2. *Similarities: Two things

Procedure: Say, "*In what way are ...... and ...... alike?*"

(a) Mosquito and sparrow.

(b) Window and door.

(c) Bread and meat.

It is often necessary to insist a little if S. is silent or says he doesn't know. It is permissible to repeat the original question or to add, "*How are they the same?*" or "*In what way are they alike?*" When a difference is given for (a) say, "*No, I want you to tell me how they are* alike. *In what way are a mosquito and a sparrow the same?*" If the child persists in giving differences, make no further comment after the other pairs.

Score: 2 plus.   See scoring standards, pages 357 f.

3. * Verbal Absurdities I

Procedure: Read each statement and, after each one, ask, *"What is foolish about that?"* If the response is ambiguous without further explanation, ask, *"Why is it (that) foolish?"*

(a) "A man had flu (influenza) twice. The first time it killed him, but the second time he got well quickly."

(b) "Walter now has to write with his left hand because two years ago he lost both his arms in an accident."

(c) "A man said, 'I know a road from my house to the city which is downhill all the way to the city and downhill all the way back home.'"

(d) "An old gentleman complained that he could no longer walk around the park as he used to; he said he could now go only halfway around and back again."

Score: 3 plus. See scoring standards, pages 358 ff.

4. Naming the Days of the Week

Procedure: Say, *" Name the days of the week for me."* If S. fails to comprehend the task and begins to name the various holidays or the like, say, *" No, that is not what I mean. I want you to name the days of the week."* It is not permissible to start S. off by naming one day. If S. names them all in correct order, give three checks by asking, *"What day comes before......?"*

(a) Tuesday, (b) Thursday, (c) Friday.

Score: All must be named in the correct order. 2 of 3 checks correct.

5. Problem Situations

Procedure: Say,

(a) "About two o'clock one afternoon a number of boys and girls dressed in their best clothes rang the bell at Alice's house. Alice opened the door. *What was happening?"*

(b) "Helen heard a big 'Bang' and came running out-doors. There were nails all over the road, and an automobile had just stopped beside the road. *What was the 'Bang'?*"

(c) "A young man and lady were sitting in a restaurant. They had nearly finished eating a big dinner. The waiter brought the bill. The young man looked at it, and then seemed worried and embarrassed. *Why?*"

Score: 2 plus. See scoring standards, pages 360 f.

6. * Opposite Analogies II

Procedure: Say,
(a) "*The rabbit's ears are long; the rat's ears are* ......"
(b) "*Snow is white; coal is* ......"
(c) "*The dog has hair; the bird has* ......"
(d) "*Wolves are wild; dogs are* ......"
Score: 3 plus. See scoring standards, page 362.

YEAR IX

1. * Memory for Designs I

Material: Card with two designs.

Procedure: Before showing the card, say, "*This card has two drawings on it. I am going to show them to you for ten seconds, then I will take the card away and let you draw from memory what you have seen. Be sure to look at both draw-ings carefully.*" Then show the card for 10 seconds, hold-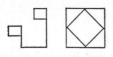ing it at right angles to the child's line of vision and with the designs in the position given in the plate. At the end of approximately 4 seconds say, quietly, "*Look at both.*" Have S. reproduce the designs immediately, and note which is the top of his drawing.

Score: 1 plus or 2 with half credit each. See scoring standards, pages 362 ff.

2. * Dissected Sentences I

Material: Cards on which disarranged words are printed in capitals.

Procedure: Show the sentences one at a time in the order indicated. Before giving S. the first sentence, say, with the card in your hand but held so that S. can't see the words until you have completed your instructions, " *Here is a sentence that has the words all mixed up so that they don't make any sense. If the words were changed around in the right order they would make a good sentence. Look carefully, and tell me how the sentence ought to read.*" Pronounce for S. any word he does not know, but give no further help.[1] For (b) and (c) say, " *Now tell me how this one ought to read.*" Time, 1 minute each

(a) A HAVE DOG I FINE.

(b) WOOL THE WAS COAT OF MADE.

(c) CHILD THE PLAYING GARDEN IN THE IS.

Score: 2 plus. See scoring standards, page 368.

3. Verbal Absurdities II (Same as XI, 3)

Procedure: Read each statement and after each one ask, "*What is foolish about that?*" If the response is ambiguous without further explanation, say, "*Why is it (that) foolish?*"

(a) "I saw a well-dressed young man who was walking down the street with his hands in his pockets and twirling a brand-new cane."

(b) "A father wrote to his son, 'I enclose ten dollars. If you do not receive this letter, please send me a telegram.'"

---

[1] The examiner should not use the first sentence for illustration in case the subject fails on it. The procedure differs in that respect from the 1916 revision.

(c) "A soldier on the march complained that every man in the regiment was out of step except himself."

(d) "A kind-hearted man who was taking a heavy bag of grain to town on his horse sat on his horse and lifted the bag to his own shoulder in order to make the load easier for the horse."

(e) "A man said to his friend, 'I hope you live to eat the chickens that scratch sand on your grave.'"

Score: 3 plus.   See scoring standards, pages 368 ff.

4. * Similarities and Differences

Procedure: Say, "*I'm going to name two things and I want you to tell me how they are* alike *and how they are* different.   *In what way are* ...... *and* ...... *alike, and how are they different?*"   If in (a) or (b) S. omits either of the comparisons, ask, "*And how are they the same* (or *different*)*?*"   Make no comment concerning omissions in (c) and (d).

(a) Honey and glue.

(b) Pencil and pen.

(c) Banana and lemon.

(d) Shoe and glove.

Score: 4 plus.   See scoring standards, pages 372 ff.

5. * Rhymes: Old form

Procedure: Say,

(a) "*You know what a rhyme is, of course.   A rhyme is a word that sounds like another word.   Two words rhyme if they end in the same sound.   For example, 'hat,' 'bat,' 'rat,' 'sat,' all rhyme with cat.   Now see how many words you can name that rhyme with* date.   *Ready; go ahead.*"

(b) "*Now see how many words you can name that rhyme with* head."

(c) " *Now see how many words you can name that rhyme with* cap."

Time limit, 30 seconds each.

Score: 2 plus with 3 rhymes each.   See scoring standards, pages 374 ff.

6. Repeating 4 Digits Reversed

Procedure: Say, "*I am going to say some numbers, and I want you to say them backwards.   For example, if I should say 5–1–4, you would say 4–1–5.   Ready now; listen carefully, and be sure to say the numbers backwards.*"   Before each series repeat, "*Ready now; listen carefully, and be sure to say the numbers backwards.*"   Pronounce the digits distinctly and with perfectly uniform emphasis at the rate of one per second.

(a) 5–8–1–3,   (b) 9–1–7–4,   (c) 3–7–2–9.

Score: 1 plus.   The series must be repeated backwards in correct order without error after a single reading.

YEAR X

1. Block Counting

Material: Card with picture of piles of cubes arranged in 2 rows.

Procedure: Show the card and, pointing to the first illustration, ask, " *How many blocks are there here?* "   Then point to the second pile of blocks and ask, " *And here there are how many?* "   Then the third and ask, " *And here?* "   These first three are for illustration only and are not counted toward the score.   Correct any errors which the subject makes on the samples and show him how the count should be made to include the unseen blocks.   Then point to the rows below and say, " *Now count them and tell me how many there are in each square, beginning here* (at the subject's left) *and working along each row.*" Point to the first square and ask, " *How many here?* " For the second square ask, "*And here?* " Record the count for each square in order from S.'s left to his right. Do not allow S. to point to each block with a pencil while counting.

Score: 8 plus.

2. * Memory for Stories I: The School Concert

Material: Card with printed selection on it.

Procedure: Say, " *Here is a story about 'The School Concert.' Listen carefully while I read it because I shall ask you questions about it.*" Give S. a copy of the selection and let him follow it as you read it aloud.

The School Concert

"On December 20th, the children of the city schools held a concert in the auditorium of the high school. All the children had some part in the program. The program consisted of singing by the school choir, fancy marching, folk dancing, and finally, a Christmas play. About 620 parents and friends attended the concert. The sale of tickets brought in nearly four hundred dollars."

Remove the child's copy of the selection and proceed to ask him the following questions:

(a) "*What was the name of that story?* "

(b) "*Where was it (the concert) held?* "

(c) "*When was it held?* "

(d) "*What did the program consist of?* " ("*What was on the program?*") (4 memories)

(e) " *How many people attended (went to) the concert?* "

(f) *" How much money was raised? "*

Score: 5 plus (9 possible memories).   See scoring standards, pages 376 f.

3. * Verbal Absurdities III

Procedure: Read each statement and after each one ask, *"What is foolish about that? "*   If the response is ambiguous without further explanation say, *"Why is it (that) foolish? "*

(a) "In the year 1915 many more women than men got married in the United States."

(b) "A man wished to dig a hole in which to bury some rubbish, but could not decide what to do with the dirt from the hole.   A friend suggested that he dig a hole large enough to hold the dirt, too."

(c) "They began the meeting late, but they set the hands of the clock back so that the meeting might surely close before sunset."

Score: 2 plus.   See scoring standards, pages 377 ff.

4. * Abstract Words I (Same as XII, 4)

Procedure: Say, *"What do we mean by ......? "* or *"What is ......? "*

(a) Pity,   (b) curiosity,   (c) grief,   (d) surprise.

Score: 2 plus.   See scoring standards, pages 380 ff.

5. Word Naming: Animals

Procedure: Say, *" Now I want to see how many different animals you can name in one minute.   When I say, 'Ready,' you begin and say them as fast as you can, and I will count them.   Ready; go ahead."*   If S. hesitates or stops, encourage him to keep on for the full time.   Time limit, 1 minute.

Score: 12 animals named.   See scoring standards, pages 382 f.

6. * Repeating 6 Digits

Procedure: Say, "*I am going to say some numbers and when I am through I want you to say them just the way I do. Listen carefully, and get them just right.*" Before each series repeat, "*Listen carefully, and get them just right.*" Pronounce the digits distinctly and with perfectly uniform emphasis at the rate of one per second.

(a) 2–9–4–8–1–6, (b) 9–6–2–7–3–8, (c) 5–1–7–2–6–9.

Score: 1 plus.   The series must be repeated in correct order without error after a single reading.

YEAR XI

1. * Finding Reasons

Procedure: Say:

(a) "*Give two reasons why children should obey their parents.*"

(b) "*Give two reasons why there should be plenty of railroads in the United States.*"

Score: 2 plus with 2 reasons each.   See scoring standards, pages 383 ff.

2. Copying a Bead Chain from Memory

Material: Box of 48 kindergarten beads all of the same color, 16 round, 16 square, and 16 cylindrical.

Procedure: Make an 11-bead chain, holding the string so that S. can see and say, "*Watch carefully what I am making because I am going to take this one away and see if you can make one just like it.*"   Make a chain like the sample, using 1 square, 3 round, 1 cylindrical, 1 round, 1 cylindrical, 3 round, 1 square.

□ ○ ○ ○ ▭ ○ ▭ ○ ○ ○ □

When complete let S. look at it for 5 seconds. Remove the chain and tell him to make one just like it. Time limit, 2 minutes.

Score: No error.

3. * **Verbal Absurdities II** (Same as IX, 3)

Procedure: Read each statement and after each one ask, *"What is foolish about that?"* If the response is ambiguous say, *"Why is it (that) funny?"*

(a) "I saw a well-dressed young man who was walking down the street with his hands in his pockets and twirling a brand-new cane."

(b) "A father wrote to his son, 'I enclose ten dollars. If you do not receive this letter, please send me a telegram.'"

(c) "A soldier on the march complained that every man in the regiment was out of step except himself."

(d) "A kind-hearted man who was taking a heavy bag of grain to town on his horse sat on his horse and lifted the bag to his own shoulder in order to make the load easier for the horse."

(e) "A man said to his friend, 'I hope you live to eat the chickens that scratch sand on your grave.'"

Score: 4 plus. See scoring standards, pages 368 ff.

4. * **Abstract Words II** [1] (Same as XIII, 4)

Procedure: Say, *"What is ......?"* or *"What do we mean by ......?"*

(a) Connection, (b) compare, (c) conquer, (d) obedience, (e) revenge.

Score: 3 plus. See scoring standards, pages 261 ff.

---

[1] This test occurs also in Form L at Year XI, Test 3.

5. * Similarities: Three things [1]

Procedure: Say, "*In what way are* ......, ..., *and*
...... *alike?*"

(a) Snake, cow, and sparrow.

(b) Rose, potato, and tree.

(c) Wool, cotton, and leather.

(d) Knife-blade, penny, and piece of wire.

(e) Book, teacher, and newspaper.

A little urging is sometimes necessary to secure a response. If S. hesitates or says he doesn't know, urge him
to try by repeating the question or asking, "*How are they
alike?*"

Score: 3 plus. See scoring standards, pages 265 ff.

6. Memory for Sentences III [2]

Procedure: Say, "*Listen, and be sure to say exactly what
I say.*"

(a) "*At the summer camp the children get up early in the
morning to go swimming.*"

(b) "*Yesterday we went for a ride in our car along the road
that crosses the bridge.*"

Score: 1 plus. No error. Errors include omissions,
substitutions, additions, changes in words or in order of
words.

YEAR XII

1. * Memory for Designs II

Material: Card with design.

Procedure: Before showing the card, say, "*This card
has a drawing on it. I am going to show it to you for ten*

---

[1] This test occurs also in Form L at Year XI, Test 6.

[2] This test occurs also in Form L at Year XI, Test 4.

seconds, then I will take the card away and let you draw from memory what you have seen. Be sure to look at the drawing carefully." Show the card for 10 seconds. Have S. reproduce the design immediately, and note which is the top of his drawing.

Score: See scoring standards, page 386.

2. Response to Pictures II [1]

Material: Picture, Messenger Boy.

Procedure: Say, *"Look at this picture and tell me all about it."*

Score: See scoring standards, pages 267 f.

3. * Minkus Completion (Same as S.A. I, 1)

Material: Selection printed in the record booklet.

Procedure: Have S. fill in the missing word for each blank in the selection printed in the booklet. Say, *"Write the missing word in each blank. Put just one word in each."*

(a) We like to pop corn ...... to roast chestnuts over the fire.

(b) Lincoln aroused no jealousy ...... he was not selfish.

(c) ...... he give me his word, I will not trust him.

(d) You must not, ..., imagine that my silence has been due to ignorance of what is going on.

If S. cannot read, it is permissible to read the words for him, indicating each. If necessary write in the missing word that S. dictates. Time limit, 5 minutes.

Score: 2 plus. See scoring standards, pages 386 f.

---

[1] This test occurs also in Form L at Year XII, Test 3.

4. * **Abstract Words I** (Same as X, 4)

   Procedure: Say, *"What do we mean by ......?"* or
   "What is ......?"
   (a) Pity, (b) curiosity, (c) grief, (d) surprise.
   Score: 3 plus. See scoring standards, pages 380 ff.

5. * **Picture Absurdities II**

   Material: Picture, The Windy Day.
   Procedure: Say, *"What's foolish about that picture?"* If
   the response is ambiguous, say, *"Why is it (that) foolish?"*
   Score: See scoring standards, page 388.

6. **Repeating 5 Digits Reversed**

   Procedure: Say, *"I am going to say some numbers, and I
   want you to say them backwards. For example, if I should
   say 5–1–4, you would say 4–1–5. Ready now; listen carefully, and be sure to say the numbers backwards."* Before
   each series repeat, *"Ready now; listen carefully, and be sure
   to say the numbers backwards."* Pronounce the digits distinctly and with perfectly uniform emphasis at the rate
   of one per second.
   (a) 5–1–3–9–4, (b) 9–2–5–1–6, (c) 2–6–3–7–1.
   Score: 1 plus. The series must be repeated backwards in
   correct order without error after a single reading.

YEAR XIII

1. * **Plan of Search**

   Material: Diamond-shaped figure with a small gap in the
   angle nearest the child (in record booklet).
   Procedure: Give S. a pencil and, showing him the figure,
   say, *"Let's suppose that your purse with a lot of money in it*

has been lost in this big field. Take this pencil and start here (pointing) *at the gate, and show me where you would go to hunt for the purse so as to be sure not to miss it."* If S. fails to understand that he is to mark the path, add, *"Mark it with the pencil to show me where you would go to hunt for the purse."*

If S. stops before there is evidence whether or not any plan governs his procedure, say, *"But suppose you hadn't found it yet, show me everywhere you would go to look for it."* No further questioning or urging.

Score: See scoring standards, pages 389 f.

2. Memory for Stories II : A Distinguished French Acrobat

Material: Card with printed selection on it.

Procedure: Say, *"Here is a story about 'A Distinguished French Acrobat.' Listen carefully while I read it because I shall ask you questions about it."* Give S. a copy of the selection and let him follow it as you read it aloud.

A Distinguished French Acrobat

"Charles won a reputation as a rope walker in his native France. His most distinguished performances, however, took place during a tour of the United States. In 1859, he crossed the Falls of Niagara, a distance of about 800 feet, on a tight-rope. This he did in the presence of a crowd of 25,000 people. On the fourth of the following July, he crossed again, blindfolded, trundling a wheelbarrow in front of him. It seems incredible that any performer should keep his head while balancing on a slender rope over a chasm 300 feet in depth when the slightest tremor or giddiness would have sent him to his death in the swirling waters below. And yet, on the 19th of August, he crossed a third time carrying a man on his back. The next year he crossed for the fourth time walking on stilts."

Remove S.'s copy of the selection and proceed to ask him the following questions:

(a) *"What was his first distinguished performance during his tour of the United States?"*

(b) *" How many people saw him do it?"*

(c) *" How did he cross Niagara the second time?"*

(d) *" How great a distance did he cross?"*

(e) *" How did he cross the third time?"*

(f) *" How deep was the chasm? (How deep was it?)"*

(g) *"How did he cross the fourth time?"*

Score: 5 plus. See scoring standards, pages 389 f.

3. * Dissected Sentences II [1]

Material: Cards on which disarranged words are printed in capitals.

Procedure: Show the sentences one at a time in the order indicated. Before giving S. the first sentence, say, with the card in your hand but held so that S. can't see the words until you have completed your instructions, *" Here is a sentence that has the words all mixed up so that they don't make any sense. If the words were turned around in the right order they would make a good sentence. Look carefully, and tell me how the sentence ought to read."* Pronounce for S. any word that he doesn't know, but give no further help.[2] For (b) and (c) say, *"Now tell me how this one ought to read."* Time, 1 minute each.

(a) FOR THE STARTED AN WE COUNTRY EARLY AT HOUR.

---

[1] This test occurs also in Form L at Year XIII, Test 5.

[2] In the present test no illustration is given. In the old revision the examiner was permitted to read the first sentence correctly if the subject was unable to succeed with it.

(b) TO ASKED PAPER MY TEACHER CORRECT I MY.

(c) A DEFENDS DOG GOOD HIS BRAVELY MASTER.

Score: 2 plus. See scoring standards, pages 276 f.

4. * **Abstract Words II** (Same as XI, 4)

Procedure: Say, *"What is ......?"* or *"What do we mean by......?"*

(a) Connection, (b) compare, (c) conquer, (d) obedience, (e) revenge.

Score: 4 plus. See scoring standards, pages 261 ff.

5. **Problems of Fact** [1]

Procedure: Say, *"Listen...."*

(a) *"A man who was walking in the woods near a city stopped suddenly, very much frightened, and then ran to the nearest policeman, saying that he had just seen hanging from the limb of a tree a...... a what?"* (If the reply is *"man,"* say, *"Tell me what you mean; explain it."*)

(b) *"My neighbor has been having queer visitors. First a doctor came to his house, then a lawyer, then a minister (preacher, priest,* or *rabbi). What do you think happened there?"* If the response is *"a death,"* etc., check by asking, *"Why did the lawyer come?"*

(c) *"An Indian who had come to town for the first time in his life saw a white boy riding along the street. As the white boy rode by the Indian said, 'The white boy is lazy; he walks sitting down.' What was the white boy riding on that caused the Indian to say, 'He walks sitting down'?"*

Score: 2 plus. See scoring standards, pages 274 ff.

[1] This test occurs also in Form L at Year XIII, Test 4.

6. * **Memory for Sentences IV**

Procedure: Say, *"Listen, and be sure to say exactly what I say."*

(a) *"The airplane made a careful landing in the space which had been prepared for it."*

(b) *"Tom Brown's dog ran quickly down the road with a huge bone in his mouth."*

Score: 1 plus.   No error.   Errors include omissions, substitutions, additions, changes in words or in order of words.

YEAR XIV

1. * **Reasoning**

Material: Card on which the problem is stated.

Procedure: Give S. a copy of the problem and let him have it to look at as you read it aloud and while he is solving it.

"My house was burglarized last Saturday.   I was at home all of the morning but out during the afternoon until 5 o'clock. My father left the house at 3 o'clock and my brother was there until 4.   At what time did the burglary take place?"

If the response is either *"after 4"* or *"before 5,"* ask S. to explain what he means.

Score: See scoring standards, page 392.

2. Picture Absurdities III [1]

Material: Picture, The Shadow.

Procedure: Showing the picture, ask, *"What's foolish about that picture?"*   If the response is ambiguous, ask, *"Why is it (that) foolish?"*

Score: See scoring standards, pages 278 f.

[1] This test occurs also in Form L at Year XIV, Test 3.

3. * Orientation: Direction I (Same as A.A., 6)

Procedure: Read the following directions distinctly, emphasizing the critical words:

(a) *"Which direction would you have to face so your* right hand would be toward the *north?"*

(If S. points or says, *" That way,"* say, *"What is the* name of the direction you would have to face etc.)?"

(b) *"Suppose you are going* east, *then turn to your* right; *what direction are you going now?"*

(c) *"Suppose you are going* south, *then turn to your* left, *then turn to your* right; *what direction are you going now?"*

(d) *"Suppose you are going* north, *then turn* right, *then turn* right *again, then turn* left; *what direction are you going now?"*

(e) *"Suppose you are going* west, *then turn* right, *then turn* right *again, then turn* right *again, then turn* left; *what direction are you going now?"*

It is permissible to repeat the directions if S. becomes confused or cannot remember the problem.

Score: 3 plus.   See scoring standards, page 392.

4. * Abstract Words III (Same as A.A., 1)

Procedure: Say, *"What is* ......*?"* or *"What do we mean by* ......*?"*

(a) Generosity, (b) independent, (c) envy, (d) authority, (e) justice.

Score: 2 plus.   See scoring standards, pages 393 ff.

5. * Ingenuity (Same as A.A., 2; S.A. II, 2)

Procedure: The problem is given orally and may be repeated if necessary. (a) *" A mother sent her boy to the river to bring back exactly 2 pints of water.   She gave him a 5-pint can and a 3-pint can.   Show me how the boy can measure out exactly 2 pints of water using nothing but these two cans and not guessing at the amount.   You should begin by filling the 5-pint can first.   Remember, you have a 5-pint can and a 3-pint can and you must bring back exactly 2 pints of water."* [1]

Use the same formula for (b) and (c).

(b) 9-pint can and 5-pint can to get 13 pints.   Begin by filling the 9-pint can.

(c) 3-pint can and 8-pint can to get 1 pint.   Begin by filling the 3-pint can.

The subject is not allowed to use pencil and paper.   If he resorts to a method that involves guessing, tell him that he must *measure* out the water without guessing.   Explain, also, if necessary, that it is a fair problem, not a catch. Encourage him to keep on trying throughout the 3-minute period allowed for each problem, but if he has failed on the first problem it is not necessary to go on to (b) and (c).

Score: 1 plus.   See scoring standards, page 395.

6. Reconciliation of Opposites (Same as S.A. I, 6)

Procedure: Say, *"In what way are ...... and ...... alike?"*

    (a) Winter and summer.   (d) Much and little.

    (b) Happy and sad.   (e) Beginning and end.

    (c) Loud and soft.

Even though S. is failing the items, all five must be given.   If, as sometimes happens, S. fails to grasp the idea until several items have been given, a correction of the preceding items is accepted if offered spontaneously.   If S. says they are opposite, repeat the question with emphasis on *alike*.

Score: 2 plus.   See scoring standards, pages 395 ff.

---

[1] If the subject fails, we do not explain the solution.   The procedure differs in this respect from the 1916 revision.

AVERAGE ADULT

1. * Abstract Words III (Same as XIV, 4)

Procedure: Say, *"What is ......?"* or *"What do we mean by ......?"*

(a) Generosity, (b) independent, (c) envy, (d) authority, (e) justice.

Score: 4 plus. See scoring standards, pages 393 ff.

2. * Ingenuity (Same as XIV, 5; S.A. II, 2)

Procedure: The problem is given orally and may be repeated if necessary. (a) *" A mother sent her boy to the river to bring back exactly 2 pints of water. She gave him a 5-pint can and a 3-pint can. Show me how the boy can measure out exactly 2 pints of water using nothing but these two cans and not guessing at the amount. You should begin by filling the 5-pint can first. Remember, you have a 5-pint can and a 3-pint can and you must bring back exactly 2 pints of water."* [1]

Use the same formula for (b) and (c).

(b) 9-pint can and 5-pint can to get 13 pints. Begin by filling the 9-pint can.

(c) 3-pint can and 8-pint can to get 1 pint. Begin by filling the 3-pint can.

The subject is not allowed to use pencil and paper. If he resorts to a method that involves guessing, tell him that he must *measure* out the water without guessing. Explain also, if necessary, that it is a fair problem, not a catch. Encourage him to keep on trying throughout the three-minute period allowed for each problem, but if he has failed on the first problem it is not necessary to go on to (b) and (c).

Score: 2 plus. See scoring standards, page 397.

[1] If the subject fails we do not explain the solution.

3. * Opposite Analogies III

Procedure: Say,

(a) *"A rabbit is timid; a lion is ......"*

(b) *"Trees are terrestrial; stars are ......"*

(c) *"A group made up of dissimilar things is heterogeneous; one made up of things which are alike is ......"*

Score: 1 plus. See scoring standards, page 398.

4. Codes I

Material: Message and code printed in capitals in the record booklet.

Procedure: Show S. the code given in the record booklet and say: *" Here is a message that has been written two ways. This is what we want to say, 'Come to London'* (pointing) *and here it is in code* (pointing and reading the letters). *Each letter here in the code stands for a letter up here in the message."* Indicate each letter, or letters, in the code and the corresponding letter in the message. *" You figure out how it goes, what the system is, and then write H U R R Y in code."*

If the first code is solved correctly, say, when presenting the second, *" Now figure this one out and then write H U R R Y in this code."* If there is more than one error on the first code, it is unnecessary to give the second. If necessary, explain to S. that a code is a way of sending secret messages. It is permissible for S. to write out the alphabet as an aid if he wishes, but E. must in no way suggest his doing so or assist him with the alphabet. Time limit, 3 minutes each.

(a) C O M E T O L O N D O N
    B N L D S N K N M C N M

(b) C O M E T O L O N D O N
    A M K C R M J M L B M L

Score: 1½ plus. See scoring standards, page 398.

5. Proverbs I

Procedure: Say, " *Here is a proverb, and you are supposed to tell what it means.   For example, this proverb, ' Large oaks from little acorns grow,' means that great things may have small beginnings.   What does this one mean?* "

(a) *"We only know the worth of water when the well is dry."*

(b) *" No wind can do him good who steers for no port."*

(c) *"Don't judge a book by its cover."*

Score: 2 plus.   See scoring standards, pages 398 ff.

6. Orientation: Direction I (Same as XIV, 3)

Procedure: Read the following directions distinctly, emphasizing the critical words:

(a) *"Which direction would you have to face so your* right hand would be toward the *north?"*

(If S. points or says, " *That way,"* say, *"What is the* name *of the direction you would have to face* etc.)*?"*

(b) *"Suppose you are going* east, *then turn to your* right; *what direction are you going now?"*

(c) *"Suppose you are going* south, *then turn to your* left, *then turn to your* right; *what direction are you going now?"*

(d) *"Suppose you are going* north, *then turn* right, *then turn* right *again, then turn* left; *what direction are you going now?"*

(e) *"Suppose you are going* west, *then turn* right, *then turn* right *again, then turn* right *again, and then* left; *what direction are you going now?"*

It is permissible to repeat the directions if S. becomes confused or cannot remember the problem.

Score: 4 plus.   See scoring standards, page 400.

7. * **Essential Differences** (Same as S.A. II, 3)

    Procedure: Say, *"What is the* principal *difference between ...... and ......?"* Repeat for each item.

    (a) Work and play.

    (b) Ability and achievement.

    (c) Optimist and pessimist.

    Score: 2 plus.   See scoring standards, pages 400 ff.

8. **Binet Paper Cutting**

    Material: Six-inch squares of paper.

    Procedure: Taking one of the sheets, say, *"Watch carefully what I do. See, I fold the paper this way* (folding it over once in the middle), *then I fold it this way* (folding it again in the middle, but at right angles to the first fold). *Now I will cut out a piece right here"* (indicating).   Cut out a small triangular piece from the middle of the side which presents but one edge.   Leave the folded paper exposed, but pressed flat against the table.   The fragments cut from the paper should be kept out of sight.   Indicating the $3'' \times 3''$ square in the booklet say, *"Make a drawing here to show how this paper would look if it were* unfolded (opened). *Draw lines to show where the paper would be creased and show how and where it would be cut."*   If S. omits either the creases or the cuts, repeat, *" Draw lines to show where the paper would be creased and show how and where it would be cut."*

    Score: The test is passed if the creases in the paper are properly represented, if the holes are drawn in the correct number, and if they are located correctly, that is, both on the same crease and each about half way between the center of the paper and the outside.   The shape of the holes is disregarded.

SUPERIOR ADULT I

1. * **Minkus Completion** (Same as XII, 3)

Material: Selection printed in the record booklet.

Procedure: Have S. fill in the missing word for each blank in the selection printed in the booklet. Say, *"Write the missing word in each blank. Put just one word in each."*

(a) We like to pop corn ...... to roast chestnuts over the fire.

(b) Lincoln aroused no jealousy ...... he was not selfish.

(c) ...... he give me his word, I will not trust him.

(d) You must not, ..., imagine that my silence has been due to ignorance of what is going on.

Time limit, 5 minutes.

Score: 3 plus. See scoring standards, pages 386 f.

2. * **Opposite Analogies IV** (Same as S.A. III, 5)

Procedure: Say,

(a) *"Ability is native; education is ......"*

(b) *"Music is harmonious; noise is ......"*

(c) *"A person who talks a great deal is loquacious; one who has little to say is ......"*

Score: 1 plus. See scoring standards, page 403.

3. * **Essential Similarities** [1]

Procedure: Say, *"What is the principal way in which ...... and ...... are alike?"* Repeat for each item.

(a) Farming and manufacturing.

(b) Melting and burning.

(c) An egg and a seed.

Score: 2 plus. See scoring standards, pages 291 f.

[1] This test occurs also in Form L at Superior Adult Level I, Test 6.

4. Repeating 6 Digits Reversed [1]

Procedure: Say, *"I am going to say some numbers, and I want you to say them backwards. For example, if I should say 5–1–4, you would say 4–1–5. Ready now; listen carefully, and be sure to say the numbers backwards."* Before each series repeat, *"Ready now; listen carefully, and be sure to say the numbers backwards."* Rate, one per second. Avoid accent or rhythm.

(a) 4–7–1–9–5–2,   (b) 5–8–3–6–9–4,   (c) 7–5–2–6–1–8.

Score: 1 plus.   The series must be repeated backwards in correct order without error after a single reading.

5. * Sentence Building II

Procedure: Say, *" Now make up a sentence that has in it the three words . . . . ."*
(a) Ceremonial, dignity, impression.
(b) Baffle, cunning, pursuit.
(c) Failure, business, incompetent.
Score: 2 plus.   See scoring standards, pages 404 f.

6. Reconciliation of Opposites (Same as XIV, 6)

Procedure: Say, *"In what way are . . . . . . and . . . . . . alike?"*

(a) Winter and summer.   (d) Much and little.
(b) Happy and sad.   (e) Beginning and end.
(c) Loud and soft.

Even though S. is failing the items, all five must be given. If, as sometimes happens, S. fails to grasp the idea until several items have been given, a correction of the preceding items is accepted if offered spontaneously.   If S. says they are opposite, repeat the question with emphasis on *alike*.

Score: 4 plus.   See scoring standards, pages 395 ff.

---

[1] This test occurs also in Form L at Superior Adult Level I, Test 4.

SUPERIOR ADULT II

1. * Proverbs II

Procedure: Say, *" Here is a proverb, and you are sup-posed to tell what it means. For example, this proverb, 'Large oaks from little acorns grow,' means that great things may have small beginnings. What does this one mean?"* If another set has preceded, say, *" Here is another proverb. What does this one mean?"*

(a) *"The mouse that has but one hole is easily taken."*

(b) *"You must not throw pearls before swine."*

Score: 1 plus.   See scoring standards, pages 405 f.

2. * Ingenuity (Same as XIV, 5; A.A., 2)

Procedure: The problem is given orally and may be repeated if necessary.   (a) *"A mother sent her boy to the river to bring back exactly 2 pints of water. She gave him a 5-pint can and a 3-pint can. Show me how the boy can measure out exactly 2 pints of water using nothing but these two cans and not guessing at the amount. You should begin by filling the 5-pint can first. Remember, you have a 5-pint can and a 3-pint can and you must bring back exactly 2 pints of water."* [1]

Use the same formula for (b) and (c).

(b) 9-pint can and 5-pint can to get 13 pints.   Begin by filling the 9-pint can.

(c) 3-pint can and 8-pint can to get 1 pint.   Begin by filling the 3-pint can.

The subject is not allowed to use pencil and paper.   If he resorts to a method that involves guessing, tell him that he must *measure* out the water without guessing.   Explain,

---

[1] If the subject fails, we do not explain the solution.

also, if necessary, that it is a fair problem, not a catch. Encourage him to keep on trying throughout the 3-minute period allowed for each problem, but if he has failed on the first problem it is not necessary to go on to (b) and (c).

Score: 3 plus. See scoring standards, page 407.

3. * **Essential Differences** (Same as A.A., 7)

Procedure: Say, "*What is the* principal *difference between* ...... *and* ......*?*" Repeat for each item.

(a) Work and play.
(b) Ability and achievement.
(c) Optimist and pessimist.

Score: 3 plus. See scoring standards, pages 400 ff.

4. * **Repeating 8 Digits**

Procedure: Say, "*I am going to say some numbers and when I am through I want you to say them just the way I do. Listen carefully, and get them just right.*" Before each series repeat, "*Listen carefully, and get them just right.*" Rate, one per second. Avoid accent and rhythm.

(a) 2–9–6–1–5–8–3–7
(b) 7–4–9–6–3–5–2–8
(c) 6–2–9–1–7–3–5–8

Score: 1 plus. The series must be repeated in correct order without error after a single reading.

5. **Codes II**

Material: Message and code printed in capitals in the record booklet.

Procedure: Show S. the code given in the record booklet and say, "*Here is a message that has been written two ways. This is what we want to say, 'Come to London'* (pointing) *and here it is in code* (pointing and reading the letters). *Each letter here in the code stands for a letter up here in the message."* Indicate each letter, or letters, in the code and the corresponding letter in the message. *" You figure out how it goes, what the system is, and then write HURRY in code."*

If the first code is solved correctly, say, when presenting the second, *"Now figure this one out and then write HURRY in this code."* If necessary, explain to S. that a code is a way of sending secret messages. It is permissible for S. to write out the alphabet as an aid if he wishes, but E. must in no way suggest his doing so or assist him with the alphabet. Time limit, 3 minutes each.

(a) C O M E   T O   L O N D O N
     D N N D   U N   M N O C P M
(b) C O M E   T O   L O N D O N
     A P K F   R P   J P L E M O

If S. gives an incorrect answer to (a), ask, *"What is the rule for this code?"* This question is used as a caution, and if a spontaneous correction on the code letters is then offered, it is accepted if it is within the time limit. The rule must be asked for (a) even though the full time has been used, in order to guard against careless error in (b). (b) should be given even in cases in which no response has been secured for (a).

Score: 1 plus or 2 with half credit each. See scoring standards, page 398.

6. Repeating Thought of Passage I: Value of Life [1]

Procedure: Say,

"I am going to read a short paragraph. When I am through you are to repeat as much of it as you can. You

---

[1] This test occurs also in Form L at Superior Adult Level II, Test 6.

*don't need to remember the exact words, but listen care-
fully so that you can tell me everything it says."* If
S.A. III has preceded, say only, *"Here is another short
selection. Repeat as much of this one as you can."*

Value of Life

"Many opinions have been given on the value of life.
Some call it good, others call it bad. It would be nearer
correct to say that it is mediocre, for on the one hand our
happiness is never as great as we should like, and on the
other hand our misfortunes are never as great as our
enemies would wish for us. It is this mediocrity of life
which prevents it from being radically unjust."

Score: See scoring standards, pages 297 f.

SUPERIOR ADULT III

1. Proverbs III

Procedure: Say, *" Here is a proverb, and you are supposed
to tell what it means. For example, this proverb, 'Large
oaks from little acorns grow,' means that great things may have
small beginnings. What does this one mean?"* If another
set has preceded, say, *" Here is another proverb. What does
this one mean?"*

(a) *"Let sleeping dogs lie."*

(b) *"A bad workman quarrels with his tools."*

(c) *"It's an ill wind that blows nobody good."*

Score: 2 plus. See scoring standards, pages 408 f.

2. * Memory for Sentences V

Procedure: Say, *"Listen, and be sure to say exactly what I say."*

(a) *"At the end of the week the newspaper published a complete account of the experiences of the great explorer."*

Score: No error.   Errors include omissions, substitutions, additions, changes in words or in order of words.

3. * Orientation: Direction II

Material: Card on which the problem is stated.

Procedure: Give S. a copy of the problem and let him have it to look at as you read it aloud and while he is solving it.   Do not allow S. to use pencil and paper.

(a) *"I drove south three miles, turned to my* left *and drove east two miles, then turned to my* left *again and drove three miles, and then to my* left *again and drove one mile.   What direction was I going then?"*

(b) *" How far was I from my starting point when I stopped?"*

Score: 2 plus.   See scoring standards, pages 409 f.

4. Repeating 9 Digits

Procedure: Say, *"I am going to say some numbers and when I am through I want you to say them just the way I do. Listen carefully, and get them just right."*   Before each series repeat, *"Listen carefully, and get them just right."*   Rate, one per second.   Avoid accent and rhythm.

(a) 3–7–1–8–2–6–4–9–5
(b) 7–3–9–4–8–1–5–2–6
(c) 8–5–2–9–6–3–1–4–7

Score: 1 plus.   The series must be repeated in correct order without error after a single reading.

5. * Opposite Analogies IV (Same as S.A. I, 2)

Procedure: Say,

(a) "*Ability is native; education is* ......"

(b) "*Music is harmonious; noise is* ......"

(c) "*A person who talks a great deal is loquacious; one who has little to say is* ...."

Score: 2 plus. See scoring standards, pages 403, 410.

6. * Repeating Thought of Passage II: Tests

Procedure: Say, "*I am going to read a short paragraph. When I am through you are to repeat as much of it as you can. You don't need to remember the exact words, but listen carefully so that you can tell me everything it says.*" If S.A. II has preceded, say only, "*Here is another short selection. Repeat as much of this one as you can.*"

"Tests such as we are now making are of value both for the advancement of science and for the information of the person who is tested. It is important for science to learn how people differ and on what factors these differences depend. If we can separate the influence of heredity from the influence of environment we may be able to apply our knowledge so as to guide human development. We may thus in some cases correct defects and develop abilities which we might otherwise neglect."

Score: See scoring standards, page 410.

PART IV
SCORING STANDARDS FOR FORM L

INTRODUCTION
SCORING THE REVISED SCALES

IN DEVISING the standards for scoring, the first consideration has been to secure objectivity without sacrificing the qualitative values of the individual test method. To this end we have made the instructions as explicit as possible. The principles involved in the scoring of each test have been explained and many illustrations given of responses that have been scored plus or minus.

Responses chosen for illustration have been selected from the standardization data and have been given for the most part in the exact words of the subjects. The basis for the selection of these responses has been to include only a few typical examples of success and failure, concerning the scoring of which there is usually little question once the scoring principle has been grasped, and to give examples chiefly of responses which are just above or just below the passing line. We have included, also, certain responses which are so ambiguous that they cannot be scored according to our standards without further questioning. Where such questioning has been necessary in the examples given, the subject's first response has been followed by a (Q.) and then the additional response recorded and classified as either plus or minus. It has been obviously impossible, of course, to include all of the doubtful and all of the ambiguous responses, but the examples given should serve as models to facilitate the scoring of obtained responses with which they are to be compared.

The importance of adherence to standard procedures can hardly be overemphasized. Standardized procedures for scoring are no less essential than standardized procedures for giving the tests, and the examiner should acquaint himself thoroughly with these standards before attempting to use the scales.[1]

[1] A general discussion of scoring has been given in Part I, Chapter IV.

YEAR II

1. Three-Hole Form Board

This simplified form board has a high interest value for young children. Gesell found it usable for the location of the easiest block (the circle) as far down in the scale as the twelve months' level. Our $5'' \times 8''$ board is smaller than the one Gesell [1] used and our bright red blocks contrast with the dark green of the board and insets. The small blocks ($1\frac{1}{2}'' \times 1\frac{1}{2}''$) are easy for small hands to handle, but it is doubtful whether the brightly colored blocks add anything of value, as children under three and a half have been found to show more interest in form than in color.[2] The test shows a good increase in per cent passing with age and is usable at several age levels when its difficulty is increased by rotating the board and by requiring two successes out of three trials. At this level, one success out of two trials is required for passing.

2. Identifying Objects by Name

One of the significant stages in the development of the use of verbal symbols in speech is the acquisition of naming habits. It is a simpler task for a child to point to an object which the examiner names than to designate and name the object himself. Comprehension of language heard precedes the ability to apply word symbols orally. In this test, we are concerned only with the child's ability to identify common objects by name. This is the easiest test in the scale and one of the most interesting to the younger children, who are delighted with the

---

[1] Gesell, Arnold. *Mental Growth of the Pre-School Child*, pp. 46 and 120. New York: Macmillan, 1925.

[2] Engel, P. "Über die teilinhaltliche Beachtung von Farbe und Form." *Z. pädag. Psychol.*, 1935, *36*, pp. 202–14; 241–51.

tiny objects and respond eagerly, usually forgetting very promptly any shyness or timidity. The test is passed if four out of six of the objects are identified.

3. Identifying Parts of the Body

This test has replaced the one used in the old scale which required the child to point to his own nose, eyes, mouth, and hair. In that form it was objectionable because by centering the child's attention on himself it tended to increase self-consciousness and embarrassment, a fault which made it a poor beginning test at an age when shyness and negativism are so marked.[1] By using a brightly colored paper doll we are able to determine whether the child comprehends simple language, without so much likelihood of arousing resistance and intensifying shyness. Three out of four must be plus to pass the test.

4. Block Building: Tower

The block-building test strongly appeals to the natural interest of children in manipulating materials. Indeed, it is necessary to make sure that the child's performance is a response to the examiner's request and in imitation of his tower rather than just a spontaneous play activity which is set off by the presence of the familiar play material. Our data agree with Gesell's in placing this test at the two-year level. The tower must be built of four or more blocks to receive credit.

---

[1] Mayer, Barbara A. The negativistic reactions of pre-school children on the new revision of the Stanford-Binet. *J. Genet. Psych.*, 1935, 46, pp. 311–34.

Barbara Mayer has made a special study of negativism in a group of pre-school children examined with the revised Stanford-Binet. Of the group she studied, aged 2 to 6, only 37 per cent showed no negativism on any of the tests. Of course, it is possible to overcome negativism to a certain extent. In the instances where negativism occurred the cooperation of the child was finally secured on that item in approximately half of the cases.

5. Picture Vocabulary (Same as II–6, 4; III, 2; III–6, 2; IV, 1)

The purpose of this test is to determine whether the sight of a familiar object in a picture provokes recognition and calls up the appropriate name. Accordingly, responses which designate the object by its use, like "sleep" for "bed," are scored minus; also, responses which give a crude description, such as "rain thing" for "umbrella," we have scored minus. Naming the part for the whole or the whole for the part, such as "finger" for "hand" or "tree" for "leaf," are scored minus. "Thing" is minus. If, however, the child uses the plural instead of the singular, saying, for example, "That's a shoes" or "Some shoes," we have scored the response plus. Likewise familiar childish names for an object, such as "patty" for "hand," have been considered satisfactory.[1]

1. *Shoe* [2]
   Plus. "That's a shoes." "Some shoes." "Boots."
   Minus. "Foot."

2. *Clock*
   Plus. "Watch." "Tockie." "A tick clock." "A time clock." "Tick-tick."
   Minus. "Wrist watch." "A time."

3. *Chair*
   Plus. "Seat."
   Minus. "Bench."

4. *Bed*
   Plus. "Cot." "Couch." "Lounge."
   Minus. "Sleep." "Pillow."

5. *Scissors*
   Plus. "A scissors." "A pair of scissors." "Shears."

---

[1] A picture-vocabulary test has been used by Baldwin and Stecher, who found it satisfactory over the five-year age range from two to six years. Baldwin, Bird T., and Stecher, Lorle I. *The Psychology of the Pre-School Child*, pp. 130–33. New York: Appleton, 1925.

[2] The obviously best response is usually not listed.

6. *House*
   Plus. "Home." "Where you go in home." "Play-house." "Dolly house." "School." "Building."
   Minus. "Some windows." "Store." "Barn."

7. *Table*
   Plus. "A sand-table."
   Minus. "Bench."

8. *Hand*
   Plus. "It's a man's hand." "Lady's hand." "Handie." "Patty."
   Minus. "A arm." "A finger." "A glove."

9. *Fork*
   Minus. "Spoon."

10. *Basket*
   Plus. "Easter basket." "Bakset." "Bassik."

11. *Glasses*
   Plus. "Glass." "A eye-glasses." "Spectacles." "Specs."
   Minus. "Eyes."

12. *Gun*
   Plus. "B. B. gun." "Rifle." "A shoot gun." "War gun." "Air rifle." "Shot gun."
   Minus. "A shoot." "Shooter." "Pistol."

13. *Tree*
   Minus. "Flowers." "Christmas tree."

14. *Cup*
   Plus. "Cup of milk." "Tea cup."
   Minus. "Dish." "Glass." "Bowl." "Pottie." "Pitcher."

15. *Umbrella*
   Plus. "Parasol." "Sun shade."
   Minus. "Rain thing." "Cane."

16. *Pocket knife*
    Plus. "Jack-knife." "Knives."
    Minus. "Butcher knife."

17. *Stool*
    Plus. "Piano stool." "Bathroom stool."
    Minus. "Chair." "High chair." "Piano chair."

18. *Leaf*
    Plus. "A tree leaf." "Maple leaf."
    Minus. "Tree." "Flower." "Bush." "Plant."
    "Weed."

The test is passed if two pictures are correctly named.

6. Word Combinations

Two or more words must be combined appropriately to meet
the requirements of this test. The repetition of two syllables
such as *dada, bebe, mama* applied to a familiar object or person
marks the emergence of true language from the babbling stage
and occurs usually before the end of the first year, but it is not
until considerably later that the child begins to use two words
meaningfully. McCarthy [1] found the mean number of words
per response for her two-year-old subjects to be 1.8. We have
found that 77 per cent of our two-year-old subjects were able
to combine at least two words into a "functionally complete"
even though "structurally incomplete" response. Such word
combinations as "See kitty," "Dat bow-wow," and "Bye-
bye car," are, according to the accompanying gestures and in-
flections, perfectly understandable as declarations, commands,
interjections, or other designations of social or affective im-
port. It is this early two-word-sentence stage that meets the
requirements for success at this level. The single-word
sentence, characteristic of a much earlier developmental level,

[1] McCarthy, D. "The Language Development of the Pre-School Child." *Instit.
Child Welfare Monog. Ser.*, No. 4. Minneapolis: Univ. of Minn. Press, 1930.

is, of course, not satisfactory, and words repeated parrot-fashion after mother or examiner do not fulfill the requirements of the test.

> *Plus.* "Mama bye-bye," "All gone," "See man," etc.
> *Minus.* "Bye-bye," "Night-night," "Bow-wow," etc.

Alternate. Obeying Simple Commands (Cf. III-6, 1)

If it is necessary to use an alternate at this age level, Obeying Simple Commands may be credited if two of the three trials are plus.

YEAR II-6

1. Identifying Objects by Use

Identifying objects by use is probably a simplified form of giving definitions by use, only here the child must fit the definition to the familiar object. At this level, language com-prehension is probably a factor in success on the test. The objects which have been chosen and their uses are familiar to children of two and a half, but knowing an object is different from identifying it in response to a verbal description of it. The task is difficult at this age and it is not until the age of three and a half that children are able to get five out of the six items of the test. At two and a half we have found that 77 per cent of the children identify three or more objects. Three of the objects must be correctly identified to pass the test.

2. Identifying Parts of the Body (Cf. II, 3)

All four parts must be correctly indicated to score plus at this level.

3. Naming Objects

Here, as in the picture-vocabulary test, we are interested in the child's ability to name common objects. This time, however, the object itself in miniature is presented. The object must be named. Responses in terms of use or description are minus. "Thing" is minus, but plural for singular, and familiar childish names are considered satisfactory. The only item of the three that presents any particular difficulties is *automobile*. Satisfactory responses include such familiar designations as "car," "'chine," "motor-car," "bus," and "ambulance." It is not, however, a "choo-choo," "bye-bye," a "dump car," "truck," etc. The test is passed if four of the objects are correctly named.

4. Picture Vocabulary (Cf. II, 5)

At this level, nine of the pictures must be correctly named to pass the test.

5. Repeating Two Digits

Repeating digits is a test which is very apt to arouse negativism in young children. Even though we begin with the repetition of a single digit, considerable urging is usually necessary and complete refusal to comply is not uncommon. The test has been retained at this level in spite of this serious disadvantage because of its value to the scale. It has a very good increase in the per cent of children passing from one age to the next and its correlation with the composite score is .62. The test is passed if one of the three series is repeated without error.

6. Three-Hole Form Board: Rotated (Cf. II, 1)

The test is passed if there is one successful response in two trials.

Alternate.   Identifying Objects by Name (Cf. II, 2)

This test may be used at this level if five of the six objects are correctly identified

YEAR III

1. Stringing Beads

Bead stringing involves complex motor coordinations.   Its interest value is high, as it fits into the child's everyday experience and utilizes familiar material and the play attitude.   Our data show the test to be one of the easiest at this age level. There is a rapid increase in difficulty; only about 50 per cent of the children of age two and a half pass the test, 73 per cent at age three, and 95 per cent at three and a half.   Descoeudres locates the test at age three and a half.[1]   A four-bead chain is scored plus.

2. Picture Vocabulary (Cf. II, 5)

Twelve plus fulfills the requirements for passing at this level.

3. Block Building: Bridge

Another of the block-building tests is building a bridge in imitation of the examiner's model.   Although our scoring of this test is a little more lenient than Gesell's (the child is not penalized for continuing to build by adding a tower to the bridging block) we find 73 per cent of our three-year-old subjects passing the test while from 65 to 85 per cent of Gesell's cases were credited with a successful performance at that level. The test is passed if the two base blocks, separated by an appreciable space, are bridged by a third.

[1] Descoeudres, Alice. *Le développement de l'enfant de deux à sept ans.*   Paris: Delachaux et Niestlé, 1922.

4. Picture Memories

This test was devised to gauge the memory span for non-verbal material by using pictures instead of words or digits. Control of attention is a very important element in success here, as is also comprehension of directions and the control of a directing idea. Making the material interesting and meaningful for this age level incurs the danger that the child may become so absorbed in the pleasure of the naming activity that he will forget the task. Of course, if he goes on to name everything else in the picture he cannot be given credit for success in picking out the objects seen on the preceding card.

Baldwin and Stecher [1] found an increase in picture memory span from two to six, and believe that the test is useful in separating "the more mature and intelligent children from the undeveloped." The test is passed if either (a) or (b) is plus.

5. Copying a Circle

Drawing from a model has always proved to be a very satisfactory test at the various age levels at which it has been used. It has come to be a standard test form for intelligence scales. At this level the design and its execution are very simple. All that is required is that the subject shall achieve a rotary motion in reproducing the circle. The circle need not be completely closed and though it must be approximately round, a somewhat elliptical form is scored plus. One satisfactory response in three passes the test. On page 202 are illustrations of satisfactory and unsatisfactory responses.

6. Repeating Three Digits

There is still some difficulty in securing willing cooperation in repeating digits at this level, and the examiner will occasionally need to exercise considerable ingenuity in securing the

[1] *Op. cit.*, pp. 113-15.

PLUS

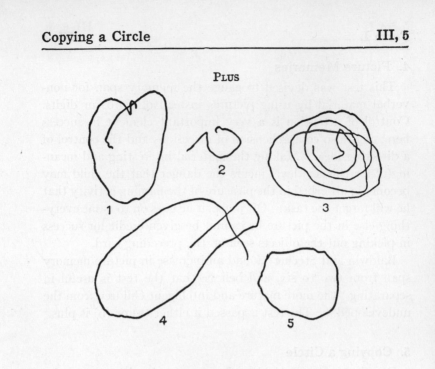

MINUS

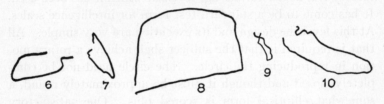

child's best effort.   The test is passed if one of the three series
is repeated without error.

Alternate.   Three-Hole Form Board: Rotated (Cf. II, 1)

If in both of the trials all three blocks are correctly placed,
the test is scored plus.

YEAR III–6

1. Obeying Simple Commands

This is a simplified form of the directions test (familiar to
users of the old scale) located at the four-and-a-half-year level.
It involves comprehending directions.   The tasks are so simple
that recall 's probably not a factor in success at this level.
The first task is the easiest; the second and third require
knowledge of the meaning of the relational words *in* and *on*, on
which success chiefly depends.   All three commands must be
carried out without error to pass the test.

2. Picture Vocabulary (Cf. II, 5)

This test is passed if fifteen of the pictures are correctly
named.

3. Comparison of Sticks

The old form of this test was comparison of lines, which,
like this one, probably gauges language comprehension rather
than actual discrimination of length.   The changed form is
more satisfactory so far as interest and variety are concerned.
Comparing two little sticks has a higher attention value than
comparing two lines printed on a card.   Three successes in
three trials or five out of six are required to pass the test.

4. Response to Pictures.   Level I

The scoring of this test should be very liberal.   The test was originally intended to differentiate the three difficulty levels represented by enumeration, description, and interpretation. However, levels II and III did not prove to be entirely satisfactory and only difficulty I has been retained in the present form.   Enumeration is a frequent form of response found at this level.   Responses that describe or interpret the picture are scored plus even when they offer inadequate explanations or are slightly inaccurate.   Purely fanciful responses which have little or no relation to the story are scored minus.   Level I, then, includes: (a) Enumeration (at least three objects must be named spontaneously, that is, without intervening questions or urging); (b) Description which may refer to a single element of the picture; and (c) Interpretation which may be inadequate and incorrect.   (Plus here corresponds to Level I in Form M at Year III–6, Test 4.)

Level I

(a) *Dutch home*

Plus.   "The kitty asleep and the little girl crying and the mother watching her."   "There's a little girl crying and there's a cat and there's a chair and there's a basket and there's two windows."   "They're Dutch.   The cat's asleep." "Here's a cat.   Here's a girl mad" (description). "Little girl crying" (description).   "Look at this kitty laying down." "There's a little girl sleepy."   "Mama, kitty, girl."   "Chair, table, dish."

Minus.   "That's a little girl, that's a little girl, here's a little kitty cat."   "She, lady, girl. (Q.)   This catty." "Little dog, grandma, these are grandma's."   "A kitty and that and that. (Q.)   That chair and thing, that and these things."

(b) *River scene*

    Plus. "There's trees and rocks and a boat and a man paddling and some buckets and a lady and a man and another man paddling in the water." "That's a man and there's a man fishing and there's a man and a lady and there's a man driving the boat." "Girl and man together and they've got a rake outside in the water." "They were out fishing and this ain't no fishing lake. They got water in the boat." "Catching fish" (inaccurate interpretation). "There's three men and a girl. They are swimming in a boat." "They're swimming. (Q.) Three men and one boy and they're swimming in the boat." "Boat going swimming" (description). "The boat went down in the water and it ain't supposed to." "Some Indians floating a boat." "Driving that boat." "Boat sailing because the wood stays up." "Riding the boat" (description). "Boys. (Q.) Boys driving that boat." "Man, lady, boat."

    Minus. "That picture goin' swimmin'. That picture you go swimmin'." "Big, big boat. What's that? Who's that?" "Boat, mans." "Boy, boy, boy, boy." "Here's a ship, a girlie. That's pretty."

(c) *Post office*

    Plus. "There's a lady and some houses and trees and a man with eggs, another man, a man with paper, another man, another man and a store." "A door and a basket with some eggs and a house and a house over here and a lady and a cat and a man holding a paper and a man without a hat and that's the butcher and a man holding some eggs." "A funny man reading a funny paper." "A man reading" (description). "That man's going down main street." "Men carrying a basket of eggs and a paper." "Man got some eggs" (description). "The woman is walking." "Man's telling stories." "Man had a hat on and this one had no hat but this man had a hat." "All men. (Q.) Looking at a paper." "Here's Listo, here's Alf, here's a man, here's daddy."

Minus. "Boy, boy, boy." "Man dere, man —, man doing." "Boys, basket, boys, basket, boy, basket, boys." "See, eggs."

Two out of three of the pictures must be scored plus at level I to pass the test.

5. Identifying Objects by Use (Cf. II–6, 1)

The score is five plus out of six.

6. Comprehension I

The purpose of these questions is to ascertain whether the child can comprehend the situation suggested and give a reasonably pertinent reply.

In evaluating the responses we take into account the fact that the child's understanding is, of course, limited to his own experience and determined by his own needs. Even his perceptions tend to be distorted by his childish interests and ideas, and especially by the personal factor which Piaget calls egocentrism. This personal character of his thinking is reflected in such replies to the question why we have stoves as, "Dickie get his supper," a perfectly adequate response. However, such "juxtaposition" of parts irrespective of their relation to the whole, as "stove's in the oven," is, of course, too distorted to count as satisfactory. In such a response we recognize the familiar tendency of a child to single out some detail, forgetting entirely the direction of his thought, and ignoring completely the place of the part with reference to the whole, like the child who draws a man and carefully arranges the teeth across the top of the head.

No one form of answer is required. It is sufficient if the question is understood and given a reasonably sensible answer according to the perceptual meanings of an adult's world.

The following are samples of typical satisfactory and unsatisfactory responses:

(a) *What must you do when you are thirsty?*

Plus. "Drink." "I ask mama for some water." "Mama give me a drink when I go up." "Drink of water." "Have some tea." "Water." "I drink last night." "Go to the sink." "Tell my mommy. (Q.) She'll give me a drink," etc.

Minus. "Thank you." "I'm hungry." "Eat. Eat dinner, don't I?" "Do nothing," etc.

(b) *Why do we have stoves?*

Plus. "To cook on." "That cook dinner." "Cause to warm." "Build a fire in." "Warm the house." "To heat things." "Stoves for eat." "Burn something, some wood." "For make our food." "So you can iron." "To play with." "Turn them on. (Q.) Cook," etc.

Minus. "Stove right there." "Mommy has those." "This is a stove." "We have stoves this way," etc.

One of the two questions must be answered correctly to pass the test.

Alternate.   Drawing a Cross

Drawing a cross is another of the designs tests which requires the eye-hand coordinations involved in executing a simple pattern.

Contrary to Gesell's findings, this imitative drawing proved to be more difficult to our subjects than the copying of a circle; 43 per cent of our three-year-old subjects succeeded in imitating the drawing of the cross as against 62 per cent of the same age group who succeeded in copying the circle. The requirement for this test is that the child shall make two lines which cross each other. We disregard the angle of crossing and the straightness and length of the lines. As will be seen from the illustration, on page 208, our scoring of this test is very lenient.

PLUS

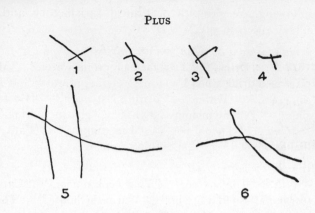

1   2   3   4

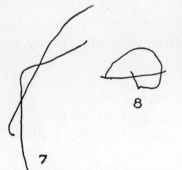   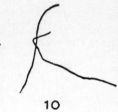

5   6

MINUS

7   8   9   10

YEAR IV

1. Picture Vocabulary (Cf. II, 5)

The test is passed at this level if sixteen pictures are correctly named.

2. Naming Objects from Memory

Success in this test depends upon immediate recall of material that is essentially interesting to a child and is within the range of his experience. The method of presentation makes of the task a game which is entered into with enthusiasm and enlists the child's best efforts. If the correct object is named in two of the three trials, the test is scored plus.

3. Picture Completion: Man

This test is one of the many forms of the completion method that have proved to be so satisfactory in measuring intelligence. We have chosen the incomplete conventionalized drawing of a man for Form L and a test of comparable difficulty, consisting of the incomplete drawing of a bird, for Form M. There is no evidence that the satisfactory completion of the picture is in any way related to drawing ability, even though success depends in part upon the development of motor coordination. Since the ability to observe details rather than artistic ability is involved here, the artistic qualities of the drawing are not taken into account in scoring the test. The significant thing is the presence or absence of arms, legs, eyes, nose, and mouth.

The child's interest in drawing a man dates from his earliest attempts to represent things symbolically. In the typical drawings at this level we can trace the characteristic stages of perceptual development of children. The child who drew

Figure 3, carefully arranging the five fingers along the arm, illustrates beautifully this phenomenon of "juxtaposition" which Piaget describes as characteristic of one stage of perceptual development. Such distortions do not invalidate the response, and credit is given for arm and hand. However, where the guiding idea of the activity is lost, as in Figure 10, no credit is given. It is obvious here that the child started to draw a leg and then got so interested in the scribbling activity that the end was lost sight of.

Credit is given for this test according to the details which are added. The total possible score is three points. Points are allotted as follows:

One point for leg, even if only crudely indicated. The child is given credit even if more than one leg is added to the original figure.

One point for both arms or for one arm and hand.

One point for attempt to fill in additional features within the outline of the head, i.e., for either nose or mouth. No additional credit for ears or hair or for completing eyes or adding the eyelashes. The test is passed if the score is one or better.

The figures on page 211 illustrate some of the various possibilities, together with the scoring credits.

4. Pictorial Identification

Like identifying objects by use, this test, too, is a variant of the use-definitions test. The difficulty of the task is increased by using pictorial symbols instead of the objects themselves, by the kind of items included, such as cow, rabbit, moon, etc., and, most of all, by increasing the number of items from which to choose. The increase in number of items makes it necessary for the subject to isolate and eliminate items, to narrow his selection to the one item that possesses the essential character-

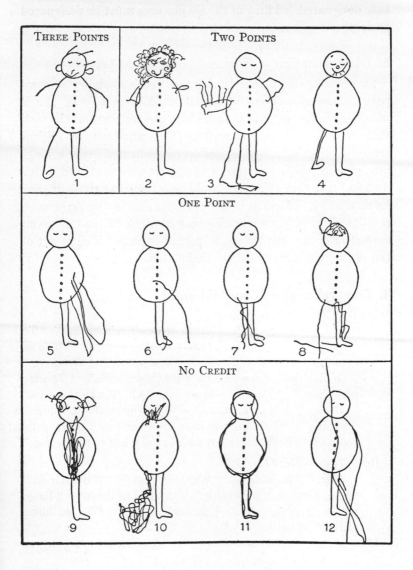

istic designated.   Three of the six pictures must be designated correctly.

5. Discrimination of Forms

Successful performance in this test involves ability to compare and contrast successive visual perceptions of form.   Lack of success is less often due to inability to understand the task than to failure to discriminate.   The undeveloped critical sense characteristic of young children is indicated in the willingness of some subjects to point to any figure at random.   Our data indicate that this test should be retained at the four-year level, where it is located in the old scale and in the Kuhlmann revision, but with the requirement of eight instead of seven correct responses out of ten.   The test is passed if eight out of ten of the forms are correctly designated.

6. Comprehension II (Cf. III–6, 6)

(a) *Why do we have houses?*

Plus. "To go in."   " 'Cause it won't rain on us."   "To cook in."   "To stay in."   "So to make us warm."   "To go in and sleep."   "To go home."   "For people."   "To eat in."   "To play in."   "Because we want to sit down."   "To play with them."   "Because you need it. (Q.) 'Cause to live in."

Minus. "This a house."   "I go in make a house." "Houses."   "In houses we have stoves and we have carpets, too, and we have tinkertoys and we have lots of things, too."

(b) *Why do we have books?*

Plus. "We read."   "Write on 'em."   "To color in." " 'Cause to teach something."   "Stories in them."   "To go to school with."   "To play with them."   "To do home works."   "For singing."

Minus. "To look around."   "Santa Claus is going to bring lots of books."

Both questions must be answered correctly to pass the test.

Alternate.   Memory for Sentences I

One of the two sentences must be repeated without error to pass the test.

YEAR IV-6

1. Aesthetic Comparisons

Surprising as it may seem, children as young as four and a half years reflect the culture patterns of the group with respect to aesthetic judgments.   Psychologically this test involves language comprehension, the process of comparison, and practical judgment.   The present pictures, which have replaced those used by Binet, are a little less primitive but involve about the same level of discriminative ability.   All three comparisons must be plus to pass the test.

2. Repeating Four Digits

The repetition of digits differs from the repetition of sentences chiefly in that the digits approximate more nearly the situations presented by nonsense syllables, the classical medium for studying retention.   Because of their relative freedom from meaning, disconnected numbers have come to be used almost universally for measuring immediate memory span.

Testing auditory memory for digits is one of the oldest of intelligence tests.   It is easy to give and it lends itself well to quantitative standardization.   The commonest aid in memorization is grouping.   The examiner should exercise particular care to avoid rhythm or accent in presenting the digits, as this tends to suggest grouping.[1]   One series of the three must be repeated without error to pass this test.

[1] A more complete discussion of the digit memory span will be found in Terman's *The Measurement of Intelligence*, p. 194 ff.   Houghton Mifflin Company, 1916.

3. Pictorial Likenesses and Differences

Success in this test depends not so much on language comprehension as on the ability to make discriminating reactions at the perceptual level. Dependence on language comprehension has been minimized by a procedure that makes use of both *same* and *alike* in the instructions and includes an illustration. Thus, the problem involves mainly the visual perception of similarities and differences pictorially presented.[1] Three of the comparisons must be correct to pass the test.

4. Materials

Giving the materials of which familiar objects are made is a test of language comprehension and of information. The test was suggested by that devised by Descoeudres [2] and located in her scale at the four-year level. Our data indicate that the test is too difficult at year four, for it is passed by only 38 per cent of our subjects at this age. It is in fact the most difficult of the tests which we have placed at the four-and-a half-year level. Lack of success more often involves failure to comprehend the question, as is indicated by such responses as "to sit" for chair, "sleeves" for dress, etc. The following samples indicate the responses which have been scored plus and minus:

(a) *Chair*
> *Plus.* "Leather." "Sticks." "Tree." "Something like stick of wood."
> *Minus.* "Brick." "To sit." "Cardboard." "Blue."

(b) *Dress*
> *Plus.* "Silk and things." "Fur." "Cloth." "Leather." "Goods." "Cotton." "Material." "Out of some other dresses. (Q.) My mommy does make a dress for me out of her dress."

---

[1] See page 228 for further discussion of similarities and differences.

[2] Descoeudres, Alice. *Le Développement de l'enfant de deux à sept ans,* p. 304. Paris: Delachaux et Niestlé. 1922.

Minus. "To put on." "Dresses are made for dressing up." "Rags." "Of clothes." "Blue and red and white." "Sleeves." "Shirt." "Made to wear." "Of flowers. See this" (flowered dress). "Sewing." "Patterns. (Q.) Make dress out of patterns. (Q.) Don't know."

(c) *Shoe*

Plus. "Leather." "Cloth." "Wool." "Snakeskin." "Of linen." "Material." "Wood." "Sheepskin." "Rubber." "Horse stuff — horse skin."

Minus. "Cardboard." "Paper." "Cotton." (Although these materials are sometimes used in making shoes, it seems more justifiable to score such responses minus. If the examiner has reason to believe the child has knowledge of this use, he should ask for an explanation.) "Tin." "Brown and black." "Board." "Pieces of hard rag." "Soles." "Laces." "Heels." "To put on."

The test is passed if two of the three are correct.

5. Three Commissions

This test samples the kind of activities demanded in everyday life situations. Success in it depends chiefly on the ability to keep the three commands in mind long enough to carry them out without confusion or error. The test is scored plus if all three commissions are executed in the proper order without further prompting, even though, in the course of carrying out the instructions, the child dawdles on the way.

Permissible variations of performance are the following:

(a) The child may pick up the box and take it with him while he places the pencil on the chair and then opens the door, lastly giving the box to the examiner as directed.

(b) He may put the pencil on the chair and then pick it up again, returning it to the examiner with the box, or he may pick it up again on his way back from the door and so return both articles to the examiner.

It will be noted that in both of the above cases the three commands are carried out in the order laid down. It is particularly important that no look or gesture of commendation or censure on the part of the examiner shall give the child any suggestion. All three commissions must be carried out in order.

6. Opposite Analogies I

This controlled association test has from every standpoint proved to be one of the most satisfactory in our entire scale. It is self-explanatory, requiring no instructions; its scoring is completely objective; it can be made simple enough for a preschool child and difficult enough for a superior adult; its interest value is high; its correlation with the composite score on both forms of the test is uniformly high at each of the various age levels at which it has been used [1]; and it shows a consistent increase in per cent passing with age.

Controlled association tests have been used for the experimental study of the thought processes since the earliest attempts to measure individual differences in the experiments of Galton,[2] Binet,[3] and Cattell.[4] The method is, indeed, the classical one for intelligence testing. We have combined the opposites test with the well-known analogies test, in which a fourth word is related to a third as a second is to a first. In this test the clue to the relationship between the second and the fourth of the critical words is that of opposites. Thus, *"An inch is short; a mile is* ...... (long)"; *"A debt is a liability; an income is* ...... (an asset).*"* In every case the exact word must be used as indicated in the following samples:

---

[1] Correlations range from .62 to .81, with an average *r* of .72, for a single age range.

[2] Galton, Francis. " Psychometric Experiments." *Brain*, 1879, *2*, 149–63.

[3] Binet, A. *L'Étude expérimentale de l'intelligence.* 1902.

[4] Cattell, J. McKeen. "Experiments in the Association of Ideas." *Mind*, 1887, *12*, 149–62; "Mental Association Investigated by Experiment." *Mind*, 1889, *14*, 230–50.

(a) *Brother is a boy; sister is a* .. .. ..
    Plus. "Girl." "Girlie." "Little girl."
    Minus. "Lady."

(b) *A table is made of wood; a window of* .. .. ..
    Plus. "Glass." "Glass and wood."

(c) *A bird flies; a fish* .. .. ..
    Plus. "Swims." "Swim."
    Minus. "Floats." "Floats in the water." "Just swims around in the water." "Likes to swim." "Goes in the water and swims."

(d) *The point of a cane is blunt; the point of a knife is* .. .. ..
    Plus. "Sharp." "Keen." "Sharper." "Pointed." "Very sharp."
    Minus. "Peaked."

(e) *An inch is short; a mile is* .. .. ..
    Plus. "Long." "Longer."
    Minus. "Too long." "Long ways."

The test is passed if two out of five are correct.

Alternate. Pictorial Identification (Cf. IV, 4)

Four out of six correct are required to pass the test.

YEAR V

1. Picture Completion: Man (Cf. IV, 3)

This test is passed if the score is two points.

2. Paper Folding: Triangle

A variation of the copying tests is the paper-folding test used by Kuhlmann,[1] of which our test is a modification. The motor

---

[1] Kuhlmann, F. *A Handbook of Mental Tests*, year VI, test 7. Baltimore: Warwick and York, 1922.

coordinations involved are not so complex as those required in the drawing of a square, but the paper folding involves the

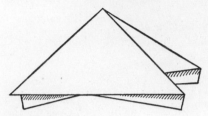

imitation of remembered movement.

The scoring of this test is rather liberal. It is not necessary for the folded edges to meet exactly to form a perfect triangle, and the diagonals may be slightly off center causing the edges to be somewhat irregular as shown in the figure. There must, however, be only two folds and the resulting figure must be approximately triangular in shape.

3. Definitions

The purpose of this test is not to determine whether the child knows the meaning of the word, but to see whether he can define it either by expressing a usage, giving a description of the object, giving the material of which it is made, or categorizing it. The words which have been chosen include only names of common objects which belong to the everyday experience of five-year-old children. The following are examples of satisfactory responses:

(a) *Ball*
   Plus. "To play with." "To play." "To roll." "Throw." "Like a balloon." "They're just like moons, balls are." "Made out of string." "Made out of rags." "A baseball to bat." "Round." "Catch the ball." "Made out of wood." "Kick." "For baby." "To knock." "Cotton." "Ball game." "It bumps."

(b) *Hat*
   Plus. "Put on you." "To go some place." "For your heads." "Straw." "Wool." "Goods." "Material."

"Wear it." "One of those kind of round things." "A thing that sticks up." "Have on boys." "Out of blue ribbon." "Sunday's cap." "On head." "To go in the rain." "Come on here" (points to head). "That means you go away." "It's round and it's got an open on the bottom." "For lady."

(c) *Stove*

   Plus. "Put wood in." "For boil the eggs on." "To burn." "Metal." "Iron." "Steel." "We put tea kettle on." "Cook." "Some of 'em gas and some ain't." "With gas burners on it." "What you get warm on." "For dinner." "For put the paper in." "Heater." "Put wood in." "My mother got one she cooks on at home." "It smokes." "To light it." "A stove is — it's built like that and it has a smoke stack like that" (illustrated with gesture). "Turn on gas."

The test is passed if two of the three definitions are plus.

4. Copying a Square

This test requires an appreciation of spatial relationships and the ability to make use of visual perception to guide a rather complex set of motor coordinations. The latter is probably the main difficulty in copying the square. The figure appears to be perceived as a whole and not simply as a group of meaningless lines. The ability to make the eye-hand coordinations involved is gauged by execution of the angles, the preservation of the proportions of the square, and the straightness of the lines. As will be seen from the sample responses, the preservation of the angles has been regarded as the most important factor. However, the figure must not be more than half again as long as it is wide, and the lines must not be broken, although they may be bowed slightly. The right angles may be formed by lines that intersect slightly, but must not be decidedly rounded and must not be made by drawing

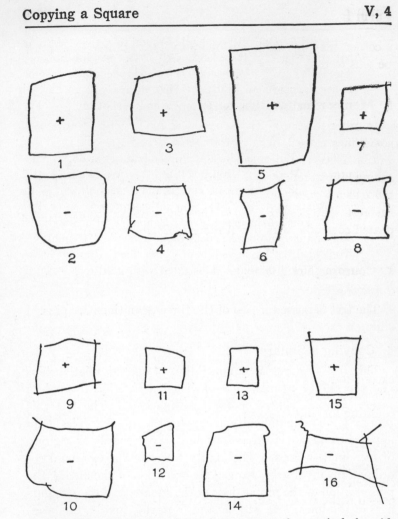

The squares have been arranged in pairs to contrast the marginal plus with the marginal failure which shows the same fault of construction exaggerated.

a corner, making ears, as in Figure 8.   One of three trials must
be plus to pass the test.

5. Memory for Sentences II

In order to secure attention and to minimize the resistance
sometimes caused by a formal warning to the child that he
will be asked to repeat something from memory, we begin by
asking him to repeat first a short phrase and then a short sentence as a sort of fore-exercise preparatory to the repetition of
the test sentences.[1]   One of the two sentences must be repeated correctly after one reading to secure plus on the test.

6. Counting Four Objects

In studying the development of the number concept,
Descoeudres[2] found that about 80 per cent of the five-year-old
children examined were able to show the same number of objects as shown by the examiner, and to show the same number
of fingers as there were objects shown, when these did not
exceed four.   Only 68 per cent of our five-year-old subjects
were able to succeed on the slightly more difficult task of
counting four objects when the criterion of success is two plus
out of three trials and the four objects used are different for
each trial.   The test is properly located at this age level since
it is passed by only 50 per cent of the four-and-a-half-year-old
children and by 91 per cent of the six-year-olds.   The test is
passed if the correct answer is given in two out of three trials.

Alternate.   Knot

Any sort of knot which does not come undone is scored plus.

---

[1] This technique was developed by Dr. Helen P. Davidson, to whom the authors
are indebted for considerable experimental work in the development and preliminary
standardization of much of the material of the memory tests throughout the scale.

[2] Descoeudres, Alice, *op. cit*

YEAR VI

1. Vocabulary (Cf. pp. 302 ff.)

The test is passed if five words are correctly defined.

2. Copying a Bead Chain from Memory I

Copying a bead chain [1] has proved to be one of the few usable genuinely non-verbal tests tried out for the scale. Whatever mental processes may be the basis for recall of the chain pattern, whether visual images are chiefly involved or the recall is primarily verbal, no language comprehension or overt language response is required for success. The test is capable of greater complication than has been made use of in the present scale. (Cf. Year XIII, Test 6.)

Success on this test consists in reproducing a very simple pattern. The subject merely has to alternate the two shapes in making his chain of round and square beads. The length of his chain may be greater than the model, but must not be made up of fewer than four beads (to enable the examiner to determine the presence or absence of a pattern). It is not necessary that the child's chain should begin with a square bead or end with a square one, as the examiner's model does. The following figures are samples of plus and minus responses:

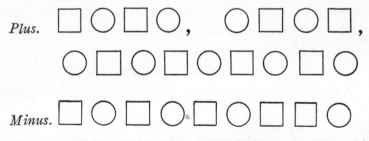

Plus.

Minus.

[1] A series of experiments involving copying bead chains from memory was carried out by Baldwin and Stecher in their studies of pre-school children. *Op. cit.*, pp. 148-49.

3. Mutilated Pictures

This test is one of the many forms of the completion method, the essential characteristic of which is that from the given parts of a whole the missing parts are to be found. In spite of early familiarity with the objects pictured in this test, it is not until the age of six that children are able to analyze the pictures and determine what part is missing. Children's perceptions are characteristically uncritical and unanalytical, becoming increasingly analytical with age and added experience. Recent studies [1] in the field of experimental child psychology emphasize the fact that child development proceeds by the analysis of wholes, and that one of the chief characteristics of perceptual growth is the tendency of percepts to become increasingly accurate, more logically organized, and more analytical in nature. The young child draws a man by making a head, arms, and legs and is perfectly satisfied with his performance. His increased intellectual development is marked by the addition of such missing details as eyes, buttons, trunk, hair, and the like. A two-year-old child can identify a wagon by name, but it is not until considerably later that he can perceive the absence of a wheel, even though he knows and can identify wheel as well as wagon.

The missing part must be named, or described verbally. Pointing is not enough. The following samples illustrate satisfactory and unsatisfactory responses:

(a) *Wagon*

    Plus. "Wheel." "No wheel on wagon." "The other wheel." "The wheel is broke." "Wagon has only three wheels." "One of the front wheels." "One tire."

    Minus. "The wheels." "Leg." "There ought to be a little horse there." "Boy."

---

[1] Cf. especially Curti, Margaret W. *Child Psychology. The Growth of Meanings,* ch. VIII. Longmans, Green & Co., 1930.

(b) *Shoes*

    Plus. "Lace." "Shoe lace." "One of the strings." "Tie." "No straps. (Q.) Like these" (points to string of other). "No shoestrings." "The laces." "One shoe tied and one not tied."

    Minus. "The tongue." "Shoe." "Shoes." "Foot."

(c) *Teapot*

    Plus. "The holder." "The handle." "The handles." "The thing that you lift it up." "Thing you hold on." "The handle's broke." "Holding thing." "Arm of the tea kettle."

    Minus. "The top" (even if handle is indicated). "Hangs on" (points correctly). "Tea." "Coffee." "Something is off" (pointing correctly).

(d) *Rabbit*

    Plus. "Ear." "Other ear." "Cat's ear." "Just one ear." "Rabbit with one ear." "No ear."

    Minus. "Ears." "Leg."

(e) *Glove*

    Plus. "No finger." "One finger broke." "Finger." "Part of the glove gone. (Q.) One of these you put your finger in." "Only has four fingers." "Other finger." "Hasn't got enough fingers."

    Minus. "Fingers." "Some fingers." "Part of this finger." "Button." "Hand." "Hasn't any snaps." "Thumb." "Glove" (points correctly). "The little finger." "Man." "It's cut."

The test is passed if four of the five items are plus.

4. Number Concepts

The purpose of this test is to determine the child's ability to utilize his concepts of number in a practical situation requiring, not only enumeration, but the carrying out of a command involving selection and differentiation based on his con-

ception of the meaning of three, nine, five, and seven.   It requires more than the ability to count by rote.   The child must
be able to count under the influence of a directing idea that
imposes definite limitations.   Three of the four trials must be
plus to pass the test.

5. Pictorial Likenesses and Differences (Cf. IV–6, 3)

All five comparisons must be correct to pass the test at this
level.

6. Maze Tracing

The game character of this test makes it intrinsically in‑
teresting to children.   At the same time, the test situation
involves comprehension, choice between different alternatives,
and the ability "to keep in mind the end to be attained," as
Binet describes one of the elements of an intelligent act.   The
test is the easiest one of this age group for our six-year-old
subjects, 81 per cent passing it.   It has a correlation of .60
with the composite score.

In scoring the test motor coordination is not heavily
weighted.   At this level of development the child may not
yet have acquired sufficiently complete control of the complex
motor coordinations involved to enable him to trace the path
without slipping out from between the two lines which mark
the boundaries.   He must, of course, choose the shortest path
to the goal, but his tracing may waver along the boundary of
the path.   The rule is that the test is scored plus if the right
path is chosen and if the marking is more inside than outside
the boundaries of the path.   Some children try to trace one of
the two lines which form the outlines of the path.   Such responses are scored plus.   Two of the three trials must be plus
to pass the test.

YEAR VII

1. Picture Absurdities I (Cf. VIII, 3)

Seeing the absurdities in pictures involves some of the same elements that are involved in pointing out the incongruities of situations presented verbally. While the visual presentation adds to the interest and variety of the tasks, the picture absurdities have never proved to be quite so good as the verbal absurdities as judged by their agreement with the scale as a whole. The average correlation with composite score is .56 as compared with .73 for the verbal presentation.

Samples of both satisfactory and unsatisfactory responses follow:

(a) *Man with umbrella*

Plus. "The umbrella is backwards, down, and it's raining on his head." "That guy he's walking in rain with the umbrella on his back." "He's letting him get wet." "About that man carrying his umbrella that way. (Q.) 'Cause the umbrella's on his back." "It's because he wants his hat to get wet and he wants his back not to get wet." "He's going through rain and he don't know it." "He's got his umbrella crooked, on his back."

Minus. "He's staying out in the rain." "The umbrella is down there and his hat is on and he's walking." "This man's walking along the street and it's raining. Umbrella leaks and he thinks it's just as well to leave it off'n his head as leave it on."

(b) *Inverted saw*

Plus. "He's sawing the wrong way." "He ain't sawing right." "He is sawing with the thing backwards." "He is sawing on the back of his saw." "He has his saw wrong, the ruffles are on top." "He is sawing a piece of wood. (Q.) He is going to sleep and sawing a piece of wood upside down."

Minus. "He's sawing wood off." "Man's sawing and there's a ball right on there." "Cutting wood. (Q.) Because the log's not over — he's standing on it."

(c) *Dog chasing the rabbit*

Plus. "The dog's chasing the rabbit the wrong way." "Because the rabbit is running and the dog doesn't know which way the rabbit is running." "The dog thinks the bunny is running over that way, the bunny is running over this way." "He thinks the rabbit's there" (points to footprints ahead of dog). "The dog thinks he's chasing the rabbit." "The dog is running after the rabbit. (Q.) The dog's running straight and the rabbit's running across." "The dog's running and he's not chasing anybody." "The little pooch he's running over here and the rabbit is running up here."

Minus. "Dog is going that way and bunny is going that way and bunny is going fast so dog can't get him." "The dog is running after those footprints." "The dog's not running after the rabbit — he's running after something else." "The dog's chasing after the rabbit's tracks." "A rabbit and a dog, the dog didn't see the little rabbit."

(d) *Sitting in the rain*

Plus. "The lady and man are sitting in the rain." "They think they're not getting wet, but they do get wet." "It's raining and they're sitting out on the porch." "They're on the porch, they haven't got an umbrella and are gettin' their clothes all wet. The house is getting all wet too." "They are sitting outdoors without any raincoat or umbrella when it's raining."

Minus. "The man is smoking a pipe in the rain." "The door is open and the man is smoking while it's raining." "It's raining inside the house."

The absurdity must be detected in three of the four pictures to pass the test.

2. Similarities: Two Things

"One of the cornerstones in the building of man's intellectual achievements"[1] is the development of the ability to make discriminating reactions. When a child exclaims "nice kitty" on first seeing a tiger in the zoo, he is making comparisons on the basis of similarity. The ability to make discriminative responses in the presence of an object is an early aspect of perceptual development which precedes the ability to react adaptively in the absence of the object. Responses to similarities and differences on both the perceptual and ideational level develop earlier than the ability to verbalize such distinctions.

Success in this test depends upon a number of factors other than mere ability to make a discriminative reaction, including the degree of familiarity of the objects presented for comparison, the ability of the child to keep in mind a directing idea (undoubtedly a much later stage of development), and comprehension of the word "alike," a word whose difficulty level is probably far beyond the actual ability to perceive similarities between familiar objects. Giving differences is a common form of failure at this level, as is giving similarities when differences are called for. Giving similarities is fairly difficult at year VII, but too easy at year VIII. The increased difficulty of giving both a similarity and a difference (year VIII) is probably due to the necessity of keeping in mind the directing idea. All forms of the comparison tests, both similarities and differences, have shown high correlation with total score.

In scoring the similarities test, any real likeness, whether fundamental or superficial, is counted satisfactory. Samples of plus and minus responses follow:

(a) *Wood and coal*
   Plus. "Both burn." "Both keep you warm." "They burn and both are wood." "You could put both of them in

[1] Dashiell, J. F. *Fundamentals of Objective Psychology*, p. 495. Houghton Mifflin Company, 1928.

the fire and coal don't burn so easy as wood does." "Burn
coal with wood." "Both come from the ground." "Both
hard." "The coal is made out of trees and the wood is made
out of trees." "You can burn coal and you can burn wood
and you can chop wood." "Both got the letter 'o.'" "Coal
is pressed wood about 100 years old."

Minus. "Both are black." "Both the same color."
"Coal's dirty and wood is dirty." "You can't break them."
"Coal burns better."

(b) *Apple and peach*

Plus. "Both of them are red. Sometimes an apple is
green." "Almost the same color." "Apple is juicy and so
is peach." "Both the same size." "Both the same shape."
"Peach is red and apple sometimes gets red. Both nearly
always have some red on them." "Both got 'a.'" "Both
have a stem" (or seeds, skin, etc.). "Both round." "They're
good."

Minus. "Both have a fuzzy skin." "Both hard" (or
soft). "Both taste the same." "Both have a lot of seeds."

(c) *Ship and automobile*

Plus. "Good to ride in." "Both go." "They both got
windows." "Ship has a horn and an automobile has a horn."
"Ship has iron in it and so does a car." "Both of 'em runs
with gas." "They both carry freight." "Both have en-
gines in them." "Both have a steering wheel."

Minus. "Machine rides on the street and boat rides on
water." "Ship goes on water and automobile sometimes
goes in water." "Both got tops on." "Both made alike."

(d) *Iron and silver*

Plus. "Both metals" (or minerals). "Both used to
make things." "Because they are hard." "Both solid"
(or strong, heavy, etc.). "You can use them. (Q.) Make
dishes out of them." "Iron don't break and silver don't
break." "They're both valuable" (or worth something).
"Both you make knives and things out of." "Can't bend

silver with your hand or you can't bend iron." "Both can
be bent." "Both shiny."

Minus. "Good to cut with." "Sometimes they are the
same shape." "Both thin." "Both thick." "Because
they both can break so easy." "Same color. (Q.) Iron is
white and silver is white."

Two of the four comparisons must be correct to pass the
test.

3. Copying a Diamond

A most puzzling topic for speculation is presented by the
fact that a child who can draw a square quite acceptably may
be totally unable to draw a diamond. Success with either
seems to hinge upon ability to break up the unitary character
of the perceptual experience when the child attempts to reproduce the figure. Difficulties in execution are involved in the
reproduction of the parts, which have been perceived not as
parts but as features of a whole. The characteristic failures
with the diamond in the case of children below seven years of
age give us valuable cues concerning the processes involved.
All may go well with the drawing until the child reaches the
corner, which presents a new problem, and he proceeds to solve
it by drawing a corner, thus producing the characteristic figure
with ears (cf. Sample 12). "Lack of mastery over the oblique
strokes," [1] which Gesell found to be characteristic of the earlier
stages in the development of motor control, is also involved in
the failure to execute the perceptual pattern.

The scoring takes account of the formation of the angles, of
the equilateral character of the sides, and of the positions of
sides and angles in relation to each other. Thus, a satisfactory
drawing must have four well-defined angles, it must be more
diamond-shaped than square or kite-shaped, and the pairs of

[1] Gesell, Arnold, *op. cit.*, p. 212.

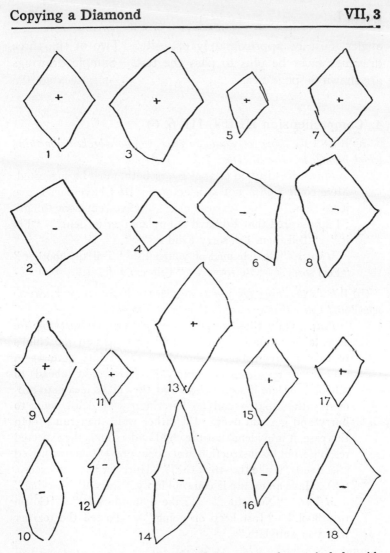

The diamonds have been arranged in pairs to contrast the marginal plus with the marginal failure which shows the same fault of construction exaggerated.

angles must be approximately opposite.   Two of the three
drawings must be plus to pass the test.   Sample drawings
are shown on page 231.

4. Comprehension III (Cf. III–6, 6)

(a) *What's the thing for you to do when you have broken something
which belongs to someone else?*

    Plus.   Restitution or apology, or both, must be suggested.
Mere confession is not satisfactory.   "If I have one, I give
it to 'em."   "Say excuse me."   "Give 'em something."
"I'd be scared that I'd have to buy another for 'em."   "Fix
it."   "Tell them I'm sorry I did it."

    Minus.   "Be ashamed of yourself."   "Tell my mother."
"Feel sorry."   "Be sorry."   "Tell 'em I did it."

(b) *What's the thing for you to do when you are on your way to
school and notice that you are in danger of being late?*

    Plus.   Only those responses which suggest hurrying are
acceptable.   Local conditions and customs and the child's
particular circumstances should be taken into account in
evaluating responses.   "Hurry."   "Go right ahead to
school."   (Here it seems clear that the child's idea is to proceed with dispatch and no loitering.)   "I don't want to
hurry and get run over.   I'd rather walk than run."   (In
this case, it is evident that the child understands the expected
response, but his instruction in accident prevention has proved
effective.)   "Take the street car."   "Hurry or have an excuse.
(Q.)   Have an excuse if you couldn't get there by hurrying."

    Minus.   "Not stop."   "Take a motorcycle."   "Go on
to school."   "Just keep on going."   "To tell the teacher
why you were late."

(c) *What's the thing for you to do if another boy* (or *girl,* depending
on sex of subject, or *another person* for adults) *hits you without meaning to do it?*

    Plus.   The only satisfactory responses are those which
suggest either excusing or overlooking the act.   "Go and tell

my mother they didn't mean to do it." "Tell them it didn't hurt." "Don't say they done it on purpose." "Go right on playing." "If they say 'excuse you,' it's all right." "Tell 'em they never meant to do it." "I wouldn't hit them back. I would say, 'Please don't do it again.'" "If they ask you to forgive them or apologize, why cake the apology." "Ask them to be more careful."

Minus. "He'd say excuse me." "I would hit them back." "Not to tell, you'd get in trouble if you did." "Leave it or go tell the teacher." "Tell my mama." "Would not play with him."

The test is passed if two of the three questions are answered correctly.

5. Opposite Analogies I (Cf. IV–6, 6)

All five items must be plus to pass the test at this level.

6. Repeating Five Digits (Cf. IV–6, 2)

One of the three series must be repeated without error to pass the test.

YEAR VIII

1. Vocabulary (Cf. pp. 302 ff.)

The score at this level must be eight to pass the test.

2. Memory for Stories: The Wet Fall (Cf. IV–6, 2)

Once there was a little girl named Betty. She lived on a farm with her brother Dick. One day their father gave them a Shetland pony. They had lots of fun with it. One day, when Dick was riding on it, the pony became frightened and ran away. Poor Dick fell into a ditch. How Betty laughed when she saw him!   He was covered with mud from head to foot.

(a) *What is the name of this story?*
Plus. "A Wet Fall."   "A Wet — something about Fall."
"One Wet Fall."
Minus. "The Wet Falls."   "A Fall."

(b) *What was Betty's brother's name?*
Plus. "Dick."   "Dickie."

(c) *Where did they live?*
Plus. "On a farm."   "On their father's ranch."
Minus.   "With their mother and father."   "In the country."

(d) *Who gave the pony to them?*
Plus. "Their father."   "Dick's father."
Minus.   "Their father and mother."

(e) *What did the pony do?*

It happens sometimes that in responding to (e) the child spontaneously gives the rest of the story, thus volunteering the answer for (f).   In such cases, of course, he receives credit for both (e) and (f), and it is unnecessary for the examiner to ask for (f).

Plus. "Became frightened and ran away."   "Gave Dick a ride."   "Ran away with Dick."   "Ran away from them." "Got frightened from Dick."   "Dumped Dick in a ditch." "Throwed him."
Minus. "Carried them on his back."   "He got mad and let Dick fall into a ditch."   "Kicked."   "They got on it and the pony went."   "Fell in a ditch."   "Fall in the mud."

(f) *What happened?*

(Dick fell into a ditch.   He was covered with mud from head to foot.   Betty laughed when she saw him.)   The expected answer for (f) varies according to what has been given for (e).

234

When a child recalls the boy's name incorrectly, e.g., Ned for Dick, his response is, of course, minus for (b); but if the incorrect name is employed in an otherwise acceptable answer for a succeeding question, the child is given credit for that question.   On the other hand, if he gives an incorrect name for (b) but uses "Dick" in later responses (b) is still scored minus.

> *Plus.* "The pony got scared" (when the response to (e) was "Gave Dick a ride").   "Then Betty laughed and laughed" (response to (e) "He got frightened and ran away.")   "Dick fell into the water and was full of mud." "John got all dirty and fell in the mud and was covered all up and the Shetland pony laughed" (where "Dick" was given in response to (b) above).   "He fell into the mud." "Mud got all over him."   "The pony ran away — he'd got frightened."
> *Minus.* "He fell into the well."   "Then Dick laughed." "They laughed."   "They both fell into a ditch."

The test is passed if five of the questions are answered correctly.

3. Verbal Absurdities I

The detection of absurdities has again shown itself to be one of the most valid and serviceable of our tests.   No other test in the scale with the exception of vocabulary yields more consistently high correlations with total score.   These range from .72 to .75 for a single age group.   The test appears to be little influenced by schooling or by differences in social status.

The purpose of the test is to discover whether the subject can point out the intellectually irreconcilable elements of the situation presented.   The only difficulty is in judging whether the response shows that the subject has seen the incongruity. The child who has seen the point instantly often indicates that fact by repeating the critical phrase, and the dull, uncomprehending child may just try to say over what you have said. For example, you ask concerning the engineer, "What's foolish about that?" and the child replies, "The faster he could go." He may be pointing out just the crucial element or he may be repeating parrot-fashion the last words you've said. Additional questioning will bring out the distinction. The following illustrations indicate the types of responses that have been scored plus and minus:

(a) *They found the young man locked in the room with his hands tied behind him and his feet bound together. They think he locked himself in.*

We expect the subject to point out either (1) that the man would not be able to tie his own hands; or (2) that having his hands tied, he could not lock the door; or (3) that someone else must have done it because he could not; or (4) that it was absurd for them to think he had done it.

Plus. "He couldn't do it. (Q.) He couldn't take and tie hisself." "'Cause he couldn't lock the door when he was tied up, couldn't tie himself up either." "He locked himself in and tied himself up — how could he though?" "Some burglars tied him up. He couldn't have got that way himself." "He couldn't because he'd have to lock and then when he tied his feet he couldn't tie his hands." "They wouldn't think that. (Q.) They would think somebody robbed the house and tied him in." "He didn't, of course. (Q.) Because a burglar had come in perhaps." "He couldn't tie himself like that." "Somebody had to tie him up like that and lock him in."

Minus. "He couldn't tie hisself — if he tied his hands he couldn't tie his feet." (Minus since there is no reason why he should tie his hands first if he is tying himself up.) "Unless he was crazy he wouldn't do that." "'Cause he locked hisself in and tied them together. (Q.) Makes people think that somebody tied him." "'Cause they think he locked himself in. (Q.) Because the lock's outside and not inside." "When they found him his hands was tied and his feet, too. (Q.) 'Cause he locked himself in. (Q.) He wouldn't do that." "He couldn't do it. (Q.) I mean that he would need somebody to help him get his legs together." "They think he locked himself in. (Q.) Because they think he locked himself in. (Q.) They thought that and they thought it was foolish."

(b) *A wheel came off Frank's automobile. As he could not get the wheel back on by himself, he drove his automobile to the shop for repairs.*

The expected response is that the car cannot be driven with only three wheels. However, here as elsewhere we find subjects who see the absurdity according to the accepted theory, but propose an explanation which reconciles the conflicting elements of the situation. Such cases are given credit.

> *Plus.* "He drove it and it was broken." "He drived it when there was only three wheels." "He couldn't drive his automobile." "How could he drive it with no wheels on it?" "How could he drive it? It would go bumpy, bumpy, bumpy." "With no wheel on!" (Laughed.) "Frank drove the automobile with one wheel off."
> *Minus.* "'Cause he couldn't get the wheel back on." "Because he didn't drive with the wheel." "His wheel didn't come off." "He drove to the shop without one wheel on. What would people think!" "He drove his auto to the shop when he had only one wheel on his car."

(c) *I read in the paper that the police fired two shots at a man. The first shot killed him, but the second did not hurt him much.*

The correct answer must take account of the statement that "the second shot did not hurt him much."

> *Plus.* "When the first one shot the man, he wouldn't be alive any more, and he couldn't be hurt." "It's wrong. (Q.)

It's backwards. (Q.) The first shot didn't hurt him much and the second killed him." "If it didn't hurt him much he couldn't be killed in the first." "How could it kill him and then the other one not hurt him much?" "He shot him and he couldn't hurt him no more." "He didn't die. (Q.) If he died the first time he wouldn't wake up the second time." "The second couldn't hurt him." "He was dead. (Q.) If he was killed he wouldn't care whether it hurt him or not."

Minus. "First shot killed him and second didn't." "He came to life again." "The first shot killed him — the next shot hurt him, too." "The first one killed him and second one didn't hurt him. (Q.) That the second one didn't hurt, too." "Because the second didn't hurt him much. (Q.) I don't know." "It should hurt him a lot." "The first shot killed him, the second shot would still keep him deader."

(d) *An engineer said that the more cars he had on his train the faster he could go.*

Plus. "He thought he could and he couldn't. (Q.) Because it was so heavy." "Too many cars on." "He couldn't go if many cars was on the train." "The more cars you don't have on your train makes you go faster." "They'd make it harder." "Going uphill he couldn't, but if he was going downhill he could." "He would go slow if he had a whole lot." "Just the opposite." "The faster he could go. (Q.) He couldn't go any faster." "The more autos, he doesn't go as fast as when he doesn't have as many automobiles." (Train loaded with automobiles.)

Minus. "He couldn't carry all those cars. (Q.) If he had some cars on his train he couldn't carry 'em." "The more cars he had on his train the faster he could go. (Q.) The engine makes it go fast." "He couldn't go fast with lots of cars unless it was a freight train." "I don't see how it could have. I think it would have made it heavier or else it was a fast engine, or maybe the cars pulled it." "He thinks he's going fast and he's pulling the train? Well, if he's pulling a train he wouldn't be going fast at all." "Because the car's heavy and the train's heavy, he can't go faster or he'll get into a wreck." "He couldn't go any faster. He could go just as fast." "Doesn't make any difference how many cars you have on, you can go fast anyway."

Three of the four absurdities must be pointed out to score plus on the test.

4. Similarities and Differences (Cf. VII, 2)

(a) *Baseball and orange*

Plus. "Both are round and baseball is a game and orange is a fruit." "Both healthy for you, one's fruit and one's wood." "An orange you can throw and a ball you can throw, a ball can sink and you can eat an orange." "You can't hit an orange and a ball you can. They both are round." "Baseball is as round as an orange. (Q.) Baseball is made of rubber." "Ball's different colors than a orange is and they're round." "A ball is hard and an orange ain't and you can play baseball with a ball and with an orange too if it don't bust open."

Minus. "Baseball is lighter than an orange and both of them are round." "Because a ball is harder than an orange. (Q.) When a ball is yellow and an orange is yellow they are alike." "The baseball and orange have tough skin and the baseball is different inside and so is the orange." "'Cause they are both round and the baseball is a little bit pointed." "You can use them both. Orange you can use for fruit and baseball to play ball with."

(b) *Airplane and kite*

Plus. "They're made out of paper and they could fly same as airplanes. (Q.) They're made out of paper and airship made out of iron." "One's up high and one's down low. (Q.) 'Cause they both go." "Airplane goes up in air and so does a kite and an airplane hasn't got sticks and a kite has." "They both fly and an airplane goes straight and a

kite doesn't" (gesturing). "Airplane can fly all the time
that it wants to and kite can't. (Q.) Both can fly." "Airplane and kite can fly — kite of paper, airship of wood."
"Difference because the kite has a different shape. Both
have wood on." "They both fly in air and kite is thin and
airship is not thin." "They fly in the air but the kite won't
fly unless you hold a string to it."

Minus. "Airplane and kite goes. (Q.) Kite's made of
paper and wood and . . . . . ." "A kite and an airplane flies
up in the air and a kite won't go up in the air if it got a hole
in it and an airplane will go up in the air if it got a hole in it."
"'Cause, they can both fly in the air and they're different because they're different colors." "Both fly and one is paper
and the other is rag."

(c) *Ocean and river*

Plus. "The ocean is water and the river is water, and
different because ocean don't run along like the river does."
"They're both water and ocean starts with 'o' and river starts
with 'r.'" "Ocean has water and river has water. Ocean
is bigger and longer and river is quite big but not as big and
not half as long." (If "longer" had been the only difference
given the response would have been unsatisfactory.) "Both
of them have water in 'em and a ocean is grayish and a river
is red and an ocean has bigger ships and bigger waves than a
river has." (We have ignored the incorrect element in view
of the satisfactory elements of the response.) "They're both
water and one's smaller than the other." "The ocean floats
like the river does, but river isn't as wide, deep, and big as
the ocean is." "They both got water in them and the rivers
are usually between the states and the oceans between the
countries." "They're both water. In the one water runs
both ways and in the river it just runs one way." "An ocean
is round and a river isn't round, is it? An ocean's got water
and river's got water." "River is same as ocean only a river
is smaller body of water and it runs through valleys to the
ocean."

Minus. "Ocean is lots of water and a river some water."
"Both have water in them but they're in different places, the
ocean is in one place and the river in another." "The ocean
is long and deep and a river is long but it isn't deep." "They
both have water and an ocean is longer than a river."
"They're both big and an ocean is bigger than a river."

(d) *Penny and quarter*

Plus. "They are money and one is silver looking and
the other looks like brass." "Both metal, but a quarter
amounts to more than a penny." "Both round. A quarter
is silver." "Both have cents and you can get more with a
quarter." "A penny is made out of hard stuff like a quarter
and a quarter is made out of silver and a penny is made out
of that tin stuff like on the gutters on your roof." "They're
both round but they haven't got the same pictures on them."
"Penny is red and quarter is gold — a quarter is silver and
they're both round. They're both small." "Penny, as soon
as you spend it you don't have any more left, and quarter,
when you spend it you have some left and they're both the
same thing and only one thing is different, when you spend
a penny you don't have nothing left and they're both round."
"Penny is little and round and quarter is big and round."

Minus. "Both of them are round and one's black and
one's white and they are bigger." "The penny is littler and
the quarter is bigger and you can buy lots of things with a
penny and more things with a quarter."

Three of the four comparisons must be correct to score plus
on the test.

5. Comprehension IV (Cf. III–6, 6)

(a) *What makes a sailboat move?*

Plus. "Wind." "Wind and water." "Wind and sails."
Minus. "Water." "The motor." "The sails. (Q.)
Sails make the boat go."

(b) *What should you say when you are in a strange city and some-one asks you how to find a certain address?*

    Plus. "Say, 'I'm a visitor.'" "Say you live somewhere else." "Tell them if I knew, and if I don't know tell them I don't know." "I'd say if I didn't know the address, 'I'll ask my folks where it is.'" "You won't know, because you don't live there." "Say I couldn't tell him." "Tell him to ask someone else."

    Minus. "Wouldn't know what to say." "Say, 'no.'" "Nothing." "Give him a 'phone book." "I'd tell him where to go if I knew."

(c) *What should you do if you found on the streets of a city a three-year-old baby that was lost from its parents?*

    Plus. "Take it to a lost and found place." "Take her home and ask her where she lives." "Ask it its name." "Find the parents." "Go look for the lady that lost the baby." "Take it to the police station." "You should try to take it home." "Keep it until I found out who owned it." "Take it home. (Q.) I'd take it home and then I'd find the mother."

    Minus. "Find it." "Don't do nothing."

Two of the three questions must be correctly answered to pass the test.

6. Memory for Sentences III (Cf. IV–6, 2)

One of the sentences must be repeated without error to pass the test.

YEAR IX

1. Paper Cutting I

Binet's paper-cutting test suggested this simplified form which has proved to be satisfactory at the present age level.

(a)

Plus

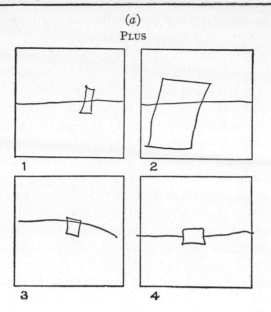

1   2

3   4

Minus

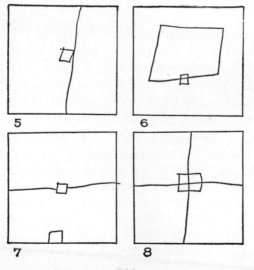

5   6

7   8

Its average correlation of .60 with the composite score ranks it as one of the best of our non-verbal tests.

Scoring is liberal. (a) There must be only one crease and it must be nearer to the center than it is to either edge of the paper. The cut must be longer than it is wide and must be intersected by the crease, but its location on the crease may be off center and it may be incorrectly placed with reference to its lengthwise dimension. The illustrations on page 243 indicate the standard of accuracy required for passing and kind of response that has been scored minus.

(b) The cut must be in the center of the square and must be approximately diamond-shaped, with each corner located approximately on the crease. Slight inaccuracies resulting from careless execution are disregarded. (Cf. illustrations on page 245.)

The test is scored plus at this level if one of the two drawings is plus.

2. Verbal Absurdities II (Cf. VIII, 3)

(a) *Bill Jones's feet are so big that he has to pull his trousers on over his head.*

This absurdity is rather difficult to explain. The point is, of course, that people and trousers just aren't made in such a way that it would be possible to pull a pair of trousers over one's head. We have scored a response plus if it indicated that the child was fumbling for this explanation and really saw the point even though he hasn't expressed it exactly.

> *Plus.* "He couldn't do that, his head would be too big." "He couldn't." "Because you usually can't put 'em on over your head." "That his trousers would stick up on his shoulders." "Because he pulls his trousers over his head. (Q.) The trousers couldn't fit his head." "Trousers don't go over his head." "'Cause his body's bigger than his feet." "He'd have to put his feet through the legs of his trousers anyway." "No hole for his head to go through."

(*b*)

PLUS

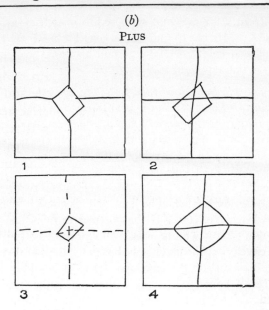

1 2

3 4

MINUS

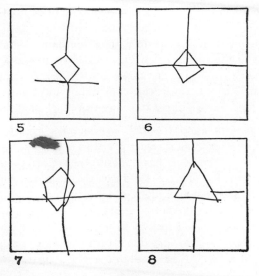

5 6

7 8

Minus. "You're not supposed to wear trousers over your head." "He has to pull 'em on over his head. (Q.) His feet would get cold." "Have to pull his pants over his head—you're not supposed to."

(b) *A man called one day at the post office and asked if there was a letter waiting for him. "What is your name?" asked the postmaster. "Why," said the man, "you will find my name on the envelope."*

Plus. "The man wouldn't know which one it was." "He doesn't know on the envelope if that's his name." "The postmaster wouldn't know what his name was." "He calls up when he's at the post office and expects him to know if there is a letter for him when he don't tell his name." "He oughta told his name. (Q.) If the postmaster found the letter he wouldn't know who he was." "You can't find his name on the envelope (child laughs), he has to tell the man." "Couldn't find his name on the envelope. (Q.) If he didn't know it." "There's bound to be more than one envelope." "That wouldn't help because there's a name on every envelope."

Minus. "Because he might take the wrong envelope. (Q.) Some one might have written the wrong name — he might have taken the letter." "He should tell him because maybe he won't find it." "They didn't have the envelope to find his name in it." "Didn't know his name — and he lived right in the town." "If he don't have any envelope there he had to tell him his name." "He should have told his name. (Q.) Because the man didn't want to look at the envelope." "Might not have been an envelope there for him."

(c) *The fireman hurried to the burning house, got his fire hose ready, and after smoking a cigar, put out the fire.*

Plus. "He should have put out the fire and then smoked." "He wouldn't do it. He'd get the hose and put it out." "Because he didn't put it out quick enough." "After he smoked a cigar the house would be all burned down." "He ought to put it out soon as he got there." "If you sit down and smoke a cigar and don't turn the water on, that don't put out a fire." "He wouldn't smoke a cigar."

246

Minus. "He shouldn't have smoked a cigar at the fire because it's liable to start another fire." "The other men would put out the fire ahead of him and he wouldn't have to." "He smoked a cigar and made all the more smoke instead of putting water on it." "He smoked his cigar while the rest of them put the fire out."

(d) *In an old graveyard in Spain they have discovered a small skull which is believed to have been that of Christopher Columbus when he was about ten years old.*

Plus. "Christopher Columbus didn't die when he was ten years old." "Christopher Columbus didn't discover nothing when he was ten years old. When he's older he discovered things." "He wasn't here when he was ten years old. (Q.) He didn't come over here yet; he was twenty-five years old when he came over." "When you was ten years old and buried you couldn't come alive again." "He didn't sail over when he was ten." "Couldn't have had two heads." "Because, how could he have sailed on his voyage?" "It couldn't be his face when he was twelve years old. (Q.) The face would be bigger — he growed up to be a big man."

Minus. "Christopher Columbus wasn't living then — so they couldn't have thought it was his." "He didn't live in Spain, he lived in Italy." "He wasn't killed like that, Christopher Columbus wasn't; he was killed in prison." "How did they know it was Christopher Columbus' skull?"

(e) *One day we saw several icebergs that had been entirely melted by the warmth of the Gulf Stream.*

Plus. "They came to some and said they saw some and they were already melted." "If they had been melted they wouldn't be there." "Wasn't any icebergs" (laughed). "There'd have been water instead of icebergs." "Said he seen them after they was melted." "'Cause you say you saw some icebergs and they was melted."

Minus. "If icebergs were in the Gulf Stream they'd get all knocked to pieces." "About icebergs that were entirely melted. (Q.) The icebergs was melted." "Icebergs can't melt because it's all wet." "The Gulf Stream couldn't be warm; it would have to be cold." "They couldn't melt that fast."

The test is passed if three out of the five absurdities are pointed out.

3. Memory for Designs

The figures are, of course, perceived as meaningful wholes; that is, the lines of the figures constitute designs and in so far as they are recalled are recalled as related. Whatever may be the processes involved — attention, visual memory, kinaesthesis — it is very certain that they differ from one individual to another and that the dependence, for instance, on visual cues is more marked in some children than in others. It is often possible to note the utilization of kinaesthetic cues as the child practices the designs with pencil in air during the ten-second exposure interval.

For *full credit* on design (a) all of the elements of the design must be reproduced and the relationship between these elements maintained. Slight irregularities due to lack of motor skill or hasty execution are disregarded.

For *half credit* all of the elements must be present, but inaccuracies due to omission or addition of details or to irregularities in size and shape of the figures are overlooked. The samples on pages 250–51 indicate the standard for plus, half credit, and minus.

For *full credit* on design (b) the essential plan of the design must have been grasped and reproduced. Ordinary irregularities due to lack of motor skill or too hasty execution are disregarded. Four conditions must be met:

(1) The outer figure must be rectangular.

(2) The inner rectangle must be off center to the right.

(3) The inner figure may appear square but must not be noticeably higher than wide.

(4) The lines from the corners of the inner rectangle must meet the corners of the outer rectangle fairly accurately.

For *half credit* no essential part must be omitted or any part added, but there is greater latitude in scoring than above.

An inverted design or one whose inner rectangle is in the center or off center to the left receives half credit.

The inner rectangle may be taller than wide in relation to the outer figure.

The outer rectangle may be square or may be rectangular in the opposite direction from the original figure. Less accuracy is required of the radiating lines, but they must show a tendency to meet the corners, otherwise the score is minus.

On pages 252-53 are samples of full-credit, half-credit, and minus responses.

The test is passed if one credit is earned on the designs.

4. Rhymes: New form

This test is a modification of one of the old controlled association tests in which the subject gives words that rhyme with the stimulus word. In the new form, the response is both limited and facilitated by the further requirement that the response word must stand also in a second relationship to the stimulus word. The requirement thus limits the correct responses to one, two, or at most three words. The following are samples of responses that have been scored plus:

(a) *Tell me the name of a color that rhymes with* head.
    Plus. "Red." "Dark red." "Lead."
(b) *Tell me a number that rhymes with* tree.
    Plus. "Three." "Twenty-three."
(c) *Tell me the name of an animal that rhymes with* fair.
    Plus. "Hare." "Bear." "Mare."
(d) *Tell me the name of a flower that rhymes with* nose.
    Plus. "Rose." "Primrose."

The test is passed if three of the four items are plus.

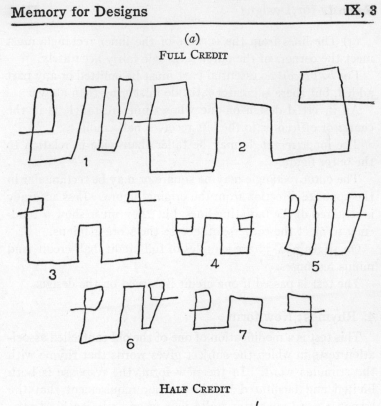

(a)
FULL CREDIT

HALF CREDIT

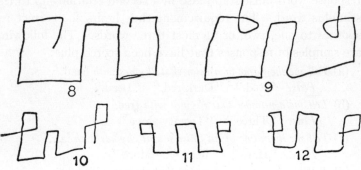

Half Credit — Continued

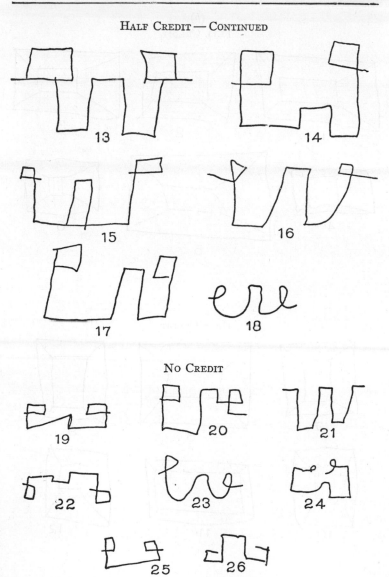

No Credit

(b)
FULL CREDIT

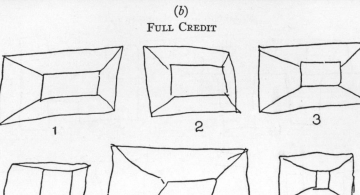

1

2

3

4

5

6

HALF CREDIT

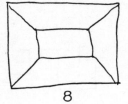

7

8

9

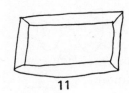

10

11

12

HALF CREDIT — CONTINUED

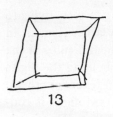

13

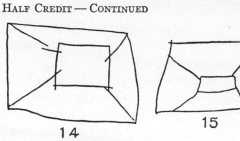

14

15

NO CREDIT

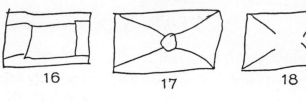

16   17   18

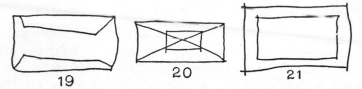

19   20   21

5. Making Change

The purpose of this test is to determine, not whether the subject can subtract 4 from 10, 12 from 15, and 4 from 25, but whether he can comprehend the problem and can apply information already acquired to a new situation. For most children of nine the simpler arithmetical computations present little difficulty; the problem consists mainly in comprehending the task and selecting the correct operations. The test is passed if two of the three problems are solved.

6. Repeating Four Digits Reversed

Certain types of failure on the reversed-digits tests indicate that comprehension of the task constitutes a larger element in success than has generally been realized. The difficulty of the task is further increased by the necessity of holding the digits in mind while performing the operation of reversing them. The result is that the memory span for reversed digits is considerably less than for digits in the direct order. The test is passed if one of the three series is repeated correctly.

YEAR X

1. Vocabulary (Cf. pp. 302 ff.)

The test is passed if eleven of the words are correctly defined.

2. Picture Absurdities II (Cf. VII, 1)

The expected response is that the white man is foolish to be shooting at the Indian farthest away when the other two are ready to attack him. However, this can be expressed so ambiguously as to cause considerable difficulty in scoring, and the examiner must be on the alert to ask for an explanation where necessary. The following are samples of satisfactory and unsatisfactory responses:

Plus. "The soldier is shooting at the Indian coming towards him. He is not paying any attention to the ones coming on the side." "This soldier is trying to shoot that Indian when two Indians here are trying to hit him." "He's just aiming at one Indian and the others could knock him over the head." "The Indian man has one feather, the hatchet of one Indian is broken, the man is killing the Indian — shooting the one farthest away instead of one closest." "He's shooting the Indian that's far away."

Minus. "Those Indians couldn't be — they'd be attacking him — they're not attacking him — they're just standing around looking while he's shooting at that one. They'd jump on him." "A fellow who was used to the woods would try and lie in ambush and wait for Indians to come by and shoot 'em all." "Other Indians are just standing there making believe they're going to hit or something. The man is shooting at another Indian." "There's a hunting man, there's Indians there, they're going to kill him, he's standing there, he ain't running." "There's a man and he's dressed too modern to be in times of Indians — got too modern a gun." "The Indians are standing there and not trying to run or anything, when the white man has his gun pointed." "These are standing right by him letting him shoot the other fella."

3. Reading and Report

That this test depends to a degree on special training does not seriously interfere with its usefulness in a scale for the measurement of intelligence. Children of ten who have had anything like normal educational advantages are able to read the selection without any difficulty. In case the subject has not attended school the equivalent of two or three years, it is our practice to omit the test from the calculation of mental age, distributing the credits for that age group among the remaining five tests of the group.

A verbatim report is not expected. The rule is to count all memories whose thought is reproduced with only minor changes in the wording. The following are some examples of responses and the amount of credit given them:

A fire	"A house was on fire" (1 memory)
last night	"one night" (no credit)
burned	"destroyed" (1 memory)
several houses	"some peoples' houses" (1 memory)
	"a lot of buildings" (no credit)

255

near the center	"in the middle" (1 memory)
of the city.	"of the town" (1 memory)
It took some time	"It took a long time" (1 memory)
to put it out.	
The loss ⎫	"the damage" (1 memory)
was 50,000 ⎬	"some people lost 50,000 dollars" (3 memories)
dollars ⎭	"a lot of money" (no credit)
and seventeen	"pretty near seventeen" (1 memory)
families	"eighteen families" (1 memory)
lost their homes.	"lost their houses" (1 memory)
In saving	"rescuing" (1 memory)
a girl	"to get a girl" (2 memories)
	"a child" "a lady" (no credit)
who was asleep	"who was sleeping" (1 memory)
in bed	"in a room" (no credit)
a fireman	"some fireman" (1 memory)
	"man" (no credit)
was burned	"burned" (1 memory)
	"got burnt" (1 memory)
on the hands	"his hands" (1 memory)

The addition of "the" before "5th" in reading the selection is not counted an error. The test is passed if the selection is read in thirty-five seconds with not more than two errors, and if the report contains at least ten memories.

4. Finding Reasons I

Finding reasons involves seeing the relationship between cause and effect in situations with which the child is familiar. The relationship pointed out needn't be an essential one, indeed at this level any plausible connection may be considered satisfactory. It often happens that the child continues to elaborate instead of being guided by the instruction to give two reasons. He thinks in terms of the particular situations which the task recalls and loses his goal in the details which present themselves, as, for instance, the child who starts out to give two reasons why children shouldn't be too noisy in school and then gets lost in his own description — "They can't do their lessons because they'd be too noisy and would run around and bump their arms and scribble all over the paper."

Our scoring standards are very lenient. We have credited the child with two reasons even when the reasons overlap somewhat, or when they belong in the same category, provided different aspects are presented that can be distinguished in any way. The following sample responses indicate the types of answers which have been scored plus and minus:

(a) *Give two reasons why children should not be too noisy in school.*
    Plus. "'Cause they'll get a lickin'. They'll have to sit in dunce chair." "Because the teacher don't want 'em to be, and then they'll have to go up to the office if they won't do what the teacher says." "So they won't disturb them working, and won't disturb them reading." "'Cause they ought not to be noisy when they have class reading. 'Cause they ought not to be noisy when the teacher's talking." "Because the other pupils couldn't hear and if they couldn't hear what the teacher was saying then they couldn't do the problems and things." "They wouldn't know what their lessons was about. Wouldn't be paying attention to the teacher and wouldn't know what she was saying." "They don't learn and they get the habit."

    Minus. "Because they're supposed to sit down and be still and do their studying when the teacher tells them to." "Because it will disturb the other classes upstairs. They might be reading, doing arithmetic, geography." "Some other children are working and they are quiet and you make them be noisy." "Because helps 'em out so they could study and they learn a lot when they grow up." "If they were noisy in school everybody would hear them over the school and it would disturb other ones from their lessons."

(b) *Give two reasons why most people would rather have an automobile than a bicycle.*

Plus. "Because an automobile can go faster than a bicycle. Because you fall down on a bicycle." "Automobile can travel more, go more miles. Bicycle can't go as fast." "People don't want bicycle because they don't last long and machines you can ride for a long time and go all over the country." "An automobile can go faster and a bicycle can get in more trouble." "Because an auto can go faster. And a bicycle is too slow. You have to pump a lot." "Because you can travel from land to land in an automobile and you can just ride around the city on a bicycle. An automobile is more convenient than a bicycle." "Can go better in an automobile and can go faster." "Automobile is easier to ride and doesn't tire you out."

Minus. "They can go faster in an auto. Don't take as much time to get there." "An auto is bigger than a bicycle. Holds more people." "An automobile can ride in the gutters and a bicycle can't, a bicycle lot of people can't stay on, but an automobile they could." "Bicycle don't run like a auto in the street because they might get runned over on street and they can't run on sidewalk because they'll run into people."

The test is passed if two reasons are given for each item.

6. Word Naming

Although scoring takes account only of the number of words given, very characteristic qualitative differences are observable between different age levels and from individual to individual in this free association test. Some subjects, more often the younger ones, give mainly isolated words. As well stated by Binet, "Little children exhaust an idea in naming it. They say, for example, hat, and then pass on to another word without noticing that hats differ in color, in form, have various parts, different uses and accessories, and that in enumerating all these they would find a large number of words."[1] Objects immediately present contribute largely to the responses of some children and abstract words are of rarer occurrence. Most responses include a mixture of isolated words, objects immediately seen, and various word groups.

The test is passed if 28 words, exclusive of repetitions, are named in one minute. Only real words are counted. As noted in the procedure, the subject is not allowed to count or to give sentences. However, he is given credit for as many as three numbers in counting and for that portion of a sentence up to the point where the examiner discovers and stops him. Sequences such as months, days of the week, etc., are allowed and proper names are credited.

6. Repeating Six Digits (Cf. IV–6, 2)

The test is passed if one of the three series is repeated correctly.

YEAR XI

1. Memory for Designs (Cf. IX, 3)

The test is scored plus at this level if one and a half credits are earned.

2. Verbal Absurdities III (Cf. VIII, 3)

(a) *The judge said to the prisoner, "You are to be hanged, and I hope it will be a warning to you."*

Plus. "After he was hung it wouldn't be any warning to him because he'd be dead." "If he is hung he can't never live again and so how would he know it?" "If he got

---

[1] For a more detailed discussion of this test, cf. Terman's *The Measurement of Intelligence*, pp. 272–77. Houghton Mifflin Company.

hanged he wouldn't be alive — he'd be dead." "Well, can't be a warning to him that he's going to be hanged because he's going to be hanged already." "That isn't a warning — judge should have said, 'Next time you do a crime like that you *will* be hanged.'" "He won't need a warning after he's hanged."

Minus. "If he's going to be hanged what's he going to warn it to him? He's just about going to die. What's warn?" "Well if he's going to be hung why should they warn him about it? They've already got him." "He warned the prisoner that he can't escape and the prisoner would have to die anyway." "The judge gave him warning he was going to be hanged." "If he warned him he couldn't get out of it anyway, if he did warn him." "If he was going to be hanged, he wouldn't know when the warning would come."

(b) *A well-known railroad had its last accident five years ago and since that time it has killed only one person in a collision.*

Plus. "If they had one five years ago and one since it would have been two accidents in five years." "He couldn't kill nobody if there was no train wreck." "It had another wreck." "It's had two accidents." "It wouldn't kill anybody if it hadn't had any wrecks."

Minus. "If it had an accident five years ago it couldn't of just killed one person since that time." "If it had a accident five years ago it couldn't have killed anybody in a collision." "And if it had it's last wreck it couldn't have any more — if it's wrecked real bad it can't be fixed." "It's had it's last accident, it is funny they're still riding on it."

(c) *When there is a collision the last car of the train is usually damaged most. So they have decided that it will be best if the last car is always taken off before the train starts.*

Plus. "There will be another last car." "Should not be taken off because the last one would be crashed most. Have to take all off." "'Cause the other one will get hurt the worst."

Minus. "Won't go if the last train is off." "They wouldn't know whether they was going to have an accident or not."

Two out of three of the absurdities must be pointed out to pass this test.

3. Abstract Words I

The ability to define abstract words has been found to have a uniformly high degree of relationship to the kind of intelligence that our scale as a whole is measuring. It is hardly surprising that the complex mental integrations which are tapped by such definitions should be so significant for the measurement of intellectual differences.

When we give the child an abstract word to define we are trying to determine whether he can respond selectively to the general characteristics which are common to a number of different ideas and can abstract by disregarding the irrelevant details. He is required to express the relationship between ideas. If you ask him, for instance, what we mean by *compare* he may say that it is "to examine two things to see how they're the same"; or he may say, "to see if someone else's arithmetic was like yours you'd compare the answers to see if they were the same." In either case, the child has expressed the meaning of *compare*, in the one case by a generalization, in the other by the selection of a typical situation in which the idea is expressed. Both involve the processes of comparison, abstraction, and generalization. The definition need not be strictly logical nor the language polished, but the definition must indicate that the meaning of the word is understood. If an illustration is used it must be appropriately explained. If the word is merely used in a sentence, or if it is defined in terms of itself the examiner should ask for further explanation. If, for example, the child says, "Compare means to compare things

261

together," say, "Yes, but what does it mean to compare things
together?" or, "What does compare mean?"   Only supplementary questions of this kind are permissible.

(a) *Connection.*   (That which joins things together.   A relationship.)

> *Plus.*   "Join two or more things together.   Sometimes
> to get in touch with someone, or also putting two parties
> together over the 'phone."   "The relation between things."
> "You're some kin to 'em."   "If somebody had a broken
> rope they'd tie the rope together, connect it."   "Like you
> connect two wires. (Q.)   Connect two things and make one."
>
> *Minus.*   "When you connect anything."   (Q.   No further
> response.)   "We go with one another."   "You connect the
> light. (Q.)   You shut off the lights."   "To fix things."
> "Means connect another car. (Q.)   Means just connect
> another, something like that."

(b) *Compare.*   (To examine for the discovery of resemblances
or differences.   To represent as similar.)

> *Plus.*   "To compare two things you match their qualities
> trying to find out which is the best thing."   "When you take
> one thing and put it along side another and see in what ways
> they're alike and in what ways they aren't alike."   "When
> you compare two things you check them as to their value —
> what they're worth."   "To show difference."   "To compare
> two things to see if they are both the same."   "You compare
> a thing. (Q.)   You look it over and compare it with other
> things.   You have two automobiles or two dresses and you
> try to decide which one you want — to compare them to-
> gether."   "You compare her to her mother. (Q.)   You liken
> her to her mother."
>
> *Minus.*   "Take two things that's just alike and put 'em
> together."   "Put together."   "To compare two answers
> together. (Q.)   To correct."   "Like two words meaning the
> same."   "Like you compare one number to another. (Q.)
> I don't know."

(c) *Conquer.* (To gain or acquire by force or by mental or moral power. To be victorious; to prevail.)

Plus. "To win over our enemies." "You capture them." "To get something. (Q.) If you're fighting you conquer the other nation if it loses." "You've got that under your power; you're going to get something and it belongs to you now." "To take something away from someone. (Q.) Like when they conquer a city they take it away from the people that own it, that are ruling it." "Conquer something, like in school if you had something you had to do like mathematics, you'd have to conquer your mathematics. (Q.) You'd have to get it, have to understand it."

Minus. "Like you had a gun and a guy says, 'I'll conquer you.' (Q.) Means you'll shoot someone." "Like if you would hurt them. (Q.) Go up and push them down just for meanness." "To make anything better." "You stop anything." "You conquer Mexico. (Q.) You discover some parts of it like Cortez." "You fight." "To surrender."

(d) *Obedience.* (Submission or compliance.)

Plus. "To mind." "To obey. (Q.) A person does what they're told." "If somebody tells you to do it, like your teacher, you do it right away, and don't hesitate." "You do what other people want you to." "Being good. (Q.) Like if you were obedient to your father and mother you'd obey them and do what they told you to." "To have manners and to do what you're told." "Keeping the law."

Minus. "Being good. (Q.) Not talk out all the time in your classroom and street car n' everything." (The explanation doesn't define obedience.) "To be quiet." (Q. No further response.) "To obey them. (Q.) To obey your parents. (Q.) To be kind." "To obey and not be bad or anything." "Obey." (Q. No further response.) "To obey. (Q.) To be good."

(e) *Revenge.* (To inflict harm in return for wrong or injury. To avenge.)

Plus. "Harming someone to make up for some evil done

263

to someone you are fond of." "The desire to return a grudge." "Get even." "Getting back at a person who's done you harm." "If somebody gets you into trouble, you want to make them get the blame for something or get into trouble for making you get into trouble." "Way people satisfy their mind. (Q.) If they've been harmed they get revenge and that satisfies 'em then." "You hate someone for something he's done and you want to get back at him some way."

Minus. "Try to get something over on somebody. (Q.) When you get ahead of somebody they want to get revenge right away." "You want to win something for yourself." "To come back at a person, double cross them." "If you're mad at someone and you wanted revenge on them you'd do something dirty to them, that's revenge." "You hate a person." "Like you revenge anything. (Q.) Keep somebody from doing what they want to do." "Like someone wants to make trouble for you because they're mad at you."

The test is passed if three of the words are correctly defined.

4. Memory for Sentences IV

Tests of memory span, whether for digits or for meaningful material, continue to show a correlation with mental age score and an increase in the per cent passing from one age to the next as far as the scale goes. This test is passed if one of the sentences is repeated without error.

5. Problem Situation

The reasoning involved in solving the problem presented by this situation consists in grasping the relationship between the given details. The solution is, then, an inference which follows when no irrelevant detail, no fact that fails to fit into the pattern, remains in the given situation. The test is another variation of the familiar completion method which permits of almost unlimited elaboration and increase in difficulty from tasks suitable for pre-school level to problems that tax the ingenuity of an adult.

The following are sample responses illustrating plus and minus scores on the problem of Donald and the skunk:

> *Plus.* "It was a skunk." "That kitty was a pole." "It was a bad smelling animal." "Because it stunk."
> *Minus.* "That the animal had a disease or something." "The animal was poison." "Because the animal probably had fleas or something." "Because his clothes were so dirty." "The animal chewed his clothes all up."

6. Similarities: Three things (Cf. VII, 2)

Any real similarity is acceptable whether fundamental or superficial. This test sometimes provokes doubtful responses such as the indefinite statements, "all are useful," "all made of the same material," etc., and in order to score these a supplementary explanation must be called for.

(a) *Snake — Cow — Sparrow*
> *Plus.* "All are animals." "All move." "They have tails" (eyes, tongue, skin, etc.). "They can eat." "All have babies." "None of them can talk." "They can all make a noise." "They all stay out in the pasture."
> *Minus.* "They can all hurt you." "All can walk." "All have legs." "They all lay down." "All animals — no, sparrow isn't an animal." "They're all mammals." "A snake crawls, a cow walks, and a sparrow flies" (or some other difference).

(b) *Rose — Potato — Tree*
> *Plus.* "They grow in the ground." "Both got leaves." "All of them bloom." "All have roots." "All are plants." "All green at the same season." "All useful. (Q.) They all produce food — rose for the bees, and potato and tree for

human being or live stock." "All part of nature." "All part of a garden."

Minus. "They all can rust." "Rose grows like a tree and potato grows underground." "All give us sap." "All grow from nearly the same things." "They're all wild plants."

(c) *Wool — Cotton — Leather*

Plus. "All used for clothing." "Make things out of them. (Q.) You can make coats out of them." "They can all make gloves." "Wool will keep you warm, cotton keeps you warm, leather will keep your feet warm." "Because they are all worn, wool and cotton makes wool and cotton dresses, and leather they make shoes out of." "All useful. (Q.) To wear." "They're all grown in the United States." "They're all cloth-like." "They're all goods."

Minus. "You use all of them. (Q.) I mean you make shoes out of leather and make clothes out of cotton and clothes out of wool." (Hasn't given a use in common.) "All soft." "Because they make clothing out of them and shoes." "Come from animals."

(d) *Book — Teacher — Newspaper*

Plus. "You learn from all." "All teach." "They all use words." "You can read a book and read a newspaper and learn something and a teacher talks to you and you learn something." "They all serve the public." "All help you get an education."

Minus. "They belong to school — newspaper has reading on it and you use it sometimes in school." "The teacher teaches you something from a book and newspaper, too, teaches you something." "To learn to read." "Teacher tells you something and newspaper does, too." "All give you news." "All read."

(e) *Knife-blade — Penny — Piece of wire*

Plus. "They are all minerals." "They're all made out of something hard." "They're made out of some kind of stuff that comes from the ground." "They're made out of different metals." "They're all made of the same thing. (Q.) All metal."

Minus. "Made of the same thing. (Q.) Copper." "They won't break." "Steel." "They are both strong." "Articles." "All made of the same metal." "You can do something with all of them. (Q.) Use 'em for different things." "They're all shiny."

Three satisfactory responses out of five are necessary for success.

YEAR XII

1. Vocabulary (Cf. pp. 302 ff.)

A score of fourteen is required at this level.

2. Verbal Absurdities II (Cf. IX, 2)

The test is passed if four of the items are plus.

3. Response to Pictures II: Messenger Boy

The three pictures of the old scale were used at the three-, seven-, and twelve-year levels. At the three-year level the characteristic response to "tell me everything you can see in the picture" was enumeration; likewise at year seven the response to "what is this picture about" was usually description; and at year twelve the picture was interpreted in response to "explain this picture." So dependent is the response on the form of the question that a child who was first given the test at a lower age level was occasionally under-rated at the higher level because his response had been in part determined by the first form of the question put to him. In order to avoid this source of error we have changed the form of question for the pictures of the revised scale to one that is usable at several levels.

The character of the pictures used is also very important in determining the type of response. Some of the pictures which were tried out in our preliminary experimentation provoked interpretation at the three- and four-year levels.

A third important factor in determining the difficulty level of the picture is the standard for scoring the responses. One picture only has been used at this level and responses have been scored plus if three points have been brought out in interpreting the picture:

(1) A message is to be delivered.

(2) Delivery has been hindered by the broken bicycle.

(3) The messenger boy is seeking help from an approaching automobile.

The following are samples of plus and minus responses:

Plus. "He's waving to get a ride to take the telegram to the house, because he had a wreck — his wheel came off." "This boy's bicycle's broken down and he's trying to stop that car. He's a telegram boy." "The wheel is off the bicycle and the messenger boy is waving his hand to stop the machine — has a telegraph in his hand. Works for Western Union." "This boy that's delivering telegrams when he was going along his wheel came off and there was a car coming and he tried to stop it so he could ride with them and take his bicycle and get it fixed." "The telegraph boy's bike broke and he's asking that car to give him a lift." "There's a boy and he's a telegraph messenger and he's hailing a motorist for help."

Minus. "There's a telegraph boy and he's got an important message for the people that's coming in this car and he is trying to stop them." "This boy's riding a bicycle and he's going to flag a car and the bicycle is broke and he's got a telegram in his hand." "The boy's had an accident and has a wheel off — out in the country and he's waving his hat to get a ride." "A boy's bike got broke and he's trying to make the car stop so he could get a lift — he must be far away from the city."

4. Repeating Five Digits Reversed (Cf. IX, 6)

The test is passed if one of the three series is repeated correctly.

5. Abstract Words II (Cf. XI, 3)

(a) *Constant.* (Firm in mind or purpose. Unchanging. Continuing without cessation, or only with such intermissions as do not interrupt continuity.)

Plus. "Steadfast." "Loyal." "You'll stand with a person in any way you can. (Q.) If he's in trouble and he asks you to help and you promise him you will and don't break your promise, you'll be constant." "Means that you keep doing anything." "Something is always keeping on and on." "Never-changing." "Everlasting." "Persistent."

Minus. "Following each other." "To repeat something." "Your mind on one thing all the time." "Like you were constant working all day." "Long. (Q.) If I were singing and I would hold it long, it would be constant." "Often." "Frequent." "When you're friends with somebody."

(b) *Courage.* (Bravery. Definitions which confuse courage with persistence or determination are scored minus.)

Plus. "The fellow's grit." "One who is brave." "You have a lot of spunk." "Someone that isn't afraid." "If you get hurt real bad, you just go on like you ain't." "Have enough courage to do something. (Q.) Do something you don't want to do 'cause you're afraid of getting hurt."

Minus. "Don't give up, you keep going. You've got courage, you don't give up." "To keep your hope up. (Q.) Don't give up." "Keep up energy to do anything — never get tired." "Keep on trying. (Q.) You don't give up what you're doing." "He has a lot of courage. (Q.) He wants to do it." "You have courage to do it, you can do it." "When one has ability to do something."

(c) *Charity*. (Love, especially with some notion of generous or spontaneous goodness. Benevolence to one's neighbors, especially the poor.)

Plus. "Kindly attitude. (Q.) Toleration and pity for one's fellow-men." "Good feeling toward one another." "Means that you help the poor." "Charity is like the community chest. The community chest gives money to charity. (Q.) Charity is something that takes care of poor people." "To love. (Q.) Like when you have charity you love people." "That helps you. (Q.) Like if you were out of work and they'd come down and give you food." "If you have to be helped by charity it means the community fund or some association would help you." "Means that you help people. (Q.) Help the poor."

Minus. "You have hope in everyone." "Something that you put money in, some kind of a club." "Out of work." "Anything free." "When people help you. (Q.) To be kind." "To be kind to people."

(d) *Defend*. (To guard from attack, protect.)

Plus. "To protect something." "To take another person's part." "If you're in a fight you should fight back and defend yourself." "Try to help yourself. (Q.) Shield yourself." "Defend means to fight for your country." "Take care of someone. (Q.) Protect them." "In a game you defend your goal, not let anybody cross it." "You help. (Q.) Help some other country in war."

Minus. "Get behind something. (Q.) Get behind a tree trunk when the Indians see you coming." "You're going to defend someone like if they got in trouble. (Q.) You'll defend someone." "Like somebody is going to capture you and you defend yourself — get away from them." "Fight it out. (Q.) To go against someone." "To try to keep up until you can't any more." "Help someone. (Q.) Help somebody with her work." "You got to watch somebody."

Two of the words must be correctly defined to pass the test.

6. Minkus Completion

This is a special form, devised by Minkus,[1] of the famous Ebbinghaus completion test.   It differs from other forms of the language-completion test in the fact that the omitted part is always a connecting word.   The idea is a clever one, for no other part of a complex or compound sentence is so crucial in the correct comprehension of the whole as the relational elements.   Such connection words as *if, although, however, for,* etc., are rather highly abstract.

The following samples include the possible choices for correct responses:

(a) *One cannot always be a hero,* ...... *one can always be a man.*
    Plus.   Although, while, yet, but, however, nevertheless, though.

(b) *The streams are dry* ...... *there has been little rain.*
    Plus.   If, therefore, where, after, because, since, for, as, when, so.

(c) ...... *either of us could speak, we were at the bottom of the stairs.*
    Plus.   Before.

(d) *He is* ...... *well grounded in geography* ...... *his brother,* ...... *he is not so quick in arithmetic.*
    Plus.   As — as — but (however, nevertheless, although, and); also — like — and (although, but); very — like — yet (although, while, but, and); considered — by — but (etc.); quite — like — but (etc.); very — unlike — but (etc.); isn't — like — and (etc.); "He is very well grounded in geography," said his brother, "but he is not so quick in arithmetic."

The test is passed if two of the four sentences are correctly completed.

---

[1] This special form of the completion method has been described by Minkus and Stern in two articles in the *Zeitschrift für Angewandte Psychologie,* 1919, 19, 1–71.

YEAR XIII

1. Plan of Search

The familiar "ball and field" problem has been changed in the present revision to the plan of search for a lost purse. The change was made in the interests of brevity of statement and simplification of directions. Scoring has been simplified by using the test at only one level and giving no credit for "inferior" plans.

The purpose of this test is to determine whether the subject can execute a plan of search that meets the logical requirements of the problem. Satisfactory evidence is based chiefly on the type of plan evolved. The paths must be almost parallel and there must be no intersections or breaks. The satisfactory types include mainly:

1. A spiral beginning either at the gate or at the center of the field and made up of fairly regular lines.

2. Concentric circles.

3. Transverse lines, parallel or almost so, and joined at the ends.

4. A line around the field which turns back on itself, then goes round again making an inner circle before turning back on itself to go round the field again, and so on covering the field.

Superimposed plans are not satisfactory unless both are clearly superior (conform to one of the above types) and are presumably given as alternative choices.

The samples on page 273 indicate the main types of satisfactory plans and give a few illustrations of the almost unlimited kinds of plans that have been scored minus because ill-adapted to the purpose.

PLUS

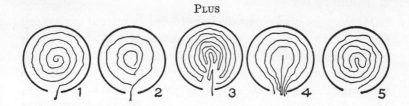

MINUS

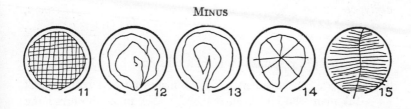

273

2. Memory for Words

Memory for discrete words is more closely related to memory for digits than it is to memory for sentences or stories in which the meaning element plays a more important rôle in recall. A number of word series were tried out, in some of which the words making up the series were related, in others were names of unrelated objects, and in others abstract words. This test includes two word series of comparable difficulty, one consisting of names of objects and the other of abstract words. The test has a correlation of .67 with the total score. One of the two series of words must be repeated without error.

3. Paper Cutting I (Cf. IX, 1)

Both drawings must be plus to pass the test.

4. Problems of Fact (Cf. XI, 5)

(a) *A man who was walking in the woods near a city stopped suddenly, very much frightened, and then ran to the nearest policeman, saying that he had just seen hanging from the limb of a tree a ......, what?*

The expected response is, a man who had been hanged.

> *Plus.* "A dead man." "A man who had been hung." "A man who had been lynched." "A man who had hung himself." "A skeleton." "A robber. (Q.) They'd hanged him." "A man. (Q.) Some robbers hung him."
>
> *Minus.* "Leaf." "A monkey." "Person. (Q.) Hanging from a tree. (Q.) Don't know." "A robber. (Q.) He was going to jump down on somebody."

(b) *My neighbor has been having queer visitors. First a doctor came to his house, then a lawyer, then a minister (preacher or priest). What do you think happened there?*

The expected answer is "a death," "someone has died," etc. However, this problem brings forth a wide variety of ingenious but rather far-fetched interpretations which are scored plus provided they can be *logically* and adequately explained by the subject.

It is almost always necessary to check the subject's response by asking what the lawyer came for and occasionally why the minister and doctor came. These must be correctly explained. The interpretation, in order to be considered satisfactory, must relate the visits of doctor, lawyer, and minister to a single event.

Plus. "Somebody died. (Q.) (Lawyer) to see about the will." "Somebody died. (Q.) (Lawyer) to see about the insurance policy." "Some one died, lawyer to settle the estate." "Got run over and killed. (Q.) (Lawyer) to try to settle the case." "A murder. (Q.) (Lawyer) came to look over the case and see what he could do about it. Minister to preach funeral sermon." "He must have got in a crash — got hurt (lawyer) to investigate what happened, (minister) maybe he died and said prayers." "Might have been some crime committed. If a man was shot the doctor came to fix his wounds, the lawyer came to see who did it and the minister to preach a sermon if he died."

Minus. "Somebody got sick and died. (Q.) (Lawyer) Because they'd have to get their doctor bills straightened." "Someone was dying. (Q.) Doctor for his money, lawyer for his money, minister came to pray for him." "Somebody died lawyer told them what to do." "A boy died or a girl or somebody. (Q.) To see about fixing up things." "They were sick. (Q.) (Lawyer) to see what the damage was done, (minister) to pray." "Someone was sick and then there was some trouble and then someone got married." "Doctor came with a baby and they have a license from the lawyer and the minister to marry them." "Maybe this lady was getting a divorce."

(c) *An Indian who had come to town for the first time in his life saw a white boy riding along the street. As the white boy rode by the*

Indian said, "The white boy is lazy; he walks sitting down." What was the white boy riding on that caused the Indian to say "he walks sitting down"?

The correct response is a bicycle.

Two of the three problems must be plus to pass the test.

5. Dissected Sentences

The task of the subject in rearranging the words of a dissected sentence is to relate the given parts to a meaningful whole. Here again is a variation of the very useful completion method.

A sentence is not counted correct if any word is omitted, altered, or inserted, or if the order given fails to make perfect sense. Certain responses are not absolutely incorrect, but are objectionable as regards sentence structure, or else fail to give the exact meaning intended. These are given half-credit.

(a) FOR THE STARTED AN WE COUNTRY EARLY AT HOUR

Plus. "We started for the country at an early hour." "At an early hour we started for the country." "We started at an early hour for the country."

Half-credit responses. "For the country at an early hour we started." "For the country we started at an early hour."

Minus. "We started early at an hour for the country." "We started early for the country." "And we started for the country at an early hour."

(b) TO ASKED PAPER MY TEACHER CORRECT I MY

Plus. "I asked my teacher to correct my paper."

Half-credit. "My teacher I asked to correct my paper." "To correct my paper I asked my teacher."

Minus. "My teacher asked to correct my paper." "I asked my teacher to correct the paper." "I asked the teacher to correct my paper."

(c) A DEFENDS DOG GOOD HIS BRAVELY MASTER

Plus. "A good dog defends his master bravely." "A good dog bravely defends his master." "A dog defends his good master bravely." "A dog bravely defends his good master."

Half-credit. "A good master bravely defends his dog." "His good dog bravely defends a master." "Bravely a master defends his good dog." "His good dog defends a master bravely."

Minus. "A dog defends his master bravely." "A bravely dog defends his master." "A good dog defends his bravely master." "A good brave dog defends his master."

A score of two is required to pass the test.

6. Copying a Bead Chain from Memory II (Cf. VI, 2)

There must be no error in the pattern to pass the test.

YEAR XIV

1. Vocabulary (Cf. pp. 302 ff.)

The score at this level must be sixteen to pass the test.

2. Induction

This test presents a series of events which affords a basis for making a generalization stating the governing principle involved. The subject must observe that each unfolded sheet contains twice as many holes as the previous one, and must infer that folding the paper again will again double the number. He must then state that doubling the number of holes contained in the preceding sheet, or multiplying that number by two, will predict the number in the succeeding sheet. It is ordinarily only after one or more mistakes have been made and have been disclosed by the examiner's unfolding the sheet for inspection that the correct principle is grasped.

The test is scored plus only if the rule is grasped and correctly stated. The criteria by which the examiner determines whether the rule has been grasped are:

1. Statement of the principle spontaneously before the sixth folding has been reached.

2. Giving the correct number of holes for the sixth folding regardless of the correctness or incorrectness of the responses for the preceding sheets, and then stating the correct principle.

Recapitulation of the correct number of holes for each folding does *not* constitute a statement of the principle. The following samples are illustrations of the standards which govern the scoring of responses to this test:

Plus. "Double it each time." "Two times the number that it is, if it was 4 when you folded it, it'd make 8." "Add the amount — like you have 8 and fold it again, add 8 more equals 16." "Every fold you make in the paper there'll be double the amount of holes."

Minus. "If you fold it once there is 1 hole, twice there's 2 holes, 3 times there's 4 holes, 4 times there's 8 holes, 5 times and there are 16 holes and then 6 times and there are 32." "By doubling it after it gets to 8." "Add more on every one." "At first you know it's 1 hole, or second it's 2 holes and on third it's 4 holes and then it gains 4 and then goes to 8 and gains 8 more and goes to 16 and gains 16 more and then goes to 32." "Multiply the last number by how many more times you fold it." "The number of times you fold it."

3. Picture Absurdities III (Cf. VII, 1)

Plus. "If the sun is shining his shadow would be on the other side of him." "His shadow wouldn't be like that — if the sun was shining that way." "His shadow's on the wrong side." "The shadow is going the wrong way." "His shadow's shining against the sun."

Minus. "The man's walking through the woods and the sun is shining and his shadow is in front of him and your shadow always goes in back of you most of the time." "His shadow is in front of him. (Q.) Because your shadow is always in back of you on a hot day." "The shadow, because it's facing a different way than he is." "He's walking this way and his shadow goes that way." "The sun hasn't risen and the man sees his shadow."

4. Ingenuity

The ingenuity test presents a task in ideational problem solving. "Mental manipulation" is involved under the guidance of a directing idea. Various methods of attack may be tried out, with the frequent result that the solution comes with a sudden flash of insight. The subject must work out his own methods. We do not solve the first problem for him in case he fails to find the solution for himself. Instead we have considerably simplified the first problem so that he will be able to solve it for himself if he is ingenious enough to hit upon the right method. The second and third problems are increasingly difficult because they involve certain complications over and above those involved in the first.

To receive credit on the test the subject must demonstrate the successive steps followed in his solution of the problem. To pass the test at this level one of the problems must be solved within the time allowed.

5. Orientation: Direction I

A number of orientation tests were experimented with in our preliminary try-outs of test items. Orientation in time and in space were the chief concepts studied, because of their significance in the development of the child's conception of the world. Various practical difficulties in formulating directions and in scoring interfered with the inclusion of the other items in the scale, so that only this rather complicated directions test remains. The test is scored plus if three of the items are passed.

6. Abstract Words II (Cf. XII, 5)

Three of the words must be correctly defined to pass the test at this level.

AVERAGE ADULT

1. Vocabulary (Cf. pp. 302 ff.)

Twenty words must be correctly defined to pass at this level.

2. Codes

The code tests used in the new revision differ from the old Stanford-Binet code test chiefly in one important particular: the problem is before the subject and the solution does not depend upon his remembering diagrams or other cues as a basis for mentally reconstructing a scheme that will give the solution. The present test has been modeled after one used in an English group test. The code test lends itself to almost indefinite complication; a more difficult problem has been included in Form M.

To receive full credit for a code there must be no error. Half-credit is allowed in either (a) or (b) where the response contains one error. One letter incorrectly coded constitutes an error. In the second code (b) where the code letters are in pairs, if either or both members of a pair are incorrect the count is one error, e.g., *IJ* TV QS QS XZ counts as one error. If R is twice coded incorrectly, it counts as two errors, e.g., I V *Q Q* Z counts as two errors.

It sometimes happens that the subject discovers an error in the first code while he is working on the second, and corrects it. Such spontaneous corrections are always credited if the time limit on that item has not already been reached. If at the end of three minutes the subject has not completed the last letter, that letter is counted as an error and, if there is no other error, he receives half-credit for the item. The requirement for plus is one and a half credits.

3. Differences between Abstract Words (Cf. VII, 2)

Success on this test depends upon the ability to point out the essential distinction between the pairs of stimulus words, a requirement which imposes a difficult task upon the powers of linguistic expression. For this reason, it is necessary in scoring to disregard clumsiness of expression and consider, rather, the essential correctness or incorrectness of the thought.

The following samples illustrate the standard for scoring responses:

(a) *Laziness and idleness*

The essential contrast is that laziness refers to unwillingness to work; idleness to inactivity. This contrast must be expressed, however clumsily.

> *Plus.* "When you're lazy you won't work and when you're idle you can't work because you haven't anything to do." "Laziness you just don't want to do anything, while idleness you stop and rest or something like that." "If you're lazy you'll do something but you don't like to do it and, if you're idle you don't do anything." "When you're lazy you don't want to do anything — just want to sit down and read or something like that, and when you're idle you're willing to do something." "If a person's out of work he's idle, but that doesn't make him necessarily lazy."

Minus. "Laziness you're too lazy to do something, idleness you're not quite lazy — just don't want to do it." "Laziness is wanting to sleep all the time and idleness is don't want to work." "Laziness you don't want to do nothing and idleness you have something to do but you don't do it — you just sit there." "They're both the same." (Frequent type of failure.) "Laziness you don't do anything at all and idleness you're just idle for the time being."

(b) *Poverty and misery*

Plus. "Poverty means to be in want; misery comes from any kind of suffering or anguish." "Misery is how you feel, like if you are cold, and poverty is when you are poor." "Poverty is to be poor, misery is to be sick or ill." "Can be poor but you don't have to be miserable." "Poverty means poor and misery means lack of food or water or to be sick." "You don't always have to be in poverty to be in misery, but poverty is usually misery."

Minus. "Misery you don't feel good and otherwise you feel good." "In poverty you're happy, in misery you're not happy." "One's in pain and the other is just the thought." "Misery — you're miserable, you don't feel good and I don't know poverty." (Frequent.) "Poverty some people owe a lot and that's their poverty, and misery you're in misery."

(c) *Character and reputation*

The essential distinction is, of course, that character is what you are and reputation is what is thought about you.

Plus. "Character is made up of all the qualities you possess and reputation is something you have acquired by acting out these qualities." "Character is what you really are and your reputation is what you're noted for." "Character tells what kind of a person you are and reputation is what you make, what people think of you." "Character is how you do things and reputation is what people think of you." "Reputation means your name and what you do, if you're good or bad, and character means yourself." "Your reputation is how you stand in your town or city and your character is your habits." "Character is what you are now and reputation is what you seem to be."

Minus. "When you have good character you're smart and know everything and have reputation, everybody knows you're doing good." "Character you do anything and reputation a lot of people know you." "Your character is yourself and reputation is the way you act." "Reputation is what you do, whether it's right or wrong, and character is your ideals and if you live up to them."

The test is passed if two of the three comparisons are correct.

4. Arithmetical Reasoning

The ability to solve these arithmetical problems correlates to the extent of .61 with the rest of the scale. The test also meets the requirements for the scale in showing a steady increase in per cent passing with age. The computations required to solve the problems are ordinarily performed easily by adults, but it is the selection of the processes to be employed and their application to the problem that constitutes the difficulty of the task. Two of the three problems must be correctly solved to pass the test.

5. Proverbs I

The proverb tests have replaced the fables of the old scale. They have the virtue of being much simpler to give and at least no harder to score, though considerable acumen and discrimination are required. We give an example to illustrate what is involved in the task and the subject is then required to explain the meaning of other proverbs in the same way.

The task is a difficult one, even for adults, since a pertinent generalization is required, based on the rather cryptic, homely situations into which folkways of thinking have become crystallized. Thus the proverb must be analyzed, abstracted, and applied to life situations. Particularized or literal interpretation is not satisfactory. The interpretation of a given proverb in terms of another pertinent proverbial saying is satisfactory because in order to arrive at such a response the subject must not only have generalized from the particular situation presented by the given proverb but have gone a step farther and reapplied the generalization. Awkwardness of verbal expression is disregarded if the generalization is correct. Failures are of three types: (a) inability to respond; (b) literal interpretation, i.e., explaining the statement without generalization; and (c) incorrect or inappropriate generalizations.

The following are samples of plus and minus responses:

(a) *A burnt child dreads the fire.*

The expected response is that a person who has had an unpleasant experience avoids the same or a similar experience in the future; that one learns by experience.

> *Plus.* "Experience is a good teacher." "If you've made a mistake, you don't like to make that mistake again." "If you do something wrong once, you learn not to do that same thing again." "After feeling the pain caused at one time, the child avoids similar occurrences." "Something hurts somebody, they got hurt or something like that and they would hate the thing, wouldn't go near it."
> *Minus.* "Because she's afraid of getting burned." "Means that after he knows what fire will do to anyone, he will stay away from it." (Not generalized.) "After you've already done something you hate it." "Everybody learns their lesson." "If somebody is in an accident, they dread another." "A child that is burnt he won't play with fire, he don't like it, he is afraid of it." "Just because you've been hurt or discouraged by something, that's no reason to be afraid to do it again or to try it." "If you try something and it hasn't been successful you won't try again."

(b) *He who would eat the kernel must crack the nut.*

For a satisfactory response the subject must suggest that one who wishes to enjoy good things must earn them, that the good things of life do not just fall into one's lap.

Plus. "Anybody who wants anything must go after it to get it." "If you want to have a good time, have enough to eat and have good beds, etc., you have to work for it. You can't get it without working." "Anybody that wants the good of things, they have to go through the bad." "To obtain a thing you have to fight for it and not get it easy." "A person can't do all the easy things, he has to do some of the hard things, too." "To succeed in anything you have to start at the bottom and do the really hard things to get at the good things of life, break through the more difficult ones." "If you want something good you've first got to get to it." "If you want to do something to make you famous, you couldn't start right at the top, you must begin at the bottom."

Minus. "If you want to get to what is inside you have to crack the outside." "One may not always play, but have to work." "If you want to get inside of anything or get to anything you have to start at the beginning." "Not to expect someone to do everything for you." "If we want anything done *well*, do it ourselves." "If you want to learn about something you must go deep into it." "If you want to do any great thing you must start it. If you want to get in the room you must open the door."

(c) *A drowning man will catch at a straw.*

A satisfactory response suggests that a person who is in desperate straights will grasp at any forlorn hope; in an extremity a person will resort to any expedient.

Plus. "Anybody that hasn't much hope will grab at anything that seems like hope." "A person will never give up until he has exhausted everything." "Person out of work will take anything." "You'll grab at anything when you're near death, but you take only bigger and best when there's no danger." "Any old port in a storm." "Any friend at all is a good friend in need." "A person will take the last hope that there is." "You always take a chance when you're in danger, when you're in deep danger."

Minus. "Any man that is going down will catch at anything small." "He will grasp at anything for life." "We don't give up until we show we're lost." "A person that's failed or anything will try to do something to pull himself up again."

Two of the three proverbs must be plus to pass the test.

6. Ingenuity (Cf. XIV, 4)

The test is passed at this level if two of the problems are correctly solved.

7. Memory for Sentences V (Cf. XI, 4)

One of the sentences must be repeated without error to pass the test.

8. Reconciliation of Opposites

Giving similarities involves the recognition of the likeness of objects that are not identical. Children of seven are able to make such comparisons and to point out some common characteristics of an apple and a peach like roundness or edibility, but it is a long step to the ability to find the identity in opposites. Indeed, it is not until the adult levels that we have found our subjects able to recognize the likeness of qualities of objects, as contrasted with the objects themselves, and of qualities that are not only not identical but which appear to be mutually exclusive or opposite in character. For the response to be satisfactory at this level some general concept must be discovered which defines an essential characteristic of the qualities. That they are opposites or antonyms or extremes would not, of course, be satisfactory, nor is a grammatical classification acceptable, like "they are both adjectives." If the subject gives such a classification the question should be repeated. The following are illustrations of satisfactory and unsatisfactory responses:

(a) *Heavy and light*

    Plus. "Both weights." "Both refer to weight." "Show weight." "Both are measures of weight." "Both measurements." "Both amounts."

    Minus. "'Cause you're still lifting." "Both words that show when you have a load." "They're both almost the same weight." "Both have the same number of letters."

(b) *Tall and short*

    Plus. "Both show size." "They tell length." "They describe your stature." "Both degrees of height." "Both height." "They're both an estimate of distance." "They're both measurements." "Both dimensions."

    Minus. "Both pertain to people." "Because you have to measure for both of them." "Both describe." "Both just so high." "Both degree. (Q.) Degree of tallness or shortness."

(c) *Sick and well*

    Plus. "Shows the condition you are in — your health." "Both express health." "The two extremes of health." "How you feel." "They're the feeling — if a person feels well, you say he's well." "Both feelings." "Both conditions of the body." "Both apply to the body." "They're both expressions of how you are."

    Minus. "They tell how." "Both ways of living." "Has to be a person." "Both happen to you." "Both have life." "You can be both." "Different ways people can get — can be well or sick."

(d) *More and less*

Plus. "Both expressions of a degree, that is to be added or subtracted." "Both extent." "They show proportion." "They're amounts." "Extremes of abundance." "Both mean how much." "Tells of quantity." "Both ways of measuring," etc.

Minus. "Both are adjectives. (Q.) Both are characteristics of property or valuation." "Both pertain to products." "Extremes in money." "Much is a greater quantity and less is a small quantity." "You can have more of one thing and less of something." "Two different sizes."

(e) *Outside and inside*

Plus. "Both tell where." "Location." "Both situations." "Pertaining to whereabouts." "They're both at some place." "Both are characteristics of a solid." "It's where you are, inside your house or outside."

Minus. "Someplace outside or inside." "Both pertaining to a building." "Both sides." "Places to walk through." "Both surroundings."

(f) *Asleep and awake*

Plus. "Consciousness." "Condition of the brain." "Just pertain to the mind of a person." "The way your mind is." "Both tell the physical condition." "Two states of being." "The two things living is divided into." "Both conditions. (Q.) The way your body is."

Minus. "Both pertaining to people." "They both mean action." "They're used in helping somebody grow." "Both movements of the body." "Both tell what you're doing." "Tells what you are."

The test is passed if three of the six comparisons are correct.

SUPERIOR ADULT I

1. Vocabulary (Cf. pp. 302 ff.)

The requirement for plus at this level is a score of twenty-three.

2. Enclosed Box Problem

The problem of the enclosed boxes requires for its solution the complex factors involved in ideational problem solving which have already been discussed in connection with other tests. This test has provoked considerable speculation concerning the kind of imagery that may make up the pattern of thinking involved. Our data are, of course, inadequate to reveal such patterns, but an analysis of errors in the test indicates that failure is usually the result of applying the wrong arithmetical operation in computing the number of boxes. One might infer that in the case of such errors, at least in the last two problems, little use has been made of visual imagery. The test is passed if three of the problems are correctly solved.

3. Minkus Completion (Cf. XII, 6)

The test is passed if three of the sentences are plus.

4. Repeating Six Digits Reversed (Cf. IX, 6)

One of the three series must be correctly repeated to pass the test.

5. Sentence Building

This test is another of the many forms of the completion test, but in the present instance success depends less upon the ability to combine isolated elements into a meaningful whole than on word comprehension. Failure is rarely due to inability to combine the words into a single sentence. All three words must, of course, be included in one sentence. The words must be correctly used and the sentence must not be ungrammatical. The only change permitted in the form of the key words is in number, plural may be used for singular. Nouns must not be changed to verbs. Failure to comprehend the meaning of a word results either in inability to respond or guessing, revealed in the bizarre character of the sentence.

The following are samples of satisfactory and unsatisfactory responses:

(a) *Benefactor — Institution — Contribution*

Plus. "A benefactor joined an institution and gave them a contribution." "They made a contribution to the benefactor of the institution." "The people gave a contribution to the institution of the benefactor." "The institution was a contribution of that benefactor." "An institution depends on the contributions of the benefactors." "The benefactor to an institution made a contribution yearly."

Minus. "The benefactor of his estate gave the institution all of his contribution." "Contribution is a great benefactor of the modern institution."

(b) *Civility — Requirement — Employee*

Plus. "Civility is one of the requirements of an employee." "The requirement for the employee was civility." "Civility of the employee was the requirement." "Civility is a requirement from an employee." "Civility is a requirement in every employee."

Minus. "The requirement for an employee is his civility." "The requirement of the office was that the employee should use civility." "The employee had a requirement of civility." "An employee depends on the requirement of civility."

(c) *Attainment — Fortune — Misery*

Plus. "The attainment of a great fortune always brings misery." "His attainment instead of bringing fortune brought misery." "Attainment of fortune may cause misery." "He was in misery but his attainment of the fortune will brighten him up." "One must go through a certain amount of misery to the attainment of fortune."

Minus. "His fortune gave him attainment for a while, but later misery." "The man went through a lot of misery to get the attainment of the fortune." "He reached his attainment by making his fortune but was only rewarded with misery." "Fortune is an attainment for misery."

Two sentences must be plus to pass the test.

6. Essential Similarities (Cf. VII, 2 and A.A., 8)

The following samples are illustrations of the standards for scoring:

(a) *Farming and manufacturing*

It is permissible to place the emphasis either on the activity of *producing*, or on *providing* that which supplies human needs.

Plus. "Both are creative." "Both make products." "Both put out something that people use." "Both produce goods from raw materials." "They both produce food and clothing for people." "They're both making something. In farming you're making new plants and manufacturing you're making new clothes or shoes or things. They're both the processes of making." "Both make things for human consumption." "They both supply the cities with goods."

Minus. "Both of them helps to make our country bigger." "You get things out of both of them." "Both employ a lot of people." "Both sell things." "They are both working places." "Both bring in money."

(b) *Melting and burning*

For this essential similarity the subject may give consideration either to the effect in changing the form of substances, or to the necessity for accompanying heat.

Plus. "The form of substances is altered by either process." "Both destroy the shapes of things." "Melting is changing that substance into a different form and fire is changing that substance into a different form." "Both changes, one chemical and the other physical." "They both change the thing that burns or melts." "Both require heat."

Minus. "When you melt something and burn something you bring it down to a smaller substance." "Both solid at the beginning and not when you get through." "They both produce a great heat." "Melting usually never comes back into the same shape and burning never does." "They both have to do with cooking and heating." "Giving off water in both processes."

(c) *Egg and seed*

Plus. "Both undeveloped plants or animals." "Both become something." "Life is hatched from egg and life grows from seed, too." "They're both for making new animals." "Both form plants or animals." "Raise more stuff with either one of 'em." "They both bring forth fruit."

Minus. "Eggs you can hatch chickens and seeds you can grow plants out of them." "They are both products of something else." "Seed is produced by the parent plant and egg is produced by the parent hen." "A plant comes out of a seed and a chicken comes out of an egg." "Both hatch out of something." "Both produce a food."

Two of the three comparisons must be correct to pass the test.

SUPERIOR ADULT II

1. Vocabulary (Cf. pp. 302 ff.)

The requirement for passing at this level is twenty-six words.

2. Finding Reasons II (Cf. X, 4)

At this level, we expect a response of a better quality than was required in the Finding Reasons test at year X. The reasons, while not limited to the most essential, must be valid, definite, and clearly differentiated. Failure is due chiefly to inability to give three reasons, and the examiner must be on the watch for the same reason repeated in different words.

(a) *Give three reasons why some people use typewriters which cost so much when they could get pen and ink for a few cents.*

Acceptable reasons include chiefly those which mention: (a) ease and convenience in use; (b) neatness and appearance; (c) speed; (d) legibility; (e) custom; and (f) economy.

Plus. "They're faster, easier, more legible." "A typewriter's so much quicker. Shows up neater. It's printed." "The typewriter is more convenient, and it can be read by other people easily, and it is cheaper to run a typewriter than it is to write with pen and ink." "They can do the work quicker, and better, and you can read it better." "You can read typewritten things better. If you've got a typewriter it's easier to get a position from some people by typing a letter to them. When you write stories to a magazine some magazines only want typewritten stories."

Minus. "A typewriter is better and it's faster, and you can do it quicker with a typewriter." "Because they can do their work faster and get more money by doing it faster and save time." "Typewriter can go faster than pen and ink. You can read it sometimes better than pen and ink. You don't have to help it."

(b) *Give three reasons why a man who commits a serious crime should be punished.*

The following categories include most of the acceptable reasons:

(a) To teach him a lesson.

(b) To set an example for others.

(c) To prevent his doing it again.

(d) To prevent his doing something worse.

(e) To protect society.

(f) To make him suffer for his wrong-doing.

(g) To uphold the law.

Plus. "So that he wouldn't do it again. To show people what they'd get if they did it themselves. To show the person who did it that that was the wrong thing to do." "'Cause if they let him go he may do it over again. Next time he might do something worse. If they don't, other people will start doing it." "So he won't do it again. So he'd repay for the crime he's done. To see how wrong the thing he's done is." "So he won't do it again. To teach a lesson for others. Doing bad is a sin." "So he won't hurt anybody else. He committed the crime and made the person suffer so he has to suffer. If you commit a crime it's against the law so you have to be punished for it." "If he isn't punished he might think he can get by with it again. It would show young boys — teach them a lesson. The laws have to be enforced." "To keep him from committing other crimes. When a man commits a crime and is not punished by law someone usually tries to punish him in some way. It wouldn't be fair to let him go." "Avenge society. To make an example of him for others. Make him pay for his folly." "If he isn't punished he'll repeat the crime. He is dangerous to the community. He is liable to influence someone else into committing crimes." (Doubtful, but probably should be plus.)

Minus. "Because if they don't punish him he might kill somebody else. And then he might steal something and then he might go and burn up something." (Stated in terms of the concrete situation.) "Because he shouldn't kill no one. And he's breakin' the law and no one lets anyone get away with committing a serious crime." "The other fellow's got as much rights as he has. He's disobeying the law. Spoiling family reputation." "A man ought to be punished so he won't think he can do anything and get away with it. He ought to be punished because it will probably give compensation to the person against whom he did the crime. And I think he ought to be punished because if he's punished it would teach him a good lesson so he won't do it again." "Because if he isn't he'll do it again and somebody else will do it again and the city won't like the people that got him free." "If he did the act willfully he should be punished, if it was against someone else's property. Because if he was let go it would serve as a bad example for the courts."

Both items must be plus to pass the test.

3. Repeating Eight Digits (Cf. IV–6, 2)

The test is passed if one of the three series is repeated correctly.

4. Proverbs II (Cf. A.A., 5)

(a) *A bird in the hand is worth two in the bush.*

A satisfactory response must convey the idea that a present benefit of which you are certain is better than a larger one of which you are not certain.

> *Plus.* "One thing which you are absolutely certain of is worth two uncertain things." "Anything that you have right now you had better take instead of taking a chance to get more — the stock market for instance." "A chance that you have is better than two you are expecting." "It's not what you hope to obtain but what you already have that counts." "When you really have something it is worth more than what you think you are going to have." "If you have something small don't let it go for anything better that might fail." "A dollar in your pocket is worth two dollars in accounts receivable." "Don't gamble."
>
> *Minus.* "If you had one bird in your hand it would be better than two in the bush where you can't get at them."

"Don't let your opportunities slip away." "A thing you own is better than something you don't." "If you got something ahead of you that you can get, get it but don't grab at anything that's not in clear view — something that you're not positive of having." "Something that you have is worth more than something that you have lost or you're working for."

(b) *You can't make a silk purse out of a sow's ear.*

An acceptable response expresses the idea that it is not possible to transcend natural limitations. A particular example is satisfactory if it is clearly applicable.

Plus. "Culture isn't just a veneer." "You can't make something wonderful that wasn't anything to begin with." "You can't make something fine out of something that wasn't naturally that way." "You can't make good things out of poor material." "You have got to have the real thing to make something." "You can't make a noble out of a peasant." "You can't make something what it isn't." "You can't make something out of nothing."

Minus. "If a person isn't good, they can't be made good." "If a person hasn't had a good environment he can't make as much out of himself as a person that has had a good environment." "You can't make something out of something when it's supposed to be made out of something else." "You can't make one thing from another which is not the same." "You can't make everything good if you haven't got things to make it out of. You can't pretend you have something when you haven't."

Both proverbs must be correctly explained to pass the test.

5. Reconciliation of Opposites (Cf. A.A., 8)

Five of the items must be plus to pass the test at this level.

6. Repeating Thought of Passage: Value of Life

This passage can be divided into the following component ideas:

(a) Many opinions have been given on the value of life.

(b) Some call it good,

(c) others call it bad.

(d) It would be nearer correct to say that it is mediocre,

(e) for on the one hand our happiness is never as great as we should like,

(f) and on the other hand our misfortunes are never as great as our enemies would wish for us.

(g) It is this mediocrity of life which prevents it from being radically unjust.

Satisfactory responses include those in which there is accurate reproduction of at least four of these seven divisions, except that in case a, b, and c are given, there must be two in addition. In any other combination four are sufficient for a satisfactory response, providing gratuitous invention does not contradict the theme and thus invalidate the response. Accurate recall is taken to be an index of comprehension of the passage. The ideas may, of course, be expressed in the subject's own language. Neither elegance of expression nor verbatim repetition is expected.

Plus. "Many opinions have been given on life. Some say it is good, some bad, but it is mediocrity. We can not have as much as our enemies wish and we can't have as much happiness as we wish." (a b c d e f) "There have been many opinions of life made. Some are good and some are bad. Our misfortunes are not as great as our enemies would like and our miseries are not as little as we would like, but these are the med — I don't know how to say it — mediocolus of life — something like that." (a b c e f) "Some — many opinions have been given about life. Some say it is good and some say it is bad but it is termed mediocre, because the goodness is not as good as we would want it to be and the badness is not as bad as our enemies would want it to be so life is unfair." (So many elements have been reproduced correctly that misunderstanding of the final idea does not invalidate this response.) (a b c d e f) "Many definitions have been given life. Some say it is good and some say it is not. But it is never as good as we could make it and is never as bad as it could be. These are both wrong. It is really medium." (a b c d e f) "Many people's opinions are that life is good or bad, but it is better to think it is medium because our misfortunes are not as great as our enemies might wish them." (b c d f) "It is better to say that life is medium than to say it is good or bad because we never have the discomforts that our enemies would wish us to have or never have the pleasant things that we and our friends would want to have." (b c d e, f slightly inaccurate.)

Minus. "There's — many things — in the value of life — some call it good and some call it bad, but it really is mediocre because our happiness is never what we like and mediocre takes in all the things." (b c d, e reproduced incorrectly.) "Great opinions have been given to life, some say it's good and some say it's bad — our misfortunes are never as great as our enemies would like for it to be." (a b c d) "There are many opinions given about our life, but even though there are many disappointments and many times our happiness is greater than might be and misfortunes are not so many but our enemies wish they were more. This keeps us medium, we can live through it if we have some happiness with our unhappiness." (Note invention.) (a f d) "Many things have been said about our life, but our happiness is never as great as we would wish it and our misfortunes are never as great as our enemies would wish it to be." (a e f)

SUPERIOR ADULT III

1. Vocabulary (Cf. pp. 302 ff.)

The requirement for plus at this level is thirty words.

2. Orientation: Direction II (Cf. XIV, 5)

(a) The correct answer is East.

(b) The only correct answer is ½ (mile).

The most frequent failure, aside from inability to answer, is 4½, at which, of course, the subject arrives by calculating the distance he has traversed rather than the actual distance that he now is from his starting point. This is the only one of our tests which presents anything like a catch question. The error mentioned is occasionally made even by a very bright subject. However, the test shows a high correlation with the composite score and an increase in the per cent passing at successive ages.

Both parts must be plus to pass the test.

3. Opposite Analogies II (Cf. IV–6, 6)

(a) *A rabbit is timid; a lion is* ......
> *Plus.* "Bold." "Brave." "Courageous." "Unafraid." "Fearless."
> *Minus.* "Not afraid." "Wild." "Ferocious." "Savage." "Vicious." "Fierce." "Dangerous."

(b) *The pine tree is evergreen; the poplar is* ......
> *Plus.* "Deciduous."
> *Minus.* "Dies in winter." "Leaf-falling tree." "Tree that sheds it's leaves." "Changeable."

(c) *A debt is a liability; an income is* ......
> *Plus.* "An asset." "Resource."
> *Minus.* "Help." "Profit." "Credit." "Salary." "Money coming in."

Two of the three items must be plus to pass the test.

4. Paper Cutting II (Cf. IX, 1)

The creases must all be represented and the holes correctly located.   The shape of the holes is disregarded; i.e., either triangular or imperfect diamond shapes are allowed, but they must be drawn so as to be intersected by the crease on which they are located.

On page 301 are samples of plus and minus drawings.

5. Reasoning (Cf. XIV, 4)

The expected answer is 40½ inches.   Since, however, one can, by considering the growth increment in terms of arithmetic ratio rather than geometric, arrive at 40 (inches) as the answer, credit is given for this response also, but *only* when the subject can satisfactorily explain how he arrived at it, for this answer is frequently only a guess.   The two methods are as follows:

Geometric:

1st year $8 + \frac{1}{2} = 12$	i.e., the tree increases each year
2d year $12 + \frac{1}{2} = 18$	at the rate of $\frac{1}{2}$ its total height
3d year $18 + \frac{1}{2} = 27$	at the beginning of the year.
4th year $27 + \frac{1}{2} = 40\frac{1}{2}$	

Arithmetic:

1st year $8 + 4 = 12$
2d year $12 + 6 = 18$ (2 inches greater increment than 1st year)
3d year $18 + 9 = 27$ (3 inches greater increment than 2d year)
4th year $27 + 13 = 40$ (4 inches greater increment than 3d year)

Guessing at the answer is very common, particularly in the case of students, and the guesses are often very close, such as "40" and "41."   However, the response "40½," not being a round number, is not likely to be guessed and does not need to be explained; nor should the examiner ask for an explanation of any other answer except "40," since to do so would be equivalent to giving the subject a second chance.

PLUS   MINUS

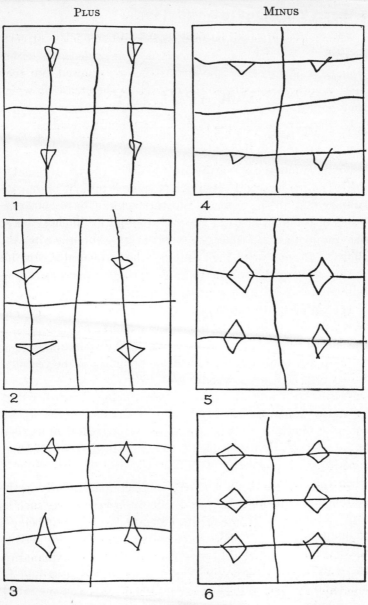

1   4

2   5

3   6

6. Repeating Nine Digits (Cf. IV–6, 2)

One of the three series must be repeated correctly to pass the test.

VOCABULARY

(VI, 1; VIII, 1; X, 1; XII, 1; XIV, 1; A.A., 1; S.A. I, 1; S.A. II, 1; S.A. III, 1)

We have found the vocabulary test to be the most valuable single test in the scale. Its interest value is high, it presents a familiar task to the subject, and the fact that it begins with words in common use and increases rapidly in difficulty gives the examiner a rapid survey method of estimating the subject's ability. It agrees to a high degree with the mental age rating on the scale as a whole; correlations for single age groups range from .65 to .91 with an average of .81.

The extension of the vocabulary downward to the six-year level as well as upward to the superior adult level has proved feasible because of the selection and present arrangement of words on the basis of their difficulty for children and for adults. Such words as *orange, envelope, straw, puddle, tap*, and *roar* are sufficiently concrete and common to the child's experience that he is able even at the age of six to formulate definitions precise enough to indicate that he knows the word. How an orange looks, what you do with an envelope, or an item of personal experience with a puddle, such as "You can get muddy in it when you step in it," refer directly to the child's world. Our scoring standards, based as they are on empirical findings, reflect to some extent successive stages in the development of thinking. In general, the more abstract and more difficult the word the more rigid the scoring requirements. Then, too, there are characteristic differences in quality of response for older and younger subjects even on the simpler words. Thus the adult gives a response which classifies a common object, but also isolates it by excluding other objects which do not belong to the class. Both a six-year-old and a sixteen-year-old know the meaning of orange — "it is round and has seeds" or "it is a citrus fruit" — but their thinking is characteristically different.[1]

It is important for the examiner to realize that the purpose of this vocabulary test is to determine whether the subject knows the meaning of the word, not whether he can give a completely logical definition. Awkwardness of expression is disregarded. It is often necessary to determine by additional questions, as indicated in the testing procedure, whether the meaning is apprehended. The examiner must determine whether, when the subject says brunette is a color of hair, he means dark hair or blonde. Of course only the former is scored plus.

[1] Since the ability to note and formulate abstract relationships, to generalize, is characteristic of the higher mental levels, it seemed to us that a scoring system which would take account of qualitative differences in responses might give a more satisfactory scoring system for the vocabulary. Accordingly special studies were made by two graduate student assistants with a view to determining the feasibility of such a scheme. A study of the first fifty words of the Stanford-Binet vocabulary (the old scale) was made by Barbara Marx in 1928. (Barbara Marx. *A Study of the First Fifty Words of the Stanford-Binet Vocabulary.* Unpublished master's thesis, 1928. Stanford University Library.) In 1931 Helen J. Green, then one of our research assistants, worked out a method of weighted scoring for each word in accordance with the relation between the quality of the response and the developmental level of the subject. (Helen J. Green. *A Qualitative Method for Scoring the Vocabulary Test of the New Revision of the Stanford-Binet.* Unpublished master's thesis, 1931. Stanford University Library.) While the study indicated that such a scheme was possible and yielded many psychologically interesting results, the method did not prove to be practical. The additional time and trouble entailed did not yield a corresponding return in increased value of the test. Correlation between mental age and score on the vocabulary was increased from .91 to .94 for the age range from seven to the adult level when weighted score was used instead of the all-or-none credit score. The scheme required more time and probably involved more subjective factors, though the reliability as indicated by the degree of agreement between two experienced examiners, one of them not specially trained in the qualitative method, was found to be .997.

Miss Green reports in her study the results of the vocabulary test for a group of 110 adults ranging in age from 19 to 84. Care was taken to secure a representative sampling according to economic and social status. Her investigation indicates that there is no great change in this ability after maturity is reached. The correlation between age and vocabulary score was found to be .09. Several other studies have shown that vocabulary remains practically unimpaired to extreme old age.

The following are illustrative of satisfactory and unsatisfactory definitions.

1. *Orange*

Plus. "A fruit." "Like a tangerine." "Tree." "A drink." "It's orange juice." "What you drink" (eat, squeeze, cut, suck). "An orange is sweet." "An orange is something to eat." "It's round." "It's yellow." "An orange is orange color."

Minus. "Lemon." "Orange. (Q.) Don't know." "Red."

2. *Envelope*

Plus. "For a letter." "Paper. (Q.) You write letters." "To read. (Q.) To mail." "To write. (Q.) A letter." "What you send." "To put things in." "An envelope is straight and it has a cover." "It's sticky on the top so you can paste it down."

3. *Straw*

Plus. "You suck it." "Paper. (Q.) When you put it in a soda it bends." "For orange juice." "To blow through." "Kind of round stick." "To eat. (Q.) For the cows." "Dried grass." "Hay." "From the oats after they've been thrashed." "It's a plant." "It's fiber of some sort." "It's used for baskets and hats." "Straw is what you make a straw house out of." "What chickens lay on." "Make chairs like this." "Brooms have it." "Play in. (Q.) You can pick up and throw it all over you and throw it all over other people." "You can put it on strawberries and things. (Q.) So the frost won't get 'em." "You tickle people with it."

Minus. "It's the same as a leaf that grows on a certain tree." "Piece of wood." "Like — bale straw. (Q.) It's a little straw." "Straw is something that's in piles." "Long." "It bends." (Q. No response.) "Piece of straw." (Q. No response.)

4. *Puddle*

Plus. "A puddle of water." "Water." "Rain makes it." "Mud." "Little pond." "A puddle is when it's raining." "What you step in." "You can sail boats in." "You can play in puddles." "For little frogs." "That's what the baby does."

Minus. "A puddle is where some fishes swim." "A plaything." "Just a puddle of water that people swim in." "You go in bathing." "To play games." "A brook of water."

5. *Tap*

Plus. "You make a little noise." "Tap on the door" (or floor, table, blocks, etc.). "Tap your foot." "You tap a bell." "Somebody is at the door." "Rain on the roof." "Dance." "Tap a shoe." "Like a heel plate on your shoes." "Tap is to hold some water in somewhere." "Something that you take out of a hole. (Q.) Like tap a barrel of cider." "Faucet." "Tap trees." "That makes music. (Q.) Have to make music — the taps." S. just illustrates tapping with hand or foot.

6. *Gown*

Plus. "A nightgown." "To sleep in." "When you go to bed." "Night — night pajamas or something." "Wear it." "Put on." "Evening gown." "Sort of a cloak." "King's wedding gown. (Q.) Big robe."

7. *Eyelash*

Plus. "Hair that protects your eyes." "When you blink your eyes the eyelash keeps it from going too far back." "Part of your eyelid" (points correctly). "To keep insects from flying into your eyes." "Hair over the eyes" (Q. points correctly). Subject points to eyelash.

Minus. "The top part of the skin that comes down over the eye." "Hair above the eye" (Q. points to eyebrows and eyelashes, both). "Hair right over your eye it's neither these (lashes) or these (brows) I always forget." "Covering of your eye" (Q. points to lid). The child should be asked to point to it because eyelash is frequently confused with eyebrow.

8. *Roar*

The examiner should take special pains to pronounce this word distinctly. If it is understood as "raw" or "oar" the word should be repeated.

> *Plus.* "Noise." "A roaring sound." "A racket." "Something that makes noise" (subject growls). "From some animal." "A lion roars." "A car roars." "When the wind roars." "A seashell roars." "A wolf or somebody goes roarrrr." "Cannon roars." "Angry. (Q.) A lion roars when he is angry." "When you're fierce." "When it thunders." "A ocean roars." "You laugh — roar."

9. *Scorch*

> *Plus.* "To apply flames to overheat." "It's to burn." "Burn your clothes with an iron." "Scorch a dress. (Q.) Means with an iron." "Burn your pants up. (Q.) When mother pressed Daddy's pants she scorched 'em." "Means you make something brown." "When something gets awful hot." "Person could be scorched by touching the stove — a part of burn." "Singe." "It's a hot day. (Q.) Scorching hot."
>
> *Minus.* "You scorch a thing. (Q.) Takes whitening out of clothes." "Scorch a potato. (Q.) Peel a potato." "You burnt yourself — with hot water." (scald) "Scorch your clothes. (Q.) You got too much blueing." "I was in a fire and I was scorched. (Q.) You were just burnt to pieces." "Scorch yourself with some hot water." "Stain. (Q.) When something like ink drops on it, it stains."

10. *Muzzle*

> *Plus.* "Anybody's nose." "Mouth." "Muzzle is for a dog. (Q.) On a dog's face." "You put it on a dog to keep him from biting — a leather strap." "Harness. (Q.) Dogs

have muzzles — kind of a harness put on 'em to stop 'em from biting." "Something to put on a dog. (Q.) Sometimes in hot weather they put them on so they won't bite." "What you put on your horse. (Q.) Because he eats when you want to plow corn." "Thing you put on a calf to keep it from sucking a cow." "A mask. (Q.) Something to keep a dog from biting." "Prevent a thing from doing something. (Q.) Shut down on it." "Muzzle of a gun. (Q.) Top of the gun barrel."

Minus. "Something you put on a dog. (Q.) So it can't get away." "Harness" (minus unless explained). "A little round thing that dogs wear — you put it around his neck." "A dog has a muzzle. (Q.) Thing you hold a dog with." "Something to put on a horse. (Q.) It holds a horse." "It's something you wear over your face." (pitcher's mask) "Thing when they play baseball they put over the face." "A muzzle on a gun. (Q.) The barrel." "The long part of a gun." "If there's a big roaring sound they'd put something over it to make it not so noisy." (muffle) "Muzzle is on hose." (nozzle)

11. *Haste*

Plus. "Hurry." "Not to lose time." "Run." "Want to do something. (Q.) Want to get something in a hurry." "Haste to get something. (Q.) Run." "If I had to haste to go I'd have to go right then." "Make haste. (Q.) Hurry up." "Better be shaking along." "Right away."

Minus. "Haste is to get ready." "When you run away. (Q.) You don't like it." "Haste away. (Q.) Do something." "Like you say haste. (Q.) It means go — like you say, haste for some water." "Haste is like you're going some place." "It means get out." "If you run away from somebody or make haste for somebody. (Q.) Like if you go after somebody."

12. *Lecture*

Plus. "A speech." "Lecture is a man who talks." "Like somebody tells you something." "Explain it to somebody."

"A lesson telling you how to do something." "Tell people not to do it." "Some place where you go and they tell you something." "Lecture — well they have that in church, somebody preaches." "If you did something. (Q.) The lecture tells you what you should do and stuff like that." "Get a lecture if you do something you shouldn't do." "Meeting of people where a person speaks."

Minus. "When you vote, elect a president." "Something you go to." (Q. No response.) "Sit straight." "Turn on the radio." "Meeting. (Q.) What you see in the movies." "Church." "They gave a lecture at the high school. (Q.) They're going to give a play." "Something like a meeting. (Q.) Sometimes they elect people for president or they talk about it." "When a man's mad."

13. *Mars*

Plus. "It's a god of war." "What the Greeks used to worship." "Man. (Q.) Mars was the man who March was named after." "Another world like this one." "A planet." "Star." "A group of stars. (Q.) Mars is something like Venus and travels around." "Some kind of a comet like the world." "Land out in space." "Up by the moon." "Scratch something that's painted."

Minus. "Some other city." "Mars is a different kind of people." "Means clouds — up near the clouds." "Things up in the sky — them round balls." "A name of a place. (Q.) Don't know." "Name of some man." "Someone in the sky." "The stars and the moon that shine at night."

14. *Skill*

Plus. "If you do something real well." "Ease and gracefulness in doing a thing." "Ability." "Means sly or smart at some tricks." "Practiced." "Like you are skilled in playing basketball. (Q.) You are successful." "You're talented." "Trained." "Brains. (Q.) They say it takes a lot of skill to be something good." "What you specialize in." "Skill means to have a great deal of knowledge." "How you do a thing." "He can work good — like he's a skilled worker." "What you can do best." "Very clever, smart." "Somebody that can do something very well and fast." "Done by energy and work — isn't luck — opposite of luck."

Minus. "Succeed. (Q.) Don't know." "People that do things with great skill. (Q.) Do many things." "Show how you can paint or whatever you know." "When you're not afraid to go up on tall buildings." "A man has great skill — he has the energy to do it." "Like you're a skilled workman. (Q.) Don't mind working." "Thoughtful." "To be brave."

15. *Juggler*

Plus. "Fellow with a fine sense of balance." "A man that juggles balls — up and down." "A man that juggles a stick — he puts his hand out like that and he has a stick balancing on it." "A man that performs tricks." "A magician, he does things. (Q.) Can spin tops on strings, and different things like that — throws tops in air." "Means you have a stick and a ball and roll the ball on the stick." "When you juggle something on your fingers." "A person talented in juggling. (Q.) Used to amuse people — something like actors." "A man who mixes up things. (Q.) If you juggle up figures you mix them all up." "Somebody knows how to juggle things and he juggles a lot of them at a time."

Minus. "Is a man. (Q.) He juggles. (Q.) Means he drinks and drinks." "A circus man. (Q.) To be quick." "To juggle anything. (Q.) Jerk it around." "Juggler goes around and tells jokes and plays an instrument." "Juggle anything. (Q.) Shake it up." "A man who juggles. (Q.) A man who juggles anything." "A man who sells jugs."

16. *Brunette*

Plus. "Somebody with black hair" (or brown). "A brunette is a woman. (Q.) A woman who has black hair and blue eyes." "You have brunette hair. (Q.) Sort of dark." "Brunette means dark." "Black hair." "Somebody that's dark in features." "Lady that isn't a blonde."

Minus. "Kind of light colored hair." "Reddish. Reddish brown. Light brown." "Sometimes if your hair's a certain color they'd call you a brunette. (Q.) If your hair was sort of brownish yellow." "Color. (Q.) Can't think of the color." "Somebody that has reddish hair." "You go to a brunette, and they curl your hair." "Something you wear on your hair." "Auburn colored."

17. *Peculiarity*

Plus. "Something somebody does and it's different from other things." "Something that's rare." "Strange." "Sort of exception." "Queer." "Odd." "Somebody that's kind of funny looking." "The different ways certain people act." "When something peculiar happens you have to see it. (Q.) Something odd happens." "Some people are peculiar. (Q.) They don't talk much and they're awful still." "Some one that is peculiar. (Q.) Somebody with pink eyes — you'd call them peculiar." "Something new — you've never seen it before. (Q.) Never seen a toy steam engine that worked by alcohol — when I saw it, it looked funny to me." "He's peculiar. (Q.) Well, if he don't act right he's peculiar." "Don't happen every time — once in awhile." "Fellow that's peculiar — he don't act like the other fellow is acting, you know." "You're peculiar. (Q.) You just want to do the opposite from everybody else." "Have some little peculiar trait about you is a peculiarity."

Minus. "Means to be peculiar about anything. (Q.) You don't know what thing it is and you are kind of peculiar about it." "Peculiar. (Q.) They're finicky." (confused with particular) "Like a man — he chews his cigar and you call that a peculiarity." "Something that is peculiar. (Q.) The things he does are sometimes peculiar." "Some people won't drink out of a dirty cup — that's peculiar." "High toned."

18. *Priceless*

Plus. "Invaluable." "Something that hasn't a price. (Q.) Something you can't buy — it's so much." "Some-

thing not to be sold." "Something that you can't buy. (Q.)
It's so costly." "When the price is out of reach." "Something very old and antique — costs very much." "Something that takes a whole lot of money to buy." "Hasn't any price. (Q.) You think a great deal of it."

Minus. "Beyond, below price, almost nothing." "Somebody gives you a bill and it's high." "Means that something's gone up real high. (Q.) Some lettuce real low and then jumped up high, the price." "If you wanted to buy something in the window and it wasn't for sale, it would be priceless." "No price. (Q.) No price on it, not marked."

19. *Regard*

The examiner in scoring this word must be sure that S. is not confusing regard with guard, a very common error and one sometimes difficult to recognize from the wording. A definition of regardless is not satisfactory.

Plus. "Can mean two things, to observe something, and then can mean compliments." "You look at something." "To watch — take notice." "You study a person or anything." "Consider." "To listen to a person when he's talking." "To think of a person." "Your feeling." "To care for something." "Regard is how you regard your friends. (Q.) Like I'd take a certain person and say I don't think she's a nice person to play with and that's how I regard her." "Respect for a person." "Like learning to regard other people's property. (Q.) Care for — not injure." "To pertain to." "Related to." "Talking about someone — talking regarding to something." "To wish luck." "To remember somebody." "When you write a letter you send regards to them. (Q.) Hope you are happy or good luck."

Minus. "Take care." "A person who watches things." (guards) "Not to heed something." "Do anything anyhow regardless of what your mother says." "Regarding anything for anyone. (Q.) In regard to anything. (Q.) To tell what it is and where it is." "When you send your

regards to somebody. (Q.)   Send your congratulations."
"Uphold. (Q.)   Like you regard a person as your friend —
you uphold him as your friend."   "You regard a person. (Q.)
You like what they do."   "Well, if you give your regards to
a person you ask about them — wonder how they are."

20. *Disproportionate*

   Plus. "Not of the right formation."   "You have an apple
and cut it in half and one half in quarters — disproportionate."   "Out of proportion — out of its natural size."
"Something that's not in shape — hasn't got the right proportions."   "Take a rich person and a poor person and that
would be disproportionate."   "Out of size — out of shape."
"Out of proportion — ungainly."   "Not in proportion."
"Opposite from proportionate."   "To give too much of —
or too less of."   "I think if somebody had a big head and
little shoulders and arms — something like that."   "To have
something on one side different from on the other side."
"They're not equal."   "Not the right proportion. (Q.) Like
you're dividing a cake and you don't give the right amount."
   Minus. "Not built right. (Q.)   Something don't fit."
"It isn't in the right place. (Q.)   Isn't where it should be
— supposed to be somewhere else and it isn't."   "Not to
have any proportion. (Q.)   Don't know."   "Not in portion."   "You haven't got quite enough of something. (Q.)
You haven't got quite enough of something you're making."
"Too much in proportion."   "A boy had something and it
wasn't the same as the other boys."

21. *Shrewd*

   Plus. "Discerning."   "Very quick thinking."   "Wise."
"Calculating."   "Wily."   "Cunning."   "Sharp."   "Intelligent."   "Sly."   "Means kind of foxy — they can do things
awful easy, or something."   "A man is a shrewd business
man. (Q.)   If he was shrewd he wouldn't put his money into
something he wasn't sure of — might mean careful sometimes."   "Not to be cheated. (Q.)   If a person is shrewd it's
a person that no one can cheat them out of something."

"Generally a very careful person, sometimes miserly."
"You can see through something quickly — not always a
desirable character." "Ingenious." "Jewish. (Q.) Best
you can get out of a deal." "Somebody that's tricky, or
something like that." "Hard to get around — hard to deal
with — and make anything out of."

Minus. "Nasty — something like a nasty person."
"Sort of queer fellow that gets by easy." "Shrewd means
shrewd person. (Q.) A mean person." "They're bad."
"Miserly." (minus without the additional characteristics of
careful or clever) "Thrifty." "Close. (Q.) Scotchman's
shrewd — they keep every penny they can get."

22. *Tolerate*

The responses to this word are considerably affected by the
prevalent use of it by school teachers in the form of "I can't
tolerate" — such and such. As a result, we have tolerate
defined as "won't stand for something," "can't stand it," etc.
In some cases this is merely a reiteration of the teacher's expression without knowledge of the connotation of the word to
be defined, and is scored minus unless it can be satisfactorily
explained.

Plus. "You don't like something and you bear it because
you have to." "Allow. (Q.) They allow a person to do
something." "To stand." "Endure." "To just barely
stand something." "You put up with something too long."
"Let anything — let them do it." "Keep someone — when
you don't really want 'em — whether you want 'em or not."
"To take something against your will." "To — if you don't
like a person you can still play up to it — not act as if you
hate it." "To be patient and to understand." "To be
kind — to tolerate another's belief is to see their side of the
question." "Take things off of people even if they do aggravate you." "Have toleration for. (Q.) If someone thinks
different than you do, do not oppress them or condemn them
because they hold different ideas than yours." "To get

along with." "You can't stand something. (Q.) The teacher says, 'I can't tolerate your noise.' Means she can't stand it."

Minus. "Like you tolerate somebody. Make friends and go around with them." "Nice or kind." "Agree with somebody — think it's all right." "Something that gets on your nerves." "To tolerate a person. (Q.) You wouldn't have to like them or have anything to do with them." "Something that you can't do — like sometimes you say you can't tolerate something you can't do it."

23. *Stave*

There is considerable confusion of the word "stave" with similar sounding words. A definition in terms of stake, stay, or picket in a fence is minus.

The noun stave is satisfactorily defined as one of the parts making up the sides of a barrel, as a stick (used as a support or weapon), staff, cane, slat, a round (rung), a musical term, or a metrical portion in poetry.

Plus. "A part of a barrel — like a curved board." "One of those boards in a barrel — is a barrel stave." "Part of a barrel." "A walking stick." "A piece of wood. (Q.) Used for a staff." "Sort of a stick that they would fight each other with — about five feet long — mostly made of oak wood." "It is a slat." "Stave in the bottom of a chair — a small rod." "A thing in music — five lines." "In a book — old fashioned book — same as calling it a chapter — call it Stave I, II, ..." "To fight away, stave off or ward off." "To break. (Q.) Stave in a barrel means you hit the barrel and broke it in."

Minus. "Ring that goes around a barrel." "Iron that binds a barrel." "Like a post." "Sort of a stick in a fence." "Something that you stick in the ground and tie a cow or horse to." "Corset stave — kind of a iron thing that supports you." "Support. (Q.) Bread is the main stave of life — thing that keeps you living."

24. *Lotus*

Plus. "Lotus is a plant — a supposed plant that whoever ate it was to forget where he came from or where he was going." "The name of a blossom." "A lily." "Chinese flower." "Some kind of a tree."

Minus. "A weed — lotus weed." (loco weed) "That is a person that eats flowers." "Some kind of a fruit or an animal. (Q.) An animal." "A bug." "A sort of food."

25. *Bewail*

Plus. "To complain." "To grieve." "Regret." "To be in despair." "You cry. (Q.) Be sorry." "When you cry for somebody." "If you lost something you want very much and it's very valuable you'd feel very badly about it." "Sad. (Q.) Feel sorry about something." "People bewail things that have gone wrong — haven't gone the way they should and bewail the fact." "Wail over something." "A cry of distress."

Minus. "Somebody is hollering. (Q.) Somebody is hurting 'em or something." "Gave a loud wail because you're frightened or something." "A shrill noise." "To wail." "Anxious."

26. *Repose*

This word is often confused with "pose." Responses which could apply equally well to "pose" and "repose" should be questioned.

Plus. "Peacefulness — of mind, or body." "To rest." "Take it easy." "To sleep or something like that." "When you're tired you lay down — say you repose." "Stay in one place. (Q.) Like the can reposes on the table." "To stand or be at ease." "Retiring — to retire." "Someone is sitting still or — not doing anything." "Some one with poise."

Minus. "Certain position that you take. (Q.) If you was in a movie you'd take a certain position, you'd repose." (pose) "Repose on something — you sit on it, I guess some

position." "Stand where you are. (Q.) Hardly know."
"To lay or sit or stand in a certain way." "You pose over
again." "To put something on a desk."

27. *Mosaic*

Mosaic may be defined as a form of art, in which pictures or
designs are made with stone, pieces of glass, tile, wool, wood,
paper, or straw; as a variety of tile; or as relating to Moses.
A definition referring to scientific uses of the term is also acceptable.

> *Plus.* "Decoration. (Q.) Pieces used to make designs."
"Work in small squares of glass or stone — color." "Little
stone. (Q.) Little stone they set into flowers and brooches."
"Painting. (Q.) Made out of little blocks." "Picture. (Q.)
In olden days people made it out of beads and glass." "In-
laid work." "Some kind of stuff used in Italy — put parts
together and make pretty things." "A form of art. (Q.)
Usually murals done in tile." "Inlaid pieces of wood. (Q.)
Make tables and things. It's wood inlaid — little different
shapes and make designs with it." "Mosaic law — the
law God gave to Moses." "Something that was in time of
Moses."

> *Minus.* "Lot of little colors. (Q.) Don't know."
"Stone — little stones they have over in Italy." "Some-
one does a little mosaic work, little figures with little mosaic."
"Type of old art. (Q.) Kind of painting — don't know
just what." "Form of architecture and drawing. (Q.) In
early Greek art the way they made tapestries and did draw-
ings on buildings." "Some sort of glass. (Q.) Don't know."
"An ornament made of stone or stucco." "A design. (Q.)
It's an odd kind of designing." "Pertaining to the Middle
Ages." "A religion. (Q.) Don't know." "Mosaic codes
— I don't know." "A character of the Bible."

28. *Flaunt*

In scoring this word, care should be taken to make sure that
flaunt has not been confused with taunt.

Plus. "To display saucily." "To flirt or — to make a show of yourself." "To be especially proud of something and to show it to everybody." "To show off." "Proud — flaunted her skirts — whisked them a certain way." "It shows its petals, a flower flaunts its petals, shows them." "To wave — something in front of somebody else." "To wave a flag — bull fighters in Spain flaunt a red flag in front of the bull."

Minus. "Make fun of." "A dare." "When you sneer at somebody." "To not think much of — to laugh at. (Q.) A rich person might flaunt a poor person — kind of ignore him." "To wave something. (Q.) If someone was going off on a boat and you waved a handkerchief to them." "To unfold." "If you go against something — flaunt it. (Q.) If somebody puts up a rule and you don't want to abide by the rule, you flaunt it." (flout)

29. *Philanthropy*

Plus. "Broad outlook toward others, helpful outlook." "Charity." "Good feeling — trying to do good." "Generousness. (Q.) Philanthropy is the act of giving out things to the poor folks." "One who gives to the public good." "Practice where people are kind to other people — sometimes they endow colleges, etc." "Giving away money to some cause." "Doing things for other people." "Brotherly — treat everybody nicely — study of love, I suppose." "A fostering of arts or better things."

Minus. "It's a place where they take in old clothes for the needy people." "A creed or something you go by." "A study." "Good natured." "Deep thinking."

30. *Ochre*

Plus. "A color. (Q.) Sort of an orange." "It's a color. (Q.) It's kind of yellow, but isn't quite yellow — medium brown and yellow color." "Kind of a tannish-reddish color." "A color used in oil paints." "Something you use for paint."

Minus. "A grayish color." "A shade of color. (Q.)

Don't know." "I don't know — is it a color? (Q.) Sort of
a mixture of colors." "Purple color." "A drug."

31. *Frustrate*

Plus. "To prevent or foil an attempt." "Not to let, or
to keep from." "Spoil — frustrate somebody's plans, means
you spoil their plans." "To stop when a person is doing
something bad and stop them in the act of doing it." "To
interfere with."

Minus. "To fool somebody. (Q.) They think you're
going to do one thing and you do another." "To be discouraged. (Q.) To have something on your mind that —
you don't think you can do." "To aggravate. (Q.) Like
someone is bothering you." "To make somebody uneasy or
uncomfortable." "To get confused." "To get excited."
(flustrate) "Means you don't know quite what to do —
you're kind of startled."

32. *Incrustation*

Plus. "Crust formed by evaporation of water from hard
particles." "The forming of a crust." "Inclosed by some
substance." "When anything is beginning to form on the
top of anything." "Something that's incrusted on a shield
or on a ship, like barnacles." "Thing gets incrusted, covered
with rust or something." "A covering. (Q.) Over the
outside of something." "Something with crust on it —
incrusted." "With a crust. (Q.) Such as on snow."
"Incrusted. (Q.) His hands were incrusted with dirt."

Minus. "To have a thing incrusted is something stuck
in it." "In a crust, maybe." "Something without a crust."
"The crust of something. (Q.) Foundation of something."
"Indented in the crust — creased or something." "Bread
in the form of a crust."

33. *Milksop*

Plus. "A mollycoddle." "A spineless creature."
"Might be a man that doesn't amount to much — hasn't got
any courage." "Some one that has no back bone and is

easily pushed about." "Somebody that's a sissy or something." "A man that is very weak — like a womanish
man." "A slang term given to a rich person or a person
that is used to having other people do things for him." "A
person that's sort of sleepy looking — seeming afraid of doing
something — of hurting themselves." "Babyish — a slang
expression." "Something that's like bread that's sopped
up — soaked in milk — call the dumb guys that."

Minus. "Term used to call somebody. (Q.) Just a name
you call them." "It's an expression of disgust. (Q.) People
call people who haven't done exactly what they wanted a
milksop." "A drunkard." "A glutton — but that isn't
right." "Bread soaked in milk." "A weed."

34. *Harpy*

The only acceptable definitions of harpy are as a mythical
character; a creature half bird and half woman; the creatures
who took food away from Ulysses or his men; birds or women
who prey on humans; a rapacious, plundering person; an ex-
tortioner; a type of eagle. Any definition of harpy as a scold
or a shrew is minus.

Plus. "Mythical being in one of the seas around Greece."
"A myth — birds — women with wings." "A harpy is a
mythical woman." "A harpy is a believed animal — something used in fairy tales — something to be afraid of."
"Name of one kind of eagle — harpy eagle." "An imag-
inary beast — part person and part animal." "Kind of bird
the Greeks believed in — had the head of a man and the body
of a bird." "The birds that took the food away from
Ulysses." "Bird that preys upon human flesh." "A person
who preys upon weaker people or upon other people."

Minus. "A certain kind of people in the ancient myths.
(Q.) They sang songs and anybody heard them never
wanted to leave." "A person of a race of people over in
Northern Africa that what's his name met on his journey. (Q.)

Aeneas." "Some one that sings and makes guys bump on rocks." "A term applied to beautiful girls who were supposed to exist in the Idylls of the Kings and other stories like that." "An old Greek character who used to sit on the rocks or sea someplace and draw people in." "A bird. (Q.) Something like a crow." "A witch." "A scold." "A loud-voiced woman." "Kind of always complaining."

35. *Ambergris*

Use, origin, or description of the substance is acceptable for ambergris.

Plus. "Some kind of jelly they take off of whales — use it to make perfume." "A product of whaling — or seal fishing valued very highly by chemists." "Something they make perfume out of." "Material from a whale — it's very valuable." "Stuff spit up from a sick whale." "Substance that comes out of a whale. I think it's kind of fat." "Substance obtained from the head of a whale." "Sort of a rather, very bad smell — it's quite valuable."

Minus. "Something that has to do with plants — no, it's a fluid." "I know it's a substance. (Q.) Don't know."

36. *Piscatorial*

Plus. "Pertaining to fishes." "Sort of fishy — study of fish or something."

37. *Depredation*

Depredation is sometimes confused with dilapidation. This confusion is readily recognized and does not present a problem of scoring.

Plus. "A raid that has done damage or something like that." "Injury to property — malicious intent to do harm — perhaps not malicious but harm done." "Outlawry, robbery, killing." "Something like marauding." "An attack made on something with a view of decreasing it's value." "To destroy." "Ruin something or nearly ruin." "Some mischievous act." "To prey upon." "Thievery — theft.

(Q.)   Could be stealing and destroying of things — not for
personal gain so much as revenge."
    Minus. "A lowering of. (Q.) Demoralizing." "Sort of
a depression." "To depreciate something, don't like it, let
it go to waste." "To deprive anybody of anything."

38. *Perfunctory*

A satisfactory definition must take cognizance of *lack of
interest* in the thing done perfunctorily.   This word is often
confused with punctual.

    Plus. "Necessarily done with a sense of duty — no feel-
ing." "In an offhand manner without particular significance." "Something you do — you don't care about it, but
it's a social necessity and you have to do it." "In a casual
manner. (Q.) You do something that you've been doing so
long it just becomes second nature — perfunctory to do it."
"Just doing something — sort of a duty — sort of a habit."
"Usually a short curt greeting or something that is done in a
mediocre sort of way." "Something that has to be done
because it has to be done." "Usual duties — perfunctory
duties." "Careless."
    Minus. "Regular." "Performing of your duties." "To
be very deliberate in everything you do. (Q.) Everything
you do, do it a certain way and always do it that way."
"Means not well — thing isn't done well if it is done in a
perfunctory manner."

39. *Limpet*
    Plus. "Some kind of a mollusk — found in the rocks —
conical shape." "Shell fish." "Sea food."
    Minus. "A man who limps." "Wilted — limp."

40. *Achromatic*
    Plus. "Without color." "Uncolored." "Refracting
light without breaking it up into its constituent colors." "A
musical scale that is not chromatic — the diatonic or whole
tone scale."

Minus. "A series of colors." "Nothing to do with chromatic is it? — means to go up by small degrees, doesn't it?" "A scale that's played on a piano. (Q.) Have one octave and play every note that is the scale." (chromatic) "Something to do with music. (Q.) Don't know."

41. *Casuistry*

Plus. "A branch of philosophy." "A branch of philosophy generally dealing with theology." "Dealing with questions of right and wrong in conduct." "Sophistry."

Minus. "Not unless it comes from casual." "A bad accident — or pertaining to death." (casualty)

42. *Homunculus*

Plus. "Some sort of variety of dwarf." "Little man."

Minus. "Pertains to a man of some sort." "Pertaining to the specie of man." "To do with man. (Q.) A homunculus pleasure is reading." "Homologous."

43. *Sudorific*

Plus. "Pertaining to perspiration." "Having to do with sweat."

Minus. "Sleepy-like."

44. *Retroactive*

Plus. "Acting back upon. (Q.) It affects events previous to a present enactment." "A retroactive law — one that governs things that happened before it was passed." "If they passed a law that if somebody stole a loaf of bread he should be put in prison, and he'd stolen the loaf of bread before they made the law, and it was a retroactive law, they'd put him in prison."

Minus. "If a thing is retroactive, it reacts." "Action that's gone on before. (Q.) Something that's happened before and you're doing it again." "Backward — going backward kind of. (Q.) A retroactive method in writing — method goes back and picks up things gone by." "To return to the action." "It acts back upon you. (Q.) In chemistry — something that reacts back — I don't know if it would be in chemistry or not — but you do something and it acts back."

45. *Parterre*

Plus. "Part of the lower floor of a theater." "Part of a theater under the balcony." "A terraced garden." "Flower beds with paths between."

Minus. "Under the ground." "Pertaining to the earth — or part of the earth." "Something about ground."

PART V

SCORING STANDARDS FOR FORM M

THE two forms of the scale are very similar. Where a test in Form M is of the same type as one in L, the comments regarding the test are not repeated, but the reader is referred to the previous discussion by page. In a few instances a test from Form L has been duplicated in Form M. Where such duplication has occurred the scoring instructions have not been repeated, but the reader has been referred to Form L.

YEAR II

1. Delayed Response

The delayed reaction experiment has been the model for this test. We have found it an excellent test with which to begin when examining young children, as they enter with eager enthusiasm into the game of finding the kitty and forget the strangeness of the situation and their own initial shyness. The purpose of the test is to determine whether the child is capable of the ideational response necessary for remembering the location of the object well enough to recall it when the situation is presented again. In order to pass the test the child's first choice in each trial must be the correct one. The required score is two successes in three trials.

2. Identifying Objects by Name (Cf. Form L, pp. 193 f.)

The task of identifying objects by name is, in this Form as it was in L, the easiest test in the scale. Here, too, the material has been chosen from the familiar everyday surroundings of the child's world. Success at this level consists in identifying four of the six objects by name.

3. Identifying Parts of the Body (Cf. Form L, p. 194)

Here we expect the child to identify three out of four of the features asked for, pointing them out on the paper doll.

4. Three-Hole Form Board (Cf. Form L, p. 193)

This test duplicates the one given in Form L at this level. In order to score plus one of the trials must be successful.

5. Picture Vocabulary (Cf. Form L, p. 195)

The object must be named. Responses in terms of use or description are scored minus. Naming a part for the whole is scored minus (i.e., hand for arm), or the whole for a part (i.e., leg for foot). "Thing" is minus. Plural may be used for singular.

1. *Automobile*
   Plus. "Auto." "Car." "'Chine."
   Minus. "Bye-bye." "Go-go." "Train." "Truck."

2. *Hat*
   Plus. "Hat." "Straw hat." "Summer hat."
   Minus. "Cap."

3. *Telephone*
   Plus. "Telephone." "Phone."
   Minus. "Hello."

4. *Key*
   Plus. "Key." "Key lock."
   Minus. "A lock." "A door locker."

5. *Airplane*
   Plus. "Airplane." "Plane." "Monoplane." "Biplane." "Flying machine." "Airship."
   Minus. "Zeppelin." "Air car." "Ship."

6. *Ball*
   Plus. "Baseball." "Ball." "Tennis ball."

Minus. "Playball thing." "Apple." "Round circle." "Balloon." "Football."

7. *Knife*

Plus. "Knife." "Butcher knife." "Paring knife." "Butter knife."

8. *Soldier's hat*

Plus. "Hat." "A big hat." "Cowboy hat." "Soldier hat." "Sailor hat." "Straw hat." "Scout hat."

Minus. "Cap." "Indian hat."

9. *Block*

Plus. "Block." "Building block."

Minus. "Box." "An A B C." "Numbers." "Letter." "A square."

10. *Flag*

Plus. "Flag." "American flag." "Flag pole." "Star Spangled Banner." "Banner."

Minus. "Pole." "Stick." "Tree." "Post." "Rag." "Kite."

11. *Horse*

Plus. "Horse." "Horsie." "Pony."

Minus. "Donkey." "Mule." "Cow."

12. *Foot*

Plus. "Foot." "Feets." "Footie." "Piece of foot." "Foot and toe."

Minus. "Shoe." "Toe." "Toes." "Leg." "Piggies."

13. *Coat*

Plus. "Coat." "Jacket."

Minus. "Suit." "Shirt." "Sweater." "Overcoat." "Smock." "Vest blouse." "Clothes." "Cape."

14. *Boat*

Plus. "Boat." "Ship." "Steamer." "Steamboat." "Ferry." "Yacht."

Minus. "Tent on top of boat." "Boat house." "House on a boat."

15. *Cane*
> *Plus.* "Cane." "Stick." "A walking stick." "Candy cane." "A hopping stick."
> *Minus.* "Part of an umbrella." "Thing that you walk with." "A walker." "Sword." "Handle."

16. *Pitcher*
> *Plus.* "Pitcher." "Cream jug." "Cream pitcher." "Creamer." "Ewer."
> *Minus.* "A mug." "Cup." "Pot." "Cream bottle." "Milk." "Bottle jar." "Dish." "Dipper." "Cream bowl."

17. *Arm*
> *Plus.* "Arm." "Arm and hand and shoulder." "Hand and a arm."
> *Minus.* "Hands." "A fist." "Muscle." "He's going to fight somebody — big hand." "Elbow." "Shoulder."

At year II the requirement is two plus out of seventeen.

6. Word Combinations (Cf. Form L, pp. 197 f.)

This is the same test that occurs at this level in Form L.

Alternate. Naming Objects (Cf. II–6, 3)

This test from II–6, scored for three instead of four successes out of six trials, may be used as an alternate at this level if necessary.

YEAR II–6

1. Identifying Objects by Use (Cf. Form L, p. 198)

The objects included in this test proved to be slightly easier than those in Form L, and the requirement for passing here is four out of six.

2. Motor Coordination

It is obviously the motor coordination involved in manipulating the toy egg-beater that constitutes the difficulty of this test.   There is a rapid increase in the per cent passing, particularly from age two to two and a half, and the correlation with the composite (.46) is satisfactory.   The standard required for success is one complete revolution of the handle in one of three trials.

3. Naming Objects (Cf. Form L, p. 199)

The scoring of this test presents few difficulties.   The same principles apply here as in the picture vocabulary.

(a) *Shoe*
   Plus. "Shoe." "Shoes."
   Minus. "Foot."

(b) *Watch*
   Plus.   "Watch."   "Clock."   "Tick-tick."   "Wrist watch."
   Minus. "A time."

(c) *Telephone*
   Plus. "Telephone." "Phone."
   Minus. "Hello." "A ring." "A talk."

(d) *Flag*
   Plus. "Flag." "American flag."

(e) *Jack-knife*
   Plus. "Jack-knife." "Knife." "Pocket knife."
   Minus. "A cutter."

(f) *Stove*
   Plus. "Stove."
   Minus. "Oven."

Four plus out of six is the standard for success at this level.

4. Picture Vocabulary (Cf. II, 5)

At this level the requirement is seven out of seventeen to score plus on the test.

5. Repeating Two Digits (Cf. Form L, p.199)

One of the three series must be repeated without error.

6. Obeying Simple Commands (Cf. Form L, p. 203)

The test is passed if there are two successes out of three.

Alternate.   Stringing Beads (Cf. Form L, p. 200)

Two or more beads must be strung to pass the test at this level.

YEAR III

1. Block Building: Bridge (Cf. Form L, p. 200)

This test is a duplicate of the block-building test in Form L at the same level.

2. Picture Vocabulary (Cf. II, 5)

The required score for success at this level is ten plus out of seventeen.

3. Identifying Objects by Use (Cf. II–6, 1)

Five plus out of six constitutes the requirement for success at this level.

4. Drawing a Vertical Line

The imitative drawing of a vertical stroke measures one of the aspects of psycho-motor development.   Gesell [1] found

Op. cit., pp. 84, 211.

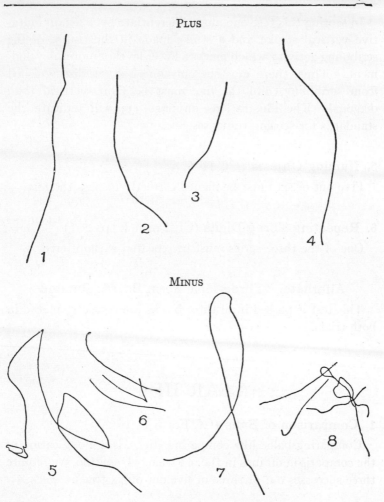

that the ability to imitate a vertical stroke was present in from 85 to 100 per cent of his three-year-old subjects. Our data agree with his in placing the test at the three-year level with 87 per cent passing. It is the easiest test at this age level for our subjects.

In scoring this test one must differentiate between an imitative vertical stroke and a stroke made in the course of the scribbling activity which marks a lower level of motor development. Thus, there must be only one line, as distinguished from scribbling, and the line must be more vertical than diagonal. The illustrations on page 333 will indicate the standards for scoring responses.

5. Naming Objects (Cf. II–6, 3)

Five out of six must be named correctly to pass the test.

6. Repeating Three Digits (Cf. Form L, p. 201)

One of the three series must be repeated without error.

Alternate.   Three-Hole Form Board: Rotated

This test is passed if all three blocks are correctly placed in both trials.

YEAR III–6

1. Comparison of Balls (Cf. Form L, p. 203)

Comparing balls, like comparing sticks, is a modification of the comparison of lines in the old scale. Here, too, we require three successes out of three or five out of six trials.

2. Patience: Pictures

This test is a simplified form of Binet's old patience test. The use of pictures to be put together instead of the two triangles makes the task easier and more concrete. Language comprehension plays very little part in success.

The task is, of course, to bring together the two halves of the figure to make a complete picture. It is rather difficult at this level and the scoring must be lenient. The child's arrangement of the cards must indicate that he is trying to make the picture. The outlines of the ball and of the pig do not need to meet exactly, but must not be out of alignment by as much as half the diameter of the ball or pig. The cards do not have to touch each other, but should meet within approximately an inch. If the two halves are slightly out of alignment they must meet, and if they do not quite meet they must not be out of alignment. The test is passed if either (a) or (b) is plus.

3. Discrimination of Animal Pictures

Discrimination of animal pictures is a variation of the form-discrimination test. (Form L, p. 212.) Making it more concrete by using meaningful material instead of the geometrical forms has so simplified the task as to place it at the three-and-a half-year level. The animal pictures are of unequal difficulty, some of them being more familiar to the younger children than others that are not so often seen. Degree of familiarity is one of the important factors determining success or failure. The test shows a rapid increase in per cent passing from one age to the next and has a correlation of .61 with the composite score. We require four correct responses for success at this level.

4. Response to Pictures I (Cf. Form L, p. 204)

Responses to pictures are scored at two difficulty levels in Form M, one of which is satisfactory at III-6, the other at year VI.

At the present level any one of the following three types of response is satisfactory:

(a) Enumeration. At least three objects must be named spontaneously, that is, without intervening questions or urging.

(b) Description, which need not refer to more than a single element of the picture.

(c) Interpretation, which may be inadequate or incorrect though not purely fanciful or bizarre.

For success at level II (year VI) the subject must bring the elements of the picture together either by describing or interpreting.

(a) *Grandmother's story*
    Level I (Year III–6)
       Plus. "Something cooking on the stove." "Water running over on the floor." "The steam is coming up out of here." "Lady sitting down." "Boy fall down." "All the boys are sitting down." "That's mother and boy and that's girl and that's girl." "She's catching the kids." "Cooking." "Her mama right here." "Here the son and here the son, don't have a tick tock." "Mother and Helen and daddy and brother and there's her little cousin." "Lady, man, baby, chair."
       Minus. "What did the lady do?" "This here girl, turn around girl." "Oh, look here — there's a choo-choo train — look at that boy." "Doing like that" (showed how girl was lying). "Little girl, big girl, thing." "Sammy, Santa Claus, and one old lady." "That'n — that'n and that'n." "Girls, lady." "About little girls." "I can't. (Q.) That a man?" "A man, a man, a lady, a boy, a cow." "Old Mother Hubbard went to the cupboard."

    Level II (Year VI)
At this level mere enumeration is not satisfactory; there must be either description or interpretation. If both description and interpretation are present a fairly low standard for each is acceptable.

       Plus. "The children are in front of the mother and the beans are burning and the hot water is boiling and they're just sitting there playing and don't do nothing about it." "It's boiling over and they don't know it." "Nobody sees that the soup is falling and it's going all over the stove." "Some children playing. Woman sitting in a chair. One of the kettles is boiling over. Tea kettle boiling." "Here's a pot and it's running over. Here's a lady and her three children. Here's a stove." "Two girls and one boy and one mama and the fire is steaming and the stuff is leaking out of the can." "A girl, a lady in a chair and stuff is boiling and things are going all out there."

Minus. Minimal responses for level I would be scored minus here.

(b) *Birthday party*
Level I (Year III–6)
Plus. "Those are candles — that's a window, that's a little girl ringing the doorbell, that's a little boy and girl. Those are birthday candles and flowers and doorbell and big tree." "Kid, kid (pointing). (Q.) Got a box and present." "Going in the door." "That's a boy and that's a girl and that's a girl — going to the door — she can't go in." "He's got the candy." "Boy and girl taking a walk." "Look — girl — clean — all the girls clean."

Minus. "Pictures — boy — boy — mama — mama." "Here the back door go out — here's the daddy." "That's a lady and that's a lady and that's a lady." "No ladies here — what the little girl doing?" "Little girl and little boy." "Boy, girl, thing." "Babies." "All the children."

Level II (Year VI)
Plus. "The girl is ringing the door bell and the boy and girl are bringing packages, there's a Christmas cake in the window." "They're going to her teacher. Today's her birthday. They're going to give her a present." "Here's one trying to go in the door on Christmas." "Three children were going visiting one day and they couldn't open the hard door so they rang the door bell and they couldn't get in." "That's a door — she's touching at the knob. This is their home. They have a present for somebody." "They went

337

to buy a box of candy and then they came home." "A boy
is bringing this girl a present." "She's ringing the doorbell
and there's a cake in the window." "There's a birthday cake
in there. Oh, a birthday cake and a present." "That little
girl's going up to the door to see if mama's in — she's ringing
the doorbell."

Minus. Minimal responses for level I would be scored
minus here.

(c) *Wash day*
Level I (Year III-6)
Plus. "The dog got loose from the lady and she couldn't
find him." "The man's shirt is on the dog." "The doggie
has some pants." "The lady pushed a dog over." "I see a
mother and a wolf fighting." "Here is a dog, and here is a
basket. Here's Dorothy." "A dog fell down — a girl and
a dog." "What's her running for?" "Doggie is fighting.'
"Here's a line with clothes on." "That is just somebody
playing, and a dog." "There's an old woman and there's a
dog running away." "Dog, mother. (Q.) Dog biting the
clothes."

Minus. "A doggie, a girl, a boy." "Dog — there's a lady,
dog, fork." "A fox — old man and another lady." "Basket, wash." "Dog. (Q.) Dresses." "Mother and this is
a doggy and this a cat and this a cat." "That's clothes —
that looks like a old rabbit." "What he doing? He's a
dog." "That's an ole dog — what's he doing — what's
that?"

Level II (Year V)
Plus. "Woman catching a dog and he had clothes, a
shirt." "The dog is running and the girl is catchin' the dog."
"She's running after these." "She's chasing the dog."
"Dog ran away with the shirt." "He's taking the clothes."
"He got the clothes down and he pulled the clothes out of the
basket." "Some clothes fell and a dog went to get the
clothes. A girl and a house and hanging out the clothes and
a basket and some grass and some wood and trees." "There's

a house and there's some clothes hanging on clothes line and there's a window and a basket and woman and a dog has got one of her clothes and a dog and a woman."

Minus. Minimal responses for level I would be scored minus here.

Two of the three pictures must meet the requirements for plus on level I or better to pass the test.

5. Sorting Buttons

Sorting black buttons into one box and white ones into another affords a simple means of gauging the ability to make discriminating reactions at the perceptual level. The test has the added virtue of being in line with the child's everyday play activities and possesses for him a high interest value. The test is passed if the buttons are classified without error.

6. Comprehension I (Cf. Form L, p. 206)

(a) *What must you do when you are hungry?*

Plus. "Eat." "My mommy cook." "I like cereal." "I drink milk" (or chocolate). "Put supper on the stove." "I want supper." "Mother gives me a piece of bread." "Say I'm hungry." "We buy bread." "Sit up to the table." "Get on my high chair." "Tell my mommy. (Q.) She gives me something to eat."

Minus. "I want a drink." "We got table down at our house."

(b) *What must you do when you are sleepy?*

Plus. "I go to sleep." "Go to bed." "Lie down." "Cover yourself up." "Take a rest." "I shut my eyes." "Fold up in the car."

Minus. "I snore." "We get a bed down there." "Take a drink of milk."

One of the two questions must be answered correctly to pass this test.

Alternate. Matching Objects

This test is passed if three of the four responses are plus.

YEAR IV

1. Picture Vocabulary (Cf. II, 5)

Twelve correct out of seventeen are required for passing at this level.

2. Stringing Beads (Cf. Form L, p. 200)

If the child succeeds in stringing seven beads of any shape, he is scored plus in the test.

3. Opposite Analogies I (Cf. Form L, p. 216)

(a) *Brother is a boy; sister is a ......*
     Plus. "Girl." "Girlie." "Little girl."
     Minus. "Lady."

(b) *In daytime it is light; at night it is .....*
     Plus. "Dark."
     Minus. "Black." "Dark time."

(c) *Father is a man; mother is a ......*
     Plus. "Woman." "Lady." "Girl."
     Minus. "Wife." "Mama."

(d) *The snail is slow; the rabbit is ......*
     Plus.   "Swift."   "Quick."   "Rapid."   "Speedy."
     "Fast." "Faster."
     Minus. "Running faster."

(e) *The sun shines during the day; the moon at ......*
     Plus.   "Night."   "The night."   "In the night."
     "Nights." "The moon shines at night." "Night time."
     "During the night."

Minus. "Midnight." "I think the moon is white in the night." "Lights up at night."

Two successes are required for plus at this level.

4. Pictorial Identification (Cf. Form L, p. 210)

Three out of six must be correct for plus at this level.

5. Number Concept of Two

The development of number concepts in children has been extensively studied, especially by Baldwin and Stecher [1] and by Descoeudres.[2] Our data are not directly comparable with the results of these experimenters because of differences in procedure and scoring. We have found that it is not until the age of four that 72 per cent of a given age group can respond correctly to the question, "How many?" when two objects are presented. The requirement for success at this level is two correct out of three trials.

6. Memory for Sentences I (Cf. Form L, p. 221)

The child must repeat two of the three sentences without error to be given credit.

Alternate. Discrimination of Animal Pictures (Cf. III–6, 3)

If it is necessary to use an alternate at this level this test may be credited if six of the animal pictures are correctly discriminated. It is advisable, however, in case one of the tests of the age group is spoiled, to score on the basis of five tests in the group rather than to weight this test so heavily. (It is used also at III–6 and IV–6.)

---

[1] *Op. cit.*, pp. 162–64. [2] *Op. cit.*, pp. 233–82.

YEAR IV-6

1. Discrimination of Animal Pictures (Cf. III–6, 3)
Seven correct responses are required at this level.

2. Definitions (Cf. Form L, p. 218)
A definition is satisfactory if it expresses a use or purpose, or if it gives an identifying description, a category, or a synonym.

(a) *Key*
    Plus. "For a door." "It's a key to the door." "Turn the door with." "Key lock in a door." "To a house." "Key, you wanta go in." "Open door." ' Key open the garage." "For my daddy's car." "It shuts." "To start things.' "A lock — er." "Wind up the clock." "It's a note that we sing on." "Piano key. (Q.) Play on it."
    Minus. "It got a handle on it." "Walk out." "Straight."

(b) *Dress*
    Plus. "What you put on." "On mama." "For girls." "Me got a dress on dollie." "A dress is to dress with and go shopping." "For getting dressed." "To get cleaned up in." "To go out." "Clothes." "Wool" (lawn, cloth, etc.). "A dress is warm." "I wear a pretty dress." "A suit." "You make a dress. (Q.) To wear."
    Minus. "Petticoat." "It's out of button." "Rag."

(c) *Bed*
    Plus. "What you sleep on." "You want to get in." "For dollies. (Q.) Sleep." "Bed to put the baby in." "Lay in." "Bed to get in." "Go to bed." "To sleep." "Made out of iron" (wood, etc.). "Made out of springs." "Bed is made of covers." "Like a couch."
    Minus. "Night-night."

Two of the three definitions must be satisfactory.

342

3. Repeating Four Digits (Cf. Form L, p. 213)

This test is passed if one of the three series is repeated without error.

4. Picture Completion: Bird (Cf. Form L, pp. 209 f.)

Credit for this test, as for the completion of the man in Form L, is given according to the details which are added. The total possible score is three points, as follows:

One point for completion of body outline.

One point for leg and an additional point for a second leg.

One point for wing and an additional point for a second wing.

The scoring for body outline is very lenient. Even a crude outline made by bringing the line up over the starting line, as shown in Sample 10, is scored one point. No credit is deducted for extra legs or wings. No extra credit is given for the addition of a tail. The test is passed at this level if the score is one or better.

The samples on page 344 illustrate some of the various possibilities together with the scoring credits.

5. Materials (Cf. Form L, p. 214)

(a) *What is a house made of?*

   Plus. "Wood." "Boards." "Bricks." "Plaster." "Adobe." "Cement." "Stucco." "Shingles." "Tile." "Stone." "Lumber." "Blocks." "Rocks."

   Minus. "Walls." "Sticks." "Nails." "Trees. (Q.) Tree houses."

(b) *What is a window made of?*

   Plus. "Glass." "Wood and glass." "Glass and steel."

   Minus. "Putty." "Wood." "Screen."

(c) *What is a book made of?*

   Plus. "Paper." "Cloth." "Leather." "Leather and paper." "Cardboard." "Pieces of paper." "Sheepskin."

THREE CREDITS

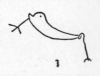

1   2   3

TWO CREDITS

4   5   6

ONE CREDIT

7   8   9   10

NO CREDIT

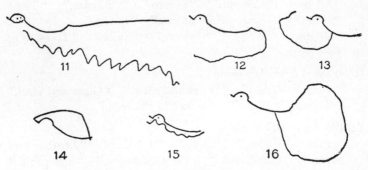

11   12   13

14   15   16

344

"Out of old rags and paper." "Pages are made out of paper and the outsides are made of something hard."

Minus. "Pictures." "Made out of pictures and covers on." "Pages." "Cards." "Pastings." "Cotton. (Q.) Made of cotton."

Two of the three questions must be answered correctly to pass the test.

6. Comprehension II

(a) *What do we do with our eyes?*

Plus. "See." "See little baby." "You can see — better." "Read." "I don't know — you blink 'em." "Shut them at night." "Keep 'em closed." "Keep them open." "Wink 'em."

Minus. "Sleep." "There — put glasses on."

(b) *What do we do with our ears?*

Plus. "Hear." "To listen." "Hear through." "To hear the radio." "Put receivers on 'em if you're telephoning anything."

Minus. "Wash them with soap." "Put glasses on them." "They're to make us pretty." "Put hair over 'em." "Keep quiet." "On our head." "This —" (moves them with hand).

One of the two questions must be answered correctly to pass the test.

Alternate. Patience: Pictures (Cf. III–6, 2)

Both pictures must be correctly assembled to score plus at this level.

YEAR V

1. Picture Vocabulary (Cf. II, 5)

The required score for passing at this level is fourteen.

2. Number Concept of Three (Cf. IV, 5)

Two out of three must be correct for plus at this level.

3. Pictorial Similarities and Differences (Cf. Form L, p. 214)

Nine of the ten comparisons must be correct to pass the test.

4. Patience: Rectangles (Cf. III–6, 2)

This is Binet's old "test of patience," so called because achievement of the desired end depends upon the child's willingness to persist in a line of action, under the control of a guiding idea. Binet,[1] in his description of the elements involved, presents a very nice analysis of the nature of an intellectual act. This one makes three demands upon the subject. "(1) To keep in mind the end to be attained, that is to say, the figure to be formed. It is necessary to comprehend this end and not lose sight of it. (2) To try different combinations under the influence of this directing idea, which guides the efforts of the child even though he be unconscious of the fact. (3) To judge the formed combination, compare it with the model, and decide whether it is the correct one."

The test is scored plus if there are two successes in three trials.

5. Comprehension II (Cf. IV–6, 6)

Both questions must be answered correctly at this level.

[1] Binet, A., and Simon, Th. "Le développement de l'intelligence chez les enfants." L'année Psychologique, 1908, 14.

6. Mutilated Pictures (Cf. Form L, p. 223)

The missing part must be named, or described verbally.

(a) *Table*

Plus. "One of the legs." "There's only one leg and two legs here. (Q.) One leg there and no leg here and two legs here." "Hasn't got four legs." "Just has three legs." "No leg." "One foot of the table." "One table stick broke." "One thing. (Q.) One leg there and no leg here and two legs here." "What holds the table up." "The other thing that it stands up on."

Minus. "The legs — the legs that stand up." "Ain't got no feet" (pointing to missing leg). "Feet."

(b) *Coat*

Plus. "Just one sleeve." "No sleeve." "The sleeve's broke." "Arm." "One where you put your arm." "Ain't got but one arm." "Part of the coat's arm."

Minus. "Hand." "One — (points to own arm) part of coat — seam." "The arms." "Half of a suit gone."

(c) *Cat*

Plus. "Tail." "Half of his tail."

(d) *Head*

Plus. "Mouth." "Teeth." "Lips." "Smile." "His mouth and two hands."

(e) *Bird*

Plus. "A wing." "His — the thing what he fly with." "He needs a wing to fly some more." "Only one wing and tail." "No wings on that side." "The other fly" (wing). "No wing." "Wing — feets."

Minus. "Wings." "His hand." "One eye."

Passed if the missing part is detected in three out of the five pictures.

Alternate. Knot (Cf. Form L, p. 221)

YEAR VI

1. Number Concepts (Cf. Form L, pp. 224 f.)

Three of the four number groups must be correctly matched to pass the test.

2. Copying a Bead Chain (Cf. Form L, p. 222)

The plan of the chain must be perceived and correctly indicated. This may be done without using as many beads as were used in the model, providing there is no error in sequence, e.g. (O O ☐ O O ☐). Also the chain may be greater in length than the model. It is permissible to alternate two round beads with one cylindrical bead, by beginning with a cylindrical bead (☐ O O ☐ O O). If the chain is correct as far as the child has gone when the end of the allotted time is reached, the trial is scored plus provided enough has been done to indicate that the child is following the correct plan, e.g. (O O ☐ O O), or (O O ☐ O O ☐ O), or (☐ O O ☐ O O).

The addition or substitution of beads not included in the model is scored minus, e.g. (O O ☐ O O ☐̣ O O). Altering the relative order of beads is minus, e.g. (O O ☐ O O O ☐ O). Omission of part of the pattern is minus, e.g. (O O ☐ O ☐ O O), or (O ☐ O O ☐ O O), or (O O ☐ O O ☐ O O ☐ O ☐). Designs which are correct as far as they go, but are insufficient to show whether the child has grasped the plan, are scored minus, e.g. (O O ☐) or (O O ☐ O).

3. Differences (Cf. Form L, p. 228)

In scoring the differences test, any real difference, whether fundamental or superficial, is counted plus. Reference may be made to just one of the words of a pair provided the distinction is evident from what is said about it.

(a) *What is the difference between a* bird *and a* dog?

Responses commonly are in terms of locomotion, size, shape, physical attributes, or type of vocalization. Specific differences in color are not satisfactory.

Plus. "A bird flies and a dog runs." "A bird flies." "A bird flies and a dog runs after the bird when he's down on the ground." (The differences here seem clearly implied.) "The dog can run and the bird can't." "A bird got wings and a dog got ears." "A bird has got two feet and a dog hasn't." "They're different shaped." "Bird's lighter than a dog." "A dog's bigger than a bird." "Bird says 'Tweet' and the dog says 'Bow-wow.'" "A bird can't bite." "It's a different kind of animal. (Q.) Birds have feathers and dogs have fur."

Minus. "A bird can go faster than a dog." "The bird is white and the dog is brown." "'Cause they don't look alike. (Q.) One is white and one is black." "If a dog went after a bird the bird would fly up." "A dog chases the bird." (These last two responses are minus because it is the relationship between the two, and not the difference between them, that is emphasized.)

(b) *What is the difference between a* slipper *and a* boot?

Satisfactory responses usually refer to relative comfort or convenience, protection, differences in shape, material, or use.

Plus. "Slipper is comfortable." "A boot is much better than a slipper because it's warmer." "You can get a slipper on faster than a boot." "Slipper leaks and boot don't." "The boot's longer." "A slipper has a little tassel on it, or a little round thing and shoe hasn't." "Slipper is wool and boot's leather." "A boot's made out of rubber." "Put on the slipper when we get up mornings." "You can't wear a slipper out-doors and you can wear a boot out-doors." "The men go out fishing with boots and the slipper people wear."

> *Minus.* "A boot is a shoe and a slipper isn't." "'Cause the boot is black and the slipper's red." "A slipper got laces and a boot hasn't." "The slipper keeps your shoes so the mud won't get on them and boot covers your leg up."

(c) *What is the difference between* wood *and* glass?

The most frequent difference given is in terms of use. Appearance and physical properties are also common bases for differentiation.

> *Plus.* "You can see through glass." "Glass breaks easier." "You drink out of a glass and you make chairs out of wood." "The glass is breakier — it will break — and the wood will crack." "Wood is to saw and make stuff and glass is to put things in." "Wood is stronger than glass." "Glass is harder than wood." "Wood will burn." "Glass can hurt you and wood can't. (Q.) Glass can cut you and wood can't." "Glass is made into a window and wood isn't." "Glass is more shinier."
>
> *Minus.* "Glass is lighter than wood. (Q.) 'Cause wood is heavy." "Glass cuts wood." "The wood is darker." "The glass gets in some one's foot when they walk on it and they are bare-footed." "Wood is brown and glass is white."

Passed if a real difference is given in two out of three comparisons.

4. Response to Pictures I (Cf. III–6, 4)

The test is passed if two of the three pictures are plus according to the scoring standards for level II. Cf. pp. 336 ff.

5. Counting Thirteen Pennies

Children usually learn to count by rote before they are able to count objects. The task here, of course, is to make the counting tally with the pointing. The test appears to depend little on specific instruction, as most children at this age have usually had enough spontaneous interest in numbers to acquire facility in counting as far as thirteen without formal teaching. The test is passed if in one of two trials the count tallies with the pointing.

6. Opposite Analogies I (Cf. IV, 3)

The test is passed if four out of five are correct.

YEAR VII

1. Giving the Number of Fingers

Like the test of counting pennies, this one, also, throws light on the child's spontaneous interest in numbers. Here we want to find out whether the child has retained this item of information from his everyday experience and observations. The test is passed if all three questions are answered correctly and promptly.

2. Memory for Sentences II (Cf. Form L, p. 221)

One of the two sentences must be repeated correctly, that is, without omissions, subtractions, or additions, after one reading.

3. Picture Absurdities I (Cf. Form L, p. 226)

(a) *Man sawing limb*

    Plus. "He is sitting on a tree sawing some wood and he will fall down won't he?" "Sawin' the tree off and he's gonna fall down." "He's gonna fall." "About the man up there — upon a limb sawing wood. (Q.) 'Cause he's setting on where he's sawing." "Sawing a limb down sitting on it." "Sawing a limb. (Q.) He's on it."

    Minus. "That man has got up on the limb of that tree and sawing it. (Q.) On the limb." "The boy got up on the

stem and it's breaking down — sitting upon it." "He's sawing a tree and he saw right there and he can't get down
again." "He has nothing to hold on, he could fall off — and
no leaves are on the tree."

(b) *Man getting weighed*

   Plus. "He's putting books under his arm so he'll weigh
more — that's what's funny." "Carrying books weighing."
"Because he has books in his hand. (Q.) Because he'd be
too heavy." "A man going on the scale and weighing himself and holding books. (Q.) Holding books when he's getting weighed."

   Minus. "The man he's weighin' hisself and he didn't even
put no penny in it." "Because that man got some books in
his arm. (Q.) Because he's weighing him." "The scale
doesn't go all the way round."

(c) *Cat and mice*

Any of the following aspects of the absurdity is scored plus:
1. The cat not going after the mice.
2. The mice not afraid of the cat.
3. An abnormal family group.

   Plus. "The mouse runs on the cat. (Q.) 'Cause they're
all running around and one is on the cat. He should get up
and eat them all." "Because the mice are so tame." "He's
coming up to the cat — the cat might bite him." "This is
on top of his back. Cats love to eat mouses. Gee, those
mouses don't seem to be very scared, do they?" "The
mouses are dumb. They don't know the cat will eat them
and they're walking all around the cat instead of running
away." "A mouse is on the cat's back. (Q.) Because the
mouse came up to the cat. He wouldn't." "A kitty has
some little mouses instead of a mama mouse having little
mouses." "'Cause the cat is with the mice. (Q.) 'Cause
cats eat mice."

   Minus. "Mouses, why are they doing that? Is cat going
to eat them up?" "A mouse, a cat, a mouse, a mouse. (Q.)

The mouse is up on top of the cat and the mouse is talking to the cat and the cat is laying down and two little mouses are eating" (description of the picture). "A mice is going on the pussy cat and there's a mice talking to him." "All the mouses are around the cat. (Q.) Here's two mouses drinking his milk up." (These two responses seem also to contain nothing beyond description.) "A mouse couldn't walk on his two hind legs." "The mice are on the cat's back. (Q.) These two eating cheese and drinking milk. (Q.) Mice don't drink milk."

Two of three must be correct to score plus on the test.

4. Repeating Three Digits Reversed (Cf. Form L, p. 254)

One of the three series must be repeated backward without error.

5. Sentence Building I

The new form of instruction for the sentence-building test makes it usable considerably lower in the scale than the old form. In the latter the child often failed simply because he did not know the meaning of the word "sentence." The test has a high correlation with the composite score (.78) and shows a rapid increase in per cent passing. It is fairly difficult at this level notwithstanding the very lenient scoring.

To be scored plus, all three key words must be included in the same sentence. The sentence must be complete, having a subject and a predicate. The number of clauses a sentence may have depends upon how well the content is unified. Three coordinate clauses are allowed if they are closely unified. A sentence with two coordinate clauses is scored minus if the clauses are totally unrelated. The words must be used meaningfully in the sentence, and the sentence must not be grossly ungrammatical. Omission of articles, or substitution of "a" for "an" and vice versa, is disregarded. The words must be used in the part of speech given; for example, a noun may not be changed to a verb, etc. A singular may be changed to a plural and vice versa, and tenses may be altered, but the number of the verb must agree with the subject.

(a) *Horse — Bigger — Dog*

Plus. "The dog is not bigger than the horse." "The horse is bigger and the dog is kinda big." "The horse is bigger and the dog will bite." "There was a horse and he was bigger than the dog and the horse ran away and the dog couldn't catch him."

Minus. "The horse started growing bigger and we lost our dog." "A dog is bigger than the horse." "A dog is littler than a horse."

(b) *Boy — Fell — Leg*

Plus. "The boy fell and broke his leg." "The boy has two legs and he fell down." "Once there was a little boy and he fell and he hurt his leg." "The boy can fall down and hurt his legs when he tips over something."

Minus. "The boy felt his leg." "Boy would hurt himself if he fell and he could walk with a leg." "A boy falls down and a leg doesn't." "The boy fell with his legs." "He fell and broke his leg."

(c) *Child — Flowers — Meadow*

Plus. "Child went to pick some flowers in the meadow." "The child got some flowers in the meadow." "The child'd be playing on the meadow and be picking flowers." "The meadow has flowers in it and the child goes in the meadow." "Children go into the meadow to get flowers." "The child picks flowers and walks in the meadow."

Minus. "The child is a whole lot different than the flower and the flower is a whole lot different than the meadow." "Flowers grow in the garden and the child can go to school and the meadow is something where the cows lay down." "A child isn't a flower or meadow." "The child went out to pick

flowers and she found a little meadow in the flowers."
"There's a garden and a child looks in and see flowers and a
meadow." "Child picked flowers and a meadow is pretty."

Two of the three sentences must be scored plus to pass the
test.

6. Counting Taps

Different forms of this test have been used by psychologists
interested in various aspects of child development, one of them
by Kuhlmann [1] in his revision of the Binet Scale. Our data
indicate that the test is very satisfactory at this level; there is
a rapid increase in per cent passing from one age to the next
and the test correlates .50 with the composite. We require
three successes in three trials for passing.

YEAR VIII

1. Comprehension III (Cf. Form L, p. 206)

(a) *What should a man do if he comes home and finds that a burglar
has robbed his house?*

A satisfactory response must suggest definite practical steps
for the capture of the burglar.

> *Plus.* "He'd send down the police." "Should report it."
> "Go and tell the cop, anyway get the money back." "He
> should go and call up the police and get his gun out of the
> house and shoot it." "The man takes the burglar to jail."
> "Bring him to the cops if he can find him." "He should look
> around for clues to see who did it and call the police to see if
> they could capture whoever robbed the house." "Get their
> fingerprints."
> *Minus.* "Find out who it was." "Put it in the paper."
> "He should get all of the money out of him." "He should

[1] Kuhlmann, F. *A Handbook of Mental Tests*, pp. 106–07; 124–25. Baltimore:
Warwick and York, 1922.

try to catch him" (no definite steps suggested).   "Go out of the house."

(b) *Why is a train harder to stop than an automobile?*

A satisfactory response must mention, at least by implication, one of the following facts: (1) the train is heavier (or bigger, longer, etc.); (2) the tracks or train wheels present less friction; (3) the train goes faster.   We overlook the fact that trains do not always go faster than automobiles, and we must be content with very crude statements about the influence of weight and traction.

> *Plus.*   "Takes more power to run a train than an automobile therefore it takes more to stop it."   (May be accepted as a reference to weight.)   "Because trains are heavy and are hard to shut off."   "Because there's so many coaches on." "There's more to stop."   "Because it runs by coal and it is bigger than an automobile."   "When a train stops it slides a little bit but when a car stops it don't."   "Because the train runs on smooth tracks and won't stop as quick."   "Because train hasn't got rubber tires on — more friction." "Train goes on a track made of iron and it could slip easier; automobile has rubber so it won't slip."   "Because it goes too fast."   "When a train's going fast the brakes won't hold so quick — won't stop it so quick."
>
> *Minus.*   "Because a train has more things to stop — an automobile you just have to push down the brakes."   "Because a train has more wheels than an automobile. (Q.) Automobile only has four and train has much more than four."   "Because trains go fast and they can't stop whenever they want because they have to stop at different stations." "Because trains go on tracks and keeps on going, there's no stop signs."   "'Cause it's much stronger."

(c) *What should a man do if he finds that he is earning less money than it takes to live on?*

For a satisfactory response the subject must suggest increasing his income.   "To economize" indicates lack of comprehension of the question and is scored minus. The ordinary methods of increasing his income are: getting a better job, advancing in the job he has, asking for a raise, increasing the number of jobs he has, having someone else in the family go to work, etc.

Plus. "Should find another job." "He should go in another business." "Should get a job that brings in more money or shouldn't spend so much." "Quit and get another job." "Have to work himself up so he can earn more." "Work some more." "He should try to work better." "Try to get some way to make more money." "Talk to the boss about it." "Have some one else in the family go to work."

Minus. "Shouldn't spend so much money to live on." "Do without." "Borrow some." "He should go out and beg." "If he earns less money than it takes to live on why he'd quit the job. (Q.) And he wouldn't work at the place any more."

This test is passed if two of the three questions are answered correctly.

2. Similarities: Two things (Cf. Form L, p. 228)

Any real likeness whether fundamental or superficial is considered satisfactory.

(a) *Mosquito and sparrow*

Plus. "Both animals." "Both have wings." "Mosquito can sing and buzz and fly and sparrow can sing and fly." "Sparrow has legs and mosquito has, too." "Both of 'em got eggs." "Both eat." "They both get their own living." "They're both the same color." "Both pests." "They both end in the same sound."

Minus. "Both of them can hop and jump." "Both have tails." "Both have small wings." "They're both little." "Both bite." "Both have long legs." "Both got a bill." "They eat about the same food." "They're both birds." "Both insects."

(b) *Window and door*

Plus. "Both keep the wind out." "What you look out." "They both got glass in them and they are both wood." "Part of both of them is wood." "They both have curtains." "You can lock a window and you can lock a door." "They're both something you can go thru'." "They both open" (or close). "A window has four corners and a door has four corners." "A window is like a rectangle and a door is like a rectangle." "They can be moved, one can be moved up and one can be opened."

Minus. "Because the window is on the door." "Both have windows in." "Both look square." "A window is glass and a door is wood with the glass on the top." "Made out of wood." "Both straight."

(c) *Bread and meat*

Plus. "You can eat both." "Both go in a sandwich." "You can cut the bread and cut the meat." "They've both been cooked." "Both sold at the store." "Both grow. (Q.) Bread from wheat which grows, meat from animals."

Minus. "Because you can put meat on bread and then you can eat it — you won't be hungry." "Both soft."

This test is passed if a similarity is pointed out in two of the three comparisons.

3. Verbal Absurdities I (Cf. Form L, pp. 235 f.)

(a) *A man had flu (influenza) twice. The first time it killed him, but the second time he got well quickly.*

Plus. "He can't have it twice if it killed him once." "If the first time it killed him, he couldn't get it again." "Just got it backwards." "It should be the first time he got well and the second time he died." "The second time he couldn't get well. (Q.) Because he was dead." "He couldn't have got well if it killed him the first time." "He can only die once. (Q.) 'Cause he got dead and got well quickly."

Minus. "When he had it the first time he couldn't have it

again." "Because the first time it killed him and the second
it didn't. (Q.) Because the first time he died and the next
time he didn't." "He got well the next day."

(b) *Walter now has to write with his left hand because two years ago
he lost both his arms in an accident.*

Plus. "He can't write if both his arms are broken."
"Writing and he's lost both hands!" "He couldn't write."
"How'd he get another one?" "If hc hurt one arm and he
wrote with the left one then how could both of them be hurt."
"He hasn't got no arms." "If he lost his arms he'd lose his
hands, too." "He couldn't write none with his left hand. (Q.)
Both arms were gone."

Minus. "He could use the other arm, too."

(c) *A man said, "I know a road from my house to the city which is
downhill all the way to the city and downhill all the way back home."*

Plus. "It can't be downhill both directions." "Have to
go uphill one way or have to change. You couldn't go down
the hill all the time." "Downhill all the way back home. (Q.)
Have to be uphill one way." "Going down to the city and
going down coming back." "If it was downhill going to
the city it would have to be uphill going home." "He'd be
taking another road if he was going home and it was downhill." "The hill can't change up and down for him — can't
be downhill coming back."

Minus. "If it's downhill to the village he'll have to
climb." "I guess it's a very crooked road." "He goes
downhill when he goes to the city and downhill when he comes
home. (Q.) 'Cause it isn't downhill all the way to the city,
it's uphill too."

(d) *An old gentleman complained that he could no longer walk
around the park as he used to; he said he could now go only halfway
around and back again.*

Plus. "Says he can't walk around and he can walk one
halfway around and back, he should be able to walk all the
way around then." "He said he couldn't walk around it all
and he said he could. (Q.) He said he couldn't walk around

it all and said he could walk around it one half way and back again." "If he could walk one half way round and back again he could walk all the way round." "If he can't walk around it how could he go one half way and back." "If he's getting too old to walk around the park he couldn't walk around one half way and back." "He could go all the way round. (Q.) If he could go half way round and back."

Minus. "Because he said he couldn't walk around the park any longer and then he said he could walk around." "'Cause if you go one half way round and back again you could walk around it twice."

The test is passed if three of the four absurdities are pointed out.

4. Naming the Days of the Week

On account of the check questions we have used, this is not a mere test of rote memory. The test has been retained because it shows a regular increase in per cent passing from one age to the next and has a good correlation with the composite score (r is .61).

The test is passed if the days of the week are all named, and in correct order, and if the child succeeds in at least two of the three check questions. It is not necessary to begin with the first day of the week.

5. Problem Situations (Cf. Form L, pp. 264 f.)

(a) *About two o'clock one afternoon a number of boys and girls, dressed in their best clothes, rang the bell at Alice's house. Alice opened the door. What was happening?*

Plus. "A party." "A dance." "It was Alice's birthday." "They were surprising her." "Some boys and girls came to visit her." "Give 'em a Valentine or a birthday party or a basket of Easter eggs." "Christmas day." "Going to be a play." "They wanted her to come to a party."

The following responses have been scored minus because they are too vague and do not indicate that account is being taken of all the elements in the situation.

> *Minus.* "They came to call." "They were coming to her house." "They came to see Alice." "They went to visit the little girl." "Some company were coming." "They wanted to play with her." "They wanted her to go somewhere."

(b) *Helen heard a big "bang" and came running outdoors. There were nails all over the road, and an automobile had just stopped beside the road. What was the "bang"?*

> *Plus.* "Puncture." "Car ran over the nails. (Q.) Punctured the tire." "Blow out." "Flat tire." "Tire busted." "The tire." "Automobile got nails in the wheels."
>
> *Minus.* "Box of nails fell out." "The nails." "Backfire." "Machine got smashed." "Wreck."

(c) *A young man and lady were sitting in a restaurant. They had nearly finished eating a big dinner. The waiter brought the bill. The young man looked at it and then seemed worried and embarrassed. Why?*

> *Plus.* "Not enough money." "Because he didn't have the money." "Didn't have no money to pay for it." "He had to pay a lot of money." "It cost too high." "Because he ate a big dinner. (Q.) Didn't have enough money to pay for it." "It was eight dollars. (Q.) He didn't have that much."
>
> *Minus.* "Because he didn't want to pay." "It might not even have had any writing on it." "He swallowed something bad and the waiter brought too much money and the stuff wasn't good." "Because the bill was wrong. (Q.) Was somebody else's."

Two of the three situations must be correctly explained.

6. Opposite Analogies II (Cf. Form L, p. 216)

(a) *The rabbit's ears are long; the rat's ears are* ......
   Plus. "Short."
   Minus. "Small."

(b) *Snow is white; coal is* ......
   Plus. "Black."
   Minus. "Dark."

(c) *The dog has hair; the bird has* ......
   Plus. "Feathers."
   Minus. "Wings."

(d) *Wolves are wild; dogs are* ......
   Plus. "Tame." "Tamed." "Domestic." "Tamed —
   or civilized." "Very tame."
   Minus. "Tameful." "Pets." "Playful." "Timid."
   "Gentle." "Calm." "Friendly." "Quiet." "Mild."

The test is passed if three of the four are correctly completed.

YEAR IX

1. Memory for Designs I (Cf. Form L, p. 248)

For *full credit* on design (a):

All of the elements must be reproduced and the relationship between these elements maintained. Slight irregularities due to lack of motor skill or hasty execution are disregarded.

The principal elements of design (a) are:

(1) The vertical uprights, the second taller than the first by the height of the square;

(2) Two similar squares at the top and to the left of the uprights;

(3) The connecting base line.

For *half credit* no essential part must be omitted, but the relationships are less well maintained.

The second upright may be only slightly taller than the first.

The squares may not be accurately formed; e.g., may be slightly rectangular or have extensions beyond the uprights.

The relative positions of the uprights may not be strictly reproduced; e.g., they may be so close together that one square may be under the other.

No credit is given when:

The second upright is shorter than the first;

Either or both squares face the wrong direction;

There are gross inaccuracies in formation and location of the squares;

Gratuitous variations have been added.

For *full credit* on design (b):

Both outer and inner figures must be approximately square;

The corners of the inner square must tend to touch the midpoints of the sides of the outer square.

For *half credit:*

The outer figure may be distinctly longer either horizontally or vertically;

The inner figure may be diamond- or kite-shaped with angles not meeting precisely;

The inner figure may not meet the midpoints of the sides of the outer figure very accurately.

No credit:

Distortion of the above proportions;

The inner figure may be entirely detached from the outer.

The test is passed if a score of one credit is earned.

On pages 364–67 are samples of plus, half-credit, and minus responses for designs (a) and (b).

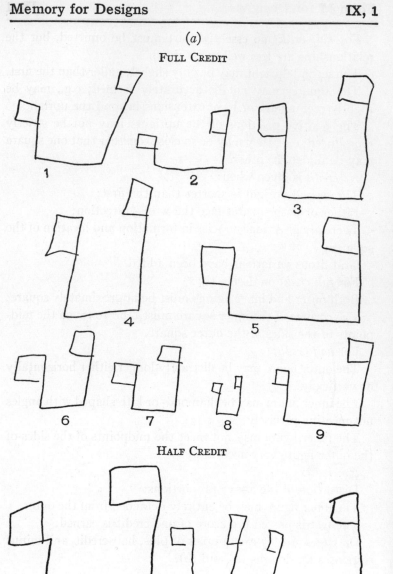

HALF CREDIT — CONTINUED

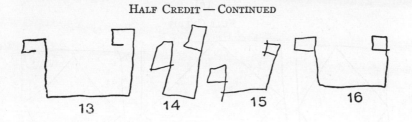

NO CREDIT

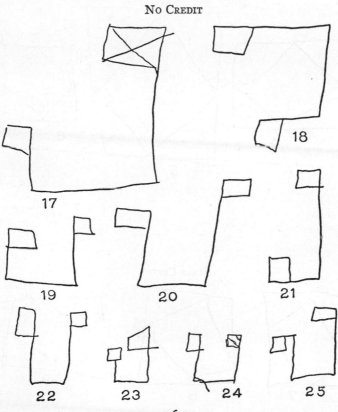

(*b*)

FULL CREDIT

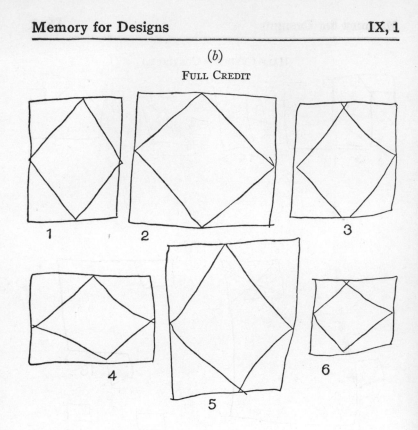

1   2   3

4   5   6

HALF CREDIT

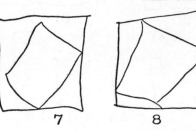
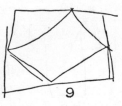

7   8   9

HALF CREDIT — CONTINUED

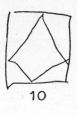

10

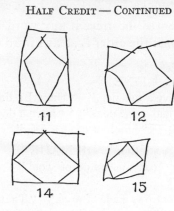

11   12

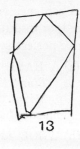

13

14   15

No CREDIT

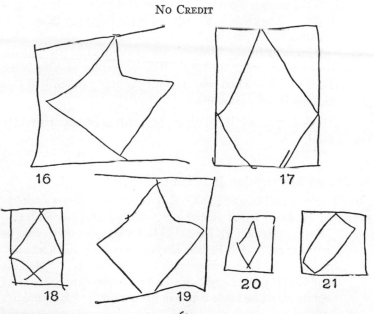

16   17

18   19   20   21

2. Dissected Sentences I (Cf. Form L, p. 276)

A sentence is counted incorrect if any word is omitted, altered, or inserted, or if the order is so awkward that it fails to make perfect sense.

(a) A HAVE DOG I FINE
> *Plus.* "I have a fine dog." "Have I a fine dog?"
> *Minus.* "I had a fine dog." "I have a dog 'Fine.'" "A fine dog have I." "Fine! I have a dog."

(b) WOOL THE WAS COAT OF MADE
> *Plus.* "The coat was made of wool." "Was the coat made of wool?"
> *Minus.* "Coat was made of wool." "That coat was made of the wool." "The coat of wool was made." "Of wool the coat was made."

(c) CHILD THE PLAYING GARDEN IN THE IS
> *Plus.* "The child is playing in the garden." "The child is in the garden playing." "Is the child playing in the garden?" "The child in the garden is playing." "In the garden the child is playing."
> *Minus.* "In the garden is the playing child." "In the garden is the child playing." "In the garden playing is the child." "The child was playing in the garden." (This response is quite common.)

The test is passed if two of the sentences are correctly transposed.

3. Verbal Absurdities II (Cf. Form L, pp. 235 f.)

(a) *I saw a well-dressed young man who was walking down the street with his hands in his pockets and twirling a brand-new cane.*
> *Plus.* "He had his hands in his pockets and how could he carry a cane?" "If he had his hands in his pocket he must have had the cane in his mouth and turning it." "Had his hands in his pocket and twirled a brand-new cane. He can't hold it, unless he made a hole in his pocket." "He wouldn't

be twirling his cane if he had his hands in his pockets." "He had his hands in his pocket twirling a cane. (Q.) He can't twirl his cane in his pocket." "He had his hands in his pockets and was twirling a cane!" (The scoring of this response depends, of course, on the inflection. Explanation is sometimes necessary.)

Minus. "He wouldn't be twirling a brand new cane if he was well-dressed and wouldn't have his hands in his pockets." "Twirling a brand new canc. (Q.) Twirling a brand-new cane." "He couldn't have his hands in his pockets with a cane on his arms." "He had his hands in his pockets and had his cane on his arm whirling it around."

(b) *A father wrote to his son, "I enclose ten dollars. If you do not receive this letter, please send me a telegram."*

Plus. "If he didn't receive the letter, he wouldn't even know his father sent it to him." "If he didn't receive it how could he know he wants a telegram." "He can't send a telegram if he didn't get the letter." "I don't see any sense in that — if he hasn't seen it yet how would he know to send the telegram." "How would the son know that?" "If he received the letter, he'd receive the ten dollars."

Minus. "He couldn't send a letter because he couldn't receive it because he didn't know when it was coming." "The letter *would* get there." "He probably can't send him a telegram unless he sent the letter." "If he gets the ten dollars he won't have to send him a telegram." "He couldn't send the telegram without ten dollars."

(c) *A soldier on the march complained that every man in the regiment was out of step except himself.*

Plus. "It means he thought he was right when he was wrong. The others were all in step." "If every one was out of step — he was out of step with them. (Q.) He was wrong instead of them." "He should be in step with the other soldiers." "He is the only one that was different." "If every one else was out of step, he couldn't be in step because there was no one for him to be in step with." "He'd

be the one out of step." "He said every man was out of step
except himself. (Q.) Why don't he tell himself that he's
out of step instead of the other people?" "He was out of
step if every man in the regiment was out of step. (Q.) He
was the one that was out of step because they were marching
differently." (This type of response becomes more frequent
with the higher ages and with brighter children. The first
part is minus unless explained.) "He wasn't in step himself.
(Q.) The rest were all together except him."

Minus. "He says every man and every man means himself." "Why, he wouldn't be in step himself, because he'd
get all mixed up with them." "If he said they were all out
of step he would be out of step too because they'd all be going
one way and he'd be going another and they'd all be out of
step." "If he wasn't out of step he wouldn't see whether the
others were out of step." "They couldn't all be out of step.
(Q.) Because they wouldn't be." "He'd be out of step —
the same as the rest of them."

(d) *A kind-hearted man who was taking a heavy bag of grain to town
on his horse sat on his horse and lifted the bag to his own shoulder in
order to make the load easier for the horse.*

In scoring this item allowance must be made for the fact that
the wording of the problem is somewhat ambiguous, because
it is not definitely stated that the man was already on the
horse when it occurred to him to shift the burden to his own
shoulder. Thus it may be pointed out that it is:

(1) Harder because of the addition of the man's weight.

(2) Harder because of concentration of previously distrib-
uted weight.

(3) Not any easier because it will make no difference.

(4) Harder for the man, but no easier for the horse.

> *Plus.* "That won't make it easier for the horse, because
> it's just as heavy with him holding it." "He sat on the
> horse, too. (Q.) Because he sat on the horse and had the
> grain too." "When he took his load and put it on his back

it would be just as heavy." "If he was trying to make the load easier for the horse he should get off his own self." "Make it all the heavier. (Q.) Because he got on the horse, too." "He wouldn't make it easier for the horse — it'd make it harder. (Q.) If he gets the bag over his shoulder it will make more weight on the same spot." "He put the grain on his shoulder to make it easier for the horse. (Q.) It wouldn't make it any easier." "It would be just the same weight."

Minus. "If he put the grain on the horse and walked himself it would be easier because he was carrying the load and the horse wasn't." "He shouldn't have lifted the grain to his shoulder because the horse could carry that just as well as the horse could carry him." "He should've left it on the horse. (Q.) He should've left the load on the horse and sat on with it." "He took it on his shoulder when he could put it on the horse." "When he got on his horse, if he wanted to make it easier and not harder he should have left the bag of grain in the wagon."

(e) *A man said to his friend, "I hope you live to eat the chickens that scratch sand on your grave."*

Either aspect of this absurdity is acceptable:

(1) If he is alive to eat the chickens he would have no grave for them to scratch sand on.

(2) If he is dead and has a grave he cannot be alive to eat them.

Plus. "If he's dead he wouldn't know whether the chickens scratch sand on his grave or not." "If he was alive they wouldn't scratch sand on his grave." "His grave wouldn't be there before he was dead." "The chickens couldn't scratch sand on his grave because he wasn't dead yet." "Because if he was dead he couldn't eat anything." "He couldn't eat 'em. (Q.) 'Cause he'd be dead."

Minus. "If he eats the chickens they won't be living to scratch sand on his grave." "I don't see how he could talk to him when he was dead." "He couldn't do it — chickens couldn't get over there 'cause they couldn't have the grave in the yard." "If he had a chicken on his grave he wouldn't be dead yet if the man was talking to him." "He hadn't died yet."

The test is passed if three of the absurdities are pointed out.

4. Similarities and Differences (Cf. Form L, p. 228)

(a) *Honey and glue*

Both the similarity and the difference must be correct.

> *Plus.* "Both of them are sticky and honey comes in combs and glue in cans." "Honey and glue are sticky but honey is sweet and glue is to use." "Honey you can eat and glue you can't — both come in bottles." "Both come from animals and you paste with glue and eat honey." "They're the same color, but glue is to stick on things and honey is not." "Honey is for bread and butter and glue is for paper. (Q.) Honey is kind of brown and glue is brown too." "The honey can flow and glue can flow, and glue you can't eat and honey you can." "They look the same but honey is a food and glue you paste with."
>
> *Minus.* "They're sticky and honey is orange and glue is brown." "Honey you can eat and glue you can't and they both smell good." "Honey is when you call any one honey you like 'em and stick to 'em and glue sticks. (Q.) Glue sticks and honey don't."

(b) *Pen and pencil*

> *Plus.* "Both of them write, and a pen writes any color you dip the pen in and a pencil doesn't write but one color." "Both to write with but a pen is plainer to write." "Both the same shape, and one has lead and one has ink." "A pen can take ink and a pencil can't, and they both have long sticks." "A pen writes with ink and a pencil writes with lead pencil. (Q.) They both have a long handle." "You can

372

write with a pen and you can write with a pencil and pen'll
stick you and a pencil won't." "Pencils are wood and pens
are celluloid, and they both write." "They begin with the
same letter and end with a different."

Minus. "Both in a set, and one writes with ink and the
pencil doesn't." "A pencil has a point and a pen has a
point, and when they ain't sharpened the pencil hasn't no
point." "A pen you keep pigs in and you write with a pencil.
How could you write in a pig pen?" "A pen writes and so
does a pencil. (Q.) A pencil is much skinnier than a pen."

(c) *Banana and lemon*

Plus. "Both are fruit, and a banana is long and a lemon
round." "Both to eat but a lemon is more for lemonade."
"You eat 'em both, and banana hasn't got big seeds and lemon
has." "Lemon tastes different than a banana and lemon is
same color as a banana." "You use them for salads, and a
banana is sweet and lemon is sour." "A banana is yellow
and a lemon is yellow, and a banana hasn't juice and a lemon
has." "The lemon is round and the banana isn't; they both
have peels." "They're both yellow — banana's long and a
lemon's round." "Banana is big and lemon is little, and
they both grow on trees."

Minus. "A lemon has brown skin and a banana has
brown skin, and a banana's long and a lemon's round."
"Their skins are alike, and a banana you eat and you make
lemonade out of a lemon and drink it." "Banana is long
and yellow and has peeling, and lemon is yellow inside and
has yellow peeling and it's round." (If it is clear that the
child is just giving a rambling general description of the objects,
mentioning, among the characteristics given, both similarities and differences, the score is minus.)

(d) *Shoe and glove*

Plus. "Both for clothing, and shoes are heavier than
gloves." "They are both made out of leather, and you wear
a shoe and don't wear a glove — you catch balls with them."
"You can wear 'em both, and shoes are made of leather and

gloves are made of wool." "The shoes keep your feet warm
and gloves keep your hands warm, and difference is — shoes
are for your feet and gloves are for your hands." "Shoes
and gloves are alike because you can put 'em on, and they're
different because shoes are harder and gloves are soft."
"Both leather, but you wear a glove and a shoe you put on
your feet." "They both got a hole in the top, but a shoe
hasn't got places for fingers."

Minus. "A shoe you wear on your foot and a glove you
wear on your hand and a glove has fingers and a shoe you
wear." "Shoes you wear and gloves you wear, and sometimes the shoe is too small and the glove can't fit you sometimes." "Shoe goes on your foot and is bigger than a glove
is and glove goes on your hand and is smaller than a shoe is."
"A glove is to keep your hands warm and a shoe has a sole
on, and a glove is leather and cloth and things like that."
"Both to keep your feet and hands clean — shoes are made
out of leather." "Shoes go on your feet and a glove goes on
your hand. A shoe keeps your feet from getting wet and a
glove keeps your hand warm." "You put a shoe on your
feet and a glove on your hand, and different because a shoe
goes on your foot and a glove on your hand."

All four comparisons must be correct to score plus on the
test.

5. Rhymes: Old form (Cf. Form L, p. 249)

This is the familiar test of finding rhymes. We have stand·
ardized new stimulus words to replace the old ones which
proved to be objectionable in some respects. As a rule the
test presents very little difficulty in scoring. There must be
three words in addition to the stimulus word. These must be
real words, not nonsense syllables or made-up words. The
child is given credit for the rhyming words even though there
may occur interspersed among the proper rhymes nonsense
syllables or words which do not rhyme. Of course, if the child

is just reeling off a list of nonsense syllables among which occur
by chance some real words, the item should be scored minus.

All common words are credited. Occasionally obscure or
rarely used words are given which are mere nonsense syllables
as far as the subject is concerned but which can be found in the
dictionary or occasionally are used as proper names. Unless
there is reason to believe that the child is using such words
meaningfully we do not give credit for them. Words of more
than one syllable are given credit when the last syllable rhymes
with the stimulus word. Words with the same pronunciation
but different meaning, when differentiated by the child, are
each given credit. Sometimes the child gives another meaning
for the stimulus word, for example, "date that you don't eat";
this does not count as a rhyme for it. A word repeated is
counted only the first time it is given. The following illustrations will serve as a guide in scoring some of the more difficult
types of responses.

(a) *Rhymes with date*
  Plus. "Rate." "Accumulate." "Concentrate." "De-
bate." "Originate." "Mate and playmate" (counted as
two). "Bait and rebate" (counted as two). "Pate."
  Minus. "Zate." "Drate." "Flate." "Sedate."

(b) *Rhymes with head*
  Plus. "Said." "Jed." "Two reds — read a book, and
red, a color" (credit for two). "Zed (a cracker)." "Ted."
"Pled." "Two sheds — shed a building, and a tree sheds its
leaves" (credit for two). "Ced — short for Cedric, you
know." "Ked (singular of keds)."
  Minus. "Married." "Med." "Ped." "Cred."
"Shredded."

(c) *Rhymes with cap*
  Plus. "Crap." "Flap." "Slap." "Hap."
  Minus. "Swap." "Drap." "Blap." "Ap." "Fap."
"Bap."

The test is passed if three rhyming words are given for each of two of the stimulus words.

6. Repeating Four Digits Reversed (Cf. Form L, p. 254)

One series of the three must be correctly reversed to pass this test.

YEAR X

1. Block Counting

The block-counting test is modeled after the cube-analysis test devised by Otis and used in Army Beta.[1] It correlates with the composite score .43 for a single age range. It is one of the few performance tests that we tried which proved to be coherent with the rest of our scale. The number of piles of cubes has been reduced to fourteen and there are three illustrations for practice. We require eight correct out of fourteen for plus.

2. Memory for Stories I: The School Concert

(a) *What is the name of the story?* (The School Concert.)
    Plus. "The School's concert." "School Concert." "A School Concert."
    Minus. "The High School Concert." "The Concert." "The Concert at School." "The Children's School Concert."

(b) *Where was it held?* (In the auditorium of the high school.)
    Plus. "At high school." "At a high school." "In the auditorium." "In the school auditorium."
    Minus. "School hall." "In the city auditorium." "Sequoia High School." "In the Junior High." "At the school."

---

[1] "Psychological Examining in the United States Army." Robert M. Yerkes, ed. *Nat'l Acad. of Sc. Mem.*, 15, 369–74; 388. Washington, Gov't Printing Office, 1921.

(c) *When was it held?*   (December 20th.)

    Plus. "December 20, 1930."

    Minus. "The 20th."   "A few days before Christmas." "December 21."   "At Christmas."   "Near Christmas." "In December."

(d) *What did the program consist of?*   (Singing by the school choir, fancy marching, folk dancing, and a Christmas play.)

The following deviations from perfectly correct responses are credited 1 point each to a maximum total of 4 points:

Singing, Choirs, Singing by choir, Songs, Folk songs, Music, Marching, Fancy dancing, Toe dancing, Play, Plays, Christmas show.

The following combinations of responses are scored as indicated:

Singing, dancing, playing (2 points).

Music, songs, marching, and a play (3 points).

Dancing, singing, marching, Christmas play (4 points).

Songs, dancing, and a Christmas show (3 points).

No credit is given for the following:

Christmas program.   Christmas party.   Santa Claus play.

(e) *How many people attended the concert?*   (620.)

    Plus. "About 620."   "About 600."   "More than 600." "Nearly 620."

(f) *How much money was raised?*   (Nearly $400.)

    Plus. "Almost $400."   "$400."   "Around $400." "Over $400."   "$400 and some dollars."

    Minus. "$401."   "$416."   "Almost $420."

Five out of nine memories are required for plus.

3. Verbal Absurdities III (Cf. Form L, pp. 235 f.)

(a) *In the year 1915 many more women than men got married in the United States.*

    Plus. "They couldn't get married if they didn't have

men." "That women have to get married to men — they
can't get married to women." "There wouldn't be enough
men married to the women. (Q.) There'd be two women
married at the same time together." "In some places that
could be possible because of polygamy but in any other place
where there aren't Mormons we need as many men as women
to get married." "'Cause there's not as many men as
women. (Q.) There has to be as many men as women to
get married."

Minus. "They couldn't do it because there wasn't as
many men. (Q.) Because there was more women than men."
"'Cause just one at a time gets married don't they?" "More
people couldn't be married because lots of people were married already." "Because the women gets married more
than the men." "Men don't get married, only women get
married because the men are the husbands and they don't do
the marrying, the wife does it." "How could there be
enough men?"

(b) *A man wished to dig a hole in which to bury some rubbish, but
could not decide what to do with the dirt from the hole. A friend suggested that he dig the hole large enough to hold the dirt, too.*

Plus. "He couldn't dig a hole big enough to put the dirt
in, too." "Well, he'd have more dirt and he'd just keep on
digging holes." "It would be foolish; a larger hole would
get more dirt." "He'd still have some dirt from the other
hole." "There'd be just as much dirt coming out." "Because if he dug a hole and put all the dirt back in the hole
there wouldn't be any room for the other rubbish." "If he
dug a hole deep it would just hold the dirt that he dug out
of it." "Because he couldn't do that. (Q.) The bigger the
hole the more dirt he'd have to put in." "He couldn't dig a
hole large enough to hold the dirt, too, unless there were a lot
of rocks in the ground he threw away." "He couldn't dig
a hole that would hold the dirt because if he dug the hole he
would have to throw the dirt aside. (Q.) Well, if you dig a
hole, if you leave the dirt in there it wouldn't be a hole at all."

Minus. "He would just have to dig it out again. (Q.) He would have to dig the dirt out." "He should put the dirt on top." "Couldn't get every scrap of the dirt back in the hole." "Don't have to dig a hole large enough to put the dirt in. Just pack the dirt in and step on it, it'll go down after a rain or two." "If he just dug a little hole the dirt would have went back in. It don't matter how big he dug it." "If he just dug one hole he could put the rubbish in that and leave the dirt where it was." "He can't bury the rubbish without putting the dirt over the top of it."

(c) *They began the meeting late, but they set the hands of the clock back so that the meeting might surely close before sunset.*

Plus. "It don't matter if they put it back. It would be sunset at the same time anyway." "They couldn't do that because it'd just be as late anyway." "The time would go on anyway. The clock would just be wrong, that's all." "They set the hands back and thought it would be later — or earlier when it's the same time." "It would be dark when they got through. (Q.) Because the clock would be slow." "It would still be late."

Minus. "It was foolish to set the hands of the clock back because then they couldn't tell what time it was." "The sun can set any time." "Then the sun would go down before the clock would strike the time it was." "It'd be sunset and past by the time they got through with the meeting." "If they started it early, they wouldn't have to set it back." "It wouldn't make any difference. (Q.) On account of they might have watches." "If they wanted the meeting to close before sunset they could watch when the sun was going down, they could stop the meeting." "It'll shorten the meeting instead of lengthening it."

The test is passed if two of the absurdities are correctly explained.

4. Abstract Words I (Cf. Form L, p. 261)

(a) *Pity.* (A feeling of compassion for the sufferings of others.)

Plus. "To feel compassion or sympathy." "Feel sorry for." "You feel for people." "Person gets hurt — you pity them — feel bad." "If a person is sick you pity them. (Q.) Means you help a person out and don't like to have 'em suffer." "Have mercy on anybody. (Q.) If somebody was awful poor or anything you'd pity 'em — might give 'em something to help 'em out." "You take mercy on some one, you'll take them in if they're hungry and give them something to eat." "You see something that's wrong and have your feelings aroused." "You pity anybody. (Q.) Feel bad for them."

Minus. "Sad." "Sorrow." "Sorry. (Q.) Pity means sorry because if someone went away to some country you'd pity them. (Q.) Because you wouldn't like them to go." "If you're liable to get a lickin' and the kids say, 'I pity you.' (Q.) You're goin' to get a whippin'." "Pity some people who are cripples. (Q.) Not start laughin' at 'em." "Somebody is going to get after you." "Take pity on a person. (Q.) Like you killed somebody and they take pity on you." "When you take pity on anybody you hope they'll do better if they've done something wrong." "Something that is going to happen to you later. (Q.) Something that is going to happen to you later and watch out."

(b) *Curiosity.* (Disposition to inquire into anything, especially something new or strange, often implying meddlesomeness; desire to know. That which is curious, or fitted to excite or reward attention.)

Plus. "Wondering what it is." "Want to know something." "You're always curious and want to look into something. If there is something, you want to see it." "It means you're very interested or anxious." "You're trying to find out about other people's business." "Means that you are nosey." "Want to know everything." "Like you think something is queer." "That they are different from other people."

Minus. "Not to know." "Asking too many questions. (Q.) You're afraid to ask, but you ask anyway." "Anxious." "If you go to see somebody for the fun of it." "Like someone is curious and never will believe you." "Somebody is always butting into someone else's business." "You hardly believe it." "Stare at people."

(c) *Grief.* (Suffering, distress, a cause of suffering, remorse, disaster.)

Plus. "Suffer." "You're in misery." "You feel hurt over something." "A feeling you have when you lose something or someone." "Like mourning." "Sorrow." "We have sadness." "You're not happy." "Sort of mournful." "You're sorry."

Minus. "When you say, 'Good grief, I've lost something.' (Q.) It means you've lost something." "Means death. (Q.) You die or somebody dies." "Sometimes you're mad and you don't know what to do and you get disgusted." "Trouble. (Q.) It's hard to get you out." "If a lady's in grief, she's sobbing. (Q.) Means pity." "To be sorry for. (Q.) Pity 'em." "When you bear anything."

(d) *Surprise.* (To be struck with wonder, astonishment, or confusion by something unexpected, sudden, or remarkable.)

Plus. "The showing of something unexpected — your emotion to that." "A sudden feeling over some one thing." "To take anyone unawares." "The feeling toward something that thrills you or amazes you." "Astonishment." "Something that comes that you didn't know about." "Something comes off suddenly." "If you didn't expect somebody you'd be surprised to see them." "Like something somebody has hidden for you — like at Christmas — they want to surprise you by giving you something." "Startled." "You are surprised — well — you are taken off your guard or something like that."

Minus. "You get alarmed by something or good news — or hear of some accident or something." "Something new that you never saw before, or heard." "Means you don't

know what to think about it." "Something to fool them."
"A present."

Two of the words must be correctly defined to pass the test
at this level.

5. Word Naming: Animals (Cf. Form L, pp. 258 f.)

This is one of the many varieties of controlled association
tests. We have used in Form L a word-naming test, but there
we have made use of the free association technique. The
guiding idea here is given in the instruction "to see how many
different animals you can name," thus facilitating the search
for ideas that belong to this class and inhibiting those which
do not belong. The effect of the directive tendency, the
Einstellung, is brought out very strikingly in contrasting the
two tests. The free association method yields a score of 28
words for ten-year-olds, whereas the effect of the limitation
imposed by the controlled association task is seen in the fact
that the score for naming animals at the same age level is
only 12.

In scoring the test it is not always easy to decide how many
animals the child has named. We have counted beasts, birds,
fish, and insects -- all animal life. If the child names "dog"
and then "collie," or "dog" and "bird dog," he is credited
with two points, both genus and species being counted toward
his score. Likewise both "ewe" and "ram," "mare" and
"stallion," etc., are given separate counts. "Cat" and "kit-
ten," "cow" and "calf" are counted separately, but it seems
to be stretching a point to allow "lion" and "baby lion," so
when the young of the species is designated as "baby ——"
we have not counted it in addition to the parent. Singular
and plural are not counted separately, as, for instance, "cat"
and "cats" or "mouse" and "mice"; "rabbit" and "bunny"
are names for the same animal and count as one.

Sample scoring: "Elephant, baby elephant" (1); "Pig, hog" (1); "Rhinosterick" (1) (mispronunciation is disregarded); "Dragon" (1); "Dinosaur" (1); "Hen, chickens" (2); "Puppy, dog" (2); "Turkey, gobbler" (2); "Rabbit, hare" (2), etc.

The test is passed if 12 animals are named.

6. Repeating Six Digits (Cf. Form L, p. 213)

One plus out of three trials passes the digit test.

YEAR XI

1. Finding Reasons (Cf. Form L, pp. 256 f.)

This test is scored very leniently. Any reason that is at all plausible is credited. Even if the reasons proposed by the child overlap or belong in the same category, provided different aspects are presented that can be distinguished, they are counted as two. Failure usually consists of inability to give two reasons and is manifested in a rambling account of some particular situation that the task recalls.

(a) *Give two reasons why children should obey their parents.*

Some of the commonest reasons mentioned are: To avoid punishment, for their own good, to avoid getting into trouble, because they should, because it is the right thing to do, because parents know best, etc.

> *Plus.* "Because their parents know best and because they might get a whipping." "Because they'll do something wrong and they'll get in trouble." "If their mother tells them not to go out on the street and they disobey they might get run over. They can get in trouble if they disobey their mother, like if they go to some house and they wreck things." "They would get things done quicker and they would leave more time to go places." "Because if they

don't then the parents won't get 'em anything. They have to obey their parents or they won't like 'em." "To be kind to the parents and because their parents want them to do it." "It'll help you learn to be good and they wouldn't have to put you in jail when you grow up." "Because they might get a whipping and they might be sent to bed." "So they wouldn't get so many whippings. They should obey their parents anyway."

Minus. "Because their parents wouldn't like it if they went off somewhere without their parents knowing where they're going and they wouldn't want them to." "Their parents know more than the children because parents was once children and they should obey them because they know better." "Because if you didn't you might get a whipping and if you do you might not." "Children should obey their parents 'cause if they don't they might not pass — they might not get good grades." "Because the mothers and daddies want to have a nice child and they would have to be ashamed." "Because the parents is bigger than the children and they should obey them."

(b) *Give two reasons why there should be plenty of railroads in the United States.*

Plus. "So they can go to a lot of towns without using their machine. Should have 'em because maybe the people haven't got machines to go in." "To carry passengers and to take fruit and cattle and things like that to different towns and cities." "So men won't have to buy automobiles in order to go down town and it's quicker than to take a taxi or bus." "To bring people from states to states and if there was a robbery and needed cops out there you could go by train — easier, quicker." "So they can carry people that have no machines and to make the United States popular." "People can get places quicker and easier." "When there's plenty of railroads there's a easy way of transportation. They'll make the country more prosperous." "To carry people. More comfortable than driving."

Minus. "So people can travel and so they can go different places." "Because there's lots of people going out of town and comin' in." "So people won't have to walk to the place — maybe they haven't got a machine and they can go by train and won't have to walk." "So the trains can run on them — there'd be too much trains to run on one track." "The trains has to haul cars and go every place and you need the railroad." "So the trains and the street cars can go on 'em."

The test is passed if two satisfactory reasons are given in each case.

2. Copying a Bead Chain from Memory (Cf. Form L, p. 222)

To score plus on the test there must be no error in pattern.

3. Verbal Absurdities II (Cf. IX, 3)

This test is passed if four out of five of the items are plus.

4. Abstract Words II (Cf. Form L, p. 261)

This is the same test that is being used in Form L at year XI, test 3. Three words must be correctly defined to pass at this level.

5. Similarities: Three things (Cf. Form L, p. 228)

This is the same test that is being used in Form L at year XI, test 6. The test is passed if three of the five comparisons are plus.

6. Memory for Sentences III (Cf. Form L, p. 264)

This is the same test that is being used in Form L at year XI, test 4. The score is one plus out of two.

YEAR XII

1. Memory for Designs II (Cf. Form L, p. 248)

This test was used in the United States Army during the World War.[1] The design is made up of three diamond-shaped figures. The plan of the design is the important thing to consider in scoring rather than neatness of execution. The diamonds may be somewhat irregular if the essential characteristics of the plan are carried out; that is, there must be an outer diamond, an inner diamond crosswise within, whose acute angles meet the obtuse angles of the outer diamond, and a still smaller diamond within the second diamond which maintains the same relationship to the second diamond as the second diamond does to the first. The latitude in scoring is indicated in the samples on page 387.

2. Response to Pictures II: Messenger Boy (Cf. Form L, pp. 267 f.)

This is the same test that is used in Form L at year XII, test 3.

3. Minkus Completion (Cf. Form L, p. 271)

(a) *We like to pop corn* ...... *to roast chestnuts over the fire.*
   Plus. And, or.

(b) *Lincoln aroused no jealousy* ...... *he was not selfish.*
   Plus. Because, since, for, as, but.

(c) ...... *he give me his word, I will not trust him.*
   Plus. Unless, although, though, if, should.

(d) *You must not,* ......, *imagine that my silence has been due to ignorance of what is going on.*

---

[1] "Psychological Examining in the United States Army." Robert M. Yerkes, ed. *Nat'l. Acad. of Sc. Mem.*, pp. 185–87; 199.

Plus

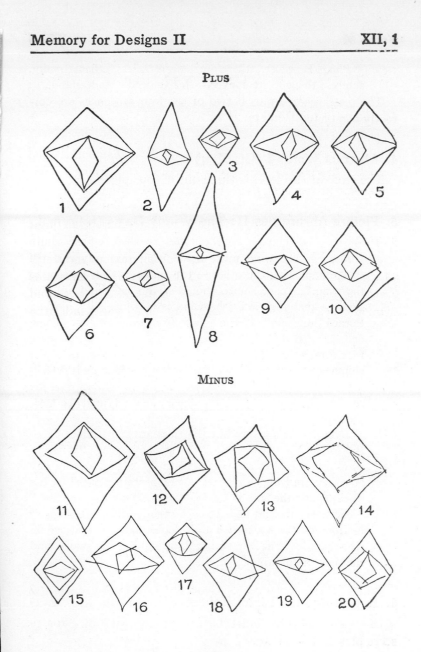

Minus

Plus. However, therefore, nevertheless, then, really, surely, though, moreover, sir, indeed, understand.

The test is scored plus if two of the four sentences are correctly completed.

4. Abstract Words I (Cf. X, 4)

The score at this level is three out of four plus.

5. Picture Absurdities II: The Windy Day (Cf. Form L, p. 226)

Plus. "The wind must be blowing that way and the smoke is blowing the other — the smoke is blowing toward the wind." "The smoke should have gone this way. (Q.) Because that's the way the wind is blowing — it's blowing toward the wind." "The smoke from the chimney is going one way and the wind is blowing another way and the gate isn't attached to the fence." "Smoke is coming out of the chimney and the wind should blow it away because it's blowing the trees and the wash on the line." "The way the smoke is blowing. (Q.) It's blowing one way and the trees the other."

Minus. "It's windy but the trees are still straight up — they're not blowing over." "The smoke is going all different ways and the trees are tipping over." "It's a stormy day and they are hanging clothes out on a stormy day." "It's smoking and the lady is leaving the clothes out on the line." "The trees are right next to each other — the clothes-line is in front of the house — and it looks like the trees go in sizes, too." "The wind's not blowing and the smoke and the trees are blowing."

6. Repeating Five Digits Reversed (Cf. Form L, p. 254)

One series of three must be reproduced without error to score plus on the test.

YEAR XIII

1. Plan of Search (Cf. Form L, p. 272)

Several figures were tried out in the process of standardization of this test. The circular field and the diamond-shaped one proved to be the most satisfactory for purposes of scoring.

Satisfactory types of plans for the diamond conform closely to the types which proved to be satisfactory for the circular field used in Form L.

The samples on page 390 indicate the main types of satisfactory plans and illustrate a few of the common types of failure.

2. Memory for Stories: The Acrobat

(a) *What was his first distinguished performance during his tour of the United States?*

> *Plus.* "He crossed the Falls of Niagara on a tight-rope." "Walking on a tight-rope." "Walking without nothing — not blindfolded — just walking across." "He went across with his eyes open." "Went across a tight-rope across the canyon." "Going across a chasm on a tight-rope."
>
> *Minus.* "Crossing the river, I guess." "Walking across a big bridge." "He crossed." "Crossed it with rope — held on to ropes and went across." "He crossed a rope blindfolded." "He was the best tight-rope walker in France."

(b) *How many people saw him do it?*

> *Plus.* "25,000." "About 25,000." "More than 25,000." "Nearly 25,000." (No other response is scored plus.)

(c) *How did he cross Niagara the second time?*

> *Plus.* "Blindfolded, trundling a wheel-barrow in front of him." "Blindfolded with a barrow in front of him — rolling a barrow." "Twirling a wheel-barrow in front of him with his face blindfolded." "Blindfolded and balancing a wheel-barrow."

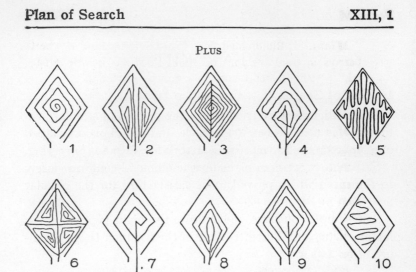

Minus. "Blindfolded." "Crossed it pushing a wheel-barrow in front of him." "Blindfolded and rolling a barrel." "Blindfolded trundling a wagon before him."

(d) *How great a distance did he cross?*
  Plus. "800 feet." "800."
  Minus. "Nearly 800 miles."

(e) *How did he cross the third time?*
  Plus. "Carrying a man on his back." "By carrying a man on his back." "With a man on his back." "With a man on his shoulders." "Carrying a man." "Carrying somebody across the tight-rope."
  Minus. "Blindfolded with a man on his back."

(f) *How deep was the chasm?*
  Plus. "300 feet." "300." "About 300 feet."
  Minus. "300 feet or inches — I think it was inches."

(g) *How did he cross the fourth time?*
  Plus. "Walking on stilts." "With some sticks — I don't know what you call them. (Q.) With them sticks what you stand on and hold them and walk across." "On stilts."
  Minus. "Walking on skiis." "On stilts — he was blindfolded." "With a man on his back and with stilts."

Five of the seven questions must be answered correctly to pass the test.

3. Dissected Sentences II (Cf. Form L, pp. 276 f.)

This is the same test that is used in Form L, year XIII, test 5. It is scored plus if two of the three responses are correct.

4. Abstract Words II (Cf. Form L, p. 261)

This test is passed if four of the five words are satisfactorily defined.

5. Problems of Fact (Cf. Form L, pp. 264 f., 274 ff.)

This test is repeated from Form L.   The score is plus if two of the three problems are correctly explained.

6. Memory for Sentences IV (Cf. Form L, p. 221)

One response of two is required for plus at this level.

YEAR XIV

1. Reasoning (Cf. Form L, p. 279)

This reasoning problem is very much simpler than a similar reasoning problem at the Superior Adult level in Form L. However, the essential processes of formal reasoning are involved.

> *Plus.* "Between four and five." "About half-past four." "Four-thirty." "Four-fifteen." "About ten minutes to five." "After four. (Q.)   Well some time between four and five o'clock." (Any specific time between four and five o'clock is plus.)
> *Minus.* "Four o'clock." "Five o'clock." "About dinner time." "About 4." "About 5." "During the afternoon." "Before 5. (Q.)   'Cause she came home at five."

2. Picture Absurdities III: The Shadow (Cf. Form L, p. 226)

This test is the same as year XIV, test 3, in Form L.

3. Orientation: Direction I (Cf. Form L, pp. 279 f.)

For plus at this level three out of five questions must be correctly answered.

4. Abstract Words III (Cf. Form L, p. 261)

(a) *Generosity.* (Liberality, magnanimity.)

Plus. "Generosity is unselfishness." "It means you're giving people a lot of things." "The art of being generous. (Q.) Not stingy." "Being generous to someone. (Q.) Well, if they ask you for anything give it to them or do what you can for them." "Means when you're generous to anyone. (Q.) When you're kind-hearted — do all you can for them." "When you're generous. (Q.) When you want to help." "Kind. (Q.) To give things to the poor."

Minus. "Be nice." "It means to be kind. (Q.) Means to be nice to people when they talk to you." "Generous. (Q.) When you're in a crowd don't push — just go on easy with everything." "Being generous. You're gentle with anybody."

(b) *Independent.* (Free from external control. Self-directing. Self-reliant.)

Independent is frequently confused with dependable. The slang use of independent as haughty, proud, or demanding is scored minus.

Plus. "Self-ruling." "Somebody don't have anybody to tell 'em what to do." "Don't belong to anybody. (Q.) Nobody owns you." "Free — if you're independent, it isn't under the rule of any other country." "Free from anything." "When you're free to do things." "Free. (Q.) You have no one bossing you around." "Can give up his job whenever he wants to — has enough money saved to live on — he's free." "Means that you earn your own living."

Minus. "You're kind of — put you're head up in the air — like that." "Always want their own way." "They want it right then." "Always particular what you get — if you get the right thing or not." "You demand your rights." "Somebody that won't do anything." "Somebody thinks they are the boss." "It's a place where you can do what you want to and nobody has to tell you what to do." "Fourth of July."

(c) *Envy*. (Envy must carry the connotation of grudging and must be distinguished from admiration.)

Plus. "It's the way you feel when you see someone with something nicer than you have." "When somebody is envied. (Q.) When somebody else has got something and you are mad you haven't got it." "Somebody has things you haven't and you get sore about it." "You don't like somebody. (Q.) Like somebody is a good talker and you're jealous you can't be one — you envy them." "Somebody got a machine and you haven't — you're not their friend — you don't like 'em and you wish you had a car." "You dislike a person — like I'd dislike a girl because she had a new dress and I didn't." "Jealous. (Q.) You hate somebody 'cause he's got more than you have."

Minus. "Means to envy somebody. (Q.) When you hate them." "Means that they don't like a person — they don't like his manner or style." "When you tell somebody that you like their hat or coat or something."

(d) *Authority*. (Jurisdiction. Power due to opinion or esteem.)

Plus. "The right to rule." "Have the privilege of commanding someone to do something." "The right to do something. (Q.) Right legally." "Like a policeman is backed by the government — policeman has authority. (Q.) He has the right to do whatever he is doing." "Authority means somebody that has high office." "Some high person in authority. (Q.) Someone has some large responsibility." "You're good on some subject and you know practically everything about it."

Minus. "Means somebody has done something and they're going to take him to court." "Authority is a man who keeps people out of trouble." "Always coming in and taking something that don't belong to them." "A company of people that decide on some of the laws of the state." "Give you a whipping." "When somebody tells you to do something. (Q.) They can do a lot that they want to."

(e) *Justice.* (Fairness. Rendering to everyone his due.)

Plus. "Doing the right thing by everybody." "To give the people their rights." "Having everyone be treated alike." "To be just. (Q.) To do the right thing by a person." "The right thing. (Q.) They look on both sides and then they think the best thing to do." "You get treated right." "Punishment given correctly and fairly." "Giving people what they have coming to them." "It's giving a person an even break." "To do what's right. (Q.) Like the judge gives justice to the man."

Minus. "Means justice of the peace." "It means we are doing the right thing — like helping other people." "To do the right thing. (Q.) Like if you tell me to do something." "Doing right. (Q.) I'll give you a sentence, 'I think I am doing justice to try to learn.'" "Right. (Q.) Don't do anything wrong." "If you've done something you would want to have justice. (Q.) You have to have somebody be lenient with you." "Just. (Q.) Well, you're nice to people."

Two of the five words must be correctly defined to score plus on the test at this level.

5. Ingenuity (Cf. Form L, p. 279)

One of the three problems must be solved to pass at this level.

6. Reconciliation of Opposites (Cf. Form L, pp. 286 f.)

(a) *Winter and summer*

Plus. "They're seasons." "They're both parts of the year." "They both get three months in 'em." "Same amount of months" (or days). "They're both time." "Both a climate." "Both weather." "Have atmospheric changes." "Both are temperatures."

Minus. "Both of them are months." "Winter is the

cold part of the year and summer is the warm part." "Summer and winter both have winds." "There are vacations in both of them — in both seasons."

(b) *Happy and sad*

Plus. "Both state of mind" (or action of mind, state of being, conditions of mind). "Both tell the mind of a person." "Both conditions, tell whether you're happy or sad." "Both emotions" (or moods, spirit, humor, disposition). "Both natures" (or characters). "Both have to do with feelings." (Two different ways people feel, etc.) "Both adjectives describing how a person feels." "Both mental."

Minus. "A way you act." "Both ways you can be." "Same capacity — sad is height of bereavement and happy is the result of joy." "Different appearance of people." "Both expressions of the face." "Both in your life."

(c) *Loud and soft*

Plus. "Vibrations." "Both detected by the senses." "Both affect the ear." "Both amount of sound" (noise, voice). "Both sounds" (noise, voice). "Both extremes of sound" (noise voice). "Both tones" (pitch). "Both a manner of making a noise or speaking."

Minus. "You can hear both of them." "Talk." "You can make a soft sound and you can make a loud sound." "Both make a noise." "Can be made by the same instrument." "Both contain the same number of letters." (Should repeat question.)

(d) *Much and little*

Plus. "Both measurements of weight" (or size). "Measurements." "Used for measuring." "Both are quantitative adjectives." "Both tell how much." "Both a certain amount of anything."

Minus. "It's some." "Both commodities." "They're something." "You can have much of something and little of something." "One's a large quantity and one's a small quantity."

(e) *Beginning and end*

This item is the hardest of the series. It is difficult to grasp the point and difficult to express the answer. The examiner must be on his guard against fine-sounding phrases which miss the point.

Plus. "They are both terminals." "Both places." "Both where some action of some sort terminates." "Both determinants." "They mark position of progress." "Both a certain point." "They're both parts in doing a thing — that isn't very clear though; time at the end of which you do something." "Tell when." "They are both times."

Minus. "Because attached on to the same thing." "Beginning and end of a thing." "Because they're both parts." (Very common.) "Both a part of something — one part beginning and other part the end." (Example of inadequate explanation.) "You can begin at both ends." "Because they are both terms of stopping." "If there's a beginning there must be an end, so they're connected." "Start with both of them." "They both determine how the thing turns out." "Both ends of stories." "Both definite proceedings."

The test is passed at this level if two out of five comparisons are correct.

AVERAGE ADULT

1. Abstract Words III (Cf. XIV, 4)

To pass at this level the subject must define correctly four of the five words.

2. Ingenuity (Cf. XIV, 5)

At this level the subject must solve two of the three problems to pass the test.

3. Opposite Analogies III (Cf. Form L, p. 216)

(a) *A rabbit is timid; a lion is* ......
> *Plus.* "Bold." "Brave." "Courageous." "Unafraid." "Fearless."
> *Minus.* "Not afraid." "Wild." "Ferocious." "Savage." "Vicious." "Fierce." "Dangerous."

(b) *Trees are terrestrial; stars are* ......
> *Plus.* "Celestrial." "Heavenly."
> *Minus.* "Spacial."

(c) *A group made up of dissimilar things is heterogeneous; one made up of things which are alike is* ......
> *Plus.* "Homogeneous."
> *Minus.* "Harmonious." "Unified."

The test is passed if one of the three is correct.

4. Codes I (Cf. Form L, pp. 280 f.)

To receive full credit for a code there must be no error. Half-credit is allowed in either (a) or (b) where the response contains one error. One letter incorrectly coded constitutes an error. If R is twice coded incorrectly, it counts as two errors; e.g., F S *Q Q* W counts as two errors.

It sometimes happens that the subject discovers an error in the first code when he is working on the second. Such spontaneous corrections are always credited if the time limit on that item *has not* already been reached. If at the end of three minutes the subject has not completed the last letter, that letter is counted as an error and, if there is no other error, he receives half-credit for the item.

A score of one and a half passes the test.

5. Proverbs I

(a) *We only know the worth of water when the well is dry.* (We don't appreciate the value of things until we are deprived of them.)

Plus. "We don't know how to appreciate a thing when it is with us." "We wait until it's too late to know the use of things." "Means the same as locking the door after the horse is stolen — means you don't know how much you want a thing 'til the chance has gone by to get it." "We don't know when we're well off until we're poor." "Might have a whole lot of money and spend it and you wouldn't care, and then when it's gone you know what it's worth." "You pay more attention to things after they're gone than when they're around you." "If you have plenty of a thing you don't care so much — just as soon as it's taken away you miss it." "Means when you have a lot of something you don't think about it until you haven't anything."

Minus. "You don't know what it means to do without water or anything 'til your well goes dry and you don't have it." "Whenever you haven't anything you realize what it is." "Do not waste when you have lots." "Should take care of things when we have them because we'll miss them when we haven't." "It's too late to begin things when they're already done." "Maybe you might have a whole lot of money and waste it and later have only a little — remember they had a whole lot and wish they hadn't been so wasteful." "We don't appreciate it when we have it." (Too vague.)

(b) *No wind can do him good who steers for no port.* (Unless one has an objective in life, assistance is of no avail.)

Plus. "No one can help a person unless they have an aim themselves and work for it." "All the advantages you have — if you don't concentrate them on something — won't amount to much." "Nothing can do you much good unless you are going some place." "Education can't do a person any good unless he goes out for some certain thing." "If a person doesn't know what he wants to do — no one can help him — until he decides." "Nothing will do him any good in life if he hasn't any ambition." "Nothing can do a person any good if he don't try to do something."

Minus. "If you don't go for a certain place, that you

won't get there." "Can't do what he don't try." "Nobody helps anybody who hasn't got any ideal." "He's got to have some goal — or he'll just blow all round." "No person can get anywhere and nobody will help him unless he shows what he wants to do and don't keep changing his ideas." "Nothing can do any good if you don't try." "No help can do him any good if he don't want to have opportunities." "Nothing will come to you if you don't get it yourself." "You have to help yourself if you want somebody else to."

(c) *Don't judge a book by its cover.* (External appearances may be deceiving.)

Plus. "Don't judge people by their clumsiness outside." "That we shouldn't judge things by their reputation or names." "Don't judge anybody by the way they dress." "Means good things sometimes don't look it." "Bad things sometimes have good outsides or don't show their bad parts." "Look into a thing before you decide what it means." "At first sight you might think things are good, but you have to learn later on." "Look into things thoroughly."

Minus. "Not to make any statements about what you see on the outside of a person or thing." "Can't tell how a person is by the way he acts." "You have to find out what's inside." "Sometimes the books don't have a good name — don't judge them by the cover — the name."

Two of the proverbs must be correctly explained to pass the test.

6. Orientation: Direction I (Cf. XIV, 3)

Success at this level consists in four correct responses out of five.

7. Essential Differences (Cf. Form L, pp. 228, 286)

(a) *Work and play*

In pointing out the difference between work and play, several characteristic contrasts appear to be about equally valid

according to one's philosophy.   One of the most frequent contrasts brought out is that of *necessity* vs. *freedom*; the *duty*
aspect of work is contrasted with the *leisure* or *recreation* aspect
of play; *usefulness* vs. *uselessness* constitutes a third contrast;
and lastly a contrast in attitudes is emphasized, the *pleasant
feeling tone* vs. the *irksomeness* or *disliked* character of the
activity.

Plus. "You work to earn money and you play for the
fun." "One is for amusement and the other for a living."
"Play is a pleasure and work is something you should do,
your duty." "Work is energy used for doing something useful and play is just wasting energy." "One's recreation —
and one's labor. I mean play is an enjoyment and work
is something you have to do. Sometimes you enjoy it and
sometimes you don't." "When you're working you're generally doing something that has to be done — when you're
playing you're just doing what you feel like." "One is
something that most people like to do and the other is
a duty." "The attitude towards whatever you're doing —
if you're playing baseball and don't like to play baseball
then it's work — if you're working at mathematics and you
like to do it — then it's not work to you anymore."
"Work you take seriously and play you don't."

Minus. "Work is hard and play is easy." "You can go
to work and make money, but when you play, you just play
games, hide-and-go-seek and things like that." "Work
you're doing something and play you're just playing around
and not working." "You'd rather play than to work."
"Work, you get tired more quickly." "One is helping you
and the other one isn't."

(b) *Ability and achievement*

Plus. "Ability is a thing you have, and achievement is
a thing you work for." "Because if you have ability you
can get somewhere and if you have achieved something
you've done it already." "Have to work to have achieve-

401

ment — don't have to work to have ability." "You're able to do it — but it is the difference — if you *do* it or not." "One, you have the ability to do something and the other — what you have done." "Achievement is a product of ability because if you have the ability most always you can achieve the thing you want." "Ability means you can or can't do it and achievement means you will or won't do it."

Minus. "If you have ability you might some day have a big achievement. (Q.) I don't know." "He has the ability to do it but he just can't achieve it. (Q.) Ability means you can try to do something and achievement is when you have accomplished it." "Ability you want to do it and achievement means you done it." "Ability is to do something and achievement is when it's already done."

(c) *Optimist and pessimist*

Plus. "Optimist is always looking at the right side of things and the pessimist always sees the wrong side." "Optimist believes he can do it and pessimist thinks he can't." "They take the exact opposite views. (Q.) Pessimist knows something bad is going to happen and the other knows it won't happen." "Pessimist is always against everything and optimist is just the opposite, thinks things are all right as they are." "A pessimist looks at the evil of the future and optimist is the opposite." "An optimist likes life and a pessimist dreads it." "An optimist looks towards better times and towards the future, and the pessimist feels that the world is all against him and owes him something."

Minus. "One is for it and the other is always against — one man would say something and they'd all agree to it and there'd be just one man in the bunch who'd say something different and wouldn't give in to them." "A pessimist isn't an optimist — a pessimist just tries to be somebody that doesn't agree — an optimist doesn't." "A pessimist is constantly bothering you while an optimist may sometimes help you." (The most common incorrect meaning given for pessimist is pest.) "Optimist is always looking ahead and

pessimist he don't look at or believe in much of anything."
"Optimistic person thinks greater thoughts than pessimists
Pessimist has a narrow mind."

The test is passed if two essential differences are given.

8. Binet Paper Cutting (Cf. Form L, pp. 242 f.)

The test is passed if the creases are drawn, if the correct
number of holes is indicated, and if the holes are correctly
located.

SUPERIOR ADULT I

1. Minkus Completion (Cf. XII, 3)

At this level the subject must complete correctly three of the
four sentences to pass the test.

2. Opposite Analogies (Cf. Form L, p. 216)

(a) *Ability is native; education is* ......
    Plus. "Acquired." "Achieved."
    Minus. "Learned." "Achievement." "Foreign."
"Something to be learned." "Culture."

(b) *Music is harmonious; noise is* ......
    Plus. "Discordant."
    Minus. "Discord." "Deafening." "Inharmonious."
"Pandimonious."

(c) *A person who talks a great deal is loquacious; one who has little
to say is* ......
    Plus. "Silent." "Quiet." "Taciturn." "Laconic."
    Minus. "Conservative." "Lackadaisical." "Not talk-
ative."

One out of three constitutes plus.

3. Essential Similarities (Cf. Form L, pp. 228, 286)

This is the same test used in Form L at Superior Adult Level I, test 6.

Two out of three comparisons must be plus to pass the test.

4. Repeating Six Digits Reversed (Cf. Form L, p. 254)

This test occurs also in Form L at Superior Adult Level I, test 4.

One series must be correctly reversed to pass the test.

5. Sentence Building II (Cf. Form L, pp. 289 f.)

(a) *Ceremonial — Dignity — Impression*

Plus. "The ceremonial dances and dignity of the Indians made an impression on the people watching." "The ceremonial had much dignity and left a big impression." "He made an impression of dignity in his ceremonial actions." "A king gave a ceremonial banquet with much dignity and made a large impression on all of his subjects." "The man had ceremonial dignity and made a good impression."

Minus. "He made an impression on their dignity at a ceremonial place." "The ceremonial rites gave an impression of dignity upon the people." "The lecture on dignity was very ceremonial and made a deep impression." "A man that has dignity sometimes likes to give a ceremonial impression." "The ceremonial was alive with dignity and the people were very much impressed with the part done by the ladies."

(b) *Baffle — Cunning — Pursuit*

Plus. "The cunning criminal will baffle the police unless they start in pursuit quickly." "The rabbit was able to baffle by his cunning the pursuit of him by hunters." "The Germans baffled the pursuit plane with cunning dexterity." "A cunning pursuit baffled the fugitive." "The criminal baffled the detectives because he was very cunning and the detectives were always in pursuit after him." "The cunning man baffled the pursuit."

Minus. "He led a baffling, cunning pursuit." "He was a cunning man and the police had to baffle the mystery to pursue him." "The police are pursuing the cunning baffler." "He was a cunning man, and the man baffled him in the pursuit." "The pursuit was very baffling and cunning." "The cunning man had to baffle the pursuit that was following him."

(c) *Failure — Business — Incompetent*

Plus. "He was a business failure and an incompetent." "The incompetent man was a failure in business." "He made a business of failure because he was incompetent." "The incompetent president caused a failure of his business." "His failure in business was due to his incompetent manner." "Because of his failure in business he was incompetent."

Minus. "My business was very incompetent and therefore it was a failure." "He made an incompetent failure in business." "Incompetent business is generally a failure."

The test is passed if two of the three sentences are satisfactory.

6. Reconciliation of Opposites (Cf. XIV, 6)

This is passed if four out of five of the items are plus.

SUPERIOR ADULT II

1. Proverbs II (Cf. Form L, pp. 283 f.)

(a) *The mouse that has but one hole is easily taken.* (Disaster is less likely where there are several alternatives.)

Plus. "It's like 'Don't put all your eggs in one basket.' If you depend too much on one thing, it may go back on you." "You should not always depend on one thing because that might easily fail. Like if you're investing your money, should not invest it all in one thing but divide it up." "A man who has just one thing to turn to, is easily broke." "If you only have one way to defend yourself you're more easily overtaken than if you had two or three ways." "Means you should make your knowledge more extensive." "Do more than one thing because that one thing may fail." "A person who has but one method is easily fooled." "A person who has a single-track mind is easily confused."

Minus. "If you have only one means of escape you're easily caught." (The proverb practically repeated.) "A person that has one place of business and one piece of property is easily taken up by a big concern or by people that are more well-to-do." "Like if you just do one thing — you'll soon be overcome with it." "Well, a person that has only one object in life is soon stopped." "A person who has but one thought may be easily persuaded." "There ought to always be two ways out of anything." "If we only have one way of learning things and know one side of anything we don't succeed so easily." "You should have several views of life."

(b) *You must not throw pearls before swine.* (Don't offer people things they can't appreciate.)

Plus. "Only people with fine sensibilities can appreciate the finer things." "It's no use to try to teach those that do not know what you're talking about and aren't interested in what you're talking about." "You shouldn't try and give beauty to ignorant things — people that don't understand — you can't show them beauty — they can't understand — so it's no use." "Swine have no appreciation of the value of pearls and if a person is uneducated he has no appreciation of fine things in life, they won't do him any good." "Should not waste good things for people that don't appreciate them, it doesn't do 'em any good." "It doesn't do any good to give some people a chance in life because they don't know what to do with it, don't know it's value." "Don't waste your time on people who don't appreciate it." "Give the people something that they can appreciate and understand."

Minus. "They wouldn't know what to do with it — you should not be giving money to people who beg for it because they don't know how to spend it — they waste it." "Not to throw away something that you could accomplish and let someone else come along and take it up and do it and get the benefit of it." "Don't make foolish offers to people who don't know what they're getting." "No use to give things away unless they are going to be made use of."

The test is passed if one of the proverbs is correctly explained.

2. Ingenuity (Cf. XIV, 5)

In order to be scored plus at this level all three of the problems must be solved correctly.

3. Essential Differences (Cf. A.A., 7)

All three differences must be given to score plus at this level.

4. Repeating Eight Digits

The test is passed if one of the three series is repeated without error.

5. Codes II (Cf. A.A., 4)

The rule is asked for as a caution against carelessness or a too hasty response. It is not scored.

The test is passed if one code is solved correctly or both are solved with half-credit (not more than one error each).

6. Repeating Thought of Passage I: Value of Life (Cf. Form L, pp. 297 f.)

This test occurs also in Form L and is repeated here without change.

SUPERIOR ADULT III

1. Proverbs III

(a) *Let sleeping dogs lie.* (Don't seek trouble if you can avoid It.)

Plus. "Leave well enough alone." "If you see something that is getting along all right left alone — leave it alone or it might cause trouble." "Don't stir up trouble." "Let anyone who isn't bothering you alone." "Don't bother trouble till trouble troubles you." "Don't bring up something that is best kept quiet." "Do not revive past happenings." "After a thing is gone and done with not to be continually bringing it up and harping on it."

Minus. "Let a person who does not care to accomplish anything alone." "Don't get into any task that would cause you great danger or injury." "You shouldn't bother with anything that's not to be bothered with." "Let something that might be dangerous alone." "Don't disturb anybody if you have nothing to say." "It's better to leave things alone that you don't know anything about." "If something is still and you disturb it, something might happen." "Let things alone that don't concern you." "Don't try to change it or make it different — leave it the way it was first."

(b) *A bad workman quarrels with his tools.* (The incompetent always finds excuses for his failure.)

Plus. "That when we make mistakes we're likely to put the blame on anything that's handy — take it out on someone else and not put the blame where it really belongs." "A man that is not doing the thing right himself finds fault with everybody else." "A person who does bad blames it on somebody else." "Because if a worker isn't a good worker he has to take his spite out on somebody or something." "A person who is incompetent blames his helpers or his tools when it is really himself that is to blame."

Minus. "If he doesn't like his work he will blame everything on to the implements he is using." "A person who is unhappy usually quarrels with what he has to do." "Because he has no one else to quarrel with, he quarrels with his tools." "A person who is unskilled at something can't get along with his associates." "He lays his failure on his tools instead of on himself." "An inefficient person will find something to fight about."

(c) *It's an ill wind that blows nobody good.* (Someone usually benefits even by a calamity which brings general misfortune.)

> *Plus.* "Everything that happens in life must do someone good so that it doesn't do to moan too much if it doesn't benefit you especially." "Nearly everything does somebody some good." "Something has to be pretty bad not to do someone some good." "Somebody always gets something out of whatever happens." "Whatever comes along ought to be an opportunity for somebody."
>
> *Minus.* "Something that's meant to do you harm never does you any good." "A person that goes around talking or whispering things about certain people doesn't bring anybody in this world any good." "An ill-minded person does nobody any good." "Something bad never does anybody any good." "Things that aren't likely to be beneficial to anyone are better left undone." "Every little something is of some importance."

The test is passed if two of the three proverbs are explained satisfactorily.

2. Memory for Sentences V

The sentence must be repeated without error to score plus on the test.

3. Orientation: Direction II (Cf. Form L, pp. 279 f.)

(a) The correct answer is West.

(b) The only correct answer is 1 mile.

The subject must answer both questions correctly to pass the test.

4. Repeating Nine Digits

One of the three series must be repeated correctly to score plus on the test.

5. Opposite Analogies IV (Cf. S.A. I, 2)

The test is passed if two of the three sentences are correctly completed.

6. Repeating Thought of Passage II: Tests

This passage may be divided into the following component ideas:

  (a) Tests such as we are now making are of value both for the advancement of science and
  (b) for the information of the person who is tested.
  (c) It is important for science to learn how people differ and
  (d) on what factors these differences depend.
  (e) If we can separate the influence of heredity from the influence of environment,
  (f) we may be able to apply our knowledge so as to guide human development.
  (g) We may thus in some cases correct defects and
  (h) develop abilities which we might otherwise neglect.

Satisfactory responses include those in which there is accurate reproduction of at least four of these eight divisions. The idea contained in the section must be stated or clearly implied, although it may of course be expressed in the subject's own way.

> *Plus.* "Tests are important both to science and to the person who takes them. They find out how people differ and they want to try out how people are in regard to heredity and

environment, and in this way they can correct defects."
(a b c e g)

"Tests of this kind aid science as well as find out about
the person who is receiving this test. Science says that certain abilities can be developed and certain defects will be
overcome. If they can take heredity instead of so much of
what comes on the home things will be better." (a b e g)

"Tests that we are taking now are good for advancing
knowledge and learning about the person who is being
tested. It advances science to learn how people differ and
it might help the person to find out defects and to have abilities in more things." (a b c g h)

"Tests such as we are now making are for the benefit of
the people who are taking them and for science. We can
separate the heredity from environment and see how much
people differ." (a b c e)

"These tests that we are having are for the help of the person given the test and we are giving them for science 'cause it
might help the development of people and science tells how
people differ and on what facts these differences depend
upon." (a b c d f)

"Tests such as we are now making are a great advantage
to us and to scientists so they may see how people differ and
thus correct the defects." (a b c g)

Minus. "Tests which we are taking are of great value to
both science and the person, to see how much he knows and
so persons can tell how people differ and the amount the
person knows who is being tested." (a b c)

"Tests which we are now making are very important.
They are useful to science to find out the difference in
people. Sometimes used to correct faults which might otherwise be neglected." (a c g)

"Examinations such as are being made are important to
science and to the knowledge of the one who is being tested.
You may in some cases fix defects and correct mistakes which
are being made." (a b g)

APPENDIX

APPENDIX
I.Q. TABLES[1] FOR THE REVISED SCALES

THESE I.Q. tables for the revised scales have been included to facilitate the calculation of intelligence quotient values for the entire range of mental ages which the new scales yield. Mental age scores in the tables range from 2–0 to 22–10 inclusive, and the chronological age range covered extends from age 2–0 to age 16–0 inclusive. Within the limits of these ages I.Q.'s between 30 and 170 have been included.[2] The intelligence quotient values in the tables are the correct values for the revised scale.

It will be recalled that not all of a subject's chronological age between 13 and 16 is counted in computing the I.Q. (See page 30.) It is important to note that this fact is allowed for in the I.Q. tables; that is, for ages above 13 the I.Q.'s given in the table are "adjusted." For example, the I.Q. of a subject whose chronological age is 15–0 and whose mental age is 15–0 is given in the table as 105. This adjustment of the I.Q. values saves the trouble of subtracting part of the chronological ages between 13 and 16.

To find the I.Q. for any mental age and chronological age, locate the column for the mental age by referring to the row of figures at the top or the bottom of the page and find the chronological age in the right or left hand column. The I.Q. for a given mental and chronological age will be found in the row to the right of the chronological age, in years and months

---

[1] Grateful acknowledgment is made to the World Book Company for their permission to use portions of the *Inglis Intelligence Quotient Values*, World Book Company, copyright 1921, 1922, and 1923.

[2] At two places in the tables, C.A. 3–6 to 3–11 for mental age six and C.A. 9–6 to 9–11 at mental age sixteen, because of limitations of space the I.Q. values beyond 150 and 160 have been omitted.

in the column under that mental age. To find the I.Q. for a child whose age is 2 years and 10 months (2–10) and whose mental age is 3 years and 4 months (3–4), first find his mental age in the table, page 1 column 18, then find his chronological age in the first column at the left of the page and in the same row find his I.Q., 118, in the column under 3–4. To find the I.Q. of a child whose chronological age is more than 13–2, follow exactly the same procedure. If, for example, you wish to find the I.Q. of a child whose chronological age is 14–6 and whose mental age is 10–0, locate the mental and chronological ages as above and find the I.Q., 71, in the row to the right of C.A. 14–6 in the column under M.A. 10–0.

MENTAL AGE

Row header (left): CHRONOLOGICAL AGE — Years and Months / Total Months
Column header (top): MENTAL AGE — given as "Years-Months (Total Months)".

Years and Months	Total Months	2-0 (24)	2-1 (25)	2-2 (26)	2-3 (27)	2-4 (28)	2-5 (29)	2-6 (30)	2-7 (31)	2-8 (32)	2-9 (33)	2-10 (34)	2-11 (35)	3-0 (36)	3-1 (37)	3-2 (38)	3-3 (39)	3-4 (40)	3-5 (41)	3-6 (42)	3-7 (43)	3-8 (44)	3-9 (45)	3-10 (46)	3-11 (47)
2-0	24	100	104	108	113	117	121	125	129	133	138	142	146	150	154	158	163	167	171						
2-1	25	96	100	104	108	112	116	120	124	128	132	136	140	144	148	152	156	160	164	168	172				
2-2	26	92	96	100	104	108	112	115	119	123	127	131	135	138	142	146	150	154	158	162	165	169	173		
2-3	27	89	93	96	100	104	107	111	115	119	122	126	130	133	137	141	144	148	152	156	159	163	167	170	
2-4	28	86	89	93	96	100	104	107	111	114	118	121	125	129	132	136	139	143	146	150	154	157	161	164	168
2-5	29	83	86	90	93	97	100	103	107	110	114	117	121	124	128	131	134	138	141	145	148	152	155	159	162
2-6	30	80	83	87	90	93	97	100	103	107	110	113	117	120	123	127	130	133	137	140	143	147	150	153	157
2-7	31	77	81	84	87	90	94	97	100	103	106	110	113	116	119	123	126	129	132	135	139	142	145	148	152
2-8	32	75	78	81	84	88	91	94	97	100	103	106	109	113	116	119	122	125	128	131	134	138	141	144	147
2-9	33	73	76	79	82	85	88	91	94	97	100	103	106	109	112	115	118	121	124	127	130	133	136	139	142
2-10	34	71	74	76	79	82	85	88	91	94	97	100	103	106	109	112	115	118	121	124	126	129	132	135	138
2-11	35	69	71	74	77	80	83	86	89	91	94	97	100	103	106	109	111	114	117	120	123	126	129	131	134
3-0	36	67	69	72	75	78	81	83	86	89	92	94	97	100	103	106	108	111	114	117	119	122	125	128	131
3-1	37	65	68	70	73	76	78	81	84	86	89	92	95	97	100	103	105	108	111	114	116	119	122	124	127
3-2	38	63	66	68	71	74	76	79	82	84	87	89	92	95	97	100	103	105	108	111	113	116	118	121	124
3-3	39	62	64	67	69	72	74	77	79	82	85	87	90	92	95	97	100	103	105	108	110	113	115	118	121
3-4	40	60	63	65	68	70	73	75	78	80	83	85	88	90	93	95	98	100	103	105	108	110	113	115	118
3-5	41	59	61	63	66	68	71	73	76	78	80	83	85	88	90	93	95	98	100	102	105	107	110	112	115
3-6	42	57	60	62	64	67	69	71	74	76	79	81	83	86	88	90	93	95	98	100	102	105	107	110	112
3-7	43	56	58	60	63	65	67	70	72	74	77	79	81	84	86	88	91	93	95	98	100	102	105	107	109
3-8	44	55	57	59	61	64	66	68	70	73	75	77	80	82	84	86	89	91	93	95	98	100	102	105	107
3-9	45	53	56	58	60	62	64	67	69	71	73	76	78	80	82	84	87	89	91	93	96	98	100	102	104
3-10	46	52	54	57	59	61	63	65	67	70	72	74	76	78	80	83	85	87	89	91	93	96	98	100	102
3-11	47	51	53	55	57	60	62	64	66	68	70	72	74	77	79	81	83	85	87	89	91	94	96	98	100
4-0	48	50	52	54	56	58	60	63	65	67	69	71	73	75	77	79	81	83	85	88	90	92	94	96	98
4-1	49	49	51	53	55	57	59	61	63	65	67	69	71	73	76	78	80	82	84	86	88	90	92	94	96
4-2	50	48	50	52	54	56	58	60	62	64	66	68	70	72	74	76	78	80	82	84	86	88	90	92	94
4-3	51	47	49	51	53	55	57	59	61	63	65	67	69	71	73	75	76	78	80	82	84	86	88	90	92
4-4	52	46	48	50	52	54	56	58	60	62	63	65	67	69	71	73	75	77	79	81	83	85	87	88	90
4-5	53	45	47	49	51	53	55	57	58	60	62	64	66	68	70	72	74	75	77	79	81	83	85	87	89
4-6	54	44	46	48	50	52	54	56	57	59	61	63	65	67	69	70	72	74	76	78	80	81	83	85	87
4-7	55	44	45	47	49	51	53	55	56	58	60	62	64	65	67	69	71	73	75	76	78	80	82	84	85
4-8	56	43	45	46	48	50	52	54	55	57	59	61	63	64	66	68	70	71	73	75	77	79	80	82	84
4-9	57	42	44	46	47	49	51	53	54	56	58	60	61	63	65	67	68	70	72	74	75	77	79	81	82
4-10	58	41	43	45	47	48	50	52	53	55	57	59	60	62	64	66	67	69	71	72	74	76	78	79	81
4-11	59	41	42	44	46	47	49	51	53	54	56	58	59	61	63	64	66	68	69	71	73	75	76	78	80

MENTAL AGE

CHRONOLOGICAL AGE

Years and Months	Total Months	2-0 (24)	2-1 (25)	2-2 (26)	2-3 (27)	2-4 (28)	2-5 (29)	2-6 (30)	2-7 (31)	2-8 (32)	2-9 (33)	2-10 (34)	2-11 (35)	3-0 (36)	3-1 (37)	3-2 (38)	3-3 (39)	3-4 (40)	3-5 (41)	3-6 (42)	3-7 (43)	3-8 (44)	3-9 (45)	3-10 (46)	3-11 (47)
5- 0	60	40	42	43	45	47	48	50	52	53	55	57	58	60	62	63	65	67	68	70	72	73	75	77	78
5- 1	61	39	41	43	44	46	48	49	51	52	54	56	57	59	61	62	64	66	67	69	70	72	74	75	77
5- 2	62	39	40	42	44	45	47	48	50	52	53	55	56	58	60	61	63	65	66	68	69	71	73	74	76
5- 3	63	38	40	41	43	44	46	48	49	51	52	54	56	57	59	60	62	63	65	67	68	70	71	73	75
5- 4	64	38	39	41	42	44	45	47	48	50	52	53	55	56	58	59	61	63	64	66	67	69	70	72	73
5- 5	65	37	38	40	42	43	45	46	48	49	51	52	54	55	57	58	60	62	63	65	66	68	69	71	72
5- 6	66	36	38	39	41	42	44	45	47	48	50	52	53	55	56	58	59	61	62	64	65	67	68	70	71
5- 7	67	36	37	39	40	42	43	45	46	48	49	51	52	54	55	57	58	60	61	63	64	66	67	69	70
5- 8	68	35	37	38	40	41	43	44	46	47	49	50	51	53	54	56	57	59	60	62	63	65	66	68	69
5- 9	69	35	36	38	39	41	42	43	45	46	48	49	51	52	54	55	57	58	59	61	62	64	65	67	68
5-10	70	34	36	37	39	40	41	43	44	46	47	49	50	51	53	54	56	57	59	60	61	63	64	66	67
5-11	71	34	35	37	38	39	41	42	44	45	46	48	49	51	52	54	55	56	58	59	61	62	63	65	66
6- 0	72	33	35	36	38	39	40	42	43	44	46	47	49	50	51	53	54	56	57	58	60	61	63	64	65
6- 1	73	33	34	36	37	38	40	41	42	44	45	47	48	49	51	52	53	55	56	58	59	60	62	63	64
6- 2	74	32	34	35	36	38	39	41	42	43	45	46	47	49	50	51	53	54	55	57	58	59	61	62	64
6- 3	75	32	33	35	36	37	39	40	41	43	44	45	47	48	49	51	52	53	55	56	57	59	60	61	63
6- 4	76	32	33	34	36	37	38	39	41	42	43	45	46	47	49	50	51	53	54	55	57	58	59	61	62
6- 5	77	31	32	34	35	36	38	39	40	42	43	44	45	47	48	49	51	52	53	55	56	57	58	60	61
6- 6	78	31	32	33	35	36	37	38	40	41	42	44	45	46	47	49	50	51	53	54	55	56	58	59	60
6- 7	79	30	32	33	34	35	37	38	39	41	42	43	44	46	47	48	49	51	52	53	54	56	57	58	59
6- 8	80	30	31	33	34	35	36	38	39	40	41	43	44	45	46	48	49	50	51	53	54	55	56	58	59
6- 9	81	30	31	32	33	35	36	37	38	40	41	42	43	44	46	47	48	49	51	52	53	54	56	57	58
6-10	82		30	32	33	34	35	37	38	39	40	41	43	44	45	46	48	49	50	51	52	54	55	56	57
6-11	83		30	31	33	34	35	36	37	39	40	41	42	43	45	46	47	48	49	51	52	53	54	55	57
7- 0	84		30	31	32	33	35	36	37	38	39	40	42	43	44	45	46	48	49	50	51	52	54	55	56
7- 1	85			31	32	33	34	35	36	38	39	40	41	42	44	45	46	47	48	49	51	52	53	54	55
7- 2	86			30	31	33	34	35	36	37	38	40	41	42	43	44	45	47	48	49	50	51	52	53	55
7- 3	87			30	31	32	33	34	36	37	38	39	40	41	43	44	45	46	47	48	49	51	52	53	54
7- 4	88			30	31	32	33	34	35	36	38	39	40	41	42	43	44	45	47	48	49	50	51	52	53
7- 5	89				30	31	33	34	35	36	37	38	39	40	42	43	44	45	46	47	48	49	51	52	53
7- 6	90				30	31	32	33	34	36	37	38	39	40	41	42	43	44	46	47	48	49	50	51	52
7- 7	91				30	31	32	33	34	35	36	37	38	40	41	42	43	44	45	46	47	48	49	51	52
7- 8	92					30	32	33	34	35	36	37	38	39	40	41	42	43	45	46	47	48	49	50	51
7- 9	93					30	31	32	33	34	35	37	38	39	40	41	42	43	44	45	46	47	48	49	51
7-10	94					30	31	32	33	34	35	36	37	38	39	40	41	43	44	45	46	47	48	49	50
7-11	95						31	32	33	34	35	36	37	38	39	40	41	42	43	44	45	46	47	48	49
Total Months		24	25	26	27	28	29	30	31	32	33	34	35	36	37	38	39	40	41	42	43	44	45	46	47

Years and Months	Total Months	3-11	3-10	3-9	3-8	3-7	3-6	3-5	3-4	3-3	3-2	3-1	3-0	2-11	2-10	2-9	2-8	2-7	2-6	2-5	2-4	2-3	2-2	2-1	2-0
8-0	96	49	48	47	46	45	44	43	42	41	40	39	38	36	35	34	33	32	31	30	....	....	....	....	....
8-1	97	48	47	46	45	44	43	42	41	40	39	38	37	36	35	34	33	32	31	30	....	....	....	....	....
8-2	98	48	47	46	45	44	43	42	41	40	39	38	37	36	35	34	33	32	31	30	....	....	....	....	....
8-3	99	47	46	45	44	43	42	41	40	39	38	37	36	35	34	33	32	31	30	....	....	....	....	....	....
8-4	100	47	46	45	44	43	42	41	40	39	38	37	36	35	34	33	32	31	30	....	....	....	....	....	....
8-5	101	47	46	45	44	43	42	41	40	39	38	37	36	35	34	33	32	31	30	....	....	....	....	....	....
8-6	102	46	45	44	43	42	41	40	39	38	37	36	35	34	33	32	31	30	....	....	....	....	....	....	....
8-7	103	46	45	44	43	42	41	40	39	38	37	36	35	34	33	32	31	30	....	....	....	....	....	....	....
8-8	104	45	44	43	42	41	40	39	38	38	37	36	35	34	33	32	31	30	....	....	....	....	....	....	....
8-9	105	45	44	43	42	41	40	39	38	37	36	35	34	33	32	31	30	30	....	....	....	....	....	....	....
8-10	106	44	43	42	42	41	40	39	38	37	36	35	34	33	32	31	30	....	....	....	....	....	....	....	....
8-11	107	44	43	42	41	40	39	38	37	36	36	35	34	33	32	31	30	....	....	....	....	....	....	....	....
9-0	108	44	43	42	41	40	39	38	37	36	35	34	33	32	31	31	30	....	....	....	....	....	....	....	....
9-1	109	43	42	41	40	39	39	38	37	36	35	34	33	32	31	30	....	....	....	....	....	....	....	....	....
9-2	110	43	42	41	40	39	38	37	36	35	35	34	33	32	31	30	....	....	....	....	....	....	....	....	....
9-3	111	42	41	41	40	39	38	37	36	35	34	33	32	32	31	30	....	....	....	....	....	....	....	....	....
9-4	112	42	41	40	39	38	38	37	36	35	34	33	32	31	30	....	....	....	....	....	....	....	....	....	....
9-5	113	42	41	40	39	38	37	36	35	35	34	33	32	31	30	....	....	....	....	....	....	....	....	....	....
9-6	114	41	40	39	39	38	37	36	35	34	33	32	32	31	30	....	....	....	....	....	....	....	....	....	....
9-7	115	41	40	39	38	37	37	36	35	34	33	32	31	30	30	....	....	....	....	....	....	....	....	....	....
9-8	116	41	40	39	38	37	36	35	34	34	33	32	31	30	....	....	....	....	....	....	....	....	....	....	....
9-9	117	40	39	38	38	37	36	35	34	33	32	32	31	30	....	....	....	....	....	....	....	....	....	....	....
9-10	118	40	39	38	37	36	36	35	34	33	32	31	31	30	....	....	....	....	....	....	....	....	....	....	....
9-11	119	40	39	38	37	36	35	34	34	33	32	31	30	....	....	....	....	....	....	....	....	....	....	....	....
10-0	120	39	38	38	37	36	35	34	33	33	32	31	30	....	....	....	....	....	....	....	....	....	....	....	....
10-1	121	39	38	37	36	36	35	34	33	32	31	31	30	....	....	....	....	....	....	....	....	....	....	....	....
10-2	122	39	38	37	36	35	34	34	33	32	31	30	30	....	....	....	....	....	....	....	....	....	....	....	....
10-3	123	38	37	37	36	35	34	33	33	32	31	30	....	....	....	....	....	....	....	....	....	....	....	....	....
10-4	124	38	37	36	35	35	34	33	32	31	31	30	....	....	....	....	....	....	....	....	....	....	....	....	....
10-5	125	38	37	36	35	34	34	33	32	31	30	30	....	....	....	....	....	....	....	....	....	....	....	....	....
10-6	126	37	37	36	35	34	33	33	32	31	30	....	....	....	....	....	....	....	....	....	....	....	....	....	....
10-7	127	37	36	35	35	34	33	32	32	31	30	....	....	....	....	....	....	....	....	....	....	....	....	....	....
10-8	128	37	36	35	34	34	33	32	31	30	30	....	....	....	....	....	....	....	....	....	....	....	....	....	....
10-9	129	36	36	35	34	33	33	32	31	30	....	....	....	....	....	....	....	....	....	....	....	....	....	....	....
10-10	130	36	35	35	34	33	32	32	31	30	....	....	....	....	....	....	....	....	....	....	....	....	....	....	....
10-11	131	36	35	34	34	33	32	31	31	....	....	....	....	....	....	....	....	....	....	....	....	....	....	....	....
Total Months		47	46	45	44	43	42	41	40	39	38	37	36	35	34	33	32	31	30	29	28	27	26	25	24

MENTAL AGE

Years and Months	Total Months	3-11	3-10	3-9	3-8	3-7	3-6	3-5	3-4	3-3	3-2	3-1	3-0	2-11	2-10	2-9	2-8	2-7	2-6	2-5	2-4	2-3	2-2	2-1	2-0
11- 0	132	36	35	34	33	33	32	31	30	30															
11- 1	133	35	35	34	33	32	32	31	30																
11- 2	134	35	34	33	33	32	31	31	30																
11- 3	135	35	34	33	33	32	31	30																	
11- 4	136	35	34	33	32	32	31	30																	
11- 5	137	34	34	33	32	31	31	30																	
11- 6	138	34	33	33	32	31	30	30																	
11- 7	139	34	33	32	31	31	30	30																	
11- 8	140	34	33	32	31	31	30																		
11- 9	141	33	32	32	31	30	30																		
11-10	142	33	32	31	31	30	30																		
11-11	143	33	32	31	31	30																			
12- 0	144	33	32	31	31	30																			
12- 1	145	32	32	31	30																				
12- 2	146	32	31	31	30																				
12- 3	147	32	31	30	30																				
12- 4	148	32	31	30	30																				
12- 5	149	32	31	30	30																				
12- 6	150	31	31	30		30																			
12- 7	151	31	30	30																					
12- 8	152	31	30	30																					
12- 9	153	31	30																						
12-10	154	31	30																						
12-11	155	30	30																						
13- 0	156	30																							
13- 1	157	30																							
13- 2	158	30																							
13- 3	159	30																							
13- 4	160	30																							
13- 5	161	30																							
13- 6	162																								
13- 7	163																								
13- 8	164																								
13- 9	165																								
13-10	166																								
13-11	167																								
Total Months		47	46	45	44	43	42	41	40	39	38	37	36	35	34	33	32	31	30	29	28	27	26	25	24

CHRONOLOGICAL AGE

MENTAL AGE

CHRONOLOGICAL AGE

Total Months	5-11	5-10	5-9	5-8	5-7	5-6	5-5	5-4	5-3	5-2	5-1	5-0	4-11	4-10	4-9	4-8	4-7	4-6	4-5	4-4	4-3	4-2	4-1	4-0	Years and Months
24	.	.	.	.	.	.	.	.	.	.	.	.	.	.	.	.	.	.	.	.	.	.	.	.	2-0
25	.	.	.	.	.	.	.	.	.	.	.	.	.	.	.	.	.	.	.	.	.	.	.	.	2-1
26	.	.	.	.	.	.	.	.	.	.	.	.	.	.	.	.	.	.	.	.	.	.	.	.	2-2
27	.	.	.	.	.	.	.	.	.	.	.	.	.	.	.	.	.	.	.	.	.	.	.	.	2-3
28	.	.	.	.	.	.	.	.	.	.	.	.	.	.	.	.	.	.	.	.	.	.	.	171	2-4
29	.	.	.	.	.	.	.	.	.	.	.	.	.	.	.	.	.	.	.	.	.	172	169	166	2-5
30	.	.	.	.	.	.	.	.	.	.	.	.	.	.	.	.	.	.	.	.	170	167	163	160	2-6
31	.	.	.	.	.	.	.	.	.	.	.	.	.	.	.	.	.	.	171	168	165	161	158	155	2-7
32	.	.	.	.	.	.	.	.	.	.	.	.	.	.	.	.	172	169	166	163	159	156	153	150	2-8
33	.	.	.	.	.	.	.	.	.	.	.	.	.	.	.	170	167	164	161	158	155	152	148	145	2-9
34	.	.	.	.	.	.	.	.	.	.	.	.	.	171	168	165	162	159	156	153	150	147	144	141	2-10
35	.	.	.	.	.	.	.	.	.	.	.	171	169	166	163	160	157	154	151	149	146	143	140	137	2-11
36	.	.	.	.	.	.	.	.	.	172	169	167	164	161	158	156	153	150	147	144	142	139	136	133	3-0
37	.	.	.	.	.	.	.	.	170	168	165	162	159	157	154	151	149	146	143	141	138	135	132	130	3-1
38	.	.	.	.	.	.	171	168	166	163	161	158	155	153	150	147	145	142	139	137	134	132	129	126	3-2
39	.	.	.	.	172	169	167	164	162	159	156	154	151	149	146	144	141	138	136	133	131	128	126	123	3-3
40	.	.	.	170	168	165	163	160	158	155	153	150	148	145	143	140	138	135	133	130	128	125	123	120	3-4
41	.	171	168	166	163	161	159	156	154	151	149	146	144	141	139	137	134	132	129	127	124	122	120	117	3-5
42	169	167	164	162	160	157	155	152	150	148	145	143	140	138	136	133	131	129	126	124	121	119	117	114	3-6
43	165	163	160	158	156	153	151	149	147	144	142	140	137	135	133	130	128	126	123	121	119	116	114	112	3-7
44	161	159	157	155	152	150	148	145	143	141	139	136	134	132	130	127	125	123	120	118	116	114	111	109	3-8
45	158	156	153	151	149	147	144	142	140	138	136	133	131	129	127	124	122	120	118	116	113	111	109	107	3-9
46	154	152	150	148	146	143	141	139	137	135	133	130	128	126	124	122	120	117	115	113	111	109	107	104	3-10
47	151	149	147	145	143	140	138	136	134	132	130	128	126	123	121	119	117	115	113	111	109	106	104	102	3-11
48	148	146	144	142	140	138	135	133	131	129	127	125	123	121	119	117	115	113	110	108	106	104	102	100	4-0
49	145	143	141	139	137	135	133	131	129	127	124	122	120	118	116	114	112	110	108	106	104	102	100	98	4-1
50	142	140	138	136	134	132	130	128	126	124	122	120	118	116	114	112	110	108	106	104	102	100	98	96	4-2
51	139	137	135	133	131	129	127	125	124	122	120	118	116	114	112	110	108	106	104	102	100	98	96	94	4-3
52	137	135	133	131	129	127	125	123	121	119	117	115	113	112	110	108	106	104	102	100	98	96	94	92	4-4
53	134	132	130	128	126	125	123	121	119	117	115	113	111	109	108	106	104	102	100	98	96	94	92	91	4-5
54	131	130	128	126	124	122	120	119	117	115	113	111	109	107	106	104	102	100	98	96	94	93	91	89	4-6
55	129	127	125	124	122	120	118	116	115	113	111	109	107	105	104	102	100	98	96	95	93	91	89	87	4-7
56	127	125	123	121	120	118	116	114	113	111	109	107	105	104	102	100	98	96	95	93	91	89	88	86	4-8
57	125	123	121	119	118	116	114	112	111	109	107	105	104	102	100	98	96	95	93	91	89	88	86	84	4-9
58	122	121	119	117	116	114	112	110	109	107	105	103	102	100	98	97	95	93	91	90	88	86	84	83	4-10
59	120	119	117	115	114	112	110	108	107	105	103	102	100	98	97	95	93	92	90	88	86	85	83	81	4-11
Total Months	71	70	69	68	67	66	65	64	63	62	61	60	59	58	57	56	55	54	53	52	51	50	49	48	Total Months

MENTAL AGE

Table for converting Mental Age and Chronological Age to an intelligence quotient. Column headings give Mental Age (in years-months and in total months); row headings give Chronological Age (in years-months and in total months).

Chron. Age (Yrs-Mos)	Total Mos	4-0 (48)	4-1 (49)	4-2 (50)	4-3 (51)	4-4 (52)	4-5 (53)	4-6 (54)	4-7 (55)	4-8 (56)	4-9 (57)	4-10 (58)	4-11 (59)	5-0 (60)	5-1 (61)	5-2 (62)	5-3 (63)	5-4 (64)	5-5 (65)	5-6 (66)	5-7 (67)	5-8 (68)	5-9 (69)	5-10 (70)	5-11 (71)
5-0	60	80	82	83	85	87	88	90	92	93	95	97	98	100	102	103	105	107	108	110	112	113	115	117	118
5-1	61	79	80	82	84	85	87	89	90	92	93	95	97	98	100	102	103	105	107	108	110	111	113	115	116
5-2	62	77	79	81	82	84	85	87	89	90	92	94	95	97	98	100	102	103	105	106	108	110	111	113	115
5-3	63	76	78	79	81	83	84	86	87	89	90	92	94	95	97	98	100	102	103	105	106	108	110	111	113
5-4	64	75	77	78	80	81	83	84	86	88	89	91	92	94	95	97	98	100	102	103	105	106	108	109	111
5-5	65	74	75	77	78	80	82	83	85	86	88	89	91	92	94	95	97	98	100	102	103	105	106	108	109
5-6	66	73	74	76	77	79	80	82	83	85	86	88	89	91	92	94	95	97	98	100	102	103	105	106	108
5-7	67	72	73	75	76	78	79	81	82	84	85	87	88	90	91	93	94	96	97	99	100	101	103	104	106
5-8	68	71	72	74	75	76	78	79	81	82	84	85	87	88	90	91	93	94	96	97	99	100	101	103	104
5-9	69	70	71	72	74	75	77	78	80	81	83	84	86	87	88	90	91	93	94	96	97	99	100	101	103
5-10	70	69	70	71	73	74	76	77	79	80	81	83	84	86	87	89	90	91	93	94	96	97	99	100	101
5-11	71	68	69	70	72	73	75	76	77	79	80	82	83	85	86	87	89	90	92	93	94	96	97	99	100
6-0	72	67	68	69	71	72	74	75	76	78	79	81	82	83	85	86	88	89	90	92	93	94	96	97	99
6-1	73	66	67	68	70	71	73	74	75	77	78	79	81	82	84	85	86	88	89	90	92	93	95	96	97
6-2	74	65	66	68	69	70	72	73	74	76	77	78	80	81	82	84	85	86	88	89	91	92	93	95	96
6-3	75	64	65	67	68	69	71	72	73	75	76	77	79	80	81	83	84	85	87	88	89	91	92	93	95
6-4	76	63	64	66	67	68	70	71	72	74	75	76	78	79	80	82	83	84	86	87	88	89	91	92	93
6-5	77	62	64	65	66	68	69	70	71	73	74	75	77	78	79	81	82	83	84	86	87	88	90	91	92
6-6	78	62	63	64	65	67	68	69	71	72	73	74	76	77	78	79	81	82	83	85	86	87	88	90	91
6-7	79	61	62	63	65	66	67	68	70	71	72	73	75	76	77	78	80	81	82	84	85	86	87	89	90
6-8	80	60	61	63	64	65	66	68	69	70	71	73	74	75	76	78	79	80	81	83	84	85	86	88	89
6-9	81	59	60	62	63	64	65	67	68	69	70	72	73	74	75	77	78	79	80	81	83	84	85	86	88
6-10	82	59	60	61	62	63	65	66	67	68	70	71	72	73	74	76	77	78	79	80	82	83	84	85	87
6-11	83	58	59	60	61	63	64	65	66	67	69	70	71	72	73	75	76	77	78	80	81	82	83	84	86
7-0	84	57	58	60	61	62	63	64	65	67	68	69	70	71	73	74	75	76	77	79	80	81	82	83	85
7-1	85	56	58	59	60	61	62	64	65	66	67	68	69	71	72	73	74	75	76	78	79	80	81	82	84
7-2	86	56	57	58	59	60	62	63	64	65	66	67	69	70	71	72	73	74	76	77	78	79	80	81	83
7-3	87	55	56	57	59	60	61	62	63	64	66	67	68	69	70	71	72	74	75	76	77	78	79	80	82
7-4	88	55	56	57	58	59	60	61	63	64	65	66	67	68	69	70	72	73	74	75	76	77	78	80	81
7-5	89	54	55	56	57	58	60	61	62	63	64	65	66	67	69	70	71	72	73	74	75	76	78	79	80
7-6	90	53	54	56	57	58	59	60	61	62	63	64	66	67	68	69	70	71	72	73	74	76	77	78	79
7-7	91	53	54	55	56	57	58	59	60	62	63	64	65	66	67	68	69	70	71	73	74	75	76	77	78
7-8	92	52	53	54	55	57	58	59	60	61	62	63	64	65	66	67	68	70	71	72	73	74	75	76	77
7-9	93	52	53	54	55	56	57	58	59	60	61	62	63	65	66	67	68	69	70	71	72	73	74	75	76
7-10	94	51	52	53	54	55	56	57	59	60	61	62	63	64	65	66	67	68	69	70	71	72	73	74	76
7-11	95	51	52	53	54	55	56	57	58	59	60	61	62	63	64	65	66	67	68	69	71	72	73	74	75

MENTAL AGE

CHRONOLOGICAL AGE

Years and Months (C.A.)	Total Months	4-0	4-1	4-2	4-3	4-4	4-5	4-6	4-7	4-8	4-9	4-10	4-11	5-0	5-1	5-2	5-3	5-4	5-5	5-6	5-7	5-8	5-9	5-10	5-11
(M.A. Total Months)		48	49	50	51	52	53	54	55	56	57	58	59	60	61	62	63	64	65	66	67	68	69	70	71
8-0	96	50	51	52	53	54	55	56	57	58	59	60	61	63	64	65	66	67	68	69	70	71	72	73	74
8-1	97	49	51	52	53	54	55	56	57	58	59	60	61	62	63	64	65	66	67	68	69	70	71	72	73
8-2	98	49	50	51	52	53	54	55	56	57	58	59	60	61	62	63	64	65	66	67	68	69	70	71	72
8-3	99	48	49	51	52	53	54	55	56	57	58	59	60	61	62	63	64	65	66	67	68	69	70	71	72
8-4	100	48	49	50	51	52	53	54	55	56	57	58	59	60	61	62	63	64	65	66	67	68	69	70	71
8-5	101	48	49	50	50	51	52	53	54	55	56	57	58	59	60	61	62	63	64	65	66	67	68	69	70
8-6	102	47	48	49	50	51	52	53	54	55	56	57	58	59	60	61	62	63	64	65	66	67	68	69	70
8-7	103	47	48	49	50	50	51	52	53	54	55	56	57	58	59	60	61	62	63	64	65	66	67	68	69
8-8	104	46	47	48	49	50	51	52	53	54	55	56	57	58	59	60	61	62	63	63	64	65	66	67	68
8-9	105	46	47	48	49	50	50	51	52	53	54	55	56	57	58	59	60	61	62	63	64	65	66	67	68
8-10	106	45	46	47	48	49	50	51	52	53	54	55	56	57	58	58	59	60	61	62	63	64	65	66	67
8-11	107	45	46	47	48	49	50	50	51	52	53	54	55	56	57	58	59	60	61	62	63	64	64	65	66
9-0	108	44	45	46	47	48	49	50	51	52	53	54	55	56	56	57	58	59	60	61	62	63	64	65	66
9-1	109	44	45	46	47	48	49	50	50	51	52	53	54	55	56	57	58	59	60	61	61	62	63	64	65
9-2	110	44	45	45	46	47	48	49	50	51	52	53	54	55	55	56	57	58	59	60	61	62	63	64	65
9-3	111	43	44	45	46	47	48	49	50	50	51	52	53	54	55	56	57	58	59	59	60	61	62	63	64
9-4	112	43	44	45	46	46	47	48	49	50	51	52	53	54	54	55	56	57	58	59	60	61	62	63	63
9-5	113	42	43	44	45	46	47	48	49	50	50	51	52	53	54	55	56	57	58	58	59	60	61	62	63
9-6	114	42	43	44	45	46	46	47	48	49	50	51	52	53	54	54	55	56	57	58	59	60	61	61	62
9-7	115	42	43	43	44	45	46	47	48	49	50	50	51	52	53	54	55	56	57	57	58	59	60	61	62
9-8	116	41	42	43	44	45	46	47	47	48	49	50	51	52	53	53	54	55	56	57	58	59	59	60	61
9-9	117	41	42	43	44	44	45	46	47	48	49	50	50	51	52	53	54	55	56	56	57	58	59	60	61
9-10	118	41	42	42	43	44	45	46	47	47	48	49	50	51	52	53	53	54	55	56	57	58	58	59	60
9-11	119	40	41	42	43	44	45	45	46	47	48	49	50	50	51	52	53	54	55	55	56	57	58	59	60
10-0	120	40	41	42	43	43	44	45	46	47	48	48	49	50	51	52	53	53	54	55	56	57	58	58	59
10-1	121	40	40	41	42	43	44	45	45	46	47	48	49	50	50	51	52	53	54	55	55	56	57	58	59
10-2	122	39	40	41	42	43	43	44	45	46	47	48	48	49	50	51	52	52	53	54	55	56	57	57	58
10-3	123	39	40	41	41	42	43	44	45	46	46	47	48	49	50	50	51	52	53	54	54	55	56	57	58
10-4	124	39	40	40	41	42	43	44	44	45	46	47	48	48	49	50	51	52	52	53	54	55	56	56	57
10-5	125	38	39	40	41	42	42	43	44	45	46	46	47	48	49	50	50	51	52	53	54	54	55	56	57
10-6	126	38	39	40	40	41	42	43	44	44	45	46	47	48	48	49	50	51	52	52	53	54	55	56	56
10-7	127	38	39	39	40	41	42	43	43	44	45	46	46	47	48	49	50	50	51	52	53	54	54	55	56
10-8	128	38	38	39	40	41	41	42	43	44	45	45	46	47	48	48	49	50	51	52	52	53	54	55	55
10-9	129	37	38	39	40	40	41	42	43	43	44	45	46	47	47	48	49	50	50	51	52	53	53	54	55
10-10	130	37	38	38	39	40	41	42	42	43	44	45	45	46	47	48	48	49	50	51	52	52	53	54	55
10-11	131	37	37	38	39	40	40	41	42	43	44	44	45	46	47	47	48	49	50	50	51	52	53	53	54

MENTAL AGE

Table of Intelligence Quotients — Chronological Age (Years and Months) by Mental Age (Years and Months). Body values are IQ; bottom row gives Total Months for each Mental Age, right-hand column gives Total Months for each Chronological Age.

Years and Months	Total Months	4-0	4-1	4-2	4-3	4-4	4-5	4-6	4-7	4-8	4-9	4-10	4-11	5-0	5-1	5-2	5-3	5-4	5-5	5-6	5-7	5-8	5-9	5-10	5-11
11- 0	132	36	37	38	39	39	40	41	42	42	43	44	45	45	46	47	48	48	49	50	51	52	52	53	54
11- 1	133	36	37	38	38	39	40	41	41	42	43	44	44	45	46	47	47	48	49	50	50	51	52	53	53
11- 2	134	36	37	37	38	39	40	40	41	42	43	43	44	45	46	46	47	48	49	49	50	51	51	52	53
11- 3	135	36	36	37	38	39	39	40	41	41	42	43	44	44	45	46	47	47	48	49	50	50	51	52	53
11- 4	136	35	36	37	38	38	39	40	40	41	42	43	43	44	45	46	46	47	48	49	49	50	51	51	52
11- 5	137	35	36	37	37	38	39	39	40	41	42	42	43	44	45	45	46	47	47	48	49	50	50	51	52
11- 6	138	35	36	36	37	38	38	39	40	41	41	42	43	43	44	45	46	46	47	48	49	49	50	51	51
11- 7	139	35	35	36	37	37	38	39	40	40	41	42	42	43	44	45	45	46	47	47	48	49	50	50	51
11- 8	140	34	35	36	36	37	38	39	39	40	41	41	42	43	44	44	45	46	46	47	48	49	49	50	51
11- 9	141	34	35	35	36	37	38	38	39	40	40	41	42	43	43	44	45	45	46	47	48	48	49	50	50
11-10	142	34	35	35	36	37	37	38	39	39	40	41	42	42	43	44	44	45	46	46	47	48	49	49	50
11-11	143	34	34	35	36	36	37	38	38	39	40	41	41	42	43	43	44	45	45	46	47	48	48	49	50
12- 0	144	33	34	35	35	36	37	38	38	39	40	40	41	42	42	43	44	44	45	46	47	47	48	49	49
12- 1	145	33	34	34	35	36	37	37	38	39	39	40	41	41	42	43	43	44	45	46	46	47	48	48	49
12- 2	146	33	34	34	35	36	36	37	38	38	39	40	40	41	42	42	43	44	45	45	46	47	47	48	49
12- 3	147	33	33	34	35	35	36	37	37	38	39	39	40	41	42	42	43	44	44	45	46	46	47	48	48
12- 4	148	32	33	34	34	35	36	36	37	38	39	39	40	41	41	42	43	43	44	45	45	46	47	47	48
12- 5	149	32	33	34	34	35	36	36	37	38	38	39	40	40	41	42	42	43	44	44	45	46	46	47	48
12- 6	150	32	33	33	34	35	35	36	37	37	38	39	39	40	41	41	42	43	43	44	45	45	46	47	47
12- 7	151	32	32	33	34	34	35	36	36	37	38	38	39	40	40	41	42	42	43	44	44	45	46	46	47
12- 8	152	32	32	33	34	34	35	36	36	37	38	38	39	39	40	41	41	42	43	43	44	45	45	46	47
12- 9	153	31	32	33	33	34	35	35	36	37	37	38	39	39	40	41	41	42	42	43	44	44	45	46	46
12-10	154	31	32	32	33	34	34	35	36	36	37	38	38	39	40	40	41	42	42	43	44	44	45	45	46
12-11	155	31	32	32	33	34	34	35	35	36	37	37	38	39	39	40	41	41	42	43	43	44	45	45	46
13- 0	156	31	31	32	33	33	34	35	35	36	37	37	38	38	39	40	40	41	42	42	43	44	44	45	46
13- 1	157	31	31	32	32	33	34	34	35	36	36	37	38	38	39	39	40	41	41	42	43	43	44	45	45
13- 2	158	30	31	32	32	33	34	34	35	35	36	37	37	38	39	39	40	41	41	42	42	43	44	44	45
13- 3	159	30	31	31	32	33	33	34	35	35	36	36	37	38	38	39	40	40	41	42	42	43	43	44	45
13- 4	160	30	31	31	32	33	33	34	34	35	36	36	37	38	38	39	39	40	41	41	42	43	43	44	44
13- 5	161	30	30	31	32	32	33	34	34	35	35	36	37	37	38	39	39	40	40	41	42	42	43	43	44
13- 6	162	30	30	31	31	32	33	33	34	35	35	36	36	37	38	38	39	40	40	41	41	42	43	43	44
13- 7	163	30	30	31	31	32	33	33	34	34	35	36	36	37	37	38	39	39	40	40	41	42	42	43	44
13- 8	164	30	30	30	31	32	32	33	34	34	35	35	36	37	37	38	38	39	40	40	41	41	42	43	43
13- 9	165	30	30	30	31	32	32	33	33	34	35	35	36	36	37	38	38	39	39	40	41	41	42	42	43
13-10	166	..	30	30	31	31	32	33	33	34	34	35	36	36	37	37	38	39	39	40	40	41	42	42	43
13-11	167	..	30	30	31	31	32	32	33	34	34	35	35	36	37	37	38	38	39	40	40	41	41	42	43
Total Months		48	49	50	51	52	53	54	55	56	57	58	59	60	61	62	63	64	65	66	67	68	69	70	71

CHRONOLOGICAL AGE

MENTAL AGE

Years and Months	4-0	4-1	4-2	4-3	4-4	4-5	4-6	4-7	4-8	4-9	4-10	4-11	5-0	5-1	5-2	5-3	5-4	5-5	5-6	5-7	5-8	5-9	5-10	5-11	Total Months
	48	49	50	51	52	53	54	55	56	57	58	59	60	61	62	63	64	65	66	67	68	69	70	71	
14-0		30	30	31	32	32	33	34	34	35	35	36	37	37	38	38	39	40	40	41	41	42	43	43	168
14-1		30	30	31	32	32	33	33	34	35	35	36	36	37	38	38	39	39	40	41	41	42	42	43	169
14-2		30	30	31	32	32	33	33	34	35	35	36	36	37	38	38	39	39	40	41	41	42	42	43	170
14-3		30	30	31	31	32	32	33	34	34	35	35	36	37	37	38	38	39	40	40	41	41	42	43	171
14-4			30	31	31	32	32	33	34	34	35	35	36	37	37	38	38	39	40	40	41	41	42	43	172
14-5			30	31	31	32	32	33	34	34	35	35	36	37	37	38	38	39	40	40	41	41	42	43	173
14-6			30	30	31	32	32	33	33	34	35	35	36	36	37	38	38	39	39	40	40	41	42	42	174
14-7				30	31	31	32	33	33	34	34	35	36	36	37	37	38	38	39	40	40	41	41	42	175
14-8				30	31	31	32	32	33	33	34	35	36	36	36	37	37	38	39	39	40	41	41	42	176
14-9				30	30	31	32	32	33	33	34	35	35	36	36	37	37	38	39	39	40	41	41	42	177
14-10				30	30	31	32	32	33	33	34	35	35	36	36	37	37	38	39	39	40	40	41	42	178
14-11				30	30	31	32	32	33	33	34	35	35	36	36	37	37	38	39	39	40	40	41	42	179
15-0				30	30	31	31	32	33	33	34	34	35	35	36	37	37	38	38	39	40	40	41	41	180
15-1					30	30	31	31	32	33	33	34	35	35	36	36	37	38	38	39	39	40	40	41	181
15-2						30	31	31	32	33	33	34	34	35	36	36	37	38	38	39	39	40	40	41	182
15-3						30	31	31	32	32	33	34	34	35	35	36	36	37	38	38	39	40	40	41	183
15-4						30	31	31	32	32	33	34	34	35	35	36	36	37	38	38	39	39	40	41	184
15-5						30	31	31	32	32	33	34	34	35	35	36	36	37	38	38	39	39	40	41	185
15-6				30	30	30	31	31	32	32	33	34	34	35	35	36	36	37	38	38	39	39	40	40	186
15-7						30	30	31	32	32	33	33	34	34	35	36	36	37	37	38	38	39	40	40	187
15-8						30	30	31	31	32	33	33	34	34	35	35	36	37	37	38	38	39	39	40	188
15-9						30	30	31	31	32	32	33	34	34	35	35	36	36	37	37	38	39	39	40	189
15-10						30	30	31	31	32	32	33	34	34	35	35	36	36	37	37	38	39	39	40	190
15-11						30	30	31	31	32	32	33	34	34	35	35	36	36	37	37	38	39	39	40	191
16-							30	31	31	32	32	33	33	34	34	35	36	36	37	37	38	38	39	39	192
Total Months	48	49	50	51	52	53	54	55	56	57	58	59	60	61	62	63	64	65	66	67	68	69	70	71	

CHRONOLOGICAL AGE

MENTAL AGE

Years and Months	6-0	6-1	6-2	6-3	6-4	6-5	6-6	6-7	6-8	6-9	6-10	6-11	7-0	7-1	7-2	7-3	7-4	7-5	7-6	7-7	7-8	7-9	7-10	7-11	Total Months
4-0	150	152	154	156	158	160	163	165	167	169	171														48
4-1	147	149	151	153	155	157	159	161	163	165	167	169	171												49
4-2	144	146	148	150	152	154	156	158	160	162	164	166	168	170											50
4-3	141	143	145	147	149	151	153	155	157	159	161	163	165	167	169	171									51
4-4	138	140	142	144	146	148	150	152	154	156	158	160	162	163	165	167	169	171							52
4-5	136	138	140	142	143	145	147	149	151	153	155	157	158	160	162	164	166	168	170						53
4-6	133	135	137	139	141	143	144	146	148	150	152	154	156	157	159	161	163	165	167	169	170				54
4-7	131	133	135	136	138	140	142	144	145	147	149	151	153	155	156	158	160	162	164	165	167	169	171		55
4-8	129	130	132	134	136	138	139	141	143	145	146	148	150	152	154	155	157	159	161	163	164	166	168	170	56
4-9	126	128	130	132	133	135	137	139	140	142	144	146	147	149	151	153	154	156	158	160	161	163	165	167	57
4-10	124	126	128	129	131	133	134	136	138	140	141	143	145	147	148	150	152	153	155	157	159	160	162	164	58
4-11	122	124	125	127	129	131	132	134	136	137	139	141	142	144	146	147	149	151	153	154	156	158	159	161	59
5-0	120	122	123	125	127	128	130	132	133	135	137	138	140	142	143	145	147	148	150	152	153	155	157	158	60
5-1	118	120	121	123	125	126	128	130	131	133	134	136	138	139	141	143	144	146	148	149	151	152	154	156	61
5-2	116	118	119	121	123	124	126	127	129	131	132	134	135	137	139	140	142	144	145	147	148	150	152	153	62
5-3	114	116	117	119	121	122	124	125	127	129	130	132	133	135	137	138	140	141	143	144	146	148	149	151	63
5-4	113	114	116	117	119	120	122	123	125	127	128	130	131	133	134	136	138	139	141	142	144	145	147	148	64
5-5	111	112	114	115	117	118	120	122	123	125	126	128	129	131	132	134	135	137	138	140	142	143	145	146	65
5-6	109	111	112	114	115	117	118	120	121	123	124	126	127	129	130	132	133	135	136	138	139	141	142	144	66
5-7	107	109	110	112	113	115	116	118	119	121	122	124	125	127	128	130	131	133	134	136	137	139	140	142	67
5-8	106	107	109	110	112	113	115	116	118	119	121	122	124	125	126	128	129	131	132	134	135	137	138	140	68
5-9	104	106	107	109	110	112	113	114	116	117	119	120	122	123	125	126	128	129	130	132	133	135	136	138	69
5-10	103	104	106	107	109	110	111	113	114	116	117	119	120	121	123	124	126	127	129	130	131	133	134	136	70
5-11	101	103	104	106	107	108	110	111	113	114	115	117	118	120	121	123	124	125	127	128	130	131	132	134	71
6-0	100	101	103	104	106	107	108	110	111	113	114	115	117	118	119	121	122	124	125	126	128	129	131	132	72
6-1	99	100	101	103	104	105	107	108	110	111	112	114	115	116	118	119	121	122	123	125	126	127	129	130	73
6-2	97	99	100	101	103	104	105	107	108	109	111	112	114	115	116	118	119	120	122	123	124	126	127	128	74
6-3	96	97	99	100	101	103	104	105	107	108	109	111	112	113	115	116	117	119	120	121	123	124	125	127	75
6-4	95	96	97	99	100	101	103	104	105	107	108	109	111	112	113	114	116	117	118	120	121	122	124	125	76
6-5	94	95	96	97	99	100	101	103	104	105	106	108	109	110	112	113	114	116	117	118	119	121	122	123	77
6-6	92	94	95	96	97	99	100	101	103	104	105	106	108	109	110	112	113	114	115	117	118	119	121	122	78
6-7	91	92	94	95	96	97	99	100	101	103	104	105	106	108	109	110	111	113	114	115	116	118	119	120	79
6-8	90	91	93	94	95	96	98	99	100	101	103	104	105	106	108	109	110	111	113	114	115	116	118	119	80
6-9	89	90	91	93	94	95	96	98	99	100	101	102	104	105	106	107	109	110	111	112	114	115	116	117	81
6-10	88	89	90	91	93	94	95	96	98	99	100	101	102	104	105	106	107	109	110	111	112	113	115	116	82
6-11	87	88	89	90	92	93	94	95	96	98	99	100	101	102	104	105	106	107	108	110	111	112	113	114	83
Total Months	72	73	74	75	76	77	78	79	80	81	82	83	84	85	86	87	88	89	90	91	92	93	94	95	

MENTAL AGE

Total Months	7-11	7-10	7-9	7-8	7-7	7-6	7-5	7-4	7-3	7-2	7-1	7-0	6-11	6-10	6-9	6-8	6-7	6-6	6-5	6-4	6-3	6-2	6-1	6-0	Years and Months
84	113	112	111	110	108	107	106	105	104	102	101	100	99	98	96	95	94	93	92	90	89	88	87	86	7-0
85	112	111	109	108	107	106	105	104	102	101	100	99	98	96	95	94	93	92	91	89	88	87	86	85	7-1
86	110	109	108	107	106	105	103	102	101	100	99	98	97	95	94	93	92	91	90	88	87	86	85	84	7-2
87	109	108	107	106	105	103	102	101	100	99	98	97	95	94	93	92	91	90	89	87	86	85	84	83	7-3
88	108	107	106	105	103	102	101	100	99	98	97	95	94	93	92	91	90	89	88	86	85	84	83	82	7-4
89	107	106	104	103	102	101	100	99	98	97	96	94	93	92	91	90	89	88	87	85	84	83	82	81	7-5
90	106	104	103	102	101	100	99	98	97	96	94	93	92	91	90	89	88	87	86	84	83	82	81	80	7-6
91	104	103	102	101	100	99	98	97	96	95	93	92	91	90	89	88	87	86	85	84	82	81	80	79	7-7
92	103	102	101	100	99	98	97	96	95	93	92	91	90	89	88	87	86	85	84	83	82	80	79	78	7-8
93	102	101	100	99	98	97	96	95	94	92	91	90	89	88	87	86	85	84	83	82	81	80	78	77	7-9
94	101	100	99	98	97	96	95	94	93	91	90	89	88	87	86	85	84	83	82	81	80	79	78	77	7-10
95	100	99	98	97	96	95	94	93	92	91	89	88	87	86	85	84	83	82	81	80	79	78	77	76	7-11
96	99	98	97	96	95	94	93	92	91	90	89	88	86	85	84	83	82	81	80	79	78	77	76	75	8-0
97	98	97	96	95	94	93	92	91	90	89	88	87	86	85	84	82	81	80	79	78	77	76	75	74	8-1
98	97	96	95	94	93	92	91	90	89	88	87	86	85	84	83	82	81	80	79	78	77	76	74	73	8-2
99	96	95	94	93	92	91	90	89	88	87	86	85	84	83	82	81	80	79	78	77	76	75	74	73	8-3
100	95	94	93	92	91	90	89	88	87	86	85	84	83	82	81	80	79	78	77	76	75	74	73	72	8-4
101	94	93	92	91	90	89	88	87	86	85	84	83	82	81	80	79	78	77	76	75	74	73	72	71	8-5
102	93	92	91	90	89	88	87	86	85	84	83	82	81	80	79	78	77	76	75	75	74	73	72	71	8-6
103	92	91	90	89	88	87	86	85	84	84	83	82	81	80	79	78	77	76	75	74	73	72	71	70	8-7
104	91	90	89	88	88	87	86	85	84	83	82	81	80	79	78	77	76	75	74	73	72	71	70	69	8-8
105	90	90	89	88	87	86	85	84	83	82	81	80	79	78	77	76	75	74	73	72	71	70	70	69	8-9
106	90	89	88	87	86	85	84	83	82	81	80	79	78	77	76	75	75	74	73	72	71	70	69	68	8-10
107	89	88	87	86	85	84	83	82	81	80	79	79	78	77	76	75	74	73	72	71	70	69	68	67	8-11
108	88	87	86	85	84	83	82	81	81	80	79	78	77	76	75	74	73	72	71	70	69	69	68	67	9-0
109	87	86	85	84	83	83	82	81	80	79	78	77	76	75	74	73	72	72	71	70	69	68	67	66	9-1
110	86	85	85	84	83	82	81	80	79	78	77	76	75	75	74	73	72	71	70	69	68	67	66	65	9-2
111	86	85	84	83	82	81	80	79	78	77	77	76	75	74	73	72	71	70	69	68	68	67	66	65	9-3
112	85	84	83	82	81	80	79	79	78	77	76	75	74	73	72	71	71	70	69	68	67	66	65	64	9-4
113	84	83	82	81	81	80	79	78	77	76	75	74	73	73	72	71	70	69	68	67	66	65	65	64	9-5
114	83	82	82	81	80	79	78	77	76	75	75	74	73	72	71	70	69	68	68	67	66	65	64	63	9-6
115	83	82	81	80	79	78	77	77	76	75	74	73	72	71	70	70	69	68	67	66	65	64	63	63	9-7
116	82	81	80	79	78	78	77	76	75	74	73	72	72	71	70	69	68	67	66	66	65	64	63	62	9-8
117	81	80	79	79	78	77	76	75	74	74	73	72	71	70	69	68	68	67	66	65	64	63	62	62	9-9
118	81	80	79	78	77	76	75	75	74	73	72	71	70	69	69	68	67	66	65	64	64	63	62	61	9-10
119	80	79	78	77	76	76	75	74	73	72	71	71	70	69	68	67	66	66	65	64	63	62	61	61	9-11
Total Months	95	94	93	92	91	90	89	88	87	86	85	84	83	82	81	80	79	78	77	76	75	74	73	72	Total Months

CHRONOLOGICAL AGE

MENTAL AGE

CHRONOLOGICAL AGE

Years and Months	6 0	6 1	6 2	6 3	6 4	6 5	6 6	6 7	6 8	6 9	6 10	6 11	7 0	7 1	7 2	7 3	7 4	7 5	7 6	7 7	7 8	7 9	7 10	7 11	Total Months
10- 0	60	61	62	63	63	64	65	66	67	68	68	69	70	71	72	73	73	74	75	76	77	78	78	79	**120**
10- 1	60	60	61	62	63	64	64	65	66	67	68	69	69	70	71	72	73	74	74	75	76	77	78	79	**121**
10- 2	59	60	61	61	62	63	64	65	66	66	67	68	69	70	70	71	72	73	74	75	75	76	77	78	**122**
10- 3	59	59	60	61	62	63	63	64	65	66	67	67	68	69	70	71	72	72	73	74	75	76	76	77	**123**
10- 4	58	59	60	60	61	62	63	64	65	65	66	67	68	69	69	70	71	72	73	73	74	75	76	77	**124**
10- 5	58	58	59	60	61	62	62	63	64	65	66	66	67	68	69	70	70	71	72	73	74	74	75	76	**125**
10- 6	57	58	59	60	60	61	62	63	63	64	65	66	67	67	68	69	70	71	71	72	73	74	75	75	**126**
10- 7	57	57	58	59	60	61	61	62	63	64	65	65	66	67	68	69	69	70	71	72	72	73	74	75	**127**
10- 8	56	57	58	59	59	60	61	62	63	63	64	65	66	66	67	68	69	70	70	71	72	73	73	74	**128**
10- 9	56	57	57	58	59	60	60	61	62	63	64	64	65	66	67	67	68	69	70	71	71	72	73	74	**129**
10-10	55	56	57	58	58	59	60	61	62	62	63	64	65	65	66	67	68	68	69	70	71	72	72	73	**130**
10-11	55	56	56	57	58	59	60	60	61	62	63	63	64	65	66	66	67	68	69	70	70	71	72	73	**131**
11- 0	55	55	56	57	58	58	59	60	61	61	62	63	64	64	65	66	67	67	68	69	70	70	71	72	**132**
11- 1	54	55	56	56	57	58	59	59	60	61	62	62	63	64	65	65	66	67	68	69	69	70	71	71	**133**
11- 2	54	54	55	56	57	58	58	59	60	60	61	62	63	63	64	65	66	66	67	68	69	69	70	71	**134**
11- 3	53	54	55	56	56	57	58	59	59	60	61	61	62	63	64	64	65	66	67	68	68	69	70	70	**135**
11- 4	53	54	54	55	56	57	57	58	59	60	60	61	62	63	63	64	65	65	66	67	68	68	69	70	**136**
11- 5	53	53	54	55	55	56	57	58	58	59	60	61	61	62	63	64	64	65	66	66	67	68	69	69	**137**
11- 6	52	53	54	54	55	56	57	57	58	59	59	60	61	62	62	63	64	64	65	66	67	67	68	69	**138**
11- 7	52	53	53	54	55	55	56	57	58	58	59	60	60	61	62	63	63	64	65	65	66	67	68	68	**139**
11- 8	51	52	53	54	54	55	56	56	57	58	59	59	60	61	61	62	63	64	64	65	66	66	67	68	**140**
11- 9	51	52	52	53	54	55	55	56	57	57	58	59	60	60	61	62	62	63	64	65	65	66	67	67	**141**
11-10	51	51	52	53	54	54	55	56	56	57	58	58	59	60	61	61	62	63	63	64	65	65	66	67	**142**
11-11	50	51	52	52	53	54	55	55	56	57	57	58	59	59	60	61	62	62	63	64	64	65	66	66	**143**
12- 0	50	51	51	52	53	53	54	55	56	56	57	58	58	59	60	60	61	62	63	63	64	65	65	66	**144**
12- 1	50	50	51	52	52	53	54	54	55	56	57	57	58	59	59	60	61	61	62	63	63	64	65	66	**145**
12- 2	49	50	51	51	52	53	53	54	55	55	56	57	58	58	59	60	60	61	62	62	63	64	64	65	**146**
12- 3	49	50	50	51	52	52	53	54	54	55	56	56	57	58	59	59	60	61	61	62	63	63	64	65	**147**
12- 4	49	49	50	51	51	52	53	53	54	55	55	56	57	57	58	59	59	60	61	61	62	63	64	64	**148**
12- 5	48	49	50	50	51	52	52	53	54	54	55	56	56	57	58	58	59	60	60	61	62	62	63	64	**149**
12- 6	48	49	49	50	51	51	52	53	53	54	55	55	56	57	57	58	59	59	60	61	61	62	63	63	**150**
12- 7	48	48	49	50	50	51	52	52	53	54	54	55	56	56	57	58	58	59	60	60	61	62	62	63	**151**
12- 8	47	48	49	49	50	51	51	52	53	53	54	55	55	56	57	57	58	59	59	60	61	61	62	63	**152**
12- 9	47	48	48	49	50	50	51	52	52	53	54	54	55	56	56	57	58	58	59	59	60	61	61	62	**153**
12-10	47	47	48	49	49	50	51	51	52	53	53	54	55	55	56	56	57	58	58	59	60	60	61	62	**154**
12-11	46	47	48	48	49	50	50	51	52	52	53	54	54	55	55	56	57	57	58	59	59	60	61	61	**155**
Total Months	**72**	**73**	**74**	**75**	**76**	**77**	**78**	**79**	**80**	**81**	**82**	**83**	**84**	**85**	**86**	**87**	**88**	**89**	**90**	**91**	**92**	**93**	**94**	**95**	

MENTAL AGE

CHRONOLOGICAL AGE

C.A. Total Months	Years and Months	7-11	7-10	7-9	7-8	7-7	7-6	7-5	7-4	7-3	7-2	7-1	7-0	6-11	6-10	6-9	6-8	6-7	6-6	6-5	6-4	6-3	6-2	6-1	6-0
M.A. Total Months		95	94	93	92	91	90	89	88	87	86	85	84	83	82	81	80	79	78	77	76	75	74	73	72
156	13-0	61	60	60	59	58	58	57	56	56	55	54	54	53	53	52	51	51	50	49	49	48	47	47	46
157	13-1	61	60	59	59	58	57	57	56	55	55	54	54	53	52	52	51	50	50	49	48	48	47	46	46
158	13-2	61	60	59	59	58	57	57	56	55	55	54	54	53	52	51	51	50	50	49	48	48	47	46	46
159	13-3	60	59	59	58	58	57	56	56	55	54	54	53	53	52	51	51	50	49	49	48	47	47	46	46
160	13-4	60	59	58	58	57	57	56	55	55	54	53	53	53	52	51	50	50	49	48	48	47	47	46	46
161	13-5	60	59	58	58	57	57	56	55	55	54	53	53	52	52	51	50	50	49	48	48	47	46	46	45
162	13-6	59	59	58	58	57	56	56	55	54	54	53	53	52	51	51	50	49	49	48	48	47	46	46	45
163	13-7	59	58	58	57	57	56	55	55	54	53	53	52	52	51	50	50	49	48	48	47	47	46	45	45
164	13-8	59	58	58	57	57	56	55	55	54	53	52	52	52	51	50	50	49	48	48	47	47	46	45	45
165	13-9	59	58	57	57	56	55	55	54	54	53	52	52	51	51	50	50	49	48	47	47	46	45	45	45
166	13-10	58	58	57	56	56	55	55	54	53	53	52	52	51	50	50	49	48	48	47	47	46	45	45	44
167	13-11	58	58	57	56	56	55	55	54	53	53	52	52	51	50	50	49	48	48	47	46	46	45	45	44
168	14-0	58	57	57	56	55	55	54	54	53	52	52	51	51	50	49	48	48	47	47	46	46	45	45	44
169	14-1	58	57	56	56	55	55	54	53	53	52	52	51	50	50	49	48	47	47	46	46	45	45	44	44
170	14-2	58	57	56	55	55	54	54	53	52	52	51	51	50	49	49	48	47	47	46	45	45	44	44	43
171	14-3	57	57	56	55	55	54	53	53	52	51	51	51	50	49	49	48	47	47	46	45	45	44	44	43
172	14-4	57	56	56	55	54	54	53	53	52	51	51	50	50	49	49	48	47	46	46	45	45	44	44	43
173	14-5	57	56	56	55	54	54	53	53	52	51	51	50	49	49	48	48	47	46	46	45	45	44	44	43
174	14-6	57	56	55	55	54	54	53	52	52	51	51	50	49	49	48	48	46	46	45	45	44	43	43	43
175	14-7	56	56	55	54	54	53	53	52	51	51	50	50	49	48	48	47	46	46	45	45	44	43	43	43
176	14-8	56	55	55	54	54	53	52	52	51	50	50	50	49	48	48	47	46	46	45	44	44	43	43	43
177	14-9	56	55	54	54	53	53	52	51	51	50	50	49	49	48	47	47	46	45	45	44	44	43	43	42
178	14-10	56	55	54	54	53	53	52	51	51	50	50	49	49	48	47	46	46	45	45	44	44	43	43	42
179	14-11	56	55	54	54	53	53	52	51	51	50	50	49	49	48	47	46	45	45	44	44	44	43	43	42
180	15-0	55	55	54	53	53	52	52	51	50	50	49	49	48	48	47	46	45	45	44	44	44	43	42	42
181	15-1	55	54	54	53	53	52	51	51	50	49	49	49	48	47	47	46	45	45	44	44	43	43	42	42
182	15-2	55	54	53	53	52	52	51	51	50	49	49	48	48	47	46	46	45	44	44	43	43	42	42	41
183	15-3	55	54	53	53	52	52	51	50	50	49	49	48	48	47	46	45	45	44	44	43	43	42	42	41
184	15-4	54	54	53	53	52	51	51	50	50	49	49	48	47	47	46	45	44	44	43	43	43	42	42	41
185	15-5	54	54	53	52	52	51	51	50	49	49	48	48	47	47	46	45	44	44	43	43	43	42	42	41
186	15-6	54	53	53	52	51	51	50	50	49	49	48	48	47	46	46	45	44	44	43	43	43	42	41	41
187	15-7	54	53	53	52	51	51	50	50	49	48	48	48	47	46	45	45	45	44	43	43	42	41	41	41
188	15-8	54	53	52	52	51	51	50	49	49	48	48	47	47	46	45	45	44	43	43	42	42	41	41	41
189	15-9	53	53	52	51	51	50	50	49	49	48	48	47	46	46	45	44	44	43	43	42	42	41	41	40
190	15-10	53	53	52	51	51	50	50	49	49	48	47	47	46	46	45	44	44	43	43	42	42	41	41	40
191	15-11	53	52	52	51	51	50	49	49	48	48	47	47	46	46	45	44	44	43	43	42	42	41	41	40
192	16-	53	52	51	51	51	50	49	49	48	48	47	47	46	46	45	44	44	43	43	42	42	41	41	40

MENTAL AGE

Years and Months	8-0	8-1	8-2	8-3	8-4	8-5	8-6	8-7	8-8	8-9	8-10	8-11	9-0	9-1	9-2	9-3	9-4	9-5	9-6	9-7	9-8	9-9	9-10	9-11	Total Months
4-0																									48
4-1																									49
4-2																									50
4-3																									51
4-4																									52
4-5																									53
4-6																									54
4-7																									55
4-8	171																								56
4-9	168	170	172																						57
4-10	166	167	169	171	172																				58
4-11	163	164	166	168	169	171																			59
5-0	160	162	163	165	167	168	170	172																	60
5-1	157	159	161	162	164	166	167	169	170	172															61
5-2	155	156	158	160	161	163	165	166	168	169	171														62
5-3	152	154	156	157	159	160	162	163	165	167	168	170	171												63
5-4	150	152	153	155	156	158	159	161	163	164	166	167	169	170	172										64
5-5	148	149	151	152	154	155	157	158	160	162	163	165	166	168	169	171									65
5-6	145	147	148	150	152	153	155	156	158	159	161	162	164	165	167	168	170	171							66
5-7	143	145	146	148	149	151	152	154	155	157	158	160	161	163	164	166	167	169	170	172					67
5-8	141	143	144	146	147	149	150	151	153	154	156	157	159	160	162	163	165	166	168	169	171	172			68
5-9	139	141	142	143	145	146	148	149	151	152	154	155	157	158	159	161	162	164	165	167	168	170	171	172	69
5-10	137	139	140	141	143	144	146	147	149	150	151	153	154	156	157	159	160	161	163	164	166	167	169	170	70
5-11	135	137	138	139	141	142	144	145	146	148	149	151	152	154	155	156	158	159	161	162	163	165	166	168	71
6-0	133	135	136	138	139	140	142	143	144	146	147	149	150	151	153	154	156	157	158	160	161	163	164	165	72
6-1	132	133	134	136	137	138	140	141	142	144	145	147	148	149	151	152	153	155	156	158	159	160	162	163	73
6-2	130	131	132	134	135	136	138	139	141	142	143	145	146	147	149	150	151	153	154	155	157	158	159	161	74
6-3	128	129	131	132	133	135	136	137	139	140	141	143	144	145	147	148	149	151	152	153	155	156	157	159	75
6-4	126	128	129	130	132	133	134	136	137	138	139	141	142	143	145	146	147	149	150	151	153	154	155	157	76
6-5	125	126	127	129	130	131	132	134	135	136	138	139	140	142	143	144	145	147	148	149	151	152	153	155	77
6-6	123	124	126	127	128	129	131	132	133	135	136	137	138	140	141	142	144	145	146	147	149	150	151	153	78
6-7	122	123	124	125	127	128	129	130	132	133	134	135	137	138	139	141	142	143	144	146	147	148	149	151	79
6-8	120	121	123	124	125	126	128	129	130	131	133	134	135	136	138	139	140	141	143	144	145	146	148	149	80
6-9	119	120	121	122	123	125	126	127	128	130	131	132	133	135	136	137	138	140	141	142	143	144	146	147	81
6-10	117	118	120	121	122	123	124	126	127	128	129	130	132	133	134	135	137	138	139	140	141	143	144	145	82
6-11	116	117	118	119	120	122	123	124	125	127	128	129	130	131	133	134	135	136	137	139	140	141	142	143	83
Total Months	96	97	98	99	100	101	102	103	104	105	106	107	108	109	110	111	112	113	114	115	116	117	118	119	

CHRONOLOGICAL AGE

MENTAL AGE

CHRONOLOGICAL AGE

Total Months	MENTAL AGE 9/11	9/10	9/9	9/8	9/7	9/6	9/5	9/4	9/3	9/2	9/1	9/0	8/11	8/10	8/9	8/8	8/7	8/6	8/5	8/4	8/3	8/2	8/1	8/0	Years and Months
84	142	140	139	138	137	136	135	133	132	131	130	129	127	126	125	124	123	121	120	119	118	117	115	114	7-0
85	140	139	138	136	135	134	133	132	131	129	128	127	126	125	124	122	121	120	119	118	116	115	114	113	7-1
86	138	137	136	135	134	133	131	130	129	128	127	126	124	123	122	121	120	119	117	116	115	114	113	112	7-2
87	137	136	134	133	132	131	130	129	128	126	125	124	123	122	121	120	118	117	116	115	114	113	111	110	7-3
88	135	134	133	132	131	130	128	127	126	125	124	123	122	120	119	118	117	116	115	114	113	111	110	109	7-4
89	134	133	131	130	129	128	127	126	125	124	122	121	120	119	118	117	116	115	113	112	111	110	109	108	7-5
90	132	131	130	129	128	127	126	124	123	122	121	120	119	118	117	116	114	113	112	111	110	109	108	107	7-6
91	131	130	129	127	126	125	124	123	122	121	120	119	118	116	115	114	113	112	111	110	109	108	107	105	7-7
92	129	128	127	126	125	124	123	122	121	120	118	117	116	115	114	113	112	111	110	109	108	107	105	104	7-8
93	128	127	126	125	124	123	122	120	119	118	117	116	115	114	113	112	111	110	109	108	106	105	104	103	7-9
94	127	126	124	123	122	121	120	119	118	117	116	115	114	113	112	111	110	109	107	106	105	104	103	102	7-10
95	125	124	123	122	121	120	119	118	117	116	115	114	113	112	111	109	108	107	106	105	104	103	102	101	7-11
96	124	123	122	121	120	119	118	117	116	115	114	113	111	110	109	108	107	106	105	104	103	102	101	100	8-0
97	123	122	121	120	119	118	116	115	114	113	112	111	110	109	108	107	106	105	104	103	102	101	100	99	8-1
98	121	120	119	118	117	116	115	114	113	112	111	110	109	108	107	106	105	104	103	102	101	100	99	98	8-2
99	120	119	118	117	116	115	114	113	112	111	110	109	108	107	106	105	104	103	102	101	100	99	98	97	8-3
100	119	118	117	116	115	114	113	112	111	110	109	108	107	106	105	104	103	102	101	100	99	98	97	96	8-4
101	118	117	116	115	114	113	112	111	110	109	108	107	106	105	104	103	102	101	100	99	98	97	96	95	8-5
102	117	116	115	114	113	112	111	110	109	108	107	106	105	104	103	102	101	100	99	98	97	96	95	94	8-6
103	116	115	114	113	112	111	110	109	108	107	106	105	104	103	102	101	100	99	98	97	96	95	94	93	8-7
104	114	113	113	112	111	110	109	108	107	106	105	104	103	102	101	100	99	98	97	96	95	94	93	92	8-8
105	113	112	111	110	110	109	108	107	106	105	104	103	102	101	100	99	98	97	96	95	94	93	92	91	8-9
106	112	111	110	109	108	108	107	106	105	104	103	102	101	100	99	98	97	96	95	94	93	92	92	91	8-10
107	111	110	109	108	107	107	106	105	104	103	102	101	100	99	98	97	96	95	94	93	93	92	91	90	8-11
108	110	109	108	107	106	106	105	104	103	102	101	100	99	98	97	96	95	94	94	93	92	91	90	89	9-0
109	109	108	107	106	106	105	104	103	102	101	100	99	98	97	96	95	95	94	93	92	91	90	89	88	9-1
110	108	107	106	105	105	104	103	102	101	100	99	98	97	96	95	95	94	93	92	91	90	89	88	87	9-2
111	107	106	105	105	104	103	102	101	100	99	98	97	96	95	95	94	93	92	91	90	89	88	87	86	9-3
112	106	105	104	104	103	102	101	100	99	98	97	96	96	95	94	93	92	91	90	89	88	88	87	86	9-4
113	105	104	104	103	102	101	100	99	98	97	96	96	95	94	93	92	91	90	89	88	88	87	86	85	9-5
114	104	104	103	102	101	100	99	98	97	96	96	95	94	93	92	91	90	89	89	88	87	86	85	84	9-6
115	103	103	102	101	100	99	98	97	97	96	95	94	93	92	91	90	90	89	88	87	86	85	84	83	9-7
116	103	102	101	100	99	98	97	97	96	95	94	93	92	91	91	90	89	88	87	86	85	84	84	83	9-8
117	102	101	100	99	98	97	97	96	95	94	93	92	91	91	90	89	88	87	86	85	85	84	83	82	9-9
118	101	100	99	98	97	97	96	95	94	93	92	92	91	90	89	88	87	86	86	85	84	83	82	81	9-10
119	100	99	98	97	97	96	95	94	93	92	92	91	90	89	88	87	87	86	85	84	83	82	82	81	9-11
Total Months	119	118	117	116	115	114	113	112	111	110	109	108	107	106	105	104	103	102	101	100	99	98	97	96	Total Months

MENTAL AGE

CHRONOLOGICAL AGE

Total Months	Years and Months	9-11	9-10	9-9	9-8	9-7	9-6	9-5	9-4	9-3	9-2	9-1	9-0	8-11	8-10	8-9	8-8	8-7	8-6	8-5	8-4	8-3	8-2	8-1	8-0
120	10-0	99	98	98	97	96	95	94	93	93	92	91	90	89	88	88	87	86	85	84	83	83	82	81	80
121	10-1	98	97	97	96	95	94	93	93	92	91	90	89	88	88	87	86	85	84	83	83	82	81	80	79
122	10-2	98	96	96	95	94	93	93	92	91	90	89	89	88	87	86	85	84	84	83	82	81	80	80	79
123	10-3	97	96	95	94	93	93	92	91	90	89	89	88	87	86	85	85	84	83	82	81	80	80	79	78
124	10-4	96	95	94	94	93	92	91	90	90	89	88	87	86	85	85	84	83	82	81	81	80	79	78	77
125	10-5	95	94	94	93	92	91	90	90	89	88	87	86	86	85	84	83	82	82	81	80	79	78	78	77
126	10-6	94	94	93	92	91	90	90	89	88	87	87	86	85	84	83	83	82	81	80	79	79	78	77	76
127	10-7	94	93	92	91	91	90	89	88	87	87	86	85	84	83	83	82	81	80	80	79	78	77	76	76
128	10-8	93	92	91	91	90	89	88	88	87	86	85	84	84	83	82	81	80	80	79	78	77	77	76	75
129	10-9	92	91	91	90	89	88	88	87	86	85	85	84	83	82	81	81	80	79	78	78	77	76	75	74
130	10-10	92	91	90	89	88	88	87	86	85	85	84	83	82	82	81	80	79	78	78	77	76	75	75	74
131	10-11	91	90	89	89	88	87	86	86	85	84	83	82	82	81	80	79	79	78	77	76	76	75	74	73
132	11-0	90	89	89	88	87	86	86	85	84	83	83	82	81	80	80	79	78	77	77	76	75	74	73	73
133	11-1	89	89	88	87	86	86	85	84	83	83	82	81	80	80	79	78	77	77	76	75	74	74	73	72
134	11-2	89	88	87	87	86	85	84	84	83	82	81	81	80	79	78	78	77	76	75	75	74	73	72	72
135	11-3	88	87	87	86	85	84	84	83	82	81	81	80	79	79	78	77	76	76	75	74	73	73	72	71
136	11-4	88	87	86	85	85	84	83	82	82	81	80	79	79	78	77	76	76	75	74	74	73	72	71	71
137	11-5	87	86	85	85	84	83	82	82	81	80	80	79	78	77	77	76	75	74	74	73	72	72	71	70
138	11-6	86	86	85	84	83	83	82	81	80	80	79	78	78	77	76	75	75	74	73	72	72	71	70	70
139	11-7	86	85	84	83	83	82	81	81	80	79	78	78	77	76	76	75	74	73	73	72	71	71	70	69
140	11-8	85	84	84	83	82	81	81	80	79	79	78	77	76	76	75	74	74	73	72	71	71	70	69	69
141	11-9	84	84	83	82	82	81	80	79	79	78	77	77	76	75	74	74	73	72	72	71	70	70	69	68
142	11-10	84	83	82	82	81	80	80	79	78	77	77	76	75	75	74	73	73	72	71	70	70	69	68	68
143	11-11	83	83	82	81	80	80	79	78	78	77	76	76	75	74	73	73	72	71	71	70	69	69	68	67
144	12-0	83	82	81	81	80	79	78	78	77	76	76	75	74	74	73	72	72	71	70	69	69	68	67	67
145	12-1	82	81	81	80	79	79	78	77	77	76	75	74	74	73	72	72	71	70	70	69	68	68	67	66
146	12-2	82	81	80	79	79	78	77	77	76	75	75	74	73	73	72	71	71	70	69	68	68	67	66	66
147	12-3	81	80	80	79	78	78	77	76	76	75	74	73	73	72	71	71	70	69	69	68	67	67	66	65
148	12-4	80	80	79	78	78	77	76	76	75	74	74	73	72	72	71	70	70	69	68	68	67	66	66	65
149	12-5	80	79	79	78	77	77	76	75	75	74	73	72	72	71	70	70	69	68	68	67	66	66	65	64
150	12-6	79	79	78	77	77	76	75	75	74	73	73	72	71	71	70	69	69	68	67	67	66	65	65	64
151	12-7	79	78	77	77	76	76	75	74	74	73	72	72	71	70	70	69	68	68	67	66	66	65	64	64
152	12-8	78	78	77	76	76	75	74	74	73	72	72	71	70	70	69	68	68	67	66	66	65	64	64	63
153	12-9	78	77	76	76	75	75	74	73	73	72	71	71	70	69	69	68	67	67	66	65	65	64	63	63
154	12-10	77	77	76	75	75	74	73	73	72	71	71	70	69	69	68	68	67	66	66	65	64	64	63	62
155	12-11	77	76	75	75	74	74	73	72	72	71	70	70	69	68	68	67	66	66	65	65	64	63	63	62
Total Months		119	118	117	116	115	114	113	112	111	110	109	108	107	106	105	104	103	102	101	100	99	98	97	96

MENTAL AGE

CHRONOLOGICAL AGE

Years and Months	Total Months	9-11	9-10	9-9	9-8	9-7	9-6	9-5	9-4	9-3	9-2	9-1	9-0	8-11	8-10	8-9	8-8	8-7	8-6	8-5	8-4	8-3	8-2	8-1	8-0
13- 0	156	76	76	75	74	74	73	72	72	71	71	70	69	69	68	67	67	66	65	65	64	63	63	62	62
13- 1	157	76	75	75	74	73	73	72	71	71	70	69	69	68	68	67	66	66	65	64	64	63	62	62	61
13- 2	158	75	75	74	73	73	72	72	71	70	70	69	68	68	67	66	66	65	65	64	63	63	62	61	61
13- 3	159	75	74	74	73	72	72	71	70	70	69	69	68	67	67	66	65	65	64	64	63	62	62	61	60
13- 4	160	74	74	73	73	72	71	71	70	69	69	68	68	67	66	66	65	64	64	63	63	62	61	61	60
13- 5	161	74	73	73	72	71	71	70	70	69	68	68	67	66	66	65	65	64	63	63	62	61	61	60	60
13- 6	162	73	73	72	72	71	70	70	69	69	68	67	67	66	65	65	64	64	63	62	62	61	60	60	59
13- 7	163	73	72	72	71	71	70	69	69	68	67	67	66	66	65	64	64	63	63	62	61	61	60	60	59
13- 8	164	73	72	71	71	70	70	69	68	68	67	66	66	65	65	64	63	63	62	62	61	60	60	59	59
13- 9	165	72	72	71	70	70	69	68	68	67	67	66	65	65	64	64	63	62	62	61	61	60	59	59	58
13-10	166	72	71	70	70	69	69	68	67	67	66	66	65	64	64	63	63	62	61	61	60	60	59	58	58
13-11	167	71	71	70	69	69	68	68	67	66	66	65	65	64	63	63	62	62	61	60	60	59	59	58	57
14- 0	168	71	70	70	69	68	68	67	67	66	65	65	64	64	63	63	62	61	61	60	60	59	58	58	57
14- 1	169	70	70	69	69	68	67	67	66	66	65	65	64	63	63	62	62	61	60	60	59	59	58	57	57
14- 2	170	70	69	69	68	68	67	66	66	65	65	64	64	63	62	62	61	61	60	59	59	58	58	57	56
14- 3	171	70	69	68	68	67	67	66	66	65	64	64	63	63	62	61	61	60	60	59	58	58	57	57	56
14- 4	172	69	69	68	67	67	66	66	65	65	64	63	63	62	62	61	60	60	59	59	58	58	57	56	56
14- 5	173	69	68	68	67	66	66	65	65	64	64	63	62	62	61	61	60	60	59	58	58	57	57	56	55
14- 6	174	68	68	67	67	66	66	65	64	64	63	63	62	61	61	60	60	59	59	58	57	57	56	56	55
14- 7	175	68	67	67	66	66	65	65	64	63	63	62	62	61	61	60	59	59	58	58	57	57	56	55	55
14- 8	176	68	67	66	66	65	65	64	64	63	63	62	61	61	60	60	59	59	58	57	57	56	56	55	55
14- 9	177	67	67	66	66	65	64	64	63	63	62	62	61	60	60	59	59	58	58	57	57	56	55	55	54
14-10	178	67	66	66	65	65	64	63	63	62	62	61	61	60	60	59	58	58	57	57	56	56	55	54	54
14-11	179	66	66	65	65	64	64	63	63	62	61	61	60	60	59	59	58	58	57	56	56	55	55	54	54
15- 0	180	66	66	65	64	64	63	63	62	62	61	61	60	59	59	58	58	57	57	56	56	55	54	54	53
15- 1	181	66	65	65	64	64	63	62	62	61	61	60	60	59	59	58	57	57	56	56	55	55	54	54	53
15- 2	182	65	65	64	64	63	63	62	62	61	60	60	59	59	58	58	57	57	56	55	55	54	54	53	53
15- 3	183	65	64	64	63	63	62	62	61	61	60	60	59	58	58	57	57	56	56	55	55	54	54	53	52
15- 4	184	65	64	64	63	63	62	61	61	60	60	59	59	58	58	57	57	56	55	55	54	54	53	53	52
15- 5	185	64	64	63	63	62	62	61	61	60	59	59	58	58	57	57	56	56	55	55	54	54	53	52	52
15- 6	186	64	63	63	62	62	61	61	60	60	59	59	58	58	57	56	56	55	55	54	54	53	53	52	52
15- 7	187	64	63	63	62	61	61	60	60	59	59	58	58	57	57	56	56	55	55	54	53	53	52	52	51
15- 8	188	63	63	62	62	61	61	60	60	59	59	58	57	57	56	56	55	55	54	54	53	53	52	52	51
15- 9	189	63	62	62	61	61	60	60	59	59	58	58	57	57	56	56	55	55	54	53	53	52	52	51	51
15-10	190	63	62	62	61	61	60	59	59	58	58	57	57	56	56	55	55	54	54	53	53	52	52	51	51
15-11	191	62	62	61	61	60	60	59	59	58	58	57	57	56	56	55	54	54	53	53	52	52	51	51	50
16- 0	192	62	61	61	60	60	59	59	58	58	57	57	56	56	55	55	54	54	53	53	52	52	51	51	50
Total Months		119	118	117	116	115	114	113	112	111	110	109	108	107	106	105	104	103	102	101	100	99	98	97	96

MENTAL AGE

CHRONOLOGICAL AGE

Years and Months	Total Months	10-0	10-1	10-2	10-3	10-4	10-5	10-6	10-7	10-8	10-9	10-10	10-11	11-0	11-1	11-2	11-3	11-4	11-5	11-6	11-7	11-8	11-9	11-10	11-11
Mental Age Total Months →		120	121	122	123	124	125	126	127	128	129	130	131	132	133	134	135	136	137	138	139	140	141	142	143
4-0	48																								
4-1	49																								
4-2	50																								
4-3	51																								
4-4	52																								
4-5	53																								
4-6	54																								
4-7	55																								
4-8	56																								
4-9	57																								
4-10	58																								
4-11	59																								
5-0	60																								
5-1	61																								
5-2	62																								
5-3	63																								
5-4	64																								
5-5	65																								
5-6	66																								
5-7	67																								
5-8	68																								
5-9	69																								
5-10	70	171																							
5-11	71	169	170	172																					
6-0	72	167	168	169	171	172																			
6-1	73	164	166	167	168	170	171																		
6-2	74	162	164	165	166	168	169	170	172																
6-3	75	160	161	163	164	165	167	168	169	171	172														
6-4	76	158	159	161	162	163	164	166	167	168	170	171	172												
6-5	77	156	157	158	160	161	162	164	165	166	168	169	170	171											
6-6	78	154	155	156	158	159	160	162	163	164	165	167	168	169	171	172									
6-7	79	152	153	154	156	157	158	159	161	162	163	165	166	167	168	170	171	172							
6-8	80	150	151	153	154	155	156	158	159	160	161	163	164	165	166	168	169	170	171						
6-9	81	148	149	151	152	153	154	156	157	158	159	160	162	163	164	165	167	168	169	170	172				
6-10	82	146	148	149	150	151	152	154	155	156	157	159	160	161	162	163	165	166	167	168	170	171	172		
6-11	83	145	146	147	148	149	151	152	153	154	155	157	158	159	160	161	163	164	165	166	167	169	170	171	172

MENTAL AGE

The left margin is labelled vertically "CHRONOLOGICAL AGE."

Years and Months	Total Months	10-0	10-1	10-2	10-3	10-4	10-5	10-6	10-7	10-8	10-9	10-10	10-11	11-0	11-1	11-2	11-3	11-4	11-5	11-6	11-7	11-8	11-9	11-10	11-11
(MA Total Months) →		120	121	122	123	124	125	126	127	128	129	130	131	132	133	134	135	136	137	138	139	140	141	142	143
7- 0	84	143	144	145	146	148	149	150	151	152	154	155	156	157	158	160	161	162	163	164	165	167	168	169	170
7- 1	85	141	142	144	145	146	147	148	149	151	152	153	154	155	156	158	159	160	161	162	164	165	166	167	168
7- 2	86	140	141	142	143	144	145	147	148	149	150	151	152	153	155	156	157	158	159	160	162	163	164	165	166
7- 3	87	138	139	140	141	143	144	145	146	147	148	149	151	152	153	154	155	156	157	159	160	161	162	163	164
7- 4	88	136	138	139	140	141	142	143	144	145	147	148	149	150	151	152	153	155	156	157	158	159	160	161	163
7- 5	89	135	136	137	138	139	140	142	143	144	145	146	147	148	149	151	152	153	154	155	156	157	158	160	161
7- 6	90	133	134	136	137	138	139	140	141	142	143	144	146	147	148	149	150	151	152	153	154	156	157	158	159
7- 7	91	132	133	134	135	136	137	138	140	141	142	143	144	145	146	147	148	149	151	152	153	154	155	156	157
7- 8	92	130	132	133	134	135	136	137	138	139	140	141	142	143	145	146	147	148	149	150	151	152	153	154	155
7- 9	93	129	130	131	132	133	134	135	137	138	139	140	141	142	143	144	145	146	147	148	149	151	152	153	154
7-10	94	128	129	130	131	132	133	134	135	136	137	138	139	140	141	143	144	145	146	147	148	149	150	151	152
7-11	95	126	127	128	129	131	132	133	134	135	136	137	138	139	140	141	142	143	144	145	146	147	148	149	151
8- 0	96	125	126	127	128	129	130	131	132	133	134	135	136	138	139	140	141	142	143	144	145	146	147	148	149
8- 1	97	124	125	126	127	128	129	130	131	132	133	134	135	136	137	138	139	140	141	142	143	144	145	146	147
8- 2	98	122	123	124	126	127	128	129	130	131	132	133	134	135	136	137	138	139	140	141	142	143	144	145	146
8- 3	99	121	122	123	124	125	126	127	128	129	130	131	132	133	134	135	136	137	138	139	140	141	142	143	144
8- 4	100	120	121	122	123	124	125	126	127	128	129	130	131	132	133	134	135	136	137	138	139	140	141	142	143
8- 5	101	119	120	121	122	123	124	125	126	127	128	129	130	131	132	133	134	135	136	137	138	139	140	141	142
8- 6	102	118	119	120	121	122	123	124	125	125	126	127	128	129	130	131	132	133	134	135	136	137	138	139	140
8- 7	103	117	117	118	119	120	121	122	123	124	125	126	127	128	129	130	131	132	133	134	135	136	137	138	139
8- 8	104	115	116	117	118	119	120	121	122	123	124	125	126	127	128	129	130	131	132	133	134	135	136	137	138
8- 9	105	114	115	116	117	118	119	120	121	122	123	124	125	126	127	128	129	130	130	131	132	133	134	135	136
8-10	106	113	114	115	116	117	118	119	120	121	122	123	124	125	125	126	127	128	129	130	131	132	133	134	135
8-11	107	112	113	114	115	116	117	118	119	120	121	121	122	123	124	125	126	127	128	129	130	131	132	133	134
9- 0	108	111	112	113	114	115	116	117	118	119	119	120	121	122	123	124	125	126	127	128	129	130	131	131	132
9- 1	109	110	111	112	113	114	115	116	117	117	118	119	120	121	122	123	124	125	126	127	128	128	129	130	131
9- 2	110	109	110	111	112	113	114	115	115	116	117	118	119	120	121	122	123	124	125	125	126	127	128	129	130
9- 3	111	108	109	110	111	112	113	114	114	115	116	117	118	119	120	121	122	123	123	124	125	126	127	128	129
9- 4	112	107	108	109	110	111	112	113	113	114	115	116	117	118	119	120	121	121	122	123	124	125	126	127	128
9- 5	113	106	107	108	109	110	111	112	112	113	114	115	116	117	118	119	119	120	121	122	123	124	125	126	127
9- 6	114	105	106	107	108	109	110	111	111	112	113	114	115	116	117	118	118	119	120	121	122	123	124	125	125
9- 7	115	104	105	106	107	108	109	110	110	111	112	113	114	115	116	117	117	118	119	120	121	122	123	123	124
9- 8	116	103	104	105	106	107	108	109	109	110	111	112	113	114	115	116	116	117	118	119	120	121	122	122	123
9- 9	117	103	103	104	105	106	107	108	109	109	110	111	112	113	114	115	115	116	117	118	119	120	121	121	122
9-10	118	102	103	103	104	105	106	107	108	108	109	110	111	112	113	114	114	115	116	117	118	119	119	120	121
9-11	119	101	102	103	103	104	105	106	107	108	108	109	110	111	112	113	113	114	115	116	117	118	118	119	120
Total Months		120	121	122	123	124	125	126	127	128	129	130	131	132	133	134	135	136	137	138	139	140	141	142	143

MENTAL AGE

Chronological Age (left column) × Mental Age (top columns); cell values are IQ. Mental ages are given as Years–Months with their equivalent Total Months shown in the bottom row.

Years and Months	10-0	10-1	10-2	10-3	10-4	10-5	10-6	10-7	10-8	10-9	10-10	10-11	11-0	11-1	11-2	11-3	11-4	11-5	11-6	11-7	11-8	11-9	11-10	11-11	Total Months
10-0	100	101	102	103	103	104	105	106	107	108	108	109	110	111	112	113	113	114	115	116	117	118	118	119	120
10-1	99	100	101	102	102	103	104	105	106	107	107	108	109	110	111	112	112	113	114	115	116	117	117	118	121
10-2	98	99	100	101	102	102	103	104	105	106	107	107	108	109	110	111	112	112	113	114	115	116	116	117	122
10-3	98	98	99	100	101	102	102	103	104	105	106	107	107	108	109	110	111	111	112	113	114	115	115	116	123
10-4	97	98	98	99	100	101	102	102	103	104	105	106	106	107	108	109	110	110	111	112	113	114	115	115	124
10-5	96	97	98	98	99	100	101	102	102	103	104	105	106	106	107	108	109	110	110	111	112	113	114	114	125
10-6	95	96	97	98	98	99	100	101	102	102	103	104	105	106	106	107	108	109	110	110	111	112	113	114	126
10-7	94	95	96	97	98	98	99	100	101	102	102	103	104	105	106	106	107	108	109	109	110	111	112	113	127
10-8	94	95	95	96	97	98	98	99	100	101	102	102	103	104	105	105	106	107	108	109	109	110	111	112	128
10-9	93	94	95	95	96	97	98	98	99	100	101	102	102	103	104	105	105	106	107	108	109	109	110	111	129
10-10	92	93	94	95	95	96	97	98	98	99	100	101	102	102	103	104	105	105	106	107	108	108	109	110	130
10-11	92	92	93	94	95	95	96	97	98	98	99	100	101	102	102	103	104	105	105	106	107	108	108	109	131
11-0	91	92	92	93	94	95	95	96	97	98	98	99	100	101	102	102	103	104	105	105	106	107	108	108	132
11-1	90	91	92	92	93	94	95	95	96	97	98	98	99	100	101	102	102	103	104	105	105	106	107	108	133
11-2	90	90	91	92	93	93	94	95	96	96	97	98	99	99	100	101	102	102	103	104	104	105	106	107	134
11-3	89	90	90	91	92	93	93	94	95	96	96	97	98	99	99	100	101	101	102	103	104	104	105	106	135
11-4	88	89	90	90	91	92	93	93	94	95	96	96	97	98	99	99	100	101	101	102	103	104	104	105	136
11-5	88	88	89	90	91	91	92	93	93	94	95	96	96	97	98	99	99	100	101	101	102	103	104	104	137
11-6	87	88	88	89	90	91	91	92	93	93	94	95	96	96	97	98	99	99	100	101	101	102	103	104	138
11-7	86	87	88	88	89	90	91	91	92	93	94	94	95	96	96	97	98	99	99	100	101	101	102	103	139
11-8	86	86	87	88	89	89	90	91	91	92	93	94	94	95	96	96	97	98	99	99	100	101	101	102	140
11-9	85	86	87	87	88	89	89	90	91	91	92	93	94	94	95	96	96	97	98	99	99	100	101	101	141
11-10	85	85	86	87	87	88	89	89	90	91	92	92	93	94	94	95	96	96	97	98	99	99	100	101	142
11-11	84	85	85	86	87	87	88	89	90	90	91	92	92	93	94	94	95	96	97	97	98	99	99	100	143
12-0	83	84	85	85	86	87	88	88	89	90	90	91	92	92	93	94	94	95	96	97	97	98	99	99	144
12-1	83	83	84	85	86	86	87	88	88	89	90	90	91	92	92	93	94	94	95	96	97	97	98	99	145
12-2	82	83	84	84	85	86	86	87	88	88	89	90	90	91	92	92	93	94	95	95	96	97	97	98	146
12-3	82	82	83	84	84	85	86	86	87	88	88	89	90	90	91	92	93	93	94	95	95	96	97	97	147
12-4	81	82	82	83	84	84	85	86	86	87	88	89	89	90	91	91	92	93	93	94	95	95	96	97	148
12-5	81	81	82	83	83	84	85	85	86	87	87	88	89	89	90	91	91	92	93	93	94	95	95	96	149
12-6	80	81	81	82	83	83	84	85	85	86	87	87	88	89	89	90	91	91	92	93	93	94	95	95	150
12-7	79	80	81	81	82	83	83	84	85	85	86	87	87	88	89	89	90	91	91	92	93	93	94	95	151
12-8	79	80	80	81	82	82	83	84	84	85	86	86	87	88	88	89	89	90	91	91	92	93	93	94	152
12-9	78	79	80	80	81	82	82	83	84	84	85	86	86	87	88	88	89	90	90	91	92	92	93	93	153
12-10	78	79	79	80	81	81	82	82	83	84	84	85	86	86	87	88	88	89	90	90	91	92	92	93	154
12-11	77	78	79	79	80	81	81	82	83	83	84	85	85	86	86	87	88	88	89	90	90	91	92	92	155
Total Months	120	121	122	123	124	125	126	127	128	129	130	131	132	133	134	135	136	137	138	139	140	141	142	143	

CHRONOLOGICAL AGE

MENTAL AGE

Years and Months	Total Months	10-0	10-1	10-2	10-3	10-4	10-5	10-6	10-7	10-8	10-9	10-10	10-11	11-0	11-1	11-2	11-3	11-4	11-5	11-6	11-7	11-8	11-9	11-10	11-11
13-0	156	77	78	78	79	79	80	81	81	82	83	83	84	85	85	86	87	87	88	88	89	90	90	91	92
13-1	157	76	77	78	78	79	80	80	81	82	82	83	83	84	85	85	86	87	87	88	89	89	90	90	91
13-2	158	76	77	78	78	79	80	80	81	82	82	83	83	84	85	85	86	87	87	88	89	89	90	90	91
13-3	159	76	77	77	78	78	79	80	80	81	82	82	83	84	84	85	85	86	87	87	88	89	89	90	91
13-4	160	75	76	77	77	78	79	79	80	81	81	82	82	83	84	84	85	86	86	87	87	88	89	89	90
13-5	161	75	76	77	77	78	79	79	80	81	81	82	82	83	84	84	85	86	86	87	87	88	89	89	90
13-6	162	75	76	76	77	78	78	79	79	80	81	81	82	83	83	84	84	85	86	86	87	88	88	89	89
13-7	163	75	75	76	76	77	78	78	79	80	80	81	81	82	83	83	84	84	85	86	86	87	88	88	89
13-8	164	75	75	76	76	77	78	78	79	80	80	81	81	82	83	83	84	84	85	86	86	87	88	88	89
13-9	165	74	75	75	76	77	77	78	78	79	80	80	81	81	82	83	83	84	85	85	86	86	87	88	88
13-10	166	74	74	75	75	76	77	77	78	79	79	80	80	81	82	82	83	83	84	85	85	86	87	87	88
13-11	167	74	74	75	75	76	77	77	78	79	79	80	80	81	82	82	83	83	84	85	85	86	87	87	88
14-0	168	73	74	74	75	76	76	77	77	78	79	79	80	80	81	82	82	83	84	84	85	85	86	87	87
14-1	169	73	73	74	75	75	76	76	77	78	78	79	79	80	81	81	82	82	83	84	84	85	85	86	87
14-2	170	73	73	74	75	75	76	76	77	78	78	79	79	80	81	81	82	82	83	84	84	85	85	86	87
14-3	171	72	73	73	74	75	75	76	77	77	78	78	79	80	80	81	81	82	83	83	84	84	85	86	86
14-4	172	72	72	73	74	74	75	75	76	77	77	78	78	79	80	80	81	81	82	83	83	84	84	85	86
14-5	173	72	72	73	74	74	75	75	76	77	77	78	78	79	80	80	81	81	82	83	83	84	84	85	86
14-6	174	71	72	73	73	74	74	75	76	76	77	77	78	79	79	80	80	81	82	82	83	83	84	85	85
14-7	175	71	72	72	73	73	74	75	75	76	76	77	78	78	79	79	80	80	81	82	82	83	83	84	85
14-8	176	71	72	72	73	73	74	75	75	76	76	77	78	78	79	79	80	80	81	82	82	83	83	84	85
14-9	177	71	71	72	72	73	74	74	75	75	76	76	77	78	78	79	79	80	81	81	82	82	83	84	84
14-10	178	70	71	71	72	73	73	74	74	75	75	76	77	77	78	78	79	80	80	81	81	82	82	83	84
14-11	179	70	71	71	72	73	73	74	74	75	75	76	77	77	78	78	79	80	80	81	81	82	82	83	84
15-0	180	70	70	71	72	72	73	73	74	74	75	76	76	77	77	78	78	79	80	80	81	81	82	83	83
15-1	181	69	70	71	71	72	72	73	73	74	75	75	76	76	77	77	78	79	79	80	80	81	82	82	83
15-2	182	69	70	71	71	72	72	73	73	74	75	75	76	76	77	77	78	79	79	80	80	81	82	82	83
15-3	183	69	70	70	71	71	72	72	73	74	74	75	75	76	76	77	78	78	79	79	80	80	81	82	82
15-4	184	69	69	70	70	71	71	72	73	73	74	74	75	75	76	77	77	78	78	79	79	80	81	81	82
15-5	185	69	69	70	70	71	71	72	73	73	74	74	75	75	76	77	77	78	78	79	79	80	81	81	82
15-6	186	68	69	69	70	70	71	72	72	73	73	74	74	75	76	76	77	77	78	78	79	80	80	81	81
15-7	187	68	68	69	69	70	71	71	72	72	73	73	74	75	75	76	76	77	77	78	79	79	80	80	81
15-8	188	68	68	69	69	70	71	71	72	72	73	73	74	75	75	76	76	77	77	78	79	79	80	80	81
15-9	189	67	68	69	69	70	70	71	71	72	72	73	74	74	75	75	76	76	77	78	78	79	79	80	80
15-10	190	67	68	68	69	69	70	70	71	72	72	73	73	74	74	75	75	76	77	77	78	78	79	79	80
15-11	191	67	68	68	69	69	70	70	71	72	72	73	73	74	74	75	75	76	77	77	78	78	79	79	80
16-	192	67	67	68	68	69	69	70	71	71	72	72	73	73	74	74	75	76	76	77	77	78	78	79	79
Total Months		120	121	122	123	124	125	126	127	128	129	130	131	132	133	134	135	136	137	138	139	140	141	142	143

CHRONOLOGICAL AGE

MENTAL AGE

CHRONOLOGICAL AGE

Years and Months	12-0	12-1	12-2	12-3	12-4	12-5	12-6	12-7	12-8	12-9	12-10	12-11	13-0	13-1	13-2	13-3	13-4	13-5	13-6	13-7	13-8	13-9	13-10	13-11	Total Months
7-0	171																								84
7-1	169	171																							85
7-2	167	169	170	171																					86
7-3	166	167	168	169	170	171																			87
7-4	164	165	166	167	168	169	170																		88
7-5	162	163	164	165	166	167	169	170	171																89
7-6	160	161	162	163	164	166	167	168	169	170	171														90
7-7	158	159	160	162	163	164	165	166	167	168	169	170	171												91
7-8	157	158	159	160	161	162	163	164	165	166	167	168	170	171											92
7-9	155	156	157	158	159	160	161	162	163	165	166	167	168	169	170	171									93
7-10	153	154	155	156	157	159	160	161	162	163	164	165	166	167	168	169	170	171							94
7-11	152	153	154	155	156	157	158	159	160	161	162	163	164	165	166	167	168	169	171						95
8-0	150	151	152	153	154	155	156	157	158	159	160	161	163	164	165	166	167	168	169	170	171				96
8-1	148	149	151	152	153	154	155	156	157	158	159	160	161	162	163	164	165	166	167	168	169	170	171		97
8-2	147	148	149	150	151	152	153	154	155	156	157	158	159	160	161	162	163	164	165	166	167	168	169	170	98
8-3	145	146	147	148	149	151	152	153	154	155	156	157	158	159	160	161	162	163	164	165	166	167	168	169	99
8-4	144	145	146	147	148	149	150	151	152	153	154	155	156	157	158	159	160	161	162	163	164	165	166	167	100
8-5	143	144	145	146	147	148	149	150	150	151	152	153	154	155	156	157	158	159	160	161	162	163	164	165	101
8-6	141	142	143	144	145	146	147	148	149	150	151	152	153	154	155	156	157	158	159	160	161	162	163	164	102
8-7	140	141	142	143	144	145	146	147	148	149	150	150	151	152	153	154	155	156	157	158	159	160	161	162	103
8-8	138	139	140	141	142	143	144	145	146	147	148	149	150	151	152	153	154	155	156	157	158	159	160	161	104
8-9	137	138	139	140	141	142	143	144	145	146	147	148	149	150	150	151	152	153	154	155	156	157	158	159	105
8-10	136	137	138	139	140	141	142	142	143	144	145	146	147	148	149	150	151	152	153	154	155	156	157	158	106
8-11	135	136	136	137	138	139	140	141	142	143	144	145	146	147	148	149	150	150	151	152	153	154	155	156	107
9-0	133	134	135	136	137	138	139	140	141	142	143	144	144	145	146	147	148	149	150	151	152	153	154	155	108
9-1	132	133	134	135	136	137	138	139	139	140	141	142	143	144	145	146	147	148	149	150	150	151	152	153	109
9-2	131	132	133	134	135	135	136	137	138	139	140	141	142	143	144	145	145	146	147	148	149	150	151	152	110
9-3	130	131	132	132	133	134	135	136	137	138	139	140	141	141	142	143	144	145	146	147	148	149	150	150	111
9-4	129	129	130	131	132	133	134	135	136	137	138	138	139	140	141	142	143	144	145	146	146	147	148	149	112
9-5	127	128	129	130	131	132	133	134	135	135	136	137	138	139	140	141	142	142	143	144	145	146	147	148	113
9-6	126	127	128	129	130	131	132	132	133	134	135	136	137	138	139	139	140	141	142	143	144	145	146	146	114
9-7	125	126	127	128	129	130	130	131	132	133	134	135	136	137	137	138	139	140	141	142	143	143	144	145	115
9-8	124	125	126	127	128	128	129	130	131	132	133	134	134	135	136	137	138	139	140	141	141	142	143	144	116
9-9	123	124	125	126	126	127	128	129	130	131	132	132	133	134	135	136	137	138	138	139	140	141	142	143	117
9-10	122	123	124	125	125	126	127	128	129	130	131	131	132	133	134	135	136	136	137	138	139	140	141	142	118
9-11	121	122	123	124	124	125	126	127	128	129	129	130	131	132	133	134	134	135	136	137	138	139	140	140	119
Total Months	144	145	146	147	148	149	150	151	152	153	154	155	156	157	158	159	160	161	162	163	164	165	166	167	

MENTAL AGE

Left margin (vertical): CHRONOLOGICAL AGE

Total Months	13-11	13-10	13-9	13-8	13-7	13-6	13-5	13-4	13-3	13-2	13-1	13-0	12-11	12-10	12-9	12-8	12-7	12-6	12-5	12-4	12-3	12-2	12-1	12-0	Years and Months
120	139	138	138	137	136	135	134	133	133	132	131	130	129	128	128	127	126	125	124	123	123	122	121	120	10-0
121	138	137	136	136	135	134	133	132	131	131	130	129	128	127	126	126	125	124	123	122	121	121	120	119	10-1
122	137	136	135	134	134	133	132	131	130	130	129	128	127	126	125	125	124	123	122	121	120	120	119	118	10-2
123	136	135	134	133	133	132	131	130	129	128	128	127	126	125	124	124	123	122	121	120	120	119	118	117	10-3
124	135	134	133	132	131	131	130	129	128	127	127	126	125	124	123	123	122	121	120	119	119	118	117	116	10-4
125	134	133	132	131	130	130	129	128	127	126	126	125	124	123	122	122	121	120	119	118	118	117	116	115	10-5
126	133	132	131	130	129	129	128	127	126	125	125	124	123	122	121	121	120	119	118	117	117	116	115	114	10-6
127	131	131	130	129	128	128	127	126	125	124	124	123	122	121	120	120	119	118	117	117	116	115	114	113	10-7
128	130	130	129	128	127	127	126	125	124	123	123	122	121	120	120	119	118	117	116	116	115	114	113	113	10-8
129	129	129	128	127	126	126	125	124	123	122	122	121	120	119	119	118	117	116	116	115	114	113	112	112	10-9
130	128	128	127	126	125	125	124	123	122	122	121	120	119	118	118	117	116	115	115	114	113	112	112	111	10-10
131	127	127	126	125	124	124	123	122	121	121	120	119	118	118	117	116	115	115	114	113	112	111	111	110	10-11
132	127	126	125	124	123	123	122	121	120	120	119	118	117	117	116	115	114	114	113	112	111	111	110	109	11-0
133	126	125	124	123	123	122	121	120	120	119	118	117	117	116	115	114	114	113	112	111	111	110	109	108	11-1
134	125	124	123	122	122	121	120	119	119	118	117	116	116	115	114	113	113	112	111	110	110	109	108	107	11-2
135	124	123	122	121	121	120	119	119	118	117	116	116	115	114	113	113	112	111	110	110	109	108	107	107	11-3
136	123	122	121	121	120	119	118	118	117	116	115	115	114	113	113	112	111	110	110	109	108	107	107	106	11-4
137	122	121	120	120	119	118	118	117	116	115	115	114	113	112	112	111	110	109	109	108	107	107	106	105	11-5
138	121	120	120	119	118	117	117	116	115	114	114	113	112	112	111	110	109	109	108	107	107	106	105	104	11-6
139	120	119	119	118	117	117	116	115	114	114	113	112	112	111	110	109	109	108	107	106	106	105	104	104	11-7
140	119	119	118	117	116	116	115	114	114	113	112	111	111	110	109	109	108	107	106	106	105	104	104	103	11-8
141	118	118	117	116	116	115	114	113	113	112	111	111	110	109	109	108	107	106	106	105	104	104	103	102	11-9
142	118	117	116	115	115	114	113	113	112	111	111	110	109	108	108	107	106	106	105	104	104	103	102	101	11-10
143	117	116	115	115	114	113	113	112	111	110	110	109	108	108	107	106	106	105	104	103	103	102	101	101	11-11
144	116	115	115	114	113	113	112	111	110	110	109	108	108	107	106	106	105	104	103	103	102	101	101	100	12-0
145	115	114	114	113	112	112	111	110	110	109	108	108	107	106	106	105	104	103	103	102	101	101	100	99	12-1
146	114	114	113	112	112	111	110	110	109	108	108	107	106	105	105	104	103	103	102	101	101	100	99	99	12-2
147	114	113	112	112	111	110	110	109	108	107	107	106	105	105	104	103	103	102	101	101	100	99	99	98	12-3
148	113	112	111	111	110	109	109	108	107	107	106	105	105	104	103	103	102	101	101	100	99	99	98	97	12-4
149	112	111	111	110	109	109	108	107	107	106	105	105	104	103	103	102	101	101	100	99	99	98	97	97	12-5
150	111	111	110	109	109	108	107	107	106	105	105	104	103	103	102	101	101	100	99	99	98	97	97	96	12-6
151	111	110	109	109	108	107	107	106	105	105	104	103	103	102	101	101	100	99	99	98	97	97	96	95	12-7
152	110	109	109	108	107	107	106	105	105	104	103	103	102	101	101	100	99	99	98	97	97	96	95	95	12-8
153	109	109	108	107	107	106	105	105	104	103	103	102	101	101	100	99	99	98	97	97	96	95	95	94	12-9
154	108	108	107	106	106	105	105	104	103	103	102	101	101	100	99	99	98	97	97	96	95	95	94	94	12-10
155	108	107	106	106	105	105	104	103	103	102	101	101	100	99	99	98	97	97	96	95	95	94	94	93	12-11
Total Months	167	166	165	164	163	162	161	160	159	158	157	156	155	154	153	152	151	150	149	148	147	146	145	144	Total Months

MENTAL AGE

CHRONOLOGICAL AGE

Years and Months	12-0	12-1	12-2	12-3	12-4	12-5	12-6	12-7	12-8	12-9	12-10	12-11	13-0	13-1	13-2	13-3	13-4	13-5	13-6	13-7	13-8	13-9	13-10	13-11	Total Months
13- 0	92	93	94	94	95	96	96	97	97	98	99	99	100	101	101	102	103	103	104	104	105	106	106	107	156
13- 1	92	92	93	94	94	95	96	96	97	97	98	99	99	100	101	101	102	103	103	104	104	105	106	106	157
13- 2	91	92	92	93	94	94	95	96	96	97	97	98	99	99	100	101	101	102	103	103	104	104	105	106	158
13- 3	91	91	92	92	93	94	94	95	96	96	97	97	98	99	99	100	101	101	102	103	103	104	104	105	159
13- 4	90	91	91	92	93	93	94	94	95	96	96	97	98	98	99	99	100	101	101	102	103	103	104	104	160
13- 5	89	90	91	91	92	93	93	94	94	95	96	96	97	98	98	99	99	100	101	101	102	102	103	104	161
13- 6	89	90	90	91	91	92	93	93	94	94	95	96	96	97	98	98	99	99	100	101	101	102	102	103	162
13- 7	88	89	90	90	91	91	92	93	93	94	94	95	96	96	97	98	98	99	99	100	101	101	102	102	163
13- 8	88	88	89	90	90	91	91	92	93	93	94	95	95	96	96	97	98	98	99	99	100	101	101	102	164
13- 9	87	88	88	89	90	90	91	92	92	93	93	94	95	95	96	96	97	98	98	99	99	100	101	101	165
13-10	87	87	88	89	89	90	90	91	92	92	93	93	94	95	95	96	96	97	98	98	99	99	100	101	166
13-11	86	87	87	88	89	89	90	90	91	92	92	93	93	94	95	95	96	96	97	98	98	99	99	100	167
14- 0	86	86	87	88	88	89	89	90	90	91	92	92	93	93	94	95	95	96	96	97	98	98	99	99	168
14- 1	85	86	86	87	88	88	89	89	90	91	91	92	92	93	93	94	95	95	96	96	97	98	98	99	169
14- 2	85	85	86	86	87	88	88	89	89	90	91	91	92	92	93	94	94	95	95	96	96	97	98	98	170
14- 3	84	85	85	86	87	87	88	88	89	89	90	91	91	92	92	93	94	94	95	95	96	96	97	98	171
14- 4	84	84	85	85	86	87	87	88	88	89	90	90	91	91	92	92	93	94	94	95	95	96	97	97	172
14- 5	83	84	84	85	86	86	87	87	88	88	89	90	90	91	91	92	92	93	94	94	95	95	96	97	173
14- 6	83	83	84	84	85	86	86	87	87	88	89	89	90	90	91	91	92	93	93	94	94	95	95	96	174
14- 7	82	83	83	84	85	85	86	86	87	87	88	89	89	90	90	91	91	92	93	93	94	94	95	95	175
14- 8	82	82	83	84	84	85	85	86	86	87	88	88	89	89	90	90	91	91	92	93	93	94	94	95	176
14- 9	81	82	82	83	84	84	85	85	86	86	87	88	88	89	89	90	90	91	92	92	93	93	94	94	177
14-10	81	81	82	83	83	84	84	85	85	86	87	87	88	88	89	89	90	90	91	92	92	93	93	94	178
14-11	80	81	82	82	83	83	84	84	85	85	86	87	87	88	88	89	89	90	91	91	92	92	93	93	179
15- 0	80	81	81	82	82	83	83	84	84	85	86	86	87	87	88	88	89	89	90	91	91	92	92	93	180
15- 1	80	80	81	81	82	82	83	83	84	85	85	86	86	87	87	88	88	89	90	90	91	91	92	92	181
15- 2	79	80	80	81	81	82	82	83	84	84	85	85	86	86	87	87	88	88	89	90	90	91	91	92	182
15- 3	79	79	80	80	81	81	82	83	83	84	84	85	85	86	86	87	87	88	89	89	90	90	91	91	183
15- 4	78	79	79	80	80	81	82	82	83	83	84	84	85	85	86	86	87	88	88	89	89	90	90	91	184
15- 5	78	78	79	79	80	81	81	82	82	83	83	84	84	85	85	86	86	87	88	88	89	89	90	90	185
15- 6	77	78	78	79	80	80	81	81	82	82	83	83	84	84	85	85	86	87	87	88	88	89	89	90	186
15- 7	77	78	78	79	79	80	80	81	81	82	82	83	83	84	84	85	86	86	87	87	88	88	89	89	187
15- 8	77	77	78	78	79	79	80	80	81	81	82	82	83	84	84	85	85	86	86	87	87	88	88	89	188
15- 9	76	77	77	78	78	79	79	80	80	81	81	82	83	83	84	84	85	85	86	86	87	87	88	88	189
15-10	76	76	77	77	78	78	79	79	80	81	81	82	82	83	83	84	84	85	85	86	86	87	87	88	190
15-11	75	76	76	77	77	78	79	79	80	80	81	81	82	82	83	83	84	84	85	85	86	86	87	87	191
16- 0	75	76	76	77	77	78	78	79	79	80	80	81	81	82	82	83	83	84	84	85	85	86	86	87	192
Total Months	144	145	146	147	148	149	150	151	152	153	154	155	156	157	158	159	160	161	162	163	164	165	166	167	

CHRONOLOGICAL AGE

Total Months	15-11	15-10	15-9	15-8	15-7	15-6	15-5	15-4	15-3	15-2	15-1	15-0	14-11	14-10	14-9	14-8	14-7	14-6	14-5	14-4	14-3	14-2	14-1	14-0	Years and Months
84																									7-0
85																									7-1
86																									7-2
87																									7-3
88																									7-4
89																									7-5
90																									7-6
91																									7-7
92																									7-8
93																									7-9
94																									7-10
95																									7-11
96																									8-0
97																									8-1
98																								171	8-2
99																							171	170	8-3
100																					171	170	169	168	8-4
101																			171	170	169	168	167	166	8-5
102																		171	170	169	168	167	166	165	8-6
103																171	170	169	168	167	166	165	164	163	8-7
104														171	170	169	168	167	166	165	164	163	163	162	8-8
105												171	170	170	169	168	167	166	165	164	163	162	161	160	8-9
106											171	170	169	168	167	166	165	164	163	162	161	160	159	158	8-10
107									171	170	169	168	167	166	165	164	164	163	162	161	160	159	158	157	8-11
108							171	170	169	169	168	167	166	165	164	163	162	161	160	159	158	157	156	156	9-0
109						171	170	169	168	167	166	165	164	163	162	161	161	160	159	158	157	156	155	154	9-1
110				171	170	169	168	167	166	165	165	164	163	162	161	160	159	158	157	156	155	155	154	153	9-2
111		171	170	169	168	168	167	166	165	164	163	162	161	160	159	159	158	157	156	155	154	153	152	151	9-3
112	171	170	169	168	167	166	165	164	163	163	162	161	160	159	158	157	156	155	154	154	153	152	151	150	9-4
113	169	168	167	166	165	165	164	163	162	161	160	159	158	158	157	156	155	154	153	152	151	150	150	149	9-5
114	168	167	166	165	164	163	162	161	161	160	159	158	157	156	155	154	154	153	152	151	150	149	148	147	9-6
115	166	165	164	163	163	162	161	160	159	158	157	157	156	155	154	153	152	151	150	150	149	148	147	146	9-7
116	165	164	163	162	161	160	159	159	158	157	156	155	154	153	153	152	151	150	149	148	147	147	146	145	9-8
117	163	162	162	161	160	159	158	157	156	156	155	154	153	152	151	150	150	149	148	147	146	145	144	144	9-9
118	162	161	160	159	158	158	157	156	155	154	153	153	152	151	150	149	148	147	147	146	145	144	143	142	9-10
119	161	160	159	158	157	156	155	155	154	153	152	151	150	150	149	148	147	146	145	145	144	143	142	141	9-11
Total Months	191	190	189	188	187	186	185	184	183	182	181	180	179	178	177	176	175	174	173	172	171	170	169	168	Total Months

MENTAL AGE

CHRONOLOGICAL AGE

Years and Months	Total Months	14-0	14-1	14-2	14-3	14-4	14-5	14-6	14-7	14-8	14-9	14-10	14-11	15-0	15-1	15-2	15-3	15-4	15-5	15-6	15-7	15-8	15-9	15-10	15-11
10-0	120	140	141	142	143	143	144	145	146	147	148	148	149	150	151	152	153	153	154	155	156	157	158	158	159
10-1	121	139	140	140	141	142	143	144	145	145	146	147	148	149	150	150	151	152	153	154	155	155	156	157	158
10-2	122	138	139	139	140	141	142	143	143	144	145	146	147	148	148	149	150	151	152	152	153	154	155	156	157
10-3	123	137	137	138	139	140	141	141	142	143	144	145	146	146	147	148	149	150	150	151	152	153	154	154	155
10-4	124	135	136	137	138	139	140	140	141	142	143	144	144	145	146	147	148	148	149	150	151	152	152	153	154
10-5	125	134	135	136	137	138	138	139	140	141	142	142	143	144	145	146	146	147	148	149	150	150	151	152	153
10-6	126	133	134	135	136	137	137	138	139	140	140	141	142	143	144	144	145	146	147	148	148	149	150	151	152
10-7	127	132	133	134	135	135	136	137	138	139	139	140	141	142	143	143	144	145	146	146	147	148	149	150	150
10-8	128	131	132	133	134	134	135	136	137	138	138	139	140	141	141	142	143	144	145	145	146	147	148	148	149
10-9	129	130	131	132	133	133	134	135	136	136	137	138	139	140	140	141	142	143	143	144	145	146	147	147	148
10-10	130	129	130	131	132	132	133	134	135	135	136	137	138	138	139	140	141	142	142	143	144	145	145	146	147
10-11	131	128	129	130	131	131	132	133	134	134	135	136	137	137	138	139	140	140	141	142	143	144	144	145	146
11-0	132	127	128	129	130	130	131	132	133	133	134	135	136	136	137	138	139	139	140	141	142	142	143	144	145
11-1	133	126	127	128	129	129	130	131	132	132	133	134	135	135	136	137	138	138	139	140	141	141	142	143	144
11-2	134	125	126	127	128	128	129	130	131	131	132	133	134	134	135	136	137	137	138	139	140	140	141	142	143
11-3	135	124	125	126	127	127	128	129	130	130	131	132	133	133	134	135	136	136	137	138	139	139	140	141	141
11-4	136	124	124	125	126	126	127	128	129	129	130	131	132	132	133	134	135	135	136	137	138	138	139	140	140
11-5	137	123	123	124	125	126	126	127	128	128	129	130	131	131	132	133	134	134	135	136	137	137	138	139	139
11-6	138	122	122	123	124	125	125	126	127	128	128	129	130	130	131	132	133	133	134	135	136	136	137	138	138
11-7	139	121	122	122	123	124	124	125	126	127	127	128	129	130	130	131	132	132	133	134	135	135	136	137	137
11-8	140	120	121	121	122	123	124	124	125	126	126	127	128	129	129	130	131	131	132	133	134	134	135	136	136
11-9	141	119	120	121	121	122	123	123	124	125	126	126	127	128	128	129	130	131	131	132	133	133	134	135	135
11-10	142	118	119	120	120	121	122	123	123	124	125	125	126	127	127	128	129	130	130	131	132	132	133	134	135
11-11	143	117	118	119	120	120	121	122	122	123	124	124	125	126	127	127	128	129	129	130	131	131	132	133	134
12-0	144	117	117	118	119	119	120	121	122	122	123	124	124	125	126	126	127	128	128	129	130	131	131	132	133
12-1	145	116	117	117	118	119	119	120	121	121	122	123	123	124	125	126	126	127	128	128	129	130	130	131	132
12-2	146	115	116	116	117	118	118	119	120	121	121	122	123	123	124	125	125	126	127	127	128	129	129	130	131
12-3	147	114	115	116	116	117	118	118	119	120	120	121	122	122	123	124	124	125	126	127	127	128	129	129	130
12-4	148	114	114	115	116	116	117	118	118	119	120	120	121	122	122	123	124	124	125	126	126	127	128	128	129
12-5	149	113	113	114	115	115	116	117	117	118	119	119	120	121	121	122	123	123	124	125	126	126	127	128	128
12-6	150	112	113	113	114	115	115	116	117	117	118	119	119	120	121	121	122	123	123	124	125	125	126	127	127
12-7	151	111	112	113	113	114	115	115	116	117	117	118	119	119	120	121	121	122	123	123	124	125	125	126	126
12-8	152	111	111	112	113	113	114	114	115	116	116	117	118	118	119	120	120	121	122	122	123	124	124	125	126
12-9	153	110	110	111	112	112	113	114	114	115	116	116	117	118	118	119	120	120	121	122	122	123	124	124	125
12-10	154	109	110	110	111	112	112	113	114	114	115	116	116	117	118	118	119	119	120	121	121	122	123	123	124
12-11	155	108	109	110	110	111	112	112	113	114	114	115	115	116	117	117	118	119	119	120	121	121	122	123	123
Total Months		168	169	170	171	172	173	174	175	176	177	178	179	180	181	182	183	184	185	186	187	188	189	190	191

MENTAL AGE

CHRONOLOGICAL AGE

Years and Months	14 0	14 1	14 2	14 3	14 4	14 5	14 6	14 7	14 8	14 9	14 10	14 11	15 0	15 1	15 2	15 3	15 4	15 5	15 6	15 7	15 8	15 9	15 10	15 11	Total Months
13- 0	108	108	109	110	110	111	112	112	113	113	114	115	115	116	117	117	118	119	119	120	121	121	122	122	156
13- 1	107	108	108	109	110	110	111	111	112	113	113	114	115	115	116	117	117	118	118	119	120	120	121	122	157
13- 2	107	108	108	109	110	110	111	111	112	113	113	114	115	115	116	117	117	118	118	119	120	120	121	122	158
13- 3	106	107	108	108	109	109	110	111	111	112	113	113	114	115	115	116	116	117	118	118	119	120	120	121	159
13- 4	106	106	107	108	108	109	109	110	111	111	112	113	113	114	114	115	116	116	117	118	118	119	119	120	160
13- 5	106	106	107	108	108	109	109	110	111	111	112	113	113	114	114	115	116	116	117	118	118	119	119	120	161
13- 6	105	106	106	107	108	108	109	109	110	111	111	112	113	113	114	114	115	116	116	117	118	118	119	119	162
13- 7	104	105	106	106	107	107	108	109	109	110	111	111	112	112	113	114	114	115	116	116	117	117	118	119	163
13- 8	104	105	106	106	107	107	108	109	109	110	111	111	112	112	113	114	114	115	116	116	117	117	118	119	164
13- 9	104	104	105	106	106	107	107	108	109	109	110	110	111	112	112	113	114	114	115	115	116	117	117	118	165
13-10	103	104	104	105	106	106	107	107	108	109	109	110	110	111	112	112	113	113	114	115	115	116	117	117	166
13-11	103	104	104	105	106	106	107	107	108	109	109	110	110	111	112	112	113	113	114	115	115	116	117	117	167
14- 0	102	103	104	104	105	105	106	107	107	108	109	109	110	110	111	112	112	113	113	114	115	115	116	116	168
14- 1	102	102	103	104	104	105	105	106	107	107	108	108	109	110	110	111	112	112	113	113	114	115	115	116	169
14- 2	102	102	103	104	104	105	105	106	107	107	108	108	109	110	110	111	112	112	113	113	114	115	115	116	170
14- 3	101	102	102	103	104	104	105	105	106	107	107	108	108	109	110	110	111	111	112	113	113	114	114	115	171
14- 4	101	101	102	102	103	104	104	105	105	106	107	107	108	108	109	110	110	111	111	112	113	113	114	114	172
14- 5	101	101	102	102	103	104	104	105	105	106	107	107	108	108	109	110	110	111	111	112	113	113	114	114	173
14- 6	100	101	101	102	102	103	104	104	105	105	106	107	107	108	108	109	110	110	111	111	112	113	113	114	174
14- 7	99	100	101	101	102	102	103	104	104	105	105	106	107	107	108	108	109	109	110	111	111	112	112	113	175
14- 8	99	100	101	101	102	102	103	104	104	105	105	106	107	107	108	108	109	109	110	111	111	112	112	113	176
14- 9	99	99	100	101	101	102	102	103	104	104	105	105	106	106	107	108	108	109	109	110	111	111	112	112	177
14-10	98	99	99	100	101	101	102	102	103	104	104	105	105	106	106	107	108	108	109	109	110	111	111	112	178
14-11	98	99	99	100	101	101	102	102	103	104	104	105	105	106	106	107	108	108	109	109	110	111	111	112	179
15- 0	98	98	99	99	100	101	101	102	102	103	103	104	105	105	106	106	107	108	108	109	109	110	110	111	180
15- 1	97	98	98	99	99	100	101	101	102	102	103	103	104	105	105	106	106	107	108	108	109	109	110	110	181
15- 2	97	98	98	99	99	100	101	101	102	102	103	103	104	105	105	106	106	107	108	108	109	109	110	110	182
15- 3	97	97	98	98	99	99	100	101	101	102	102	103	103	104	105	105	106	106	107	107	108	109	109	110	183
15- 4	96	97	97	98	98	99	99	100	101	101	102	102	103	103	104	105	105	106	106	107	107	108	109	109	184
15- 5	96	97	97	98	98	99	99	100	101	101	102	102	103	103	104	105	105	106	106	107	107	108	109	109	185
15- 6	95	96	97	97	98	98	99	99	100	101	101	102	102	103	103	104	105	105	106	106	107	107	108	109	186
15- 7	95	95	96	97	97	98	98	99	99	100	101	101	102	102	103	103	104	105	105	106	106	107	107	108	187
15- 8	95	95	96	97	97	98	98	99	99	100	101	101	102	102	103	103	104	105	105	106	106	107	107	108	188
15- 9	94	95	96	96	97	97	98	98	99	99	100	101	101	102	102	103	103	104	104	105	106	106	107	107	189
15-10	94	94	95	96	96	97	97	98	98	99	99	100	101	101	102	102	103	103	104	104	105	106	106	107	190
15-11	94	94	95	96	96	97	97	98	98	99	99	100	101	101	102	102	103	103	104	104	105	106	106	107	191
16-	93	94	94	95	96	96	97	97	98	98	99	99	100	101	101	102	102	103	103	104	104	105	106	106	192
Total Months	168	169	170	171	172	173	174	175	176	177	178	179	180	181	182	183	184	185	186	187	188	189	190	191	

MENTAL AGE

CHRONOLOGICAL AGE

Total Months	17-11	17-10	17-9	17-8	17-7	17-6	17-5	17-4	17-3	17-2	17-1	17-0	16-11	16-10	16-9	16-8	16-7	16-6	16-5	16-4	16-3	16-2	16-1	16-0	Years and Months
120												170	169	168	168	167	166	165	164	163	163	162	161	160	10-0
121										170	169	169	168	167	166	165	164	164	163	162	161	160	160	159	10-1
122									170	169	168	167	166	166	165	164	163	162	161	161	160	159	158	157	10-2
123							170	169	168	167	167	166	165	164	163	163	162	161	160	159	159	158	157	156	10-3
124					170	169	169	168	167	166	165	165	164	163	162	161	160	160	159	158	157	156	156	155	10-4
125				170	169	168	167	166	166	165	164	163	162	162	161	160	159	158	158	157	156	155	154	154	10-5
126		170	169	168	167	167	166	165	164	163	163	162	161	160	160	159	158	157	156	156	155	154	153	152	10-6
127	169	169	168	167	166	165	165	164	163	162	161	161	160	159	158	157	157	156	155	154	154	153	152	151	10-7
128	168	167	166	166	165	164	163	163	162	161	160	159	159	158	157	156	155	155	154	153	152	152	151	150	10-8
129	167	166	165	164	164	163	162	161	160	160	159	158	157	157	156	155	154	153	153	152	151	150	150	149	10-9
130	165	165	164	163	162	162	161	160	159	158	158	157	156	155	155	154	153	152	152	151	150	149	148	148	10-10
131	164	163	163	162	161	160	160	159	158	157	156	156	155	154	153	153	152	151	150	150	149	148	147	147	10-11
132	163	162	161	161	160	159	158	158	157	156	155	155	154	153	152	152	151	150	149	148	148	147	146	145	11-0
133	162	161	160	159	159	158	157	156	156	155	154	153	153	152	151	150	150	149	148	147	147	146	145	144	11-1
134	160	160	159	158	157	157	156	155	154	154	153	152	151	151	150	149	149	148	147	146	146	145	144	143	11-2
135	159	159	158	157	156	156	155	154	153	153	152	151	150	150	149	148	147	147	146	145	144	144	143	142	11-3
136	158	157	157	156	155	154	154	153	152	151	151	150	149	149	148	147	146	146	145	144	143	143	142	141	11-4
137	157	156	155	155	154	153	153	152	151	150	150	149	148	147	147	146	145	145	144	143	142	142	141	140	11-5
138	156	155	154	154	153	152	151	151	150	149	149	148	147	146	146	145	144	143	143	142	141	141	140	139	11-6
139	155	154	153	153	152	151	150	150	149	148	147	147	146	145	145	144	143	142	142	141	140	140	139	138	11-7
140	154	153	152	151	151	150	149	149	148	147	146	146	145	144	144	143	142	141	141	140	139	139	138	137	11-8
141	152	152	151	150	150	149	148	148	147	146	145	145	144	143	143	142	141	140	140	139	138	138	137	136	11-9
142	151	151	150	149	149	148	147	146	146	145	144	144	143	142	142	141	140	139	139	138	137	137	136	135	11-10
143	150	150	149	148	148	147	146	145	145	144	143	143	142	141	141	140	139	138	138	137	136	136	135	134	11-11
144	149	149	148	147	147	146	145	144	144	143	142	142	141	140	140	139	138	138	137	136	135	135	134	133	12-0
145	148	148	147	146	146	145	144	143	143	142	141	141	140	139	139	138	137	137	136	135	134	134	133	132	12-1
146	147	147	146	145	145	144	143	142	142	141	140	140	139	138	138	137	136	136	135	134	134	133	132	132	12-2
147	146	146	145	144	144	143	142	142	141	140	139	139	138	137	137	136	135	135	134	133	133	132	131	131	12-3
148	145	145	144	143	143	142	141	141	140	139	139	138	137	136	136	135	134	134	133	132	132	131	130	130	12-4
149	144	144	143	142	142	141	140	140	139	138	138	137	136	136	135	134	134	133	132	132	131	130	130	129	12-5
150	143	143	142	141	141	140	139	139	138	137	137	136	135	135	134	133	133	132	131	131	130	129	129	128	12-6
151	142	142	141	140	140	139	138	138	137	136	136	135	134	134	133	132	132	131	130	130	129	128	128	127	12-7
152	141	141	140	139	139	138	138	137	136	136	135	134	134	133	132	132	131	130	130	129	128	128	127	126	12-8
153	141	140	139	139	138	137	137	136	135	135	134	133	133	132	131	131	130	129	129	128	127	127	126	125	12-9
154	140	139	138	138	137	136	136	135	134	134	133	132	132	131	131	130	129	129	128	127	127	126	125	125	12-10
155	139	138	137	137	136	135	135	134	134	133	132	132	131	130	130	129	128	128	127	126	126	125	125	124	12-11
Total Months	215	214	213	212	211	210	209	208	207	206	205	204	203	202	201	200	199	198	197	196	195	194	193	192	Total Months

MENTAL AGE

Total Months	16-0	16-1	16-2	16-3	16-4	16-5	16-6	16-7	16-8	16-9	16-10	16-11	17-0	17-1	17-2	17-3	17-4	17-5	17-6	17-7	17-8	17-9	17-10	17-11	Years and Months
156	123	124	124	125	126	126	127	128	128	129	129	130	131	131	132	133	133	134	135	135	136	137	137	138	13-0
157	122	123	124	124	125	125	126	127	127	128	129	129	130	131	131	132	132	133	134	134	135	136	136	137	13-1
158	122	122	123	123	124	125	125	126	127	127	128	128	129	130	130	131	132	132	133	134	134	135	135	136	13-2
159	121	121	122	123	123	124	125	125	126	126	127	128	128	129	130	130	131	131	132	133	133	134	135	135	13-3
160	120	121	121	122	123	123	124	124	125	126	126	127	128	128	129	129	130	131	131	132	133	133	134	134	13-4
161	119	120	121	121	122	122	123	124	124	125	125	126	127	127	128	129	129	130	130	131	132	132	133	134	13-5
162	119	119	120	120	121	122	122	123	123	124	125	125	126	127	127	128	128	129	130	130	131	131	132	133	13-6
163	118	118	119	120	120	121	121	122	123	123	124	125	125	126	126	127	128	128	129	129	130	131	131	132	13-7
164	117	118	118	119	120	120	121	122	122	123	123	124	125	125	126	126	127	127	128	129	129	130	130	131	13-8
165	116	117	118	118	119	119	120	121	121	122	122	123	124	124	125	125	126	127	127	128	128	129	130	130	13-9
166	116	116	117	117	118	119	119	120	120	121	122	122	123	123	124	125	125	126	127	127	128	128	129	130	13-10
167	115	116	116	117	117	118	119	119	120	120	121	122	122	123	123	124	125	125	126	126	127	128	128	129	13-11
168	114	115	115	116	117	117	118	118	119	120	120	121	121	122	123	123	124	124	125	126	126	127	127	128	14-0
169	114	114	115	115	116	117	117	118	119	120	120	121	121	122	122	123	124	124	125	125	126	126	127	127	14-1
170	113	114	114	115	115	116	116	117	118	118	119	119	120	121	121	122	122	123	124	124	125	125	126	126	14-2
171	112	113	113	114	115	115	116	116	117	118	118	119	119	120	120	121	122	122	123	123	124	125	125	126	14-3
172	112	112	113	113	114	115	115	116	116	117	117	118	119	119	120	120	121	122	122	123	123	124	124	125	14-4
173	111	112	112	113	113	114	114	115	116	116	117	117	118	119	119	120	120	121	121	122	123	123	124	124	14-5
174	110	111	111	112	113	113	114	114	115	116	116	117	117	118	118	119	120	120	121	121	122	122	123	124	14-6
175	110	110	111	111	112	113	113	114	114	115	115	116	117	117	118	118	119	119	120	121	121	122	122	123	14-7
176	109	110	110	111	111	112	113	113	114	114	115	115	116	116	117	118	118	119	119	120	120	121	122	122	14-8
177	108	109	110	110	111	111	112	113	113	114	114	115	115	116	116	117	118	118	119	119	120	120	121	121	14-9
178	108	108	109	110	110	111	111	112	112	113	113	114	115	115	116	116	117	117	118	119	119	120	120	121	14-10
179	107	108	108	109	110	110	111	111	112	112	113	113	114	115	115	116	116	117	118	118	119	119	120	120	14-11
180	107	107	108	108	109	109	110	111	111	112	112	113	113	114	114	115	116	116	117	117	118	118	119	119	15-0
181	106	107	107	108	108	109	109	110	111	111	112	112	113	113	114	114	115	115	116	117	117	118	118	119	15-1
182	105	106	107	107	108	108	109	109	110	110	111	112	112	113	113	114	114	115	115	116	116	117	118	118	15-2
183	105	105	106	107	107	108	108	109	109	110	110	111	111	112	113	113	114	114	115	115	116	116	117	117	15-3
184	104	105	105	106	107	107	108	108	109	109	110	110	111	111	112	113	113	114	114	115	115	116	116	117	15-4
185	104	104	105	105	106	106	107	108	108	109	109	110	110	111	111	112	112	113	114	114	115	115	116	116	15-5
186	103	104	104	105	105	106	106	107	108	108	109	109	110	110	111	111	112	112	113	113	114	115	115	116	15-6
187	103	103	104	104	105	105	106	106	107	107	108	109	109	110	110	111	111	112	112	113	113	114	114	115	15-7
188	102	103	103	104	104	105	105	106	106	107	107	108	109	109	110	110	111	111	112	112	113	113	114	114	15-8
189	102	102	103	103	104	104	105	105	106	106	107	107	108	108	109	110	110	111	111	112	112	113	113	114	15-9
190	101	102	102	103	103	104	104	105	105	106	106	107	107	108	108	109	109	110	111	111	112	112	113	113	15-10
191	101	101	102	102	103	103	104	104	105	105	106	106	107	107	108	108	109	109	110	110	111	112	112	113	15-11
192	100	101	101	102	102	103	103	104	104	105	105	106	106	107	107	108	108	109	109	110	110	111	111	112	16-
Total Months	192	193	194	195	196	197	198	199	200	201	202	203	204	205	206	207	208	209	210	211	212	213	214	215	Total Months

CHRONOLOGICAL AGE

MENTAL AGE

CHRONOLOGICAL AGE

Total Months	19-11	19-10	19-9	19-8	19-7	19-6	19-5	19-4	19-3	19-2	19-1	19-0	18-11	18-10	18-9	18-8	18-7	18-6	18-5	18-4	18-3	18-2	18-1	18-0	Years and Months
120																									10-0
121																									10-1
122																									10-2
123																									10-3
124																									10-4
125																									10-5
126																									10-6
127																								170	10-7
128																					170	170	169	10-8
129																				170	169	168	167	10-9
130																			170	169	168	168	167	166	10-10
131																	170	169	169	168	167	166	166	165	10-11
132															170	170	169	168	167	167	166	165	164	164	11-0
133														170	169	168	168	167	166	165	165	164	163	162	11-1
134												170	169	169	168	167	166	166	165	164	163	163	162	161	11-2
135										170	170	169	168	167	167	166	165	164	164	163	162	161	161	160	11-3
136									170	169	168	168	167	166	165	165	164	163	163	162	161	160	160	159	11-4
137							170	169	169	168	167	166	166	165	164	164	163	162	161	161	160	159	158	158	11-5
138					170	170	169	168	167	167	166	165	164	164	163	162	162	161	160	159	159	158	157	157	11-6
139				170	169	168	168	167	166	165	165	164	163	163	162	161	160	160	159	158	158	157	156	155	11-7
140		170	169	169	168	167	166	166	165	164	164	163	162	161	161	160	159	159	158	157	156	156	155	154	11-8
141	170	169	168	167	167	166	165	165	164	163	162	162	161	160	160	159	158	157	157	156	155	155	154	153	11-9
142	168	168	167	166	165	165	164	163	163	162	161	161	160	159	158	158	157	156	156	155	154	154	153	152	11-10
143	167	166	166	165	164	164	163	162	162	161	160	159	159	158	157	157	156	155	155	154	153	152	152	151	11-11
144	166	165	165	164	163	163	162	161	160	160	159	158	158	157	156	156	155	154	153	153	152	151	151	150	12-0
145	165	164	163	163	162	161	161	160	159	159	158	157	157	156	155	154	154	153	152	152	151	150	150	149	12-1
146	164	163	162	162	161	160	160	159	158	158	157	156	155	155	154	153	153	152	151	151	150	149	149	148	12-2
147	163	162	161	161	160	159	159	158	157	156	156	155	154	154	153	152	152	151	150	150	149	148	148	147	12-3
148	161	161	160	159	159	158	157	157	156	155	155	154	153	153	152	151	151	150	149	149	148	147	147	146	12-4
149	160	160	159	158	158	157	156	156	155	154	154	153	152	152	151	150	150	149	148	148	147	146	146	145	12-5
150	159	159	158	157	157	156	155	155	154	153	153	152	151	151	150	149	149	148	147	147	146	145	145	144	12-6
151	158	158	157	156	156	155	154	154	153	152	152	151	150	150	149	148	148	147	146	146	145	144	144	143	12-7
152	157	157	156	155	155	154	153	153	152	151	151	150	149	149	148	147	147	146	145	145	144	143	143	142	12-8
153	156	156	155	154	154	153	152	152	151	150	150	149	148	148	147	146	146	145	144	144	143	142	142	141	12-9
154	155	155	154	153	153	152	151	151	150	149	149	148	147	147	146	145	145	144	144	143	142	142	141	140	12-10
155	154	154	153	152	152	151	150	150	149	148	148	147	146	146	145	145	144	143	143	142	141	141	140	139	12-11
Total Months	239	238	237	236	235	234	233	232	231	230	229	228	227	226	225	224	223	222	221	220	219	218	217	216	Total Months

MENTAL AGE

Total Months	19-11	19-10	19-9	19-8	19-7	19-6	19-5	19-4	19-3	19-2	19-1	19-0	18-11	18-10	18-9	18-8	18-7	18-6	18-5	18-4	18-3	18-2	18-1	18-0	Years and Months
156	153	153	152	151	151	150	149	149	148	147	147	146	146	145	144	144	143	142	142	141	140	140	139	138	13-0
157	152	152	151	150	150	149	148	148	147	146	146	145	145	144	143	143	142	141	141	140	139	139	138	138	13-1
158	151	151	150	149	149	148	147	147	146	146	145	144	144	143	142	142	141	141	140	139	139	138	137	137	13-2
159	150	150	149	148	148	147	147	146	145	145	144	143	143	142	142	141	140	140	139	138	138	137	136	136	13-3
160	149	149	148	148	147	146	146	145	144	144	143	143	142	141	141	140	139	139	138	138	137	136	136	135	13-4
161	148	148	147	147	146	145	145	144	143	143	142	142	141	140	140	139	139	138	137	137	136	135	135	134	13-5
162	148	147	146	146	145	144	144	143	143	142	141	141	140	140	139	138	138	137	136	136	135	135	134	133	13-6
163	147	146	145	145	144	144	143	142	142	141	140	140	139	139	138	137	137	136	136	135	134	134	133	133	13-7
164	146	145	145	144	143	143	142	141	141	140	140	139	138	138	137	137	136	135	135	134	134	133	132	132	13-8
165	145	144	144	143	142	142	141	141	140	139	139	138	138	137	136	136	135	135	134	133	133	132	132	131	13-9
166	144	143	143	142	142	141	140	140	139	139	138	137	137	136	136	135	134	134	133	133	132	131	131	130	13-10
167	143	143	142	141	141	140	140	139	138	138	137	137	136	135	135	134	134	133	132	132	131	131	130	129	13-11
168	142	142	141	140	140	139	139	138	138	137	136	136	135	135	134	133	133	132	132	131	130	130	129	129	14-0
169	141	141	140	140	139	138	138	137	137	136	136	135	134	134	133	133	132	131	131	130	130	129	128	128	14-1
170	141	140	139	139	138	138	137	136	136	135	135	134	134	133	132	132	131	131	130	129	129	128	128	127	14-2
171	140	139	139	138	137	137	136	136	135	135	134	133	133	132	132	131	130	130	129	129	128	127	127	126	14-3
172	139	138	138	137	137	136	135	135	134	134	133	133	132	131	131	130	130	129	128	128	127	127	126	126	14-4
173	138	138	137	136	136	135	135	134	134	133	132	132	131	131	130	129	129	128	128	127	127	126	125	125	14-5
174	137	137	136	136	135	134	134	133	133	132	132	131	130	130	129	129	128	128	127	126	126	125	125	124	14-6
175	137	136	135	135	134	134	133	133	132	131	131	130	130	129	129	128	127	127	126	126	125	125	124	123	14-7
176	136	135	135	134	134	133	132	132	131	131	130	130	129	128	128	127	127	126	126	125	124	124	123	123	14-8
177	135	134	134	133	133	132	132	131	131	130	129	129	128	128	127	127	126	125	125	124	124	123	123	122	14-9
178	134	134	133	133	132	131	131	130	130	129	129	128	128	127	126	126	125	125	124	124	123	122	122	121	14-10
179	134	133	132	132	131	131	130	130	129	128	128	127	127	126	126	125	125	124	123	123	122	122	121	121	14-11
180	133	132	132	131	131	130	129	129	128	128	127	127	126	126	125	124	124	123	123	122	122	121	121	120	15-0
181	132	131	131	130	130	129	129	128	128	127	127	126	125	125	124	124	123	123	122	122	121	120	120	119	15-1
182	131	131	130	130	129	129	128	127	127	126	126	125	125	124	124	123	123	122	121	121	120	120	119	119	15-2
183	131	130	130	129	128	128	127	127	126	126	125	125	124	123	123	122	122	121	121	120	120	119	119	118	15-3
184	130	129	129	128	128	127	127	126	126	125	124	124	123	123	122	122	121	121	120	120	119	118	118	117	15-4
185	129	129	128	128	127	126	126	125	125	124	124	123	123	122	122	121	121	120	119	119	118	118	117	117	15-5
186	128	128	127	127	126	126	125	125	124	124	123	123	122	122	121	120	120	119	119	118	118	117	117	116	15-6
187	128	127	127	126	126	125	125	124	124	123	122	122	121	121	120	120	119	119	118	118	117	117	116	116	15-7
188	127	127	126	126	125	124	124	123	123	122	122	121	121	120	120	119	119	118	118	117	116	116	115	115	15-8
189	126	126	125	125	124	124	123	123	122	122	121	121	120	120	119	119	118	117	117	116	116	115	115	114	15-9
190	126	125	125	124	124	123	123	122	122	121	121	120	119	119	118	118	117	117	116	116	115	115	114	114	15-10
191	125	125	124	124	123	123	122	121	121	120	120	119	119	118	118	117	117	116	116	115	115	114	114	113	15-11
192	124	124	123	123	122	122	121	121	120	120	119	119	118	118	117	117	116	116	115	115	114	114	113	113	16-0
Total Months	239	238	237	236	235	234	233	232	231	230	229	228	227	226	225	224	223	222	221	220	219	218	217	216	Total Months

(Left margin label, read vertically: CHRONOLOGICAL AGE)

MENTAL AGE

Years and Months	20-0	20-1	20-2	20-3	20-4	20-5	20-6	20-7	20-8	20-9	20-10	20-11	21-0	21-1	21-2	21-3	21-4	21-5	21-6	21-7	21-8	21-9	21-10	21-11	Total Months
11-6																									138
11-7																									139
11-8																									140
11-9	170																								141
11-10	169	170	170																						142
11-11	168	169	169	170																					143
12-0	167	167	168	169	169	170																			144
12-1	166	166	167	168	168	169	170	170																	145
12-2	164	165	166	166	167	168	168	169	170																146
12-3	163	164	165	165	166	167	167	168	169	169	170														147
12-4	162	163	164	164	165	166	166	167	168	168	169	170	170												148
12-5	161	162	162	163	164	164	165	166	166	167	168	168	169	170	170										149
12-6	160	161	161	162	163	163	164	165	165	166	167	167	168	169	169	170									150
12-7	159	160	160	161	162	162	163	164	164	165	166	166	167	168	168	169	170	170							151
12-8	158	159	159	160	161	161	162	163	163	164	164	165	166	166	167	168	168	169	170	170					152
12-9	157	158	158	159	159	160	161	161	162	163	163	164	165	165	166	167	167	168	169	169	170				153
12-10	156	156	157	158	158	159	160	160	161	162	162	163	164	164	165	166	166	167	168	168	169	169	170		154
12-11	155	155	156	157	157	158	159	159	160	161	161	162	163	163	164	165	165	166	166	167	168	168	169	170	155
Total Months	240	241	242	243	244	245	246	247	248	249	250	251	252	253	254	255	256	257	258	259	260	261	262	263	

CHRONOLOGICAL AGE

MENTAL AGE

CHRONOLOGICAL AGE

Total Months	21-11	21-10	21-9	21-8	21-7	21-6	21-5	21-4	21-3	21-2	21-1	21-0	20-11	20-10	20-9	20-8	20-7	20-6	20-5	20-4	20-3	20-2	20-1	20-0	Years and Months
156	169	168	167	167	166	165	165	164	163	163	162	162	161	160	160	159	158	158	157	156	156	155	154	154	13-0
157	168	167	166	166	165	164	164	163	162	162	161	161	160	159	159	158	157	157	156	155	155	154	154	153	13-1
158	166	166	165	165	164	163	163	162	161	161	160	159	159	158	158	157	156	156	155	154	154	153	153	152	13-2
159	165	165	164	164	163	162	162	161	160	160	159	158	158	157	157	156	155	155	154	153	153	152	152	151	13-3
160	164	164	163	163	162	161	161	160	159	159	158	158	157	156	156	155	154	154	153	153	152	151	151	150	13-4
161	163	163	162	161	161	160	160	159	158	158	157	157	156	155	155	154	153	153	152	152	151	150	150	149	13-5
162	162	162	161	160	160	159	159	158	157	157	156	156	155	154	154	153	152	152	151	151	150	149	149	148	13-6
163	161	161	160	160	159	158	158	157	156	156	155	155	154	153	153	152	152	151	150	150	149	148	148	147	13-7
164	160	160	159	159	158	157	157	156	155	155	154	154	153	152	152	151	151	150	149	149	148	148	147	146	13-8
165	159	159	158	158	157	156	156	155	155	154	153	153	152	152	151	150	150	149	148	148	147	147	146	145	13-9
166	158	158	157	157	156	155	155	154	154	153	152	152	151	151	150	149	149	148	148	147	146	146	145	145	13-10
167	157	157	156	156	155	154	154	153	153	152	151	151	150	150	149	149	148	147	147	146	146	145	144	144	13-11
168	157	156	155	155	154	154	153	152	152	151	151	150	149	149	148	148	147	146	146	145	145	144	143	143	14-0
169	156	155	154	154	153	153	152	151	151	150	150	149	149	148	147	147	146	146	145	144	144	143	143	142	14-1
170	155	154	154	153	152	152	151	151	150	149	149	148	148	147	146	146	145	145	144	144	143	142	142	141	14-2
171	154	153	153	152	151	151	150	150	149	149	148	147	147	146	146	145	144	144	143	143	142	142	141	140	14-3
172	153	152	152	151	151	150	149	149	148	148	147	147	146	145	145	144	144	143	142	142	141	141	140	140	14-4
173	152	151	151	150	150	149	149	148	147	147	146	146	145	145	144	143	143	142	142	141	140	140	139	139	14-5
174	151	151	150	149	149	148	148	147	147	146	145	145	144	144	143	143	142	141	141	140	140	139	139	138	14-6
175	150	150	149	149	148	147	147	146	146	145	145	144	143	143	142	142	141	141	140	139	139	138	138	137	14-7
176	149	149	148	148	147	147	146	145	145	144	144	143	143	142	141	141	140	140	139	139	138	138	137	136	14-8
177	149	148	147	147	146	146	145	145	144	144	143	142	142	141	141	140	140	139	138	138	137	137	136	136	14-9
178	148	147	147	146	146	145	144	144	143	143	142	142	141	140	140	139	139	138	138	137	137	136	135	135	14-10
179	147	146	146	145	145	144	144	143	142	142	141	141	140	140	139	139	138	137	137	136	136	135	135	134	14-11
180	146	146	145	144	144	143	143	142	142	141	141	140	139	139	138	138	137	137	136	136	135	134	134	133	15-0
181	145	145	144	144	143	143	142	141	141	140	140	139	139	138	138	137	136	136	135	135	134	134	133	133	15-1
182	145	144	143	143	142	142	141	141	140	140	139	138	138	137	137	136	136	135	135	134	134	133	132	132	15-2
183	144	143	143	142	142	141	140	140	139	139	138	138	137	137	136	136	135	134	134	133	133	132	132	131	15-3
184	143	142	142	141	141	140	140	139	139	138	138	137	136	136	135	135	134	134	133	133	132	132	131	130	15-4
185	142	142	141	141	140	139	139	138	138	137	137	136	136	135	135	134	134	133	132	132	131	131	130	130	15-5
186	141	141	140	140	139	139	138	138	137	137	136	135	135	134	134	133	133	132	132	131	131	130	130	129	15-6
187	141	140	140	139	139	138	137	137	136	136	135	135	134	134	133	133	132	132	131	130	130	129	129	128	15-7
188	140	139	139	138	138	137	137	136	136	135	135	134	134	133	132	132	131	131	130	130	129	129	128	128	15-8
189	139	139	138	138	137	137	136	135	135	134	134	133	133	132	132	131	131	130	130	129	129	128	128	127	15-9
190	138	138	137	137	136	136	135	135	134	134	133	133	132	132	131	131	130	129	129	128	128	127	127	126	15-10
191	138	137	137	136	136	135	135	134	134	133	132	132	131	131	130	130	129	129	128	128	127	127	126	126	15-11
192	137	136	136	135	135	134	134	133	133	132	132	131	131	130	130	129	129	128	128	127	127	126	126	125	16-0
Total Months	263	262	261	260	259	258	257	256	255	254	253	252	251	250	249	248	247	246	245	244	243	242	241	240	Total Months

CHRONOLOGICAL AGE

Years and Months	22-0	22-1	22-2	22-3	22-4	22-5	22-6	22-7	22-8	22-9	22-10	22-11	Total Months
13- 0	169	170											156
13- 1	168	169	169	170									157
13- 2	167	168	168	169	170								158
13- 3	166	167	167	168	169	169	170						159
13- 4	165	166	166	167	168	168	169	169	170				160
13- 5	164	165	165	166	166	167	168	168	169	170			161
13- 6	163	164	164	165	165	166	167	167	168	169	169		162
13- 7	162	163	163	164	164	165	166	166	167	167	168		163
13- 8	161	162	162	163	163	164	165	165	166	166	167		164
13- 9	160	161	161	162	162	163	164	164	165	165	166		165
13-10	159	160	160	161	161	162	163	163	164	164	165		166
13-11	158	159	159	160	160	161	162	162	163	163	164		167
14- 0	157	158	158	159	160	160	161	161	162	163	163		168
14- 1	156	157	157	158	159	159	160	160	161	162	162		169
14- 2	155	156	156	157	158	158	159	159	160	161	161		170
14- 3	154	155	156	156	157	157	158	158	159	160	160		171
14- 4	153	154	155	155	156	156	157	158	158	159	159		172
14- 5	153	153	154	154	155	155	156	157	157	158	158		173
14- 6	152	152	153	153	154	155	155	156	156	157	157		174
14- 7	151	151	152	153	153	154	154	155	155	156	157		175
14- 8	150	151	151	152	152	153	153	154	155	155	156		176
14- 9	149	150	150	151	151	152	153	153	154	154	155		177
14-10	148	149	149	150	151	151	152	152	153	153	154		178
14-11	147	148	149	149	150	150	151	151	152	153	153		179
15- 0	147	147	148	148	149	149	150	151	151	152	152		180
15- 1	146	146	147	148	148	149	149	150	150	151	151		181
15- 2	145	146	146	147	147	148	148	149	149	150	151		182
15- 3	144	145	145	146	146	147	148	148	149	149	150		183
15- 4	143	144	145	145	146	146	147	147	148	148	149		184
15- 5	143	143	144	144	145	145	146	146	147	148	148		185
15- 6	142	142	143	144	144	145	145	146	146	147	147		186
15- 7	141	142	142	143	143	144	144	145	145	146	147		187
15- 8	140	141	141	142	143	143	144	144	145	145	146		188
15- 9	140	140	141	141	142	142	143	143	144	144	145		189
15-10	139	139	140	141	141	142	142	143	143	144	144		190
15-11	138	139	139	140	140	141	141	142	142	143	143		191
16- 0	138	138	139	139	140	140	141	141	142	142	143		192
Total Months	264	265	266	267	268	269	270	271	272	273	274		

INDEX OF NAMES

INDEX

Abbreviated scales, validity of, 31–32; probable errors of I.Q.'s in, 47; use of, 64

Abstract words, (L, XI, 3), 109; *scoring*, 261; (L, XII, 5), 112; *scoring*, 269; (L, XIV, 6), 120; *scoring*, 269; (M, X, 4), 165; *scoring*, 380; (M, XI, 4), 167; *scoring*, 261; (M, XII, 4), 170; *scoring*, 380; (M, XIII, 4), 173; *scoring*, 261; (M, XIV, 4), 175; (M, A.A., 1), 177; *scoring*, 393; differences between, (L, A. A., 3), 121; *scoring*, 281

Absurdities, picture, (L, VII, 1), 97; *scoring*, 226; (L, X, 2), 106; *scoring*, 254; (L, XIV, 3), 118; *scoring*, 278; (M, VII, 3), 156; *scoring*, 351; (M, XII, 5), 170; *scoring*, 388; (M, XIV, 2), 174; *scoring*, 392

Absurdities, verbal, (L, VIII, 3), 101; *scoring*, 235; (L, IX, 2), 103; *scoring*, 244; (L, XI, 2), 108; *scoring*, 259; (L, XII, 2), 111; *scoring*, 244; (M, VIII, 3), 159; *scoring*, 358; (M, IX, 3), 161; *scoring*, 368; (M, X, 3), 165; *scoring*, 377; (M, XI, 3), 167; *scoring*, 368; Rulon's study of, 8

"Adjusted" chronological age, 68

Administering tests, examiner's procedure in, 52–55; desirable conditions for, 60–68

Adult mental age, 29–31

Aesthetic comparison, (L, IV-6, 1), 89; *scoring*, 213

Age. *See* Mental age, Chronological age

Age levels, relative difficulty of Forms at, 37, 38; basal, 63

Age scale, standardization of, 22–23

Alternative tests, use of, 66

"Altitude" scores, 24

Ambiguous responses, scoring of, 54–55, 191–92

Analogies, opposite, (L, IV-6, 6), 91; *scoring*, 216; (L, VII, 5), 98: *scoring*, 216; (L, S.A. III, 3), 131; *scoring*, 299; (M, IV, 3), 146; *scoring*, 340; (M, VI, 6), 155; *scoring*, 340; (M, VIII, 6), 160; *scoring*, 362; (M, A.A., 3), 178; *scoring*, 398; (M, S.A. I, 2), 181; *scoring*, 403; (M, S.A. III, 5), 188; *scoring*, 403

Animal pictures, discrimination of, (M, III–6, 3), 143; (M, IV, alt.), 148; (M, IV-6, 1), 148; *scoring*, 335

Animals, naming, (M, X, 5), 165; *scoring*, 382

Arithmetical reasoning, (L, A.A., 4), 121; *scoring*, 283

Arrangement of materials for testing, 62

Association, controlled, 382

Attention, maintenance of subject's, 60–61, 70

Ball and field test. *See* Plan of search.

Balls, comparison of, (M, III 6, 1), 142; *scoring*, 334

Barr rating scale, for classification of occupations, 13

Basal age level, 63

Bead chain, copying from memory, (L, VI, 2), 95; *scoring*, 222; (L, XIII, 6), 116; *scoring*, 277; (M, VI, 2), 154; *scoring*, 348; (M, XI, 2), 166; *scoring*, 385

Beads, stringing, (L, III, 1), 80; (M, II-6, alt.), 139; (M, IV, 2), 146; *scoring*, 200

Beginning point of testing, 63

Binet paper cutting, (M, A.A., 8), 180; *scoring*, 403

Bird, picture completion of, (M, IV-6, 4), 149; *scoring*, 343

Block building, tower, (L, II, 4), 76; *scoring*, 194; bridge, (L, III, 3), 81; (M, III, 1), 140; *scoring*, 200

Block counting, (M, X, 1), 163; *scoring*, 376

453